SOUTH-WESTERN

GED

WRITING SKILLS

Publisher:	Betty B. Schechter
Developmental Editor:	Mark Linton
Coordinating Editor:	Karen Roberts
Marketing Manager:	Barbara Baker
Consultant:	Wendy Harris
Software Manager:	Kenneth Tamarkin
CONNECTIONS Developer:	Learning Unlimited
Design Coordinator:	Darren Wright
Production Manager:	Carol Sturzenberger
Production Editors:	June Davidson, Melanie Blair
Photo Coordinator:	Devore Nixon

Cover Design: Graphica, Design and Communications Group
Internal Design: Rosa + Wesley Design Associates

ISBN: 0-538-71083-7
Library of Congress Catalog Card Number: 94-065926

1 2 3 4 5 6 PR 99 98 97 96 95 94
Printed in the United States of America

International Thomson Publishing Company

South-Western Publishing Co. is an ITP Company.
The ITP trademark is used under license.

 This book is printed on recycled, acid-free paper that meets Environmental Protection Agency standards.

SOUTH-WESTERN
GED

WRITING SKILLS

Susan Nicoles
Winterstein Adult Center
San Juan Unified School District
Sacramento, CA

Consulting Editor
Catherine A. Hoyt, Los Angeles, CA

Reviewers
Louetta Bowman, Folson State Prison, Placerville, CA
Trudy Herriron, Atlantic County Adult Education, Ventnor, NJ
Donna Miller-Parker, Seattle University, Seattle, WA
Susan Olsen, Eastern Correctional Institute, Westover, MD
Peter Burton Ross, Washington Technical Institute, Rockville, MD

South-Western Publishing Co.

Introduction

How have adults who have prepared for and passed the GED Tests described their experience? A major life achievement. A milestone. A turning point.

This introduction will give you general information about the GED Tests and answer some basic questions you may have, such as

- What Are the GED Tests?
- What Do the GED Tests Look Like?
- What Does It Take to Pass the GED Tests?
- What Do I Need to Know to Pass the GED Tests?
- How Long Will It Take Me to Get My GED?

You will also find out what is included in the South-Western GED Preparation System to help you successfully pass the GED Tests. Specific information on the GED Writing Skills Test begins on page 1.

What Are the GED Tests?

The Tests of General Educational Development (GED) are developed and administered by the GED Testing Service of the American Council on Education. Each year the council provides close to 1 million adults with the chance to earn a certificate or diploma that is widely recognized as the equivalent of a high school diploma. Since 1942, when the GED program began, more than 12 million adults have earned their GED credentials. Among them are names as familiar as Bill Cosby, Waylon Jennings, Mary Lou Retton, and Dave Thomas.

Because the GED credential is recognized and accepted by over 95 percent of businesses, industries, and educational institutions, it frequently is a step to further achievement. Perhaps most importantly, the GED credential proves to those who succeed that they are indeed achievers with the potential for further success. "The experience taught me that it is never too late to change the circumstances of your life," said one adult who earned the GED diploma at the age of thirty.

The GED Tests are five separate tests: Writing Skills, Social Studies, Science, Interpreting Literature and the Arts, and Mathematics. A GED certificate or diploma is earned by obtaining a passing score based on the results of all five tests.

What Do the GED Tests Look Like?

The GED Tests are entirely multiple choice, with the exception of the Writing Skills Test, which includes an essay section. The following chart describes each of the GED Tests. This book focuses on Test 1—the highlighted portion of the chart.

TEST NUMBER	TEST NAME	NUMBER OF TEST ITEMS	TIME	CONTENT AREAS
Test 1	Writing Skills: Part I Part II	55 items 1 topic	75 min. 45 min.	Sentence Structure: 35% Usage: 35% Mechanics: 30% Essay Writing
Test 2	Social Studies	64 items	85 min.	History: 25% Geography: 15% Economics: 20% Political Science: 20% Behavioral Science: 20%
Test 3	Science	66 items	95 min.	Life Sciences: 50% Physical Sciences: 50%
Test 4	Interpreting Literature and the Arts	45 items	65 min.	Popular Literature: 50% Classical Literature: 25% Commentary: 25%
Test 5	Mathematics	56 items	90 min.	Arithmetic: 50% Algebra: 30% Geometry: 20%

NOTE: In Canada, 20 percent of the GED Social Studies Test is based on geography and 15 percent on behavioral science.

What Does It Take to Pass the GED Tests?

To earn a GED credential, you need to earn a minimum passing score on each of the five tests as well as a passing average score overall. If you do not achieve a passing score on any one test or an overall passing score on all five tests, it is possible to retake one or more of the individual tests. By retaking a test, you can improve individual test scores, and that will increase your overall average score.

NOTE: *You will want to find out more about the requirements of the GED Tests where you live. Each state, U.S. territory, and Canadian province sets its own specific requirements for taking and passing the GED Tests. This region-*

specific information is available by contacting a local adult education center, community college, or library or simply by calling the toll-free number 1-800-62-MY GED.

What Do I Need to Know to Pass the GED Tests?

In general, you need to have the skills of an average graduating high school senior to pass the GED Tests. You will be tested on your knowledge of broad concepts and generalizations, not on how well you can remember exact details or facts. Your ability to *use* knowledge, information, and skills to *solve* problems is the key to passing the Tests.

Certain key skills will help you pass the Tests. Reading is the most important; however, reasoning and problem solving are also important skills. Writing, too, is very important. A good test preparation tip is to read as much as you can of everything that interests you—general and specific. Studies show that GED candidates who read more tend to do better on the Tests. Read newspapers and magazines—whatever you enjoy reading. Just read!

How Long Will It Take Me to Get My GED?

It's up to you to decide how long it will take to get your GED. You probably already have many of the skills and possess much of the knowledge you need. Getting ready for the tests means finding out what you already know and what you need to work on, choosing a study plan for self-improvement, and spending the time you need to follow through on your plan. The more concentrated your preparation efforts, the sooner you will be ready to take the Tests.

Most people prepare for the GED Tests with review classes, books, software review programs, or practice tests. Although many adults need only a quick review, others may need more extensive work in specific areas where their skills may be less developed.

The South-Western GED Preparation System

The South-Western GED Preparation System gives you your *connection to success* on the GED Tests. A full range of materials, from instructional books and exercise books to state-of-the-art software, meets the varied needs of adult learners. This system has been prepared by a team of professionals and reviewed by experienced adult educators who know what GED candidates need to *know* and *do* to pass the Tests. The instruction and GED practice exercises also have been tested by GED candidates across the United States.

GED Test Preparation Books

Five test preparation books, one for each of the GED Tests, are the core of the system. Their design, consisting of three distinctive sections plus the unique CONNECTIONS theme pages at the back of the book, provides for flexible use in individualized learning situations as well as in classrooms.

Recognizing the immediate and practical needs of GED candidates, these books are interspersed with test-taking tips for passing the GED Tests. To help foster further development of the higher-order thinking skills so much in demand in our society, real-life writing activities are included in every lesson. To help sharpen the skills needed to work with small groups of people, in the workplace and in the home, group activities are included.

Section One: Introducing the Test. This section provides specific test information for the adult learner. In this book, this information focuses on Test 1: Writing Skills. It contains

- A detailed description of the GED Writing Skills Test
- A Skills Survey Pretest
- A Skills Analysis Chart to help pinpoint less-developed skills
- An explanation of the structure and use options for this book

Section Two: Foundation Skills for the Test. This section provides instruction and practice in the areas most frequently identified as *foundations for success.* Each lesson focuses on a particular skill, showing its relationship to success on the Test. Each lesson ends with a Skill Checkup, which enables learners to measure their progress specifically. In this book, Section Two is devoted to the writing process. It contains

- Thorough instruction on every step of the writing process
- Models of good writing
- Frequent skills practice exercises for reinforcement
- A Skill Checkup at the end of every lesson to check progress

Section Three: Preparing for the Test. This section provides extensive instruction and practice on every major content area covered by the Test. In this book, it is organized into three units: Building Sentences, Using Language, and Handling Mechanics. Each lesson in a unit covers a specific topic of that content area with instruction, examples, explanations, and practice exercises. In addition, it contains

- Unit overviews, which forecast the topics and introduce key terms
- Achievement goals, which focus learning
- Test-taking tips, which relate to specific lesson topics
- Group activities, which facilitate cooperative learning and build real-life problem-solving skills
- Write on Target activities, which promote higher-order thinking skills
- CONNECTIONS activities, which link lessons to real-life themes
- Unit reviews, which summarize learning and check GED readiness
- Skills Analysis Charts, which measure specific skill and content area progress

Simulated GED Test. A full-length simulated GED Test is provided near the end of each book to help you determine if you are ready for the GED Tests.

CONNECTIONS. This unique high-interest section of information and activities that relate to current issues of our society appears in full color at the back of the book. Each lesson is "connected" to this special resource through an activity that accesses one of the real-world themes. Additional activities within this section challenge adults to "make the connection" with each of the areas addressed by the GED Tests—writing, social studies, science, literature, and mathematics—to their daily lives.

GED Exercise Books

Five exercise books deliver 100 percent GED exercise items. The items in the exercise books are arranged in units that correspond to the units in their companion test preparation books. For added content reinforcement and writing skill development, each unit of exercises ends with an *optional writing activity*. Finally, a full-length GED posttest is also included to measure GED readiness.

GED *Advantage* Software

South-Western's GED *Advantage* software is state-of-the-art instructional software that is easy to use and gives adult learners a software advantage for passing the GED Tests. GED *Advantage* makes adult learners active participants in determining their own courses of action by allowing them to select lessons and GED practice exercises that coordinate with sections in the test preparation texts.

GED *Advantage* delivers GED instruction with selected animation and abundant GED practice. Diagnostic as well as prescriptive reports quantitatively and visually direct learners toward effective GED preparation. Learners control their own instruction through the use of *bookmarks* and *branching*, or they can follow the recommended "Plan of Action" based on the actual results of their practice.

South-Western's GED *Advantage* software offers the following special features:

- A pretest to evaluate skills and content knowledge
- Foundation and Content modules to deliver instruction with selected animation and abundant GED practice
- GED mini-tests for each lesson to evaluate progress and development
- Pull-down menus, comprehensive graphic reports, and student management features to put the learner in control
- A complete teacher management system to provide individual student, teacher, or group with diagnostic and prescriptive reports
- A mini word processor, pop-up calculator, complete glossary, and e-mail (network version), all with on-line help, to enhance self-paced instruction
- One full-length and two half-length posttests to measure GED readiness

Packaging Options. GED *Advantage* is available for both DOS and Macintosh computers and can be installed on the hard drive of individual computers or used on networked systems. The software is available for *each* of the five individual GED Tests or as a complete package.

Hardware/Programming Requirements. South-Western's GED *Advantage* is designed to operate on the following microcomputer platforms:

DOS Versions:

- 80286 CPU minimum; 386 or better CPU recommended
- DOS 3.1 or higher and 640K RAM for standalone version
- DOS 5.0 or higher and at least 1 M RAM (500K free RAM) for Novell network version
- Hard drive installation required
- VGA adapter, with color or monochrome display, and at least 256K RAM installed
- Mouse recommended

Macintosh®[1] Versions:

- Macintosh II, SE, SE30, Classic, LC, Performa, Centris, Quadra System 6.0.7 or higher required
- Hard drive installation required

Black and White

- 1 M RAM (System 6.0.7, non-MultiFinder) for standalone version
- 2 M RAM (System 6.0.7, non-MultiFinder) for AppleTalk network version

256 — Color

- 2 M RAM (System 6.0.7, non-MultiFinder, with 32-bit Color QuickDraw installed) for standalone version
- 4 M RAM (either System 6.0.7, with 32-bit Color QuickDraw installed, or System 7) for AppleTalk network version

GED Assessment Booklets

Two GED assessment booklets—pretests and posttests—facilitate the ongoing diagnosis and assessment of GED readiness. The pretest assessment booklet contains skills surveys that can be used to determine capabilities before a plan of focused instruction begins. The posttest assessment booklet contains Simulated GED Tests that can be used to measure progress and readiness for the actual GED Test.

A Note from the Author

Adult education instructors, writing skills experts, and GED candidates from across the nation who tried these materials during their development have shaped the writing of this book. South-Western and the author gratefully acknowledge the contributions of these individuals: Louetta Bowman, Trudy Herriron, Cathy Hoyt, Donna Miller-Parker, Susan Olsen, Peter Burton Ross, Caren Van Slyke, and Sarah Williams. A special thanks also goes to all the GED candidates who tested these materials and provided valuable feedback.

---

[1] Macintosh is a registered trademark of McIntosh Laboratory, Inc.

Table of Contents

GED WRITING SKILLS

Introduction   v

SECTION ONE **Introducing the Test**   **1**

What Will I Find on the GED Writing Skills Test?   2
What Do I Already Know?   7
     SKILLS SURVEY PRETEST   7
     ANSWERS AND EXPLANATIONS   15
How Can I Prepare for the GED Writing Skills Test?   18

SECTION TWO **Foundation Skills for the Test**   **25**

Skill 1 Think About Your Essay   26
Skill 2 Organize Your Material   36
Skill 3 Write Your Essay   46
Skill 4 Revise Your Work   56
Skill 5 Edit Your Work   64
     ANSWERS AND EXPLANATIONS   68

SECTION THREE **Preparing for the Test**   **75**

Unit 1 Building Sentences   77
     OVERVIEW   78
     Lesson 1   Avoiding Sentence Fragments   80
     Lesson 2   Avoiding Run-on Sentences   94

Lesson 3 Linking Ideas of Equal Importance **106**

Lesson 4 Linking Ideas of Unequal Importance **118**

Lesson 5 Using Modifers to Add Information **128**

Lesson 6 Understanding Parallel Structure **140**

REVIEW **148**

ANSWERS AND EXPLANATIONS **154**

Unit 2 Using Language **167**

OVERVIEW **168**

Lesson 1 Does the Verb Match the Subject? **170**

Lesson 2 Placing Verbs in Sentences **180**

Lesson 3 Recognizing Parts of Verbs **188**

Lesson 4 When Does the Action Take Place? **198**

Lesson 5 Looking at Noun Substitutes **206**

Lesson 6 Does the Pronoun Fit the Rest of the Sentence? **216**

REVIEW **222**

ANSWERS AND EXPLANATIONS **228**

Unit 3 Handling Mechanics **241**

OVERVIEW **242**

Lesson 1 Using Capital Letters **244**

Lesson 2 What About Commas? **252**

Lesson 3 Using Commas to Set Off Parts of Sentences **262**

Lesson 4 Overcoming Spelling Problems **276**

Lesson 5 Adding Syllables to Words **284**

Lesson 6 What Is the Apostrophe For? **290**

Lesson 7 Words to Watch Out For **296**

REVIEW **308**

ANSWERS AND EXPLANATIONS **314**

Simulated GED Writing Skills Test   329

Simulated Test Answers and Explanations   344

Scoring Guide: Simulated GED Writing Skills Test Part II   349

Glossary   355

Acknowledgments   359

Index   361

CONNECTIONS Answer Guide   A1–A4

CONNECTIONS	**C1–C16**
Technology	C2 – C3
Employment	C4 – C5
Cultures	C6 – C7
Family Life	C8 – C9
News Media	C10 – C11
Leisure	C12 – C13
Lifestyles	C14 – C15
The GED Essay: 45-Minute Plan for Success	C16

1 Introducing the GED
WRITING SKILLS TEST

What Will I Find on the GED Writing Skills Test? — **2**

What Do I Already Know? — **7**

SKILLS SURVEY PRETEST — 7

ANSWERS AND EXPLANATIONS — 15

How Can I Prepare for the GED Writing Skills Test? — **18**

What Will I Find on the GED Writing Skills Test?

This section of *GED Writing Skills* will help you understand what you will find on the GED Writing Skills Test, what you already know, and what you need to review and practice to be completely ready to take the test.

The Writing Skills Test is Test One of the GED tests. It measures your knowledge of written English and your ability to write. The GED Writing Skills Test is *not* a measure of how many grammar rules you know and how well you know them. It does *not* ask you to rewrite long lists of poorly constructed sentences as you may have had to do in English classes. It does *not* contain trick questions designed to make you doubt what you think is correct. Finally, it does *not* make you write an impossibly long essay.

The GED Writing Skills Test *is* an opportunity for you to demonstrate your ability to read, to think logically, and to express yourself clearly in written English.

The GED Writing Skills Test is divided into two parts. Each part is discussed on the pages that follow.

Part I of the GED Writing Skills Test

Part I of the GED Writing Skills Test measures your ability to use the conventions of standard written English. These conventions are the basic language tools you use to communicate effectively. These conventions are sentence structure, usage, and mechanics.

All items in Part I are multiple-choice questions. Each question has five answer choices. You are first asked to read a paragraph or two. A series of questions that focuses on certain sentences within those paragraphs follows. The paragraphs cover topics of general interest to adults, and a deliberate emphasis is placed on three key topics: technology, the global nature of our society, and the world of work.

Three types of multiple-choice questions appear on the test: sentence correction questions, sentence revision questions, and construction shift questions. Each type is described in the following paragraphs. A sample of each question type and an explanation of how to determine the correct answer is also provided.

Sentence Correction Questions

These questions ask you to find what is wrong with a sentence and to determine how it can be corrected. Close to half of all questions in Part I (about twenty-five items) are sentence correction questions. Here is a sample:

SAMPLE

1. Sentence 2: **Dorothy and her assistant evaluates 20 applications every day.**

What correction should be made to this sentence?

(1) insert a comma after <u>Dorothy</u>
(2) insert a comma after <u>assistant</u>
(3) change the spelling of <u>assistant</u> to <u>assistent</u>
(4) change <u>evaluates</u> to <u>evaluate</u>
(5) no correction is necessary

When you encounter this type of question, it may include, as the sample shows, the answer choice *no correction is necessary.*

To find the correct answer to this sample, you need to know something about commas, spelling, and verbs because those are the kinds of changes covered by the choices. If you know when and why to use commas, you will know that options (1) and (2) are not correct. Option (3) is also incorrect. Spelling errors either illustrate a spelling rule or misspell a word from the GED Master List of Frequently Misspelled Words (see Unit 3, Lesson 7). For option (4), you must determine what, if anything, is wrong with the verb in the original sentence. In the sample sentence, the verb doesn't agree in number with the subject. Option (4), therefore, is the correct answer. It changes the singular verb *evaluates* to the plural form *evaluate.* The plural verb *evaluate* agrees with the plural subject of the sample sentence: *Dorothy and her assistant.*

NOTE: *If you are offered an answer choice that says no correction is necessary, do not assume that it is the correct choice. Occasionally it will be, but not always. You must consider all answer choices as possibilities.*

Sentence Revision Questions

These questions have *a specific portion of a sentence underlined.* Your task is to choose the answer that best improves the underlined portion of the sentence. About 35 percent of the questions in Part I (seventeen to eighteen items) are sentence revision questions. Here is a sample:

SAMPLE

2. Sentence 4: **After they attended the technology <u>workshop the accounting clerks felt</u> more confident about using computers.**

Which of the following is the best way to write the underlined portion of the sentence? If you think the original is the best way, choose option (1).

(1) workshop the accounting clerks felt
(2) workshop, the accounting clerks felt
(3) workshop the Accounting Clerks felt
(4) workshop the accounting clerks will feel
(5) workshop. The accounting clerks felt

To find the correct answer to this sample, you need to know something about punctuation, capitalization, and verb tense because those are the kinds of changes offered by the choices. The correct answer is option (2). It inserts a comma after the dependent clause that introduces the sentence. Option (1) does not contain the necessary comma. Option (3) does not contain the necessary comma, and it contains two incorrectly capitalized words, *Accounting Clerk.* Option (4) does not contain the necessary comma, and it contains an incorrect verb tense. Option (5) uses a period where the necessary comma belongs, thereby creating a sentence fragment.

Construction Shift Questions

These questions ask you to choose a better way to write a sentence mentally without changing its meaning. Although the original sentence contains no mechanical errors, it may be awkwardly written. In a construction shift question, you are asked to select another way of saying what is expressed. About 15 percent of the questions in Part I (seven to eight items) are construction shift questions. Here is a sample:

SAMPLE

3. Sentence 5: **Schools all across America are seeking ways to address the needs of children who have a wide range of ethnic backgrounds, which is a major problem that educators struggle to solve.**

If you rewrote sentence 5 beginning with

American educators seek ways to

the next word should be

(1) struggle
(2) need
(3) help
(4) separate
(5) employ

Construction shift questions may apply to more than one sentence. You may be asked to find the most effective combination of two sentences.

To find the correct answer to this sample, you must understand the meaning of the original sentence. Although the correct answer choice does not actually appear in the original sentence, the idea it conveys does. The original poorly constructed sentence tells you that *educators want to find ways to meet the needs of students with varying ethnic backgrounds.* The answer that most closely expresses this idea is option (3): *helps.*

ONE FINAL NOTE ON PART I: *It is in your best interest to answer every question on the test whether you know the answer or not. There is no penalty for guessing. When you are "stuck," relax and then make your best guess. It may be correct.*

Part II of the GED Writing Skills Test

Part II of the GED Writing Skills Test measures your ability to state an opinion on a given topic or to explain something. You will need to write an essay that clearly states ideas and supports them effectively with detailed reasons and examples. Your essay will be evaluated on how clear, well organized, and free of mechanical errors it is. Your essay will need to be about 200 words in length.

You will not have a choice of topics to write about on the GED test. You will make decisions, however, on how to respond to the topic that is given to you. There is no right or wrong way to respond to a topic if you support your ideas with reasons and examples. Here is a sample:

SAMPLE ESSAY TOPIC

As electronic devices become easier to use, more and more homes will have such things as telephone answering machines, compact disc players, computerized games, and personal computers. One of the most popular electronic inventions is the videocassette recorder (VCR).

In an essay of 200 words, discuss the advantages, disadvantages, or both of owning a VCR. Be sure to support your ideas with details and examples.

TEST-TAKING TIP

It is okay to add extra things as you look over what you have written. As you write, it is okay to cross out words or sentences; but you should keep your changes and corrections neat. And by all means, correct any spelling, capitalization, or other errors you find.

Notice that the GED essay topic has two parts. The first part introduces the topic by giving you some background information about it. The second part tells what the topic is; that is, it tells you what you must write about. In the sample essay topic, the topic is the advantages and/or disadvantages of owning a VCR.

For the sample topic, you could choose to write about the convenience of a VCR (advantage) and contrast that convenience with some disadvantages. To support your views, you could discuss the convenience of watching movies at home, which saves money, time, and the hassle of going to a theater. You could also mention the convenience of using a VCR to record favorite television programs to watch at more suitable times. For the disadvantages, you might talk about the high cost of purchasing video equipment, the temptation to spend too much time in front of television screens, and the frustration of operating VCRs.

What Do I Already Know?

You already know a great deal of what you need to take the GED Writing Skills Test. Your own life experiences have prepared you for this test more than you may think. The GED Writing Skills Test measures your ability to read information, to think about it, and to use it.

The Skills Survey Pretest that follows lets you practice answering some typical GED test questions as well as other questions designed to help you discover what you already know. The pretest is only about half as long as the actual GED Writing Skills Test.

Completing this pretest and analyzing your results will help you focus your preparation efforts on the skills you need to be fully prepared for the test.

Skills Survey Pretest

Part I

Part I of the pretest consists of paragraphs with numbered sentences. Some of the sentences contain errors in sentence structure, usage, or mechanics (mechanics includes spelling, punctuation, and capitalization). Some sentences do not have errors. After reading the numbered sentences, answer the questions that follow.

Take as much time as you need to complete this pretest. Answer every question, but do not spend too much time on any one question. Each question has only one right answer; there are no trick questions. If a question refers to a sentence that is correct as written, the best answer choice is the one that leaves the sentence as written. If you don't know the answer to a question, try eliminating choices that you know are wrong and then select the best remaining choice. If you are "stuck" on a question, skip it and come back to it later, but be sure to answer every question.

Directions: Choose the <u>one best answer</u> to each item.

<u>Items 1 to 7</u> refer to the following paragraph.

(1) Advances in miniaturization and computer technology have revolutionized our world, they have also saved our lives. (2) Machines play an important roll in medical treatment. (3) Computers monitor the pulse, heartbeat and respiration of patients during surgery and recovery. (4) Nurse's stations stay in constant contact with patients via computer hookups. (5) Surgery has benefitted a great deal from new technology. (6) Pacemakers, organ transplants, and artificial hearts have literally give people life. (7) After they make a small incision surgeons can insert tiny cameras and surgical instruments into people's bodies. (8) Then they can perform operations by looking at the surgical area on a television monitor. (9) Less trauma to the patient speeds recovery from this type of surgery. (10) Clearly, increased use of high-tech tools have resulted in marvelous advances in medicine today.

1. Sentence 1: **Advances in miniaturization and computer technology have revolutionized our world, they have also saved our lives.**

A group of words that *looks like* a sentence because it begins with a capital letter and ends with a period may not actually be a sentence. A word group that looks like a sentence may sometimes only be a sentence fragment, or it may actually be two or more sentences incorrectly written as one. Sentence 1 is a word group, but it is not a correct sentence. Identify the problem and write sentence 1 correctly.

2. Sentence 2: **Machines play an important roll in medical treatment.**

What correction should be made to this sentence?

(1) change the spelling of <u>Machines</u> to <u>Mashines</u>
(2) change <u>play</u> to <u>plays</u>
(3) change the spelling of <u>roll</u> to <u>role</u>
(4) insert a comma after <u>roll</u>
(5) change <u>medical treatment</u> to <u>Medical Treatment</u>

3. Sentence 3: **Computers monitor the <u>pulse, heartbeat and respiration of patients during surgery</u> and recovery.**

Which of the following is the best way to write the underlined portion of this sentence? If you think the original is the best way, choose option (1).

(1) pulse, heartbeat and respiration of patients during surgery
(2) pulse, heartbeat, and respiration of patients during surgery
(3) pulse heartbeat and respiration of patients during surgery
(4) pulse, heartbeat and respiration of patients, during surgery
(5) pulse, heartbeat and respiration, of patients during surgery

4. Sentence 4: **Nurse's stations stay in constant contact with patients via computer hookups.**

What correction should be made to this sentence?

(1) change <u>Nurse's</u> to <u>Nurses</u>
(2) change <u>Nurse's</u> to <u>Nurses'</u>
(3) change <u>stations</u> to <u>station's</u>
(4) change <u>patients</u> to <u>patient's</u>
(5) change <u>patients</u> to <u>patients'</u>

5. Sentence 6: **Pacemakers, organ transplants, and artificial hearts have literally give people life.**

What correction should be made to this sentence?

(1) insert a comma after <u>organ</u>
(2) remove the comma after <u>transplants</u>
(3) change <u>give</u> to <u>gave</u>
(4) change <u>give</u> to <u>given</u>
(5) no correction is necessary

6. Sentence 7: **After they make a small incision surgeons can insert** tiny cameras and surgical instruments into people's bodies.

Which of the following is the best way to write the underlined portion of this sentence? If you think the original is the best way, choose option (1).

(1) After they make a small incision surgeons can insert

(2) After they make a small incision, surgeons can insert

(3) After they make a small incision surgeons, can insert

(4) After they makes a small incision surgeons can insert

(5) After they make a small incision Surgeons can insert

7. Sentence 10: **Clearly, increased use of high-tech tools have resulted in marvelous advances in medicine today.**

Which of the following is the best way to write the underlined portion of this sentence? If you think the original is the best way, choose option (1).

(1) increased use of high-tech tools have resulted

(2) increased use of high-tech tools have result

(3) increased use of high-tech tools, have resulted

(4) increased, use of high-tech tools have resulted

(5) increased use of high-tech tools has resulted

<u>Items 8 to 14</u> refer to the following paragraphs.

(1) Many social critics worrying about a decline in reading among Americans. (2) They cite surveys that show that 72 percent of eighth graders watch three or more hours of television a day. (3) Only 27 percent of eighth graders say they spend time. (4) Reading for pleasure. (5) Television is not the only factor contributing to a population that doesnt read. (6) Computers also plays a role. (7) People are becoming used to flashing, noisy, and instantaneous electronic information. (8) Reading, on the other hand, is private and quiet. (9) Electronic communication lacks the subtlety of the written word, but reading demands more effort than watching television.

(10) Nevertheless, the number of bookstores increases 76 percent in the 1980s. (11) Independent bookstores, especially, try to entice customers with a wide selection of titles and a homelike atmosphere. (12) Many install wooden shelves for their books and provide comfortable chairs so consumers can read while they browse through books.

8. Sentence 1: **Many social critics worrying about a decline in reading among Americans.**

A sentence must contain a subject and a complete verb and express a complete thought. If one of these criteria is missing, you have only a piece of a sentence, or a sentence fragment. Sentence 1 is a fragment rather than a complete sentence. Determine what is missing (the subject? the verb or part of the verb? a complete thought?). Rewrite the sentence by supplying whatever is missing.

9. Sentences 3 and 4: **Only 27 percent of eighth graders say they spend time. Reading for pleasure.**

Which of the following is the best way to write the underlined portion of these sentences? If you think the original is the best way, choose option (1).

(1) they spend time. Reading for pleasure.

(2) they spend time reading. For pleasure.

(3) they spend time, reading for pleasure.

(4) they spend time reading for pleasure.

(5) he or she spends time. Reading for pleasure.

10. Sentence 5: **Television is not the only factor contributing to a population that doesnt read.**

What correction should be made to this sentence?

(1) insert a comma after <u>factor</u>
(2) change the spelling of <u>contributing</u> to <u>contributeing</u>
(3) change <u>contributing</u> to <u>contributed</u>
(4) change <u>doesnt</u> to <u>does'nt</u>
(5) change <u>doesnt</u> to <u>doesn't</u>

11. Sentence 6: **Computers also plays a role.**

What correction should be made to this sentence?

(1) insert a comma after <u>Computers</u>
(2) change <u>plays</u> to <u>play</u>
(3) change <u>plays</u> to <u>will play</u>
(4) insert a comma after <u>plays</u>
(5) no correction is necessary

12. Sentence 9: **Electronic communication lacks the subtlety of the written <u>word, but reading demands</u> more effort than watching television.**

Which of the following is the best way to write the underlined portion of this sentence? If you think the original is the best way, choose option (1).

(1) word, but reading demands
(2) word, if reading demands
(3) word, or reading demands
(4) word, so reading demands
(5) word, even though reading demands

13. Sentence 10: **Nevertheless, the number of bookstores increases 76 percent in the 1980s.**

What correction should be made to this sentence?

(1) remove the comma after <u>Nevertheless</u>
(2) change <u>increases</u> to <u>increase</u>
(3) change <u>increases</u> to <u>increased</u>
(4) change <u>increases</u> to <u>will increase</u>
(5) insert a comma after <u>increases</u>

14. Sentence 12: **Many install wooden shelves for their books and provide comfortable chairs so consumers can read while they browse through the books.**

If you rewrote sentence 12 beginning with

<u>Wooden shelves and comfortable chairs</u>

the next word should be

(1) encourage
(2) repel
(3) browse
(4) read
(5) install

<u>Items 15 to 21</u> refer to the following paragraph.

(1) Checking accounts offer convenience to many people. (2) When you pay bills by mail, it's much safer to mail a check than mailing cash. (3) Checking accounts do, however, require some care. (4) Balancing a checkbook is the most important way of keeping your account in good shape. (5) Being confusing and frustrating, many people simply don't bother to reconcile their accounts. (6) Don't despair, however; bank statements include forms to guide you through the process of balancing your account. (7) You do have to solve some addition and subtraction problems, but it usually isn't complicated. (8) The main reason to reconcile your account with the bank's monthly statement is to be sure you have the funds you think you have. (9) Errors carry over from month to month, so you might end up with a Bounced Check even though you thought you had enough money in your account to cover it. (10) Bouncing a check makes things difficult for the person you wrote the check for, and it can be expensive for you because most places charge a penalty for bounced checks. (11) It's important to use the account wisely and carefully. (12) That way, you had all the benefits of a checking account and none of its perils.

15. Sentence 2: **When you pay bills by mail, it's much safer to mail a check than mailing cash.**

Sentence 2 contains an error in parallel structure. Errors in parallel structure occur when words or word groups perform similar functions in a sentence but take different forms. Rewrite sentence 2 to correct the error in parallel structure.

16. Sentence 3: **Checking accounts do, however, require some care.**

What correction should be made to this sentence?

(1) remove the comma after <u>do</u>
(2) remove the comma after <u>however</u>
(3) remove <u>however</u>
(4) change <u>require</u> to <u>required</u>
(5) no correction is necessary

17. Sentence 5: <u>**Being confusing and frustrating, many people**</u> **simply don't bother to reconcile their accounts.**

Which of the following is the best way to write the underlined portion of this sentence? If you think the original is the best way, choose option (1).

(1) Being confusing and frustrating, many people
(2) Being confused and frustrating, checking accounts
(3) Because people are confusing and frustrating, many
(4) Because balancing a checking account is often confusing and frustrating, many people
(5) Because they confuse and frustrate them, many people

18. Sentence 7: **You do have to solve some addition and subtraction problems, <u>but it usually isn't complicated.</u>**

Which of the following is the best way to write the underlined portion of this sentence? If you think the original is the best way, choose option (1).

(1) but it usually isn't complicated
(2) but it usually wasn't complicated
(3) and it usually isn't complicated
(4) but they usually aren't complicated
(5) it usually isn't complicated

19. Sentence 9: **Errors carry over from month to month, so you might end up with a Bounced Check even though you thought you had enough money in your account to cover it.**

What correction should be made to this sentence?

(1) remove the comma after <u>month</u>
(2) change <u>Bounced Check</u> to <u>bounced check</u>
(3) insert a comma after <u>Check</u>
(4) replace <u>it</u> with <u>them</u>
(5) no correction is necessary

20. Sentence 10: **Bouncing a check makes things difficult for the person you wrote the check for, and it can be expensive for you because most places charge a penalty for bounced checks.**

If you rewrote sentence 10 beginning with

<u>Bouncing a check creates many problems and costs</u>

the next word should be

(1) little
(2) nothing
(3) them
(4) me
(5) you

21. Sentence 12: **That way, you had all the benefits of a checking account and none of its perils.**

What correction should be made to this sentence?

(1) remove the comma after <u>way</u>
(2) change <u>had</u> to <u>have</u>
(3) insert a comma after <u>account</u>
(4) change <u>its</u> to <u>it's</u>
(5) change <u>perils</u> to <u>peril's</u>

<u>Items 22 to 28</u> refer to the following paragraphs.

(1) Tuberculosis once thought eradicated from the civilized world is returning. (2) The disease is spreading in American slums and poor cities throughout the world. (3) TB is not the only returning disease doctors thought they had conquered. (4) New strains of cholera that doesn't respond to vaccines have been seen in Africa and Asia. (5) The World Health Organization, an agency of the United Nations, says malaria is another one. (6) Typhoid and diphtheria has resurfaced in Russia. (7) Although these diseases appear mostly in underdeveloped countries, they threaten developed nations too. (8) There, tuberculosis already worries health officials.

(9) Health professionals blame the threatening epidemics on three things. (10) First, they blame poverty and poor health care in overpopulated third world countries. (11) Second, new strains of bacteria resist drugs. (12) Third, the growth in world travel spreads diseases across continents and oceans. (13) The world must improve sanitation, step up vaccination programs, and practice better hygiene. (14) To prevent epidemics.

22. Sentence 1: **Tuberculosis once thought eradicated from the civilized world is returning.**

Sentence 1 contains a punctuation error. Words that add information to a sentence but do not affect its main idea should be set off from the rest of the sentence with commas. This lets the reader understand that those words are nonessential to the main idea. Rewrite sentence 1, inserting the commas.

23. Sentence 3: **TB is not the only returning disease doctors thought they had conquered.**

If you rewrote sentence 3 beginning with

<u>Doctors thought they had conquered TB and many other diseases,</u>

the next word should be

(1) so
(2) or
(3) and
(4) but
(5) if

24. Sentence 4: **New strains of cholera that doesn't respond to vaccines have been seen in Africa and Asia.**

What correction should be made to this sentence?

(1) replace <u>that</u> with <u>who</u>
(2) replace <u>doesn't</u> with <u>don't</u>
(3) insert a comma after <u>vaccines</u>
(4) change <u>seen</u> to <u>saw</u>
(5) no correction is necessary

25. Sentence 5: **The World Health Organization, an agency of the United Nations, <u>says malaria is another one.</u>**

Which of the following is the best way to write the underlined portion of this sentence? If you think the original is the best way, choose option (1).

(1) says malaria is another one
(2) say malaria is another one
(3) says malaria was another growing health problem
(4) say malaria is another growing health problem
(5) says malaria is another growing health problem

26. Sentence 6: **Typhoid and diphtheria <u>has resurfaced in Russia</u>.**

Which of the following is the best way to write the underlined portion of this sentence? If you think the original is the best way, choose option (1).

(1) has resurfaced in Russia
(2) have resurfaced in Russia
(3) has resurface in Russia
(4) has resurfaced in russia
(5) will resurface in Russia

27. Sentences 7 and 8: **Although these diseases appear mostly in underdeveloped countries, they threaten developed nations too. There, tuberculosis already worries health officials.**

The most effective combination of sentences 7 and 8 would include which of the following groups of words?

(1) Underdeveloped countries don't worry about disease
(2) mostly tuberculosis
(3) Underdeveloped diseases worry health officials
(4) where health officials already worry about tuberculosis
(5) because developed nations are free of these diseases

28. Sentences 13 and 14: **The world must improve sanitation, step up vaccination programs, and practice better hygiene. To prevent epidemics.**

What correction should be made to these sentences?

(1) remove the comma after <u>sanitation</u>
(2) remove the comma after <u>programs</u>
(3) insert a comma after <u>and</u>
(4) change <u>hygiene. To</u> to <u>hygiene to</u>
(5) change <u>hygiene. To</u> to <u>hygiene, to</u>

Part II

Part II of the pretest consists of a sample essay topic. Read the entire sample essay topic carefully to determine the topic you are to write about.

After you're sure you understand the topic, take some time to plan what you want to say. Be sure to check your essay after you write it to correct any errors in structure, content, or mechanics.

SAMPLE ESSAY TOPIC

Political campaigns can cost candidates hundreds of thousands or even millions of dollars. To reach voters, politicians spend huge amounts of money to hire professional advertising firms and to buy television time. Through the technology of television, candidates can speak to the American people right in their own homes. Sometimes, however, we get more image than substance through televised politics.

In an essay of about 200 words, discuss the value of television as a source of information during political campaigns.

After you finish this pretest, turn to the Answers and Explanations section on the pages that follow to check your answers. Use the Skills Analysis Chart on page 17 and circle the number of each item you answered correctly. Directions for using the Skills Analysis Chart explain how to interpret your pretest results.

NOTE: *After you have checked your answers, turn to page 18 to learn how this book can help you prepare for the GED Writing Skills Test.*

Answers and Explanations

Part I

1. **Advances in miniaturization and computer technology have revolutionized our world. They have also saved our lives.** Sentence 1 is a run-on sentence; that is, it is two sentences written as one. To correctly punctuate a run-on sentence, a period (or a semicolon) is required at the end of the first complete thought. It is incorrect to separate two independent clauses, or complete thoughts, with only a comma.

2. **(3) change the spelling of <u>roll</u> to <u>role</u>** Option (3) uses the correct sound-alike word. Option (1) introduces a spelling error. Option (2) lacks subject-verb agreement. There is no reason for the comma in option (4), and there is no reason to capitalize the words in option (5).

3. **(2) pulse, heartbeat, and respiration of patients during surgery** Option (2) includes a comma before the last item in a series of three. Option (1) omits that comma. Option (3) omits all series commas. Option (4) inserts a comma before a prepositional phrase that follows the main clause. There is no reason for the comma in option (5).

4. **(2) change Nurse's to Nurses'** Option (2) places the apostrophe in the correct place to show a plural possessive. Option (1) changes the possessive to a plural, and the other options change plurals to possessives.

5. **(4) change <u>give</u> to <u>given</u>** Option (4) uses the correct past participle. Option (1) changes the meaning of the sentence, option (2) removes the comma before the last item in a series, and option (3) shifts to the past tense.

6. **(2) After they make a small incision, surgeons can insert** Option (2) places a comma after the introductory dependent clause. Option (1) omits this comma. Option (3) wrongly uses a comma to separate the subject (*surgeons*) from its verb (*can insert*), option (4) uses the singular verb *makes* with the plural subject *they*, and there is no reason to capitalize the general term in option (5).

7. **(5) increased use of high-tech tools has resulted** Option (5) matches the singular subject (*use*) with a singular verb (*has*). Option (2) uses an incorrect verb form for the past participle, option (3) incorrectly inserts a comma between the subject and the verb, and there is no reason for the comma in option (4).

8. **Many social critics are worrying about a decline in reading among Americans** As written, part of the verb is missing, and that's why this word group is a sentence fragment. It can be corrected by changing the form of the verb.

9. **(4) they spend time reading for pleasure** Option (4) corrects the fragment by eliminating the period at the end of sentence 3 and the capital letter at the beginning of sentence 4. Option (1) is a fragment. Options (2) and (5) do not correct the fragment, and option (5) uses pronouns incorrectly. Option (3) uses a comma inappropriately to join the fragment to the preceding sentence.

10. **(5) change <u>doesnt</u> to <u>doesn't</u>** Option (5) indicates a contraction by replacing the missing letter with an apostrophe. There is no reason for the comma in option (1), option (2) doesn't drop the *e* before adding *ing*, option (3) uses a past participle instead of a present participle, and option (4) puts the apostrophe in the wrong place.

11. **(2) change <u>plays</u> to <u>play</u>** Option (2) uses a verb that agrees with the subject. Option (1) separates the subject and verb with a comma, option (3) shifts to the future tense, and there's no reason for the comma in option (4).

12. **(4) word, so reading demands** Option (4) uses a connecting word that shows the correct relationship between the two ideas stated in this compound sentence. The other options use inappropriate connecting words.

13. **(3) change <u>increases</u> to <u>increased</u>** Option (3) uses the past tense, which is appropriate because the action being described took place in the 1980s. Option (1) removes a comma after an introductory word, option (2) lacks subject-verb agreement, option (4) shifts to the future tense, and there is no reason for the comma in option (5).

14. **(1) encourage** Option (1) is the only word that maintains the meaning of the original sentence.

15. **When you pay bills by mail, it's much safer to mail a check than to mail cash.** Repeating the verb *to mail* makes the parts of the sentence parallel.

16. **(5) no correction is necessary**

17. (4) Because balancing a checking account is often confusing and frustrating, many people Option (4) corrects the misplaced modifier by making it clear that balancing checking accounts is often confusing and frustrating. The misplaced modifier in option (1) makes it seem as if people, not the task of balancing checking accounts, are confusing and frustrating. Option (2) puts *checking accounts* near the modifier, which does not make sense. Option (3) incorrectly states that people are confusing. Option (5) uses unclear pronoun references.

18. (4) but they usually aren't complicated Option (4) uses a pronoun that agrees in number with its antecedent. Option (1) lacks pronoun-antecedent agreement, option (2) shifts to the past tense, option (3) uses an inappropriate connecting word between the clauses, and option (5) creates a run-on sentence because it deletes a connecting word and a comma.

19. (2) change Bounced Check to bounced check. Option (2) is correct because there is no reason to capitalize *bounced check*. Option (1) removes a comma that is required with the connecting word *so that* separates two independent clauses. Option (3) incorrectly inserts a comma before a dependent clause, and option (4) uses the plural pronoun *them* with the singular antecedent *bounced check*.

20. (5) you Option (5) is the only choice that maintains the meaning of the original sentence: bouncing a check costs *you* money.

21. (2) change <u>had</u> to <u>have</u> Option (2) continues the paragraph's use of the present tense. Option (1) removes a comma that is required after an introductory phrase, there is no reason for the comma in option (3), option (4) changes the possessive to a contraction, and option (5) changes a plural to a possessive.

22. Tuberculosis, once thought eradicated from the civilized world, is returning. The main idea of the sentence is that tuberculosis is returning. The other words add information but are not necessary for the sentence to be complete. Such interrupting elements must be set off with commas.

23. (4) but Option (4) is the only choice that shows the contrast between what doctors thought (diseases had been eradicated) and what is really happening (diseases are returning).

24. (2) replace <u>doesn't</u> with <u>don't</u> Option (2) uses the plural form of the verb to agree with the plural subject (*strains*). Option (1) uses the wrong pronoun (*who* instead of *that*) to refer to a thing, there's no reason for the comma in option (3), and option (4) changes the past participle (*seen*) of the verb *to see* to the past tense (*saw*).

25. (5) says malaria is another growing health problem Option (5) replaces the pronoun *one,* which had no clear antecedent, with a noun. None of the other options corrects *one's* vague reference.

26. (2) have resurfaced in Russia Option (2) uses the plural verb *have* to agree with the plural subject *Typhoid and diphtheria.* Options (1), (3), and (4) do not correct this subject-verb agreement error, and option (5) shifts to the future tense.

27. (4) where health officials already worry about tuberculosis Option (4) is the only choice that maintains the meaning of the original sentences.

28. (4) change <u>hygiene. To</u> to <u>hygiene to</u> Option (4) eliminates the sentence fragment by joining it to the complete sentence. Option (5) eliminates the fragment but joins the words to the complete sentence with incorrect punctuation. Options (1) and (2) omit commas between items in a series of three, and option (3) inserts a comma after the *and* at the end of the series.

Part II

Although it is difficult to evaluate your own essay, the scoring information on page 349 will help you estimate a score for your essay. For your use, make a list of your essay's strengths and weaknesses based on the self-evaluation checklist that follows. If you can, ask an instructor to read and score your essay as well.

Self-Evaluation and Revision: Answer the questions below to help you evaluate your essay.

- Did you write about the topic?
- Does your essay have a clear controlling idea that is developed throughout?
- Does your essay have a clear structure (introduction, body, and conclusion)?
  - Does your introduction tell the reader what the topic is and what you are going to say about it?
  - Does your body contain details and examples to support each point?
  - Does your conclusion sum up what you have written?
- Did you revise your essay to correct errors?

SKILLS ANALYSIS CHART

This chart will help you determine your strengths and identify the areas where your skills are less developed. It will also help you identify which types of test items you answer best and which are more difficult for you.

CATEGORIES	SENTENCE CORRECTION	SENTENCE REVISION	CONSTRUCTION SHIFT	SCORE
Part I Sentence Structure (pp. 77–165)	8, 15	9, 12, 17, 28	20, 23, 6	_____ of 9
Usage (pp. 167–238)	5, 11, 13, 21, 24	7, 18, 25, 27	14	_____ of 10
Mechanics (pp. 241–327)	1, 2, 4, 10, 16, 19, 22	3, 6	6	_____ of 9
SCORE	_____ of 14	_____ of 10	_____ of 4	_____ of 28
Part II GED Essay (pp. 25–73)	Strengths: Weaknesses:			

Finding the Results

To use the Skills Analysis Chart, circle the item number of each pretest question you answered *correctly*. Add each column *down* to find the number correct for each type of test question. Then add each row *across* to find the number correct for each major content area. Be sure to write comments about your essay in the bottom portion of this chart.

Using the Results

After you have totaled your scores, make a list of the areas you want to work on. Page references for instruction and practice on each area are provided on the chart. To understand how to use the materials you will find on these pages, turn to the next page.

How Can I Prepare for the GED Writing Skills Test?

This book has been specially designed to help you prepare for the GED Writing Skills Test. It will help you discover what you need to do to prepare for the test. It will provide you with the explanations, guided practice, and exercises you need. It will give you a "sneak preview" of what you can expect to see on the actual GED Writing Skills Test.

You can use this book however you choose based on your needs. Whether you are working with an instructor, a tutor, or on your own, this book will help you plan the course of study that will work best for you. The descriptions below tell you how you may want to use Sections 2 and 3 of this book and the special CONNECTIONS section at the end of the book.

Section 2: Foundation Skills for the Test

This section gives you a short review and plenty of opportunity to practice the basic, or "foundation," skills everyone needs for success on the GED Writing Skills Test. In this book, the writing process is presented as the foundation for success.

Foundation Skills

These lessons take you through the process of writing an essay. You'll see how to plan and organize your essay. You'll see how to write good paragraphs that develop one idea with detail and examples. You'll see how to write clear sentences with standard English usage and correct punctuation.

Skill Checkup

A Skill Checkup is provided at the end of every Foundation Skill lesson. This checkup gives you an opportunity to practice what you learned in the lesson.

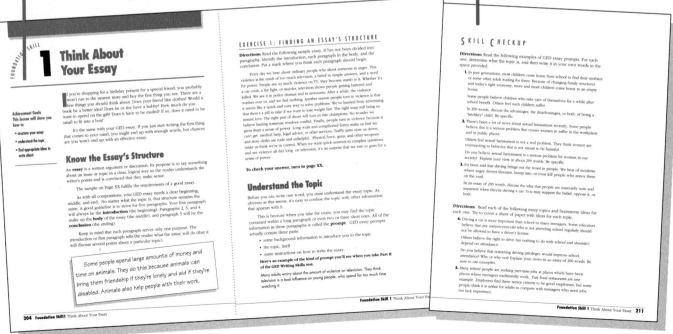

Section 3: Preparing for the Test

This section gives you thorough instruction, with plenty of opportunity for practice, in the three major content areas of Part I of the Writing Skills Test: sentence structure, usage, and mechanics. You may begin on the unit of your choice. There's no need to work through the lessons in a particular unit if you feel confident about your skills in that area. Each unit is self-contained, so it provides all the instruction and practice you need to be prepared in the content area it covers.

Unit Overview

Each unit begins with an overview. The unit lessons that follow cover specific topics you will find on the GED Writing Skills Test.

GED Test Preview

Every lesson contains a "preview" of typical GED-type questions. These questions test your knowledge of what is covered in the lesson.

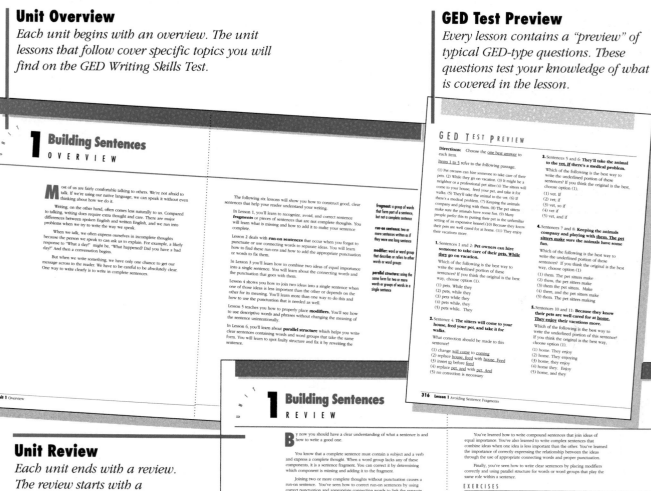

Unit Review

Each unit ends with a review. The review starts with a summary of the unit's content, followed by a comprehensive list of the terms encountered in the lessons. The exercises that follow simulate actual GED test questions. Each unit review is approximately half the length of the actual GED test.

Lesson Format

Within unit lessons, you will find instruction, examples, explanations, and a variety of practice opportunities. Practice exercises clarify your understanding of the lesson materials and allow you to practice with GED-type questions. Some allow you to work together with others to solve a problem. Every exercise in every lesson ends with a page reference to the answers and explanations you need to check your learning.

Lesson Openers

Lessons begin by identifying the learning goals and the relevance of the lesson material to your life.

Test-Taking Tips

Tips from instructors and others who have taken the test in the past are provided in the margin.

Practice Exercises and Write on Target

Each exercise begins with a challenging question or problem followed by several multiple-choice questions typical of what you might find on the actual GED Writing Skills Test. A Write on Target activity lets you apply some aspect of the writing process to a real-life writing task.

Interactive Instruction

The lesson instruction is written in a problem-solving approach. It includes questions you might be asking yourself, sample problems you might encounter, and answers to those questions and problems.

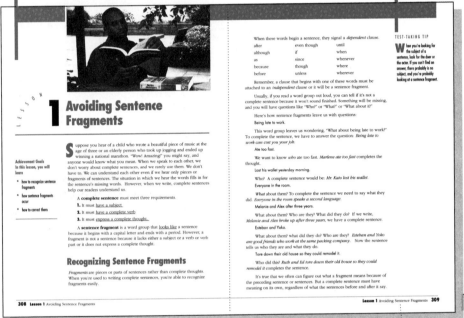

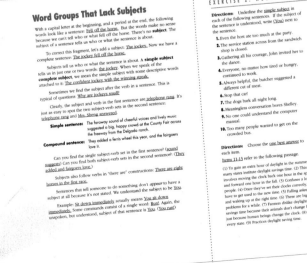

CONNECTIONS

CONNECTIONS is a unique, high-interest section of information, colorful graphic displays, and activities that appears in the back of the book. CONNECTIONS integrates information from all areas of the GED tests— writing, literature, social studies, science, and mathematics—around themes that are important to adults.

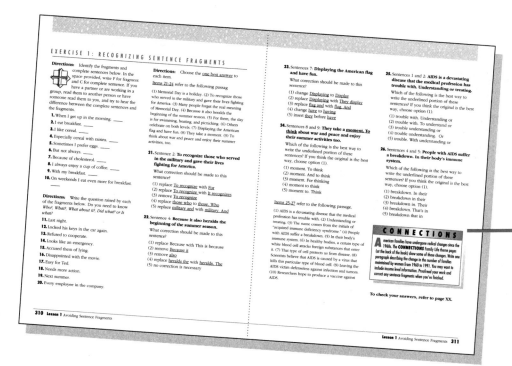

CONNECTIONS
Lesson Activity

Every lesson is "connected" to important life issues through a unique activity that sends you to the full-color pages at the back of the book.

CONNECTIONS
Theme Pages and Activities

Each of the theme pages covers a topic such as employment, family life, technology, and health and fitness. Every one has an employment information box called Working World, a writing activity called The Writing Connection, and a math activity called Problem Solver.

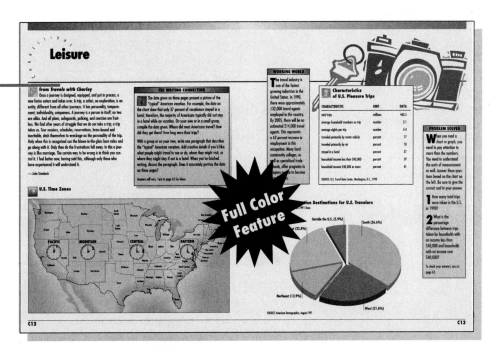

The Simulated GED Writing Skills Test

The Simulated GED Writing Skills Test, near the end of the book, provides a real-life testing situation in which you practice answering typical GED Writing Skills Test questions. It is identical in length to the actual GED Writing Skills Test. Like the actual test, it is a timed test. Completing this simulated test and analyzing your results will help you see if you are fully prepared for the actual GED Writing Skills Test.

Test Preparation Tips

The secret to passing the GED Writing Skills Test is knowing what to expect and being prepared to meet the challenge. Following are some tips that have helped many other adults.

Before the Day of the Test

1. **Read a variety of materials.** Although you don't need to know specific data to write the GED essay, it helps to be familiar with issues in the news. The more you read, the more confidence you will have about GED essay topics. Besides, the more you read, the better you will write. Reading informs you and makes you feel comfortable with the written word.

2. **Talk about what you are learning.** Studies have shown that adults may remember only 20 percent of what they hear. When adults talk about something with others and apply it to their lives, memory retention increases to 90 percent.

3. **Practice writing.** You might enjoy keeping a daily journal in which you write your thoughts, observations, and feelings. This activity not only increases your comfort about writing but also raises your awareness of the world around you. Raising your awareness will help you feel at ease with essay topics.

On the Day of the Test

1. Eat well so that you won't be tired or distracted by hunger during the test.

2. Bring the materials you will need: identification, admission ticket, three or four sharpened No. 2 pencils, an eraser, and a watch.

3. Arrive early enough to find the testing room and to relax before the test starts.

4. Read test directions carefully to be sure you understand what is being asked.

5. Don't spend a lot of time on questions you can't answer easily. Skip those and finish the test. Go back to difficult questions and guess at the answers if you have to. Don't leave any questions unanswered.

6. Allow yourself plenty of time to plan your essay. Planning can take up to a third of your essay writing time. Remember, if you plan and organize your essay, the actual writing will be much easier.

7. Although handwriting will not be scored on the test, try to keep your answer sheet neat. Erase or cross out with a single line. Carefully correct mistakes and make changes you feel will improve your essay.

8. If you become anxious, take a deep breath, stretch, relax for a few minutes, and remember that you are prepared.

9. Believe in yourself. After having practiced essay writing (Section 2: Foundation Skills), having worked through the lessons in areas that needed review and practice (Section 3: Preparing for the Test), and having answered the many questions posed to you Sections 1, 2, and 3 of this book, you will be well prepared for the GED Writing Skills Test.

2 Foundation Skills for the GED
WRITING SKILLS TEST

Skill 1 Think About Your Essay   26

Know the Essay's Structure, 26 • Understand
the Topic, 30 • Collect Ideas, 31

Skill 2 Organize Your Material   36

Group Ideas, 36 • Limit the Number of Groups,
37 • Make a Point, 38 • Create an Outline, 40

Skill 3 Write Your Essay   46

Introduce the Subject, 46 • Develop the Body,
50 • Tie It Up, 53

Skill 4 Revise Your Work   56

Stick to the Subject, 56 • Does Your Essay Have
a Clear Structure? 58 • Did You Use Clear and
Interesting Examples? 60 • Did You Choose the
Best Words? 61

Skill 5 Edit Your Work   64

Are the Sentences Complete? 64 • Is the Essay
Free of Spelling, Capitalization, and Punctuation
Errors? 65 • Have You Used Standard English? 66

ANSWERS AND EXPLANATIONS   68

1 Think About Your Essay

ACHIEVEMENT GOALS
This lesson will show you how to

- structure your essay

- understand the topic

- find appropriate ideas to write about

If you're shopping for a birthday present for a special friend, you probably won't run to the nearest store and buy the first thing you see. Before selecting a gift, you should think about a few things. Does your friend like clothes? Would a book be a better idea? Does he or she have a hobby? How much do you want to spend on the gift? Does it have to be mailed? If so, does it need to be small to fit into a box?

You should use the same care with your GED essay. If you just start writing the first thing that comes to your mind, you might end up with enough words, but chances are you won't end up with an effective essay.

Know the Essay's Structure

An **essay** is a written argument or discussion. Its purpose is to say something about an issue or a topic in a clear, logical way so that the reader understands the writer's points and is convinced that they make sense. The sample in Figure 1-1 fulfills the requirements of a good essay.

As with all compositions, your GED essay needs structure. It needs a clear beginning, middle, and end. No matter what the topic is, this structure remains the same. A good way to achieve this structure is to strive for five paragraphs. Your first paragraph, then, will be the **introduction** (the beginning). Paragraphs 2, 3, and 4 will make up the **body** of the essay (the middle), and paragraph 5 will be the **conclusion** (the ending).

Keep in mind that each paragraph in your essay should serve only one purpose. The introduction, or first paragraph, tells the reader what the essay will do (that it will discuss several points about a particular topic). Each of the body paragraphs discusses one of those points. The concluding paragraph briefly sums up the discussion to end the essay.

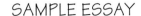

SAMPLE ESSAY

Some people spend large amounts of money and time on animals. They do this because animals can bring them friendship if they're lonely and aid if they're disabled. Animals also help people with their work.

People who live alone might count on a pet for company. An eager dog, wagging its tail, might welcome them home from a tiring day at work. A warm kitten might snuggle up and keep them company while they read or watch television.

For the physically disabled, an animal can make life easier. Seeing-eye dogs help blind people get around. Highly skilled dogs and chimpanzees can turn lights on and off and get food for people who are paralyzed.

Besides appreciating animals for friendship and aid, some people depend on animals in their work. The police rely on dogs to help catch criminals. Scientists use dolphins and other animals to study behavior. People who work in the wilderness can use pack animals such as horses and llamas, to provide transportation or carry heavy loads.

Animals serve as friends, as helpers, and as workers. That's why people are willing to spend time and money caring for them.

Introduction

Body

Conclusion

Figure 1-1 This sample meets all the criteria for a good essay.

> Some people spend large amounts of money and time on animals. They do this because animals can bring them friendship if they're lonely and aid if they're disabled. Animals also help people with their work.

This introductory paragraph lets the reader know that animals provide people with three things: friendship, aid to the disabled, and help with work. Notice that no specific examples or details are given in the introduction to support those three points. An introduction is general.

> People who live alone might count on a pet for company. An eager dog, wagging its tail, might welcome them home from a tiring day at work. A warm kitten might snuggle up and keep them company while they read or watch television.

The second paragraph opens with a topic sentence, or a general statement, about animals as friends. Then the entire paragraph illustrates ways in which animals serve people as friends. The paragraph talks about nothing else.

> For the physically disabled, an animal can make life easier. Seeing-eye dogs help blind people get around. Highly skilled dogs and chimpanzees can turn lights on and off and get food for people who are paralyzed.

The third paragraph opens with a general statement about the ability of animals to ease the lives of disabled people. The remaining sentences show the reader how animals can help the blind and the paralyzed. Nothing in the paragraph deals with subjects other than animals helping the disabled.

> Besides appreciating animals for friendship and aid, some people depend on animals in their work. The police rely on dogs to help catch criminals. Scientists use dolphins and other animals to study behavior. People who work in the wilderness can use pack animals, such as horses and llamas, to provide transportation or carry heavy loads.

The fourth paragraph opens with a general statement about animals doing work for people, which is the topic of this paragraph. The rest of the sentences, again, illustrate the main idea.

> Animals serve as friends, as helpers, and as workers. That's why people are willing to spend time and money caring for them.

The fifth paragraph is the conclusion, which ties together everything in the essay. Like the introduction, it is general. Examples and illustrations appear only in the body of the essay.

EXERCISE 1: FINDING ESSAY STRUCTURE

Directions: Read the following sample essay. It has not been divided into paragraphs. Identify the introduction, each paragraph in the body, and the conclusion. Put a mark where you think each paragraph should begin.

Every day we hear about ordinary people who shoot others in anger. This violence is the result of viewing too much mayhem on television, a belief in simple answers, and a need for power. People see so much violence on television that they become numb to it. Whether it's a car crash, a fist fight, or a murder, television shows people getting battered and killed. We see violence in police dramas and in newscasts. After a while, the violence washes over us, and we feel nothing. Another reason people turn to violence is that it seems like a quick and easy way to solve problems. We've learned from advertising that a pill may be taken if we want to lose weight fast. The right soap will bring us instant love. The right pair of shoes will turn us into champions. No wonder we believe beating someone resolves conflict. Finally, people turn to violence because it gives them a sense of power. Long waits and complicated forms make us feel we can't get medical help, legal advice, or other services. Traffic jams slow us down, and store clerks are rude and unhelpful. Physical force, guns, and other weapons make us think we're in control. When we want quick answers to complex questions and see violence all day long on television, it's no surprise that we turn to guns for a sense of power.

To check your answer, turn to page 68.

Understand the Topic

Before you begin writing your essay, you must understand the topic. As obvious as this advice seems, it's easy to confuse the topic of an essay with other information that appears with it.

When you take the GED exam, a series of paragraphs, called the **prompt,** will assign a topic on which an essay must be written. You may find the topic buried within a long paragraph or perhaps stretched across two or three short ones. Regardless of their particular construction, GED essay prompts actually contain three parts:

- some *background* information to introduce you to the topic
- the *topic* itself
- some *instructions* on how to write the essay

Here's an example of the kind of prompt you'll see when you take Part II of the GED Writing Skills Test:

> Many adults worry about the amount of violence on television. They think television is a bad influence on young people, who spend far too much time watching it. Others take a different view, believing that television has many good features for children and teenagers.
>
> Write an essay of about 200 words in which you discuss the positive effects television has on young people. Be sure to use examples.

At first glance, you might assume the essay topic is violence on television because that's the topic of the first sentence you read. Violence on television would be a good essay topic. It's a controversial subject, and you might have many ideas and opinions about it. But, in this prompt, violence on television is *background* to the topic itself.

If you read the entire prompt carefully, you'll realize that the mention of violence on television simply *prepares* you to consider the real topic, which is *the positive effects television has on young people.* If you don't read everything in the prompt, you could mistakenly write about the wrong topic, and even if your essay were otherwise perfect, you'd get no credit because you didn't write about the assigned topic.

Use these guidelines to find the topic when you read a GED essay prompt:

- Look for a statement that tells you to do something.
- Look for a question that you must answer.

Notice that the prompt also tells you how long the essay should be and reminds you to use examples. As noted above, these specific *instructions* make up the third part of a GED essay prompt.

Directions: Read the following example of a GED essay prompt. Determine what the topic is, then write it in your own words to be sure you understand it.

In recent years, only a small percentage of eligible voters have turned out for local and national elections. Many people think their votes don't make a difference, so they don't bother to go to the polls. Yet voting is a major right granted to citizens in a democracy.

Citizens of a democracy also enjoy many other rights. In an essay of 200 words, discuss some of the other rights individuals have in America. Be sure to illustrate your ideas.

To check your answer, turn to page 68.

Collect Ideas

After you read a prompt and understand the topic, you need to decide what to say about it. There is a way to see that you have a great deal to say. To discover your own ideas, all you have to do is start with one idea (the topic) and **brainstorm.** To brainstorm means to write down every single thought that comes into your mind that relates to a topic. Brainstorming is a good way to collect ideas for later use in your essay.

Brainstorming is a time to let yourself be free and open. One thought will probably trigger another. It doesn't matter whether these thoughts are good ideas. It's important just to get something down on paper so that you'll see that you actually have plenty to say about a topic.

Brainstorming is not the time to judge your ideas or to worry about how they could fit into an essay. The goal is to write down everything you think, to build your idea pool. Some ideas you'll keep, and others you'll discard, but those decisions will come later.

Let's return to the topic of the positive effects television has on young people. (To see the full prompt, turn to page 30.) Perhaps the first thing that comes to your mind when you consider this topic is that you like to watch television. Write that idea down. Maybe then you'll ask yourself why you enjoy watching television and will follow with some answers to that question. Maybe you'll write down names of programs you watch, and those titles will suggest other ideas.

While brainstorming, beginning writers should place ideas randomly all over the page. Random placement helps keep ideas flowing, letting one idea stimulate another and freeing you from restrictions that occur when you list ideas. Figures 1-2 and 1-3 on the next page show some results of brainstorming and how random placement works.

Figure 1-2 As you begin to write down ideas, your paper will resemble this illustration.

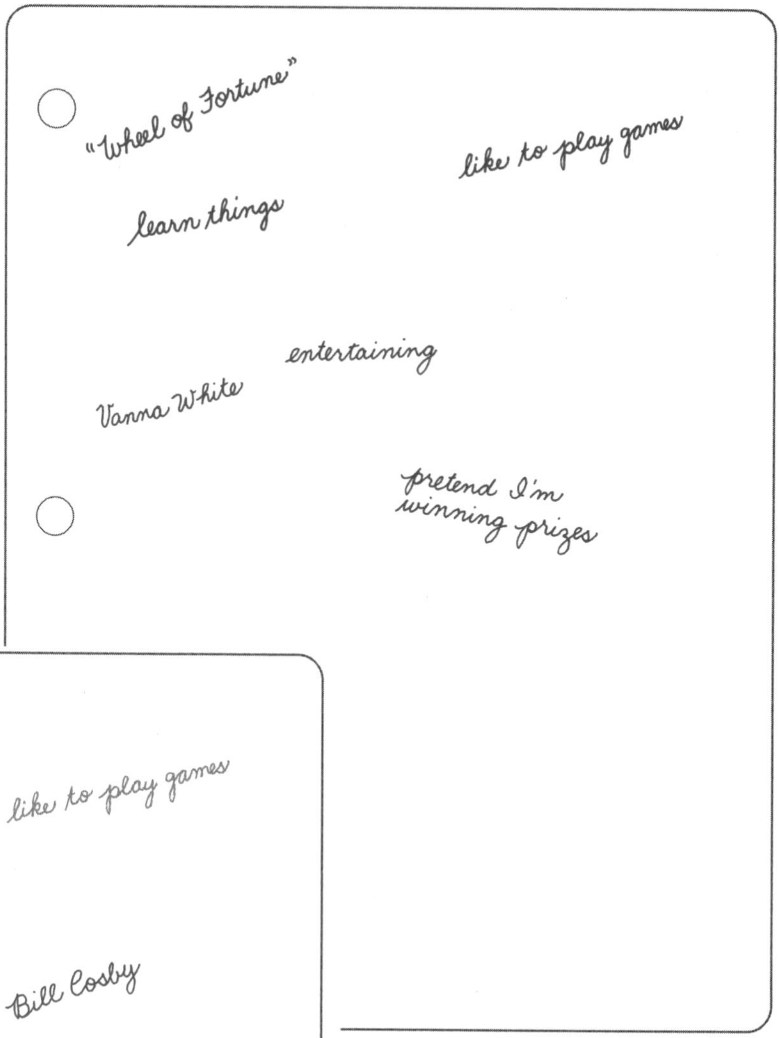

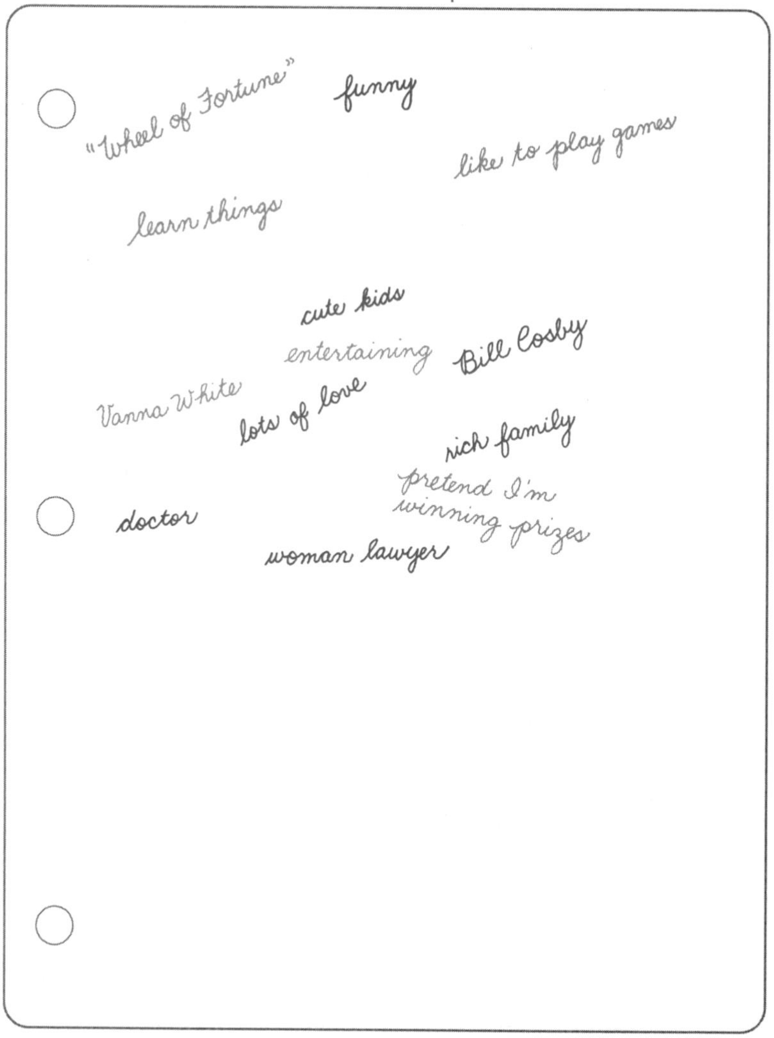

"Wheel of Fortune"

like to play games

learn things

Vanna White   entertaining

pretend I'm winning prizes

"Wheel of Fortune"   funny

like to play games

learn things

cute kids

entertaining   Bill Cosby

Vanna White   lots of love

rich family

pretend I'm winning prizes

doctor

woman lawyer

Figure 1-3 As you brainstorm new ideas, add them randomly to your paper.

As your mind roams freely about the topic, you may think of words such as *murder, car chases, blood,* and *shootings.* Go ahead and write them down, but when you look at these words later, you'll realize that they're inappropriate for this essay because they relate to violence, a negative impact of television. Your job is to discuss television's *good* effects.

When you've finished brainstorming, your paper will look similar to Figure 1-4.

Figure 1-4 The goal of brainstorming is to cover your paper with ideas that relate to the topic.

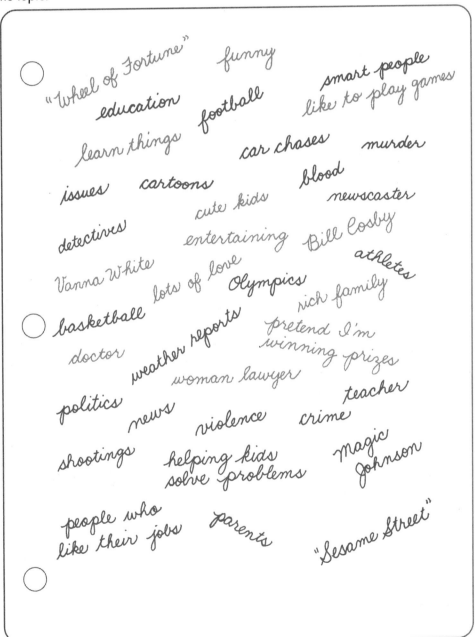

"Wheel of Fortune" funny smart people like to play games
education football
learn things
issues cartoons car chases murder
detectives cute kids blood newscaster
entertaining Bill Cosby
Vanna White lots of love Olympics athletes
basketball rich family
doctor weather reports pretend I'm winning prizes
politics woman lawyer
news teacher
shootings violence crime
helping kids solve problems magic Johnson
people who like their jobs parents "Sesame Street"

Directions: Read the following GED essay prompt:

Many states have lotteries in which people can win huge amounts of money. States use part of the lottery money for prizes and part of it to pay for state services, such as education. Because lotteries are a form of gambling, some people disapprove of governments supporting them.

What is your opinion of this issue? In an essay of about 200 words, discuss the pros, cons, or both of state lotteries. Be sure to use details and examples in your essay.

Now write down the first idea that comes to your head when you think of state lotteries. Continue to brainstorm, covering a sheet of paper with your ideas.

To check your answer, turn to page 68.

NOTE: *Save your answer. You'll need it to complete an exercise in Foundation Skill 2.*

S KILL C HECKUP

Directions: Read the following examples of GED essay prompts. For each prompt, determine the topic, then write it in your own words.

1. In past generations, most children came home from school to find their mothers or some other adult waiting for them. Because of changing family structures and today's tight economy, more and more children come home to empty houses. Some people believe children who take care of themselves for a while after school benefit. Others feel these children suffer.

In 200 words, discuss the advantages, the disadvantages, or both of being a latchkey child. Be specific.

2. A lot of reports about sexual harassment have recently appeared in the newspapers. Some people believe that sexual harassment is a serious problem that causes women to suffer in the workplace and in other public places. Others feel that sexual harassment is not a real problem. They think women are overreacting to behavior that is not meant to be harmful.

Do you believe sexual harassment is a serious problem for women in our society? Explain your view in about 200 words. Be specific.

3. It's been said that driving brings out the worst in people. We hear of incidents where angry drivers threaten, bump into, or even kill people who annoy them on the road.

In an essay of 200 words, discuss the idea that people are especially rude and impatient when they're driving a car. You may support the belief, oppose it, or both.

Directions: Read each of the following essay topics and brainstorm ideas for each one. Try to cover a sheet of paper with ideas for each topic.

4. Driving a car is more important to many teenagers than attending school. Some educators believe that any sixteen year old who is not attending school regularly should not be allowed to have a driver's license. Others believe the right to drive has nothing to do with school and shouldn't depend on attendance.

Do you believe that restricting driving privileges would improve school attendance? Why or why not? Explain your views in an essay of 200 words. Be sure to use examples.

5. Many retired people seek part-time jobs at places where teenagers traditionally work. Fast-food restaurants are one example. Employers find senior citizens to be good employees, but some people think it is unfair for adults to compete with teenagers who need jobs but lack experience.

In an essay of 200 words, explain your views on senior citizens and teenagers seeking jobs at the same places.

6. Most cities have at least one daily newspaper, and many cities have more than one. Newspapers are available by subscription and are delivered to people's homes, or they are available at newsstands.

Still, many people never read a newspaper. Do you think it's important to read a daily newspaper? Explain your view in 200 words. Be specific.

To check your answers, turn to page 68.

NOTE: *Save your answers. You will need them to complete the Skill Checkup in Foundation Skill 2.*

2 Organize Your Material

Running errands, buying groceries, making appointments, and scheduling kids' activities all require a certain amount of organization and planning. In your daily life, you organize and plan all the time. Now you will learn how to do it in an essay.

ACHIEVEMENT GOALS
This lesson will show you how to

- make sense out of a jumble of ideas

- be sure your essay makes a point

- plan what you're going to say before you start writing

Group Ideas

In Foundation Skill 1, you covered a page with a random collection of ideas resulting from brainstorming. Now you need to put these ideas into *groups* as a first step toward organizing an essay.

To see how this works, let's look again at Figure 1-4 on page 33, the brainstorming sample for our topic, the positive effects television has on young people. (See page 30 for the complete prompt.) As you look over the ideas you've collected, you'll see that most of them fall naturally into groups. Somehow they seem related to other ideas on the page. Now is the appropriate time to arrange your ideas into lists.

For example, you might put *shootings, car chases, murder,* and *crime* into a group labeled *TV Violence.* Maybe you'll group *funny, like to play games, Bill Cosby,* and *"Sesame Street"* and label the collection *Entertainment.* You'll probably find that some ideas fall into more than one group and that some ideas stand alone, not forming a group at all. You may end up with several lists that look similar to the lists illustrated in Figure 2-1 on page 37.

EXERCISE 1: GROUPING IDEAS

Directions: In Foundation Skill 1, Exercise 3 (page 34), you were asked to brainstorm ideas for an essay on state lotteries. Look at your paper from that exercise and find ideas that seem to be related to each other. Put them into groups. Give each group a label. If you didn't save your work, redo the exercise now.

To check your answer, turn to page 68.

NOTE: *Save your answer. You will need it to complete the next exercise.*

Figure 2-1 Your new sheet of paper will group ideas that seem to belong together. You can give the groups labels.

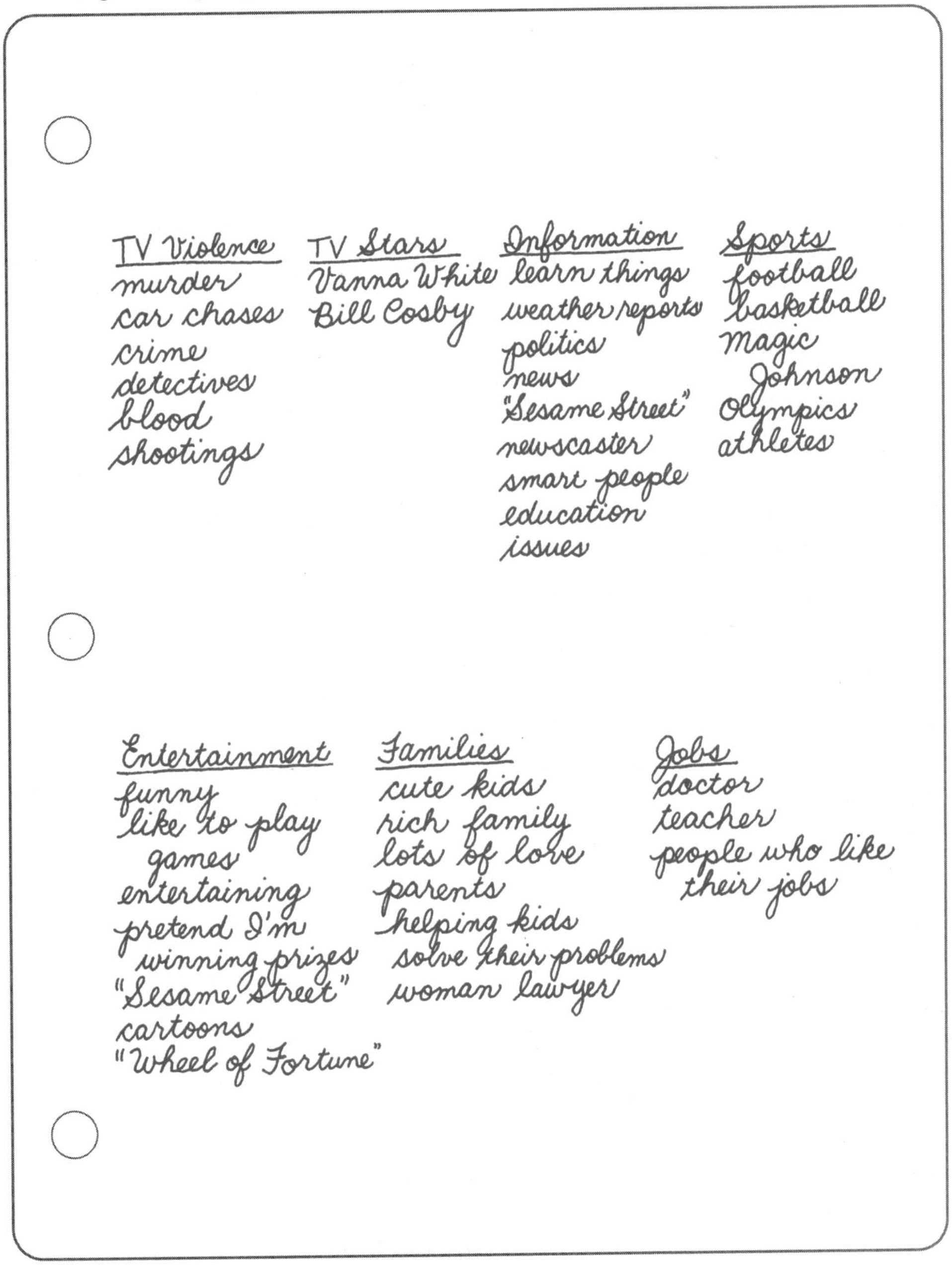

<u>TV Violence</u>
murder
car chases
crime
detectives
blood
shootings

<u>TV Stars</u>
Vanna White
Bill Cosby

<u>Information</u>
learn things
weather reports
politics
news
"Sesame Street"
newscaster
smart people
education
issues

<u>Sports</u>
football
basketball
Magic
 Johnson
Olympics
athletes

<u>Entertainment</u>
funny
like to play
 games
entertaining
pretend I'm
 winning prizes
"Sesame Street"
cartoons
"Wheel of Fortune"

<u>Families</u>
cute kids
rich family
lots of love
parents
helping kids
solve their problems
woman lawyer

<u>Jobs</u>
doctor
teacher
people who like
 their jobs

Limit the Number of Groups

We want your essay on the good effects of television to make three major points. (See "Know the Essay's Structure" in Foundation Skill 1 on page 26.) Your next task, then, is to reduce the number of groups to only three. Later, these three groups will become the three paragraphs in the body of your essay.

Here are some ways to get your material to fit into three groups:

- Eliminate groups that are short, inappropriate, or don't interest you.
- Take ideas from some groups and put them into others.
- Combine two groups into one and give it a new label.

With a computer, you can easily move ideas around among groups, using the cut-and-paste technique. Likewise, you can eliminate groups you don't want simply by deleting them from the screen. With a partner, you can discuss different ways to group ideas and how best to label each group.

After you have finished reducing the number of groups to three, your page of groups will look something like Figure 2-2 on page 39.

In our sample we've ended up with three groups, labeled *Entertainment, Information,* and *Goals.*

NOTE: *Although our essay about the positive effects of television will make three points, some essays may need only two. For example, if you're asked to compare life in the city with life in the country, you may want to write an essay with only four paragraphs: an introduction, a paragraph about city life, a paragraph about country life, and a conclusion.*

E X E R C I S E 2 : R E G R O U P I N G I D E A S

Directions: Look at the groups you formed for the essay on state lotteries in Exercise 1 on page 36. Work with these groups until you have reduced them to only three.

To check your answer, turn to page 70.

NOTE: *Save your answer. You will need it to complete the next exercise.*

Make a Point

Now that you have narrowed your ideas about television down to three main groups, you're ready to make a point about the essay's topic. In other words, now you can see where your essay is going and what it will do.

Actually, the topic has already determined your point: *television is not all bad for kids,* or *television does some good things for kids.* Your job is to say something about that point, and you can do that in one sentence. This sentence, called a **thesis statement,** forms the central idea of your entire essay. A thesis statement is essential to your writing because it gives your essay direction, focus, and control.

Figure 2-2 Move items around to condense your ideas into three groups. *TV Violence* is not an appropriate group for this essay, but you may use some of the ideas from that group in other groups. The asterisks show the three groups you'll keep.

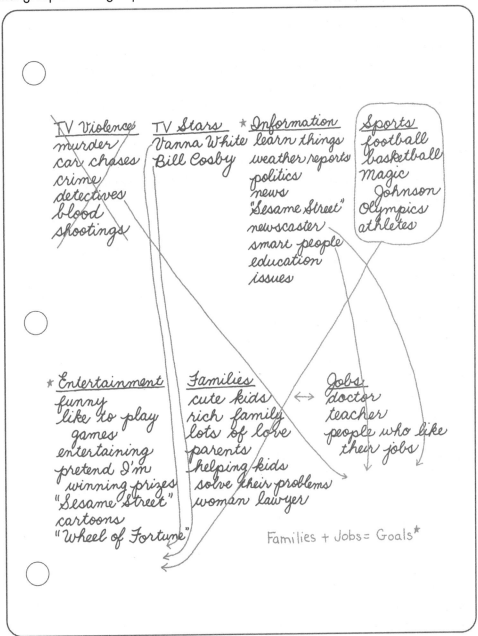

Once you have three groups of ideas, it's easy to create a thesis statement. All you have to do is combine the topic (the positive effects television has on young people) with the three groups you developed (entertainment, information, and goals).

Here's a possible thesis statement for your essay:

Television is sometimes good for young people because it entertains them, keeps them informed, and helps them set positive goals.

Another possible thesis might be:

Although adults worry that television is bad for children, actually television provides entertainment and information for young people and helps them set goals.

Fifteen writers on the same topic will probably write fifteen different thesis statements, but each statement must contain the topic and the main points each writer wants to make about the topic.

With some topics, two or three points to discuss may come to your mind right away. If that happens, as it often does with more experienced writers, you actually begin to plan your essay with group labels rather than with brainstormed ideas. You will need, however, to fill in details, or ideas, for each label.

For example, suppose your topic is how to help the homeless. It may occur to you immediately that homeless people need shelter, jobs, and emotional support. Thus, you already have three points for your thesis, which might read as follows:

To help the homeless, we must provide inexpensive housing, job training, and psychological counseling.

Now you can brainstorm ideas that relate to each of these three points (housing, jobs, and counseling).

Once you've written a thesis statement, you have taken control of the essay.

EXERCISE 3: WRITING THESIS STATEMENTS

Directions: Look at your work from Exercise 2 (page 38) in which you created groups and labels for ideas about state lotteries (see page 34 for the complete prompt). Using those labels, write two different thesis statements for the essay. If you didn't do Exercise 2, do it now.

To check your answer, turn to page 70.

Create an Outline

Just as a map can keep you from getting lost if you're driving to a place for the first time, an outline, or written guide, can keep you from wandering off track when you write an essay.

An **outline** is simply a plan to get you from the beginning of your essay to the end. It helps you stick to the subject of each paragraph and keeps your essay organized and under control.

Some people are comfortable with a traditional outline that uses numbers, letters, and words to keep track of ideas. Others prefer pictures to guide them on the road to a complete, well-structured essay. Whichever type of guide you use, you're far more likely to reach your goal if you follow a plan that you can look at as you write.

The outline needn't be complicated nor long. For a five-paragraph essay, you only need five main points, one for each paragraph (or four points if you are writing a four-paragraph essay). Let's look at an outline (Figure 2-3) for the sample essay about why people spend time and money on animals. The sample essay appears on page 27.

Figure 2-3 The outline numbers each paragraph that will appear in the essay. The main point of the paragraph appears first, and below it are the supporting details.

Outline of Sample Essay

1. Introduction
   a. Attention-grabber (people spend money and time on animals)
   b. Thesis (friendship, aid, help with work)

2. Pets offer company
   a. dog awaits eagerly at the end of workday
   b. kitten snuggles by television

3. Animals help disabled
   a. seeing-eye dogs
   b. dogs and chimps do things around house
      - lights
      - get food for paralyzed

4. Animals help with work
   a. police
   b. scientists study behavior (dolphins)
   c. pack animals in wilderness

5. Conclusion
   a. Restate thesis (use different words)
   b. Closing thought

There's no mystery to creating an outline. In fact, for your essay about the positive effects of television, you've already done most of the work. You've learned that an essay, regardless of the topic, must begin with an introduction; therefore, your first paragraph will always be an introduction. Likewise, a good essay will end with a conclusion, which will be your fifth paragraph in a five-paragraph essay. The three paragraphs in the middle, the body of the essay, come from the three points made in your thesis. An outline simply maps out each of these paragraphs.

Because your essay won't be very effective if each paragraph contains only one sentence, you must support each point in your thesis with details and examples. In other words, you must show your reader what each part of your thesis means by using examples that you have jotted down in an outline.

Once again, you've already done most of the necessary work. When you separated your brainstorming ideas into groups, you were collecting details to put into the essay. The outline helps you put those details into a logical order, ensuring that you write a logically developed essay.

To see how an outline works, let's outline one of the paragraphs for your essay on the positive effects television has on young people (see page 30 for the complete prompt). We'll use television informs, the second point in the thesis, to develop that section of the outline.

NOTE: *It might be necessary to do some more brainstorming at the outline stage to get more detail*.

Look again at Figure 2-2 on page 39. The group labeled *Information* contains nine items. Your task now is to organize those items into subgroups. You organize subgroups in the same way that you grouped your brainstorming ideas.

Let's assume that, as you look at the group, you think of more things you learn from watching television (more brainstorming), and you add those new ideas to the group. Now the group contains fourteen items: *learn things, weather reports, politics, news, "Sesame Street," education, issues, documentaries, Big Bird, new cars, cold medicines, credit cards, talk shows,* and *candidates*.

Your essay won't be very well organized if you simply *list* all these ideas in a paragraph about information. Instead, you need to subgroup them. You may now notice that several items are related to commercials. Others, such as *candidates, news,* and *talk shows,* have to do with current events. Still others have to do with learning the kinds of things kids learn in school: *documentaries* and *"Sesame Street."*

To make a more useful outline, fill in examples and supporting details for each subpoint as shown in the example below:

3. Television informs

   a. Current events

     - News programs—local, national, international

     - Elections—know candidates and issues

     - Talk shows—current issues

      - Oprah, Donahue, etc.

      - Weird lifestyles, victims of crime, etc.

   b. School-type learning

     - Documentaries

      - Animals

      - Other countries

     - Children's programs

      - "Sesame Street"

      - Reading, songs, numbers

   c. Commercials

     - Consumer products—cars, toys, food

     - Services—credit cards, banks, telephone companies

     - Other programs to watch for

You may think of even more ideas to include in your essay when you begin to subgroup and to organize ideas within the outline. You also might find that some of your earlier ideas no longer fit. That's okay. Just throw them out. You'll have plenty to write without them.

The important thing about creating an outline is that you will now have all your material jotted down in a logical order. If you follow the steps in your outline, you will know your essay will stay on topic, will move forward logically, and will be easy for your reader to follow. And what is better, you won't have to worry about what to write because you will have the entire essay mapped out. All you have to do is follow the map.

At the outline stage, you may find that you have too much material for a 200-word essay. If that happens, eliminate one or two subgroups. But, remember, it's always better to go into the writing stage knowing you won't be at a loss for something to say rather than worrying that you'll have too little to say.

The preliminary steps in writing an essay are so important that *you should expect to spend one-third to one-half of your time on this part of the project.* You will not need more than half the time to write if you use the first half for careful planning and organizing.

EXERCISE 4: WRITING OUTLINES

Directions: Look at the other two groups for the essay on the positive effects television has on young people (see Figure 2-2 on page 39). Outline paragraphs that will be based on the groups labeled *Entertainment* and *Goals*.

To check your answer, turn to page 70.

S KILL C HECKUP

Directions: Complete each of the following steps in the essay writing process.

1. In the Skill Checkup for Foundation Skill 1, you brainstormed ideas for three GED topics (see page 35 for the prompts). Put the items from each of those sets of ideas into groups. Label each group. If you didn't do the brainstorming, do it now.

2. Combine the topic with the three labels you have just written and write thesis statements for each essay.

3. Turn the thesis statements you've just written into outlines for five-paragraph essays. Brainstorm, as needed, to fill in details for the body of your essays.

To check your answers, turn to page 70.

NOTE: *Save your answers. You will need them to complete the Skill Checkup in Foundation Skill 3 and an exercise in Foundation Skill 4.*

3 Write Your Essay

By the time you're actually ready to write your essay, you've already done the hardest part of the job—planning and organizing. Now your job is to put your ideas into sentences and paragraphs.

ACHIEVEMENT GOALS
This lesson will show you how to write the essay's

• introduction

• body

• conclusion

Introduce the Subject

Your essay's first paragraph, the introduction, tells the reader two things: (a) what the topic is and (b) what you are going to say about that topic (in other words, your thesis). At the same time, the introduction should capture the readers' attention. You can generate interest by writing a sentence or two to "hook" the readers; that is, by giving them some background information about the topic to engage their curiosity. The sample essay in Figure 1-1 on page 27 opens with this sentence: *Some people spend large amounts of money and time on animals.* That sentence is the **hook**. From that point, the introduction tells your readers what the essay will say about this idea.

Let's return to the topic of the positive impact of television on young people. (To see the complete prompt, turn to page 30.) You've decided, through brainstorming, grouping, and outlining, that *what you are going to say about the topic* is this: that television has a positive impact on young people because it entertains them, informs them, and helps them establish goals. This is, in fact, your thesis statement, or controlling idea. All you have to do to write the introduction, then, is to catch the reader's attention and then state your thesis.

A simple outline structure for an introduction would look like this:

1. Introduction

    a. Attention-grabber (or hook)

    b. Thesis

Based on this simple outline, here's how your essay's first paragraph might look:

> Many adults think television is the cause of all society's problems. They think television is a terrible influence because children watch too much of it. But, in some ways, television actually does good things for young people. It not only entertains them, but it keeps them informed and helps them set goals for the future.

Notice that four sentences were used to introduce the essay. The first two sentences serve to hook the reader, or get the reader's attention. The second two sentences express the thesis. You could do this with only two sentences. A two-sentence introduction could be written as follows:

Many people think television is a bad influence on young people. However, television entertains children, keeps them informed, and helps them establish goals for their future.

The four-sentence introduction is more complete and more interesting than the two-sentence introduction, but both paragraphs do a good job of introducing the essay. Both paragraphs accurately tell the reader *what the topic is* and *what the writer is going to say about the topic.*

Notice what the introductory paragraph does *not* do:

- **It doesn't announce what it will say.** It doesn't say *"In this essay, I will show . . ."* If you have a clearly stated thesis, you don't need to *tell* the reader what you are going to say, you *just say it.*

- **It doesn't apologize for not being a good essay.** It doesn't say *"I'll do the best I can, but this is a hard topic."*

- **It doesn't wander away from the topic.** It doesn't say *"We have two television sets in our house, but my sister and I still fight over what to watch. I wouldn't spend five minutes watching the stuff she likes. I don't even like the same music she listens to. And I can't stand her clothes. Even her friends are hard to take."*

- **It doesn't contain specific details or examples.** The introduction must be general; examples will come later.

Let's write an introduction to an essay on this topic: Are team sports good for children?

Let's assume you've already completed the planning stages for your essay and you've decided to make *three points about the topic.* What you are going to say is this:

1. Team sports are a good way to make friends.

2. Team sports are good for health and fitness.

3. Team sports can put too much pressure on young athletes.

The thesis statement might be stated as follows:

Participating in team sports is a good way for children to make friends and to promote health and fitness, but team sports sometimes put too much pressure on some kids.

Remember, the thesis statement serves two important functions:

1. It gives your essay focus and direction. You know exactly what you are going to write about.

2. You can use it, exactly as written, in your introduction.

Now it's time to make use of an outline. Let's look at an outline for the essay on children and team sports. Refer to Figure 3-1. Following the outline, the introduction might read as follows:

> There are all kinds of after-school and weekend sports opportunities for kids. Participating in team sports is a good way for children to make friends and to promote health and fitness, but team sports sometimes put too much pressure on some kids.

NOTE: *When you write an introduction, you don't have to use the exact words you wrote to list the points that you are going to make about a topic. Nor do you have to use the words exactly as they appear in your thesis statement. You may change words as long as you don't change ideas. As a writer, you are free to choose the words you prefer, but be sure they convey the same ideas that you put into your thesis statement.*

The following example changes the words in the thesis statement about team sports, but does not change the ideas:

> Team sports provide great social opportunities. They also help children stay healthy and fit. But if the competition creates too much pressure, league sports can be harmful.

EXERCISE 1: WRITING AN INTRODUCTION

Directions: Read the following GED essay prompt:

America is facing a health care crisis. Many politicians and health care professionals believe we can keep medical costs down only if we take better care of ourselves and try to prevent illness.

Write a 200-word essay in which you show how people can accept responsibility for their own health care.

Your topic: Show how people can accept responsibility for their own health to keep medical costs down.

Your main points:

- People must become informed.
- People must look at diet and exercise.
- People must create a safe home environment.

Now use this information to write an introduction. When you have written your introduction, check for the following:

- Will the opening grab the reader's attention?
- Will the reader know what the topic is?
- Will the reader know what you intend to say about the topic?

In other words, is your thesis clear?

To check your answer, turn to page 70.

Figure 3-1 An outline creates a logical plan for each paragraph in your essay.

1. Introduction
   a. Hook
   b. Thesis

2. Good way to make friends
   a. Part of team
      - Work together
      - Share goals
      - Practice regularly
      - Get to know teammates well
   b. Parties
      - Celebrate victories (out for pizza)
      - Visit each other's houses (overnights)
      - Meetings to discuss games and plans
   c. Varied backgrounds
      - At school, kids from other classes
      - Maybe from other schools

3. Good for health and fitness
   a. Exercise
      - Running
      - Warm-ups
      - Frequent practice
      - Stay fit to stay skilled
      - Burn fat
   b. Improved diet
      - Coach teaches about nutrition
      - No time to sit around and eat junk
      - Want to eat well to stay strong

4. Too much pressure
   a. Competition scares kids
      - Hate to lose
      - Afraid of making mistakes
      - Afraid to let down team
      - Afraid to disappoint coach and parents
   b. Interference with school
      - Worrying about games
      - Neglecting homework to practice
   c. Pregame tension
      - Can't eat
      - Obsessed with winning
      - Game no longer fun

5. Conclusion
   a. Thesis
   b. Closing thought

Develop the Body

Once you've written the introduction, you're ready to develop the body of the essay. These middle paragraphs are the most complicated paragraphs in your essay because they contain the details and examples you thought of when brainstorming.

You can feel confident, however, that you will be able to develop the body of your essay because you have an outline to follow. Your outline maps out a logical order for the ideas that will support each part of your thesis. Your job now is to expand that outline into sentence and paragraph form.

Use Topic Sentences

Try to begin each paragraph in the body with a sentence that is general. That sentence, sometimes called the **topic sentence**, tells the reader what the paragraph is about, but it doesn't contain any examples. Examples come after the topic sentence.

Let's look at the outline for the second paragraph in the essay on whether team sports are good for children (Figure 3-1 on page 49). The first point of your thesis, which is the subject of your second paragraph, is that team sports help children make friends. The subheadings underneath represent the details and examples that will be used to support the main point, or subject, of the paragraph.

To write the paragraph, then, you must first turn the main point into a topic sentence. Here's a possible topic sentence for this paragraph:

One reason team sports are good for children is that they offer a chance to make friends.

Notice that the sentence does more than tell the reader that this paragraph is about team sports helping children make friends. It also reminds the reader that the entire essay is about whether team sports are good for kids.

The rest of the paragraph develops from the outline. Here's how it might look:

As members of a team, kids *work with others* to improve their playing skills and win games. At *daily practice,* members *get to know each other well.* After games, teams sometimes *go out for pizza.* Between games, team members might *visit at each other's homes, stay overnight,* or *meet* with the coach *to discuss* future games.

Notice that the paragraph doesn't include everything on the outline. It's okay to end a paragraph, if it seems complete, before you've included everything on your outline. On the other hand, you might think of something you'd like to include that is not on the outline. That's okay, too, as long as the new material fits into the outline and doesn't take you in a different direction.

Notice, also, that some words were changed. The words *share goals* (from the outline) became *improve their playing skills and win games.* The new wording carries the same idea as the first, but the second expression is more specific and, therefore, more interesting.

EXERCISE 2: USING TOPIC SENTENCES

Directions: Following the outline shown on page 49, write topic sentences for the third and fourth paragraphs of the essay on children and team sports.

Be sure your topic sentences do the following:

- make the point indicated by the outline
- remain general, that is, do not contain any examples

To check your answers, turn to page 70.

Use Transitions

When an essay moves from one paragraph to another, it's important that smooth **transitions,** or connections, allow the essay to flow easily from one paragraph to the next.

Transitional words and phrases, such as *therefore, furthermore, besides, in addition, however,* and *on the other hand,* remind the reader of the main idea in the preceding paragraph by linking it to the upcoming paragraph. For example, your essay needs to move from *making friends,* its first point, to the next point, *good for health and fitness.* A topic sentence for the third paragraph might include a transitional phrase to link it to the second paragraph:

Besides making friends, children who participate in team sports improve their health and fitness.

Then you would follow your outline for the health and fitness paragraph to continue writing the body of your essay.

When it's time to move to the fourth paragraph, the one about *creating too much pressure,* you'll be changing from a positive to a negative viewpoint. The first two points made about the topic discussed good outcomes of team sports. But your last point, *too much pressure,* is a bad consequence of team sports, so your transition should reflect that shift in perspective.

You might begin your fourth paragraph with this topic sentence:

Even though there are social and health benefits to team sports, some children can't handle the pressure.

Then you would go on to write a paragraph (following the outline) that supports the idea that participating in team sports can put too much pressure on some kids.

Table 3-1 lists some transitional words. Pay attention to the differences in their meanings.

Table 3-1 Transitional words and phrases show readers that an essay is moving to a new point. Transitions also tell the reader something about the relationship between the point just discussed and the one about to be discussed.

TRANSITIONAL WORD OR PHRASE	SUGGESTS
however	a different way to look at an issue **Example:** We expect rain Monday and Tuesday. However, Wednesday should be warm and sunny.
on the other hand	another point of view **Example:** Everyone enjoyed dancing on Cinco de Mayo. On the other hand, we ate far too much.
nevertheless	another point of view **Example:** The speaker should have arrived on time. Nevertheless, we're glad she's here.
but	another point of view **Example:** Kim Jun and Marco can't stay late, but they can be here for an hour.
furthermore	another point, similar to preceding ones **Example:** The requirements for the job were too difficult. Furthermore, the pay was much too low.
in addition	another similar point **Example:** Most people wore native dress and brought food from their countries on Culture Day. In addition, there was a beautiful multicultural crafts display.
finally	a last, similar point **Example:** The camping trip was cancelled because no one had the proper equipment. In addition, there were no campsites available that weekend. Finally, we couldn't find enough drivers.
therefore	a point that results from the preceding one **Example:** Serena watered her garden every day. Therefore, her tomatoes grew large and delicious.

EXERCISE 3: USING TRANSITIONS

Directions: Following the outline on page 49, write paragraphs 3 and 4 for the essay on kids and team sports. Remember, you may add or delete ideas, but stick to the point of the paragraph.

When you have written the paragraphs, check for the following:

- Did you begin each paragraph with a topic sentence?
- Did you use transitions to let the reader know whether you were changing viewpoint?
- Did you include supporting details from your outline?
- If you chose to use details other than those itemized on the outline, do they support the topic sentence?

To check your answer, turn to page 71.

Tie It Up

As you know now, the last paragraph of an essay will always be a conclusion. Regardless of what the topic is, a conclusion, like an introduction, does two things:

1. It restates the thesis or, at least, the ideas contained in the thesis.

2. It contains a **closing thought**, something the reader can think about after reading the essay.

Think of the conclusion as a bow or knot that ties up a package.

Now look at the outline for the last paragraph for the essay on whether team sports are good for children (Figure 3-1 on page 49). Let's see how to wrap up this particular essay.

Recall the thesis:

Participating in team sports is a good way for children to make friends and to promote health and fitness, but team sports sometimes put too much pressure on some kids.

In the concluding paragraph, you want to convey the ideas of the thesis without using the exact words used to state the thesis in the introduction. You also want to leave the reader with something to think about.

Here's one possible conclusion to this essay:

Team sports give kids a great opportunity to make friends while they improve their health and fitness. However, parents and coaches shouldn't apply too much pressure because it's more important to have fun than to win every game.

Notice that the first sentence reminds the reader of the essay's topic (children and team sports). It also mentions the first two points of the thesis (friendship and health and fitness). The third point (too much pressure) appears in the last sentence, along with the closing thought that sports, above all, should be fun for kids.

Notice what the concluding paragraph does *not* do:

- **It doesn't report what it just said.** It doesn't say "*In this essay, I talked about what's good and what's bad about team sports for kids.*"
- **It doesn't apologize for not being a good essay.** It doesn't say "*This probably isn't very clear, but I hope you understand it.*"
- **It doesn't change the subject at the very end.** It doesn't say "*I never had a chance to play sports because we moved all the time. My father kept changing jobs.*"

Note that you can write a conclusion to an essay even if you haven't written the essay yet. All you have to do is think of a closing thought that's appropriate to your topic and combine it with your thesis.

Let's try to write a conclusion before writing the body of an essay for a topic on how people can take more responsibility for their own health. (To see the complete prompt, turn to Exercise 1 on page 48.)

Let's assume you've written the following thesis statement:

To solve health care problems, people must take responsibility for their own health by becoming informed, looking at their diet and exercise habits, and creating a safe home environment.

Here's a possible conclusion:

People must learn all they can about healthful living. They must eat well, exercise regularly, and make sure that their homes are safe places to live. This is the best way to solve our country's health care problems.

If your essay's last paragraph restates your thesis (the topic plus whatever you are saying about the topic) and contains a closing thought, *without changing the subject,* you will have written an acceptable conclusion.

EXERCISE 4: WRITING CONCLUSIONS

Directions: Write two possible conclusions for an essay that asks you to consider why people enjoy horror movies. The essay has the following thesis statement: *Horror movies help me forget my problems, entertain me with special effects, and let me enjoy fantastic drama.*

Be sure your conclusion

- restates the thesis
- contains a closing thought
- does not change the subject

If possible, try out different conclusions on a classmate or partner to determine which have the most impact. Read the possibilities and ask what works and what doesn't. Encourage your partner to explain why one ending seems more effective than another.

To check your answer, turn to page 71.

S KILL C HECKUP

Directions: Complete each of the following steps in the essay writing process.

1. In Foundation Skill 2, the second Skill Checkup item (page 45) asked you to write thesis statements for three essay topics. Now use those thesis statements to write three essay introductions. If you didn't write thesis statements earlier, do so now.

You may also exchange thesis statements with a partner and write introductory paragraphs for each other's essays. You'll see that you can write a first paragraph on *any* topic, if you have a point to make (a thesis statement) and can write an opening sentence or two to grab the reader's attention.

2. Using the outlines created in the third Skill Checkup item for Foundation Skill 2 (page 45), write the *body,* or three middle paragraphs, for each of those essays. If you didn't create outlines earlier, do so now.

3. Using the outlines created in the third Skill Checkup item for Foundation Skill 2 (page 45), write a *conclusion* for each of those essays.

Try to write more than one possible conclusion and see which you prefer. Ask your classmates what they think about each conclusion.

To check your answers, turn to page 71.

NOTE: *Save your work. You will need it to complete exercises in Foundation Skill 4.*

4 Revise Your Work

ACHIEVEMENT GOALS
This lesson will show you how to make sure your essay

- discusses the topic

- has a thesis, or central idea

- has a clear structure

- contains plenty of good illustrations

- uses the right words

Life doesn't always offer second chances. If you're building something out of wood and you cut a board too short, there's not much you can do about it. Writing is different. When you write, you can give yourself second chances. In fact, a good essay demands that you take time to revise your work. When taking the GED Writing Skills Test, plan to spend about ten minutes of your allotted time revising your essay.

Stick to the Subject

Your GED essay must be unified and easy to follow. With careful planning and organizing, you should have no trouble keeping your essay focused on one subject. The reader must be able to tell from the beginning what the essay is about and where you are going with the topic. Revising allows you to clear up fuzzy writing and check for logic and appropriate content.

Did You Write About the Topic?

The first step in revising an essay is to make sure you have written about the assigned topic. It's unlikely that you'll have time to rewrite the entire essay if you realize, at this point, that you didn't write about the assigned topic. The best way to deal with this crisis is *prevention*. Never begin to construct an essay until you are able to state the topic in your own words. Stating the topic in your own words forces you to examine the prompt closely to make sure you understand what you've been asked to discuss.

If, despite your careful efforts, you discover that you did not write about the assigned topic, you can try to modify what you've written to make it fit the topic. If you can't change a paragraph to make it work, you may have to rewrite that paragraph. If only a part of a paragraph is off the topic, cross out that part.

Let's look again at the sample essay shown in Figure 1-1 on page 27. The essay's thesis is

Animals offer friendship, aid to disabled people, and help with work.

A first attempt to develop the point that animals provide help with work might be written as follows:

> Besides appreciating animals for friendship and aid, some people depend on animals in their work. Scientists use dolphins and other animals to study behavior. For example, greyhounds and horses run very fast. Some people like to go to the races, but that can be a big problem for gamblers, who could lose all their money. If you like to gamble, it's a good idea to watch the races on television or not to take any money when you go to the track.

Notice that after talking about scientists using animals for research, the writer wanders off in another direction. Suddenly the paragraph discusses the dangers of gambling. Gambling has nothing to do with the topic of why people are willing to spend time and money caring for their animals.

In the case of this sample essay, the writer realized what had happened and removed the sentences about gambling. The writer then added other sentences to support the point that animals help people work.

Do You Have a Thesis and Did You Develop It As Promised?

The next step in revising an essay is to read through it entirely. Read the introduction to make sure it contains a clearly defined thesis. From this first paragraph, the reader must be able to tell what the topic is and what you are going to say about the topic; that is, the reader must be able to grasp the essay's thesis.

After making sure the introduction clearly states your thesis, you should check that your essay truly develops the thesis as stated. What can you do if you find yourself with an essay that contradicts its thesis? You have two choices. You can rewrite the essay, or you can revise the thesis. In the revision stage, it is usually easier to change the thesis to make it fit what has been written than to rewrite the essay.

To see how to revise a thesis, let's assume the writer of the sample essay had brainstormed a group of ideas about animal racing and gambling. Imagine that the writer's original thesis was expressed in this way:

> Animals offer friendship and aid to disabled people, but they also inspire gambling.

After writing the fourth paragraph that you now see in the final essay (the paragraph about work), instead of crossing it out the writer changed the thesis to match the essay as written:

> Animals offer friendship, aid to disabled people, and help with work.

Remember, when a writer *states* one thesis but *develops* a different one, the entire essay is spoiled. Such a flaw destroys an essay's unity.

Directions: Follow the instructions given in items 1 and 2 to complete this exercise.

1. Look at the introductions you wrote for the first Skill Checkup item in Foundation Skill 3 on page 55. Underline the parts of the thesis (the topic and the three points made about the topic) in each introduction.

If you didn't write the introductions, do the exercise now.

2. Look at the outlines you wrote for the third Skill Checkup item in Foundation Skill 2 on page 45. Circle or underline the three points of the thesis in each outline. Now read the supporting details for each point. Do the details truly support the point under which they appear in the outline?

If you didn't write the outlines, do the exercise now.

To check your answers, turn to page 71.

Does Your Essay Have a Clear Structure?

To satisfy the GED requirement for a clearly structured essay, your composition must have a beginning, a middle, and an end. Each point must follow logically from preceding points.

You have learned that your composition will stay on track if you develop and follow a simple outline, or plan. Using an outline, you logically move from one point to the next.

Let's check a sample essay to see if it has a clear structure. The essay should *explain why fast food restaurants are popular in America.* The writer decides that the thesis should be stated in this manner:

Americans love fast-food restaurants because they are convenient, economical, and fun for kids.

Here's the essay:

I've loved fast-food restaurants ever since I was a little kid. We hardly ever go out to dinner. I'd like to go to restaurants more often and not just to fast-food ones either. If I want Mexican food instead of a hamburger, there are lots of fast-food taco places, but McDonald's is my favorite. Sometimes we just use the drive-up window, but you have to check to be sure they give you what you order.

We had a party at McDonald's for my fourth birthday. It was so neat. I got to go back into the kitchen and help them bring out the cake. We played games, too. I'd rather order a cheeseburger because it tastes better and fills me up more. I like fries and a soft drink, but I think the desserts are gross, even if they are inexpensive.

My aunt makes the best pies. Especially pumpkin pies for Thanksgiving. My sister doesn't like them, so I always get her piece, which makes Thanksgiving even more special. Some fast-food restaurants have salad bars. You can get breakfast and other things there, too. There are so many fast-food restaurants, I wonder how they all stay in business. I guess because my friends and I go there a lot.

This essay lacks structure, order, logic, and form. It's just a jumble of ideas. The essay does mention each point in the thesis, but points seem to have found their way into the essay by accident rather than by good planning:

- The drive-up window illustrates convenience, although the writer doesn't mention convenience.

- A comment that desserts might be inexpensive suggests economy, but the writer doesn't make a point about economy.

- Talk of a birthday party refers to entertaining kids, but the writer doesn't state the point that fast-food restaurants entertain kids.

- The essay has no clear introduction nor a thesis to tell readers where the essay is going.

- None of the paragraphs sticks to one subject.

- The essay lacks a single paragraph to discuss convenience, one to discuss economy, and one to discuss fun for kids.

- Wanting to go out to dinner, Thanksgiving, and the aunt's pies have nothing to do with the topic.

- Gross desserts is a negative comment, but the thesis mentions only positive points (convenience, economy, and fun).

Directions: Read the following well-written essay and construct the outline the writer apparently followed.

Almost every American family goes to a fast-food restaurant occasionally. These restaurants are popular because they're convenient, inexpensive, and entertaining for children.

Families are too busy to spend a lot of time at a restaurant, so they like the convenience of fast food. You only have to wait a few minutes for a meal. If you're really in a hurry, you can stay right in your car and order at the drive-through window. In the morning, you can even get a fast bacon-and-eggs breakfast. If you want a quick snack, you can order a drink or fries any time. You'll find a fast-food restaurant in almost every neighborhood.

Not only are fast-food places convenient, they have inexpensive food. A family of four can eat an entire meal for around ten dollars. Special deals for children save even more money, and the kids usually get a free toy, like a movie character doll, with their meal.

Giving away toys is not the only way fast-food restaurants entertain children. Many have playgrounds right outside the door. Children can climb and slide while their parents drink a cup of coffee or relax a little bit. Some fast-food places host birthday parties for children. But even without a party, kids think it's fun just to go out for a hamburger or taco.

Some people think Americans eat too much fast food. But as long as fast-food restaurants are convenient, inexpensive, and fun, they're here to stay.

Check the following:

- Were you able to come up with the thesis?
- Was each point of the thesis outlined?
- Were there supportive details?

To check your answer, turn to page 71.

Did You Use Clear and Interesting Examples?

Often a GED essay prompt includes instructions to use examples, to be specific, or to be sure to illustrate. Before you turn in your essay, check to be sure it includes good, clear, interesting examples.

In a well-written essay, it's not enough simply to state that cars harm the environment. You should illustrate the statement with examples:

Car exhaust pollutes the air. Gas and oil use up natural resources, and rusty, broken car parts create ugly junk yards.

If you're writing about the many ways computers affect our lives and if one of your points is that we use computers all the time without even realizing it, illustrate with examples. *We use computers to carry out all sorts of daily business* is a good general topic sentence, but it requires detail to show the reader what you mean. You might say,

> When we pump our own gasoline, use automated teller machines, or even dial a long-distance phone number, we are using computers, although we may not realize it.

Let's look at the paragraph on the low cost of fast food in the essay on fast-food restaurants on page 60. Instead of merely saying that fast food is inexpensive, the writer used a dollar figure (ten dollars) to illustrate the point. Even if you had to guess at the price of a fast-food dinner for four, it's better to use a specific amount than to keep your essay vague and general.

EXERCISE 3: USING EXAMPLES

Directions: Look at the essay on fast-food restaurants on page 60. Circle the specific details that illustrate main points. Try this with your own writing as well.

To check your answers, turn to page 72.

Did You Choose the Best Words?

The last check to make when you revise your essay concerns word choice. It's most important that you use correct words. But as you read your finished essay, you may decide to change some words for more sophisticated, colorful, or powerful ones. For example, instead of using the expression *all the time,* you may say *daily* or *frequently.*

You also should avoid repetition. For example, if you're writing about children, you won't want to use that word more than once or twice in a paragraph. You should look for words that mean the same thing: *kids, youngsters, boys and girls*. When you're talking about a number, instead of writing *a lot,* try phrases like *several dozen, countless,* or *more than a thousand.*

Sometimes writers change words just to add variety and interest. If the topic asks you to write about *automobiles,* you'll probably be more comfortable using the word *cars* because it is the more common word today. But you can add variety to your essay by using both words.

Avoid slang or clichés. If you find any slang words, change them during revision. For example, the sentence *Bad drivers are a pain in the neck* may be colorful, but its language is too informal. You might change it to *Bad drivers can be very annoying.* (Then, of course, be sure to illustrate the point with some good examples of drivers' annoying habits.)

Watch out for words that sound like other words but are spelled differently and have different meanings. Examples of commonly misused words that sound alike are *they're, their,* and *there; our, hour,* and *are; your* and *you're;* and *too, to,* and *two.* Pay special attention to these words. (See page 296 for more information about words that sound alike.)

EXERCISE 4: CHOOSING THE BEST WORDS

Directions: Replace the underlined words in the following passages. They are either inappropriate, misspelled, incorrect, or used too often.

1. Television <u>effects</u> people negatively by exposing them to <u>a lot of</u> violence. They see so much <u>icky stuff</u> on TV, no <u>wander</u> they go out and <u>blow some guy's head off</u> just because <u>their</u> mad.

2. <u>A lot of</u> people dislike seat belt laws and helmet laws. These people think they should decide <u>four</u> themselves how safe they want <u>too</u> be. <u>Some people</u> figure it's <u>there</u> own business if they want to risk <u>there</u> lives. <u>Other people</u> say other people should <u>butt out</u>. But <u>these people</u> forget that society might have to pay to take care of them if they are seriously injured in an accident.

To check your answers, turn to page 72.

S KILL C HECKUP

Directions: Read the following GED-type essay prompts.

1. Choose one of the prompts and write an essay.

a. Many people spend more money than necessary in the grocery store because they buy the first item they see. One reason is that grocers deliberately display high-priced items in prominent places, and consumers buy the first thing they see.

In an essay of about 200 words, discuss ways consumers can reduce their grocery expenses. Support your views with specific examples.

b. In the 1950s, Americans began to move out of the cities into the suburbs, seeking a different lifestyle.

Write a composition of about 200 words, comparing life in the suburbs with life in the cities. Be sure to use examples to support your views.

c. Many states have passed laws limiting cigarette smoking to certain areas or banning it altogether in public places. In a 200-word essay, tell why you approve or disapprove of such laws. Be sure to use examples.

2. Revise the essay, using the checklist below:

- Did you write about the topic?
- Can you find the thesis?
- Is there an introductory paragraph?
- Does each paragraph in the body discuss one point from the thesis?
- Is there a conclusion?
- Did you use clear and interesting examples?
- Did you use the best words?

To check your answers, turn to page 72.

5 Edit Your Work

Have you ever hesitated before dropping an important letter into a mailbox? You double-check that you've put the correct address on the envelope and included a stamp and your return address. You might even hold the envelope up to the light to make sure the contents are in it.

You should exercise similar caution with your GED essay by double-checking it before you submit it to the examiner. When you write an essay, some errors may occur because you're writing quickly. These errors are easy to correct. Others may be more difficult to detect. It's important to take the time to edit your essay before you turn it in.

Are the Sentences Complete?

We often learn what's correct by listening to people around us. A good way to test for sentence completeness is to read your essay out loud. Of course, in the exam, you can't do that, but during practice, you can. If you are working in groups or with partners, let someone else read your essay to you so that you can hear what you have actually written and not what you think you have written.

It's also important that you read sentences as they are punctuated, not as you *think* they should sound, because that's how your readers will read them. When you read a group of words that begins with a capital letter, don't stop reading until you come to a period. If you've written more then one sentence without punctuating, you'll run out of breath. On the other hand, if you put a period before a sentence is finished, you'll hear that the thought is not complete. You'll learn to recognize that all the words in a sentence must make sense as a single unit.

Refer to pages 80–93 in Unit 1, "Building Sentences," for more information on complete sentences.

Directions: Read the following passage, stopping when you come to a period. If you do not hear complete thoughts between capital letters and periods, make the necessary changes to complete the thoughts. You may have to add or change words, punctuation, or capitalization. If there are too many thoughts between a capital letter and a period, insert periods to make separate sentences.

Americans feel compelled to diet because they see pictures of thin people everywhere these are movie stars, models, and people having fun. Like television commercials. Everyone in television commercials. Looks so good all the time it makes us want to be thin and beautiful like them. Running to the store. We buy diet food and diet pills and we decide to get thin. No matter what happens we ruin our health and can get sick doing this we don't care if we can look good. Like Madonna, for example. that's all that seems to matter.

To check your answer, turn to page 73.

Is the Essay Free of Spelling, Capitalization, and Punctuation Errors?

Although readers can usually tell what is meant even if words are misspelled, misspelled words distract the reader and weaken an essay's overall effect.

Capitalization and punctuation errors not only distract the reader, but they often change a writer's meaning. Consider the following sets of sentences that contain the same words but are punctuated differently:

I'm sorry. That won't help us.   That's all. She's done.

I'm sorry that won't help us.   That's all she's done.

Refer to pages 244–275 in Unit 3, "Handling Mechanics," for more information on capitalization and punctuation.

Directions: Punctuate the following group of words in two different ways. Make changes in capitalization as needed.

it's a miracle their team won with only seconds to go Jones ran the last twelve yards for a touchdown

To check your answer, refer to page 73.

Have You Used Standard English?

No matter how well-organized your essay is, if you consistently misuse the English language, your score will drop considerably. Using **standard English** means correctly using proper English words and following the grammatical conventions of the language.

If you remember grammar rules, you'll recognize errors more easily than writers whose grammar skills are rusty. Section 3 of this book includes a basic review of English grammar. For now, let's check your knowledge. Table 5-1 lists some examples of the kinds of grammatical errors writers commonly make.

Table 5-1 Watch for these types of errors when you edit your essay.

TYPE OF ERROR	EXAMPLES
Subject-Verb Agreement	**Correct:** The *dogs walk* fast, but their *master walks* slowly. **Incorrect:** They *is* angry about the assignment.
Verb Tense	**Correct:** Yesterday we *ate* the cake, so tomorrow we *will eat* pie for dessert. **Incorrect:** They *will want* to finish early tonight, so they *worked* faster.
Pronouns	**Correct:** Sharon gave the book to Tom. *He* thanked *her* for *it*. **Incorrect:** Each student had *their* own book.
Capitalization	**Correct:** We'll go skiing in *February* in the mountains. **Incorrect:** we swim during the summer at *lake quinault*.
Commas	**Correct:** Three chickens, two ducks, and five geese crossed the street, stopping traffic. **Incorrect:** Jamie was good at baseball basketball and hockey.

E X E R C I S E 3 : U S I N G S T A N D A R D E N G L I S H A N D F I N D I N G E R R O R S

Directions: Correct the italicized errors in the following passage. Use Table 5-1 to help, but remember, you'll learn all the skills you need to proofread your essay in Section 3.

Last summer, in *august*, we took our vacation. We went to a resort at a nearby *lake it* was the first time we *go* there. The lake is beautiful. The resort has mountains in the *background trees all around good hiking trails and great picnic spots.*

The one bad thing about our summer vacation *were* packing too many fishing poles. We thought we would go fishing, but we never *did they* were never used. My uncle was angry because we *will take* so long to get all those things packed in the car, and then didn't use *it*. Next year we *had* a better idea of what to take.

To check your answers, turn to page 73.

SKILL CHECKUP

Directions: Read the following sample paragraphs, which were written using the outline shown on page 49. Use Table 5-1 to correct the italicized errors.

Americans of all ages *loves* team sports. *being* on an athletic team benefits children as well as adults. Through *there* team, children can *make friends develop good health and stay fit*. However, participating in team sports could be *to* much pressure for some.

Sports teams *gave* kids many opportunities to make *Friends*. The players get to know each other well through many practice *sessions they* also enjoy each other's company at after-game parties. If the players come from different schools or neighborhoods, *he has* a chance to meet people they don't see every day.

To check your answers, turn to page 73.

Answers and Explanations

Foundation Skill 1: Think About Your Essay

Exercise 1 (page 29)

Paragraph 1: Every day we hear about ordinary people who shoot others in anger. This violence is the result of viewing too much mayhem on television, a belief in simple answers, and a need for power.

Paragraph 2: People see so much violence on television that they become numb to it. Whether it's a car crash, a fist fight, or a murder, television shows people getting battered and killed. We see violence in police dramas and in newscasts. After a while, the violence washes over us, and we feel nothing.

Paragraph 3: Another reason people turn to violence is that it seems like a quick and easy way to solve problems. We've learned from advertising that a pill may be taken if we want to lose weight fast. The right soap will bring us instant love. The right pair of shoes will turn us into champions. No wonder we believe beating someone resolves conflict.

Paragraph 4: Finally, people turn to violence because it gives them a sense of power. Long waits and complicated forms make us feel we can't get medical help, legal advice, or other services. Traffic jams slow us down, and store clerks are rude and unhelpful. Physical force, guns, and other weapons make us think we're in control.

Paragraph 5: When we want quick answers to complex questions and see violence all day long on television, it's no surprise that we turn to guns for a sense of power.

Exercise 2 (page 31)

The topic for this essay is rights that individuals have in America, other than voting.

At first glance, you might think the essay is about voting or about democracy because you see those words early in the prompt and you probably recognize that they would be good subjects for an essay. But, remember, all GED essay prompts begin with background information to prepare you for the actual topic. The actual topic comes later and is usually somewhat different from the background material.

Exercise 3 (page 34)

Even if your paper looks different from the answer given in Figure A-1, you have done your work correctly if your ideas are scattered randomly on the page.

Skill Checkup (page 34)

1. What are the advantages and/or disadvantages of being a latchkey child?

Figure A-1

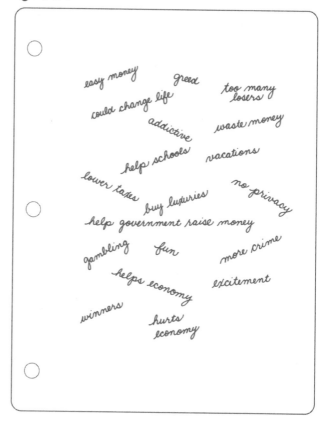

2. Is sexual harassment a serious problem in our society?

3. Agree and/or disagree with the idea that people behave especially badly when they are driving a car.

4. Your papers should be covered with ideas, placed in no particular order, as shown in Figure A-2.

Foundation Skill 2: Organize Your Material

Exercise 1 (page 36)

Answers will vary. Answer these questions to check your work:

- Have you formed groups with ideas that all seem related to each other?

- Does each group have a label? Your labels might include gambling, eliminating poverty, and helping the state.

- Do your groups include pros and cons of state lotteries (the prompt said to discuss both)?

If you can answer yes to each of these questions, you have done the work correctly.

Figure A-2

Exercise 2 (page 38)

Answers will vary. Your answer depends on the groups you formed in Exercise 1. Answer these questions to check your work:

- Do you have three groups? (If you were able to come up with only two groups, that's okay. You would then write a four-paragraph essay.)

- Does each group have a label?

- Have you taken useful ideas from some groups and put them into others?

- Have you eliminated groups that do not fit the topic?

If you can answer yes to each of these questions, you have done the work correctly. Your paper should resemble Figure 2-2 on page 39.

Exercise 3 (page 40)

Answers will vary. One possible thesis statement might be expressed as follows: A state lottery can bring money into the state treasury and may end poverty for a few people, but it also encourages gambling. Answer these questions to check your work:

- Does your thesis statement mention the topic?

- Does your thesis statement include the labels of the final groups you formed in Exercise 2?

If you can answer yes to these questions, you've done the work correctly.

Exercise 4 (page 44)

Answers will vary. Your outline will be different from anybody else's because it is based on your brainstorming ideas and the way you chose to group them. Answer these questions to check your work:

- Do you have a numbered section for each paragraph in your essay?

- Is the first heading "Introduction"?

- Is the last heading "Conclusion"?

- Do you have a numbered heading for each point in your thesis statement?

- Have you listed details under each numbered heading?

If you can answer yes to these questions, you've done the work correctly.

Skill Checkup (page 45)

1. Answers will vary. (See the checklist for Exercise 1 above.)

2. Answers will vary. (See the checklist for Exercise 3 above.)

3. Answers will vary. (See the checklist for Exercise 4 above.)

Foundation Skill 3: Write Your Essay

Exercise 1 (page 48)

Answers will vary. Answer these questions to check your work:

- Is your introduction one paragraph?

- Does it start with a hook?

- Does it contain your thesis?

If you can answer yes to each of these questions, you have done the work correctly. Here's one possible introduction:

> Many Americans are worried about the rising cost of health care, and they want the government to do something about it. To keep medical costs down, however, people must accept responsibility for their own health. They need to stay informed about the latest health trends and take a look at their diet and exercise habits. They should also create a safe home environment to prevent injury.

The first sentence is the hook. The rest of the paragraph is the thesis.

Exercise 2 (page 51)

Answers will vary. Answer these questions to check your work:

- Are your topic sentences general, with no examples?

- Do the topic sentences reflect the points listed next to numbers 3 and 4 on the outline?

If you can answer yes to each of these questions, you have done the work correctly. Here are possible topic sentences:

Paragraph 3: Team sports also help children stay healthy and fit.

Paragraph 4: On the other hand, team sports can create too much pressure for children.

Exercise 3 (page 52)

Answers will vary. Answer these questions to check your work:

- Did you begin each paragraph with a topic sentence?

- Did you use transitions to let the reader know that you were moving to a new point and to show the relationship between that point and the preceding one?

- Did you use some or all of the supporting detail from the outline?

- If you added details not found in the outline, do they support the main point of the paragraph?

If you can answer yes to each of these questions, you have done the work correctly. Paragraphs 3 and 4 might look something like this:

> Team sports also help children stay healthy and fit. On a team, kids get plenty of exercise, warming up with a run around the field, for example. To develop skill for their sport, they practice several times a week, which helps them stay fit. They also eat well because they understand the importance of good nutrition. Besides, they don't have time to sit around and eat junk food.

> On the other hand, team sports can create too much pressure for children. Competition can make them afraid to lose and fearful of making mistakes. They could worry so much about winning that their schoolwork would suffer. Pregame tension could make it difficult for them to eat, and the game would no longer be fun.

Exercise 4 (page 54)

Answers will vary. Answer these questions to check your work:

- Do your conclusions restate the thesis?

- Do they contain a closing thought?

- Do they stick to the subject of the essay?

If you can answer yes to each of these questions, you have done the work correctly. Here is one possible conclusion for this essay:

> If I can forget my own problems and be thrilled by terrifying special effects, I will always enjoy horror movies. I like the fun of a good scare when I know I can't really be harmed. People who don't go to horror movies are missing a great escape.

The first two sentences restate the thesis. The last sentence is the closing thought.

Skill Checkup (page 55)

Answers will vary. Your essays will depend on the work you've done in earlier steps. To check your answers, ask the questions suggested in the answers to Exercises 1–4 above. If you can answer yes to those questions, you have done the work correctly.

Foundation Skill 4: Revise Your Work

Exercise 1 (page 58)

1. Answers will vary. Answer these questions to check your work:
   - Does the introduction mention the topic of the essay?
   - Does the introduction mention each point of the thesis?

If you can answer yes to each of these questions, you have done the work correctly.

2. Answers will vary. Answer these questions to check your work:
   - After the introduction and before the conclusion, does each section of the outline reflect a point in the thesis?
   - Have you eliminated any details that do not illustrate the point of the section?

If you can answer yes to each of these questions, you have done the work correctly.

Exercise 2 (page 60)

The outline probably looked something like this:

1. Introduction
   a. Hook
   b. Thesis

2. Convenience
   a. Short wait
   b. Drive-through window
   c. Breakfast
   d. Quick snacks
   e. Fast-food places in most neighborhoods

3. Inexpensive
   a. Family eats for ten dollars
   b. Special kids' deals with toys

4. Entertain children
   a. Playgrounds
   b. Birthday parties
   c. Fun to go out to eat

5. Conclusion
   a. Thesis
   b. Closing thought

Exercise 3 (page 61)

You should have circled all the specific foods: hamburger, taco, eggs, bacon, drink, and fries. Other specific examples that illustrate your main points include ten dollars, movie character doll, playgrounds, climb and slide, parents drink a cup of coffee, and birthday parties.

Exercise 4 (page 62)

1. Change inappropriate words: *a lot of* to *too much; icky stuff* to *shooting, dangerous driving, fighting, and killing; blow some guy's head off* to *shoot a stranger.*

Correct spelling: *wander* to *wonder; their* to *they're*

Use correct word: *effects* to *affects*

2. Change inappropriate words: *A lot of* to *Many; butt out* to *worry about their own safety.*

Correct spelling: *four* to *for; too* to *to; there* to *their* (twice).

Replace repeated words: *Some people* to *Others; Other people* to *These opponents of the law; these people* to *they.*

Notice that some of the words were misspelled, whereas others were inappropriate, too vague, or used too often.

Skill Checkup (page 63)

1. a. The topic is, How can people spend less money on groceries? Upon first reading, you might think you're supposed to write about the way grocery store items are displayed. But keep reading. The actual topic usually appears after the words *write an essay, . . . discuss, . . .* or *explain. . . .*

   b. The topic is, How does life in the city compare with life in the suburbs?

   c. The topic is, Argue for or against laws that limit or ban smoking in public places. You are not being asked to write about the evils of smoking nor are you asked to defend smoking. You are to write about *laws.* The essay should deal with questions of individual rights, public health, and government control. You should use *antismoking* laws as the focus for your examples.

2. Answers will vary. Answer these questions to check your work:
   - Does the entire essay stick to the topic?
   - Is the thesis apparent in the introduction?
   - Is there a paragraph for each point in the thesis?
   - Does the conclusion restate the thesis?
   - Are examples clear and interesting?
   - Did you use appropriate words, spell them correctly, and change those that were repeated frequently?

If you can answer yes to each of these questions, you have done the work correctly.

Foundation Skill 5: Edit Your Work

Exercise 1 (page 65)

Americans feel compelled to diet because they see pictures of thin people everywhere. These are movie stars, models, and people having fun. In television commercials, for example, everyone looks so good all the time, it makes us want to be thin and beautiful like them. Running to the store, we buy diet food and diet pills, and we decide to get thin no matter what happens. We ruin our health and get sick doing this. We don't care. If we can look good, like Madonna, that's all that seems to matter.

Exercise 2 (page 65)

1. It's a miracle their team won with only seconds to go. Jones ran the last twelve yards for a touchdown.

2. It's a miracle their team won. With only seconds to go, Jones ran the last twelve yards for a touchdown.

Exercise 3 (page 66)

- august—August

- lake it—lake. It

- go—went

- background trees all around good hiking trails and great picnic spots—background, trees all around, good hiking trails, and great picnic spots.

- were—was

- did they—did. They

- will take—took

- it—them

- had—will have

Skill Checkup (page 67)

- loves—love

- being—Being

- there—their

- make friends develop good health and stay fit.—make friends, develop good health, and stay fit.

- to—too
- gave—give
- Friends—friends
- sessions they—sessions. They
- he has—they have

3 Preparing for the GED
WRITING SKILLS TEST

Unit 1 Building Sentences **77**
OVERVIEW 78
REVIEW 148
ANSWERS AND EXPLANATIONS 154

Unit 2 Using Language **167**
OVERVIEW 168
REVIEW 222
ANSWERS AND EXPLANATIONS 228

Unit 3 Handling Mechanics **241**
OVERVIEW 242
REVIEW 308
ANSWERS AND EXPLANATIONS 314

1 Building Sentences

OVERVIEW   78

Lesson 1   Avoiding Sentence Fragments   80

Recognizing Sentence Fragments, 81 • Word Groups That
Lack Subjects, 84 • Word Groups That Lack Verbs or
Parts of Verbs, 86 • Word Groups That Do Not Express a
Complete Thought, 88

Lesson 2   Avoiding Run-on Sentences   94

Recognizing Run-on Sentences, 94 • Recognizing Run-
ons with Commas, 96 • Using Punctuation to Correct
Run-ons, 98 • Is It Really a Run-on? Recognizing
Compound Subjects and Verbs, 100 • Using Connecting
Words to Correct Run-on Sentences, 102

Lesson 3   Linking Ideas of Equal Importance   106

Identifying Compound Sentences, 106 • Connecting
Ideas That Are Closely Related, 110 • Understanding the
Relationship Between Equal Ideas, 112

Lesson 4   Linking Ideas of Unequal Importance   118

Identifying Complex Sentences, 118 • Choosing
Appropriate Connecting Words, 122

Lesson 5   Using Modifiers to Add Information   128

Recognizing Modifiers, 128 • Putting Modifiers in the
Right Place, 132 • Making Sure There's Something to
Modify, 136

Lesson 6   Understanding Parallel Structure   140

Keeping the Meaning Clear with Parallel Structure, 141 •
Balancing Your Writing with Parallel Structure, 144

See page 165 for   REVIEW   148
SKILLS ANALYSIS
CHART   ANSWERS AND EXPLANATIONS   154

1 Building Sentences
O V E R V I E W

Most of us are fairly comfortable talking to others. We're not afraid to talk. If we're using our native language, we can speak it without even thinking about how we do it.

Writing, on the other hand, often comes less naturally to us. Compared to talking, writing does require extra thought and care. There are major differences between spoken English and written English, and we run into problems when we try to write the way we speak.

When we talk, we often express ourselves in incomplete thoughts because the person we speak to can ask us to explain. For example, a likely response to "What a day!" might be, "What happened? Did you have a bad day?" And then a conversation begins.

But when we write something, we have only one chance to get our message across to the reader. We have to be careful to be absolutely clear. One way to write clearly is to write in complete sentences.

The following six lessons will show you how to construct good, clear sentences that help your reader understand your writing.

In Lesson 1, you'll learn to recognize, avoid, and correct sentence **fragments,** or pieces of sentences that are not complete thoughts.

Lesson 2 deals with **run-on sentences,** which occur when you forget to punctuate or use connecting words to separate ideas.

In Lesson 3 you'll learn how to combine two ideas of equal importance into a single sentence.

Lesson 4 shows you how to join two ideas into a single sentence when one of those ideas is less important than the other or depends on the other for its meaning.

Lesson 5 teaches you how to properly place **modifiers.** You'll see how to use descriptive words and phrases without changing the meaning of the sentence unintentionally.

In Lesson 6, you'll learn about **parallel structure,** which helps you write clear sentences containing words and word groups that take the same form.

fragment: a group of words that form part of a sentence but not a complete sentence

run-on sentence: two or more sentences written as if they were one long sentence

modifier: word or word group that describes or refers to other words or word groups

parallel structure: using the same form for two or more words or groups of words in a single sentence

LESSON 1

Avoiding Sentence Fragments

ACHIEVEMENT GOALS
In this lesson, you will learn

- how to recognize sentence fragments

- how sentence fragments occur

- how to correct them

Suppose you hear of a child who wrote a beautiful piece of music at the age of three or an elderly person who took up jogging and ended up winning a national marathon. "Wow! Amazing!" you might say, and anyone would know what you mean.

When we speak to each other, we don't worry about complete sentences, and we rarely use them. We don't have to. We can understand each other even if we hear only pieces or fragments of sentences. The situation in which we hear the words fills in for the sentence's missing words.

When we write, complete sentences help our readers understand us.

A **complete sentence** must meet three requirements:

1. It must *have a subject.*

2. It must *have a complete verb.*

3. It must *express a complete thought.*

A **fragment** is a word group that *looks like* a sentence because it begins with a capital letter and ends with a period. However, a fragment is not a sentence because it lacks either a subject or a verb or a verb part or because it does not express a complete thought.

Recognizing Sentence Fragments

Fragments are pieces or parts of sentences rather than complete thoughts. If you're used to writing complete sentences, you're able to recognize fragments easily.

Usually, if you read a word group out loud, you can tell if it's not a complete sentence because it won't sound finished. Something will be missing, and you will have questions like Who? or What? or What about it?

The following examples show how sentence fragments leave us with questions:

Being late to work.

This word group leaves us wondering What about being late to work? To complete the sentence, we have to answer the question: *Being late to work can cost you your job.*

Ate too fast.

We want to know *who* ate too fast. *Marlene ate too fast* completes the thought.

Lost his wallet yesterday morning.

Who? A complete sentence would be *Mr. Kato lost his wallet yesterday morning.*

Everyone in the room.

What about them? To complete the sentence we need to say something about everyone in the room: *Everyone in the room speaks a second language.*

Melanie and Alex after three years.

What about them? Who are they? What did they do? If we write *Melanie and Alex broke up after three years,* we have a complete sentence.

Esteban and Yoko.

What about them? What did they do? Who are they? *Esteban and Yoko are good friends who work at the same packing company.* Now the sentence tells us who they are and what they do.

Tore down their old house so that they could remodel it.

Who did this? *Ruth and Ed tore down their old house so that they could remodel it* completes the sentence.

It's true that we often can figure out what a fragment means because of the preceding sentence or sentences. But a complete sentence must have meaning on its own, regardless of what the sentences before and after it say.

Directions: Identify the fragments and complete sentences below using an *F* for fragment and *C* for complete sentence. Reading the items aloud may help. If you have a partner or are working in a group, read them to another person or have someone read them to you, and try to hear the difference between the complete sentences and the fragments.

1. When I get up in the morning.

2. I eat breakfast.

3. I like cereal.

4. Especially cereal with raisins.

5. Sometimes I prefer eggs.

6. But not always.

7. Because of cholesterol.

8. I always enjoy a cup of coffee.

9. With my breakfast.

10. On weekends I eat even more for breakfast.

Directions: Write the question raised by each of the fragments below. Do you need to know *Who? What? What about it? Did what?* or *Is what?*

11. Last night.

12. Locked his keys in the car again.

13. Refused to cooperate.

14. Looks like an emergency.

15. Accused them of lying.

16. Disappointed with the movie.

17. Easy for Ted.

18. Needs more action.

19. Next summer.

20. Every employee in the company.

Directions: Choose the one best answer to each item.

Items 21 to 24 refer to the following paragraph.

(1) Memorial Day is a holiday. (2) To recognize those who served in the military and gave their lives fighting for America. (3) Many people forget the real meaning of Memorial Day. (4) Because it also heralds the beginning of the summer season. (5) For them, the day is for swimming, boating, and picnicking. (6) Others celebrate on both levels. (7) Displaying the American flag and have fun. (8) They take a moment. (9) To think about war and peace and enjoy their summer activities too.

21. Sentence 2: **To recognize those who served in the military and gave their lives fighting for America.**

    What correction should be made to this sentence?

    (1) replace <u>To recognize</u> with <u>For</u>
    (2) replace <u>To recognize</u> with <u>It recognizes</u>
    (3) remove <u>To recognize</u>
    (4) replace <u>those who</u> to <u>those. Who</u>
    (5) replace <u>military and</u> with <u>military. And</u>

22. Sentence 4: **Because it also heralds the beginning of the summer season.**

    What correction should be made to this sentence?

    (1) replace <u>Because</u> with <u>This is because</u>
    (2) remove <u>Because it</u>
    (3) remove <u>also</u>
    (4) replace <u>heralds the</u> with <u>heralds. The</u>
    (5) no correction is necessary

23. Sentence 7: **Displaying the American flag and have fun.**

    What correction should be made to this sentence?

    (1) change <u>Displaying</u> to <u>Display</u>
    (2) replace <u>Displaying</u> with <u>They display</u>
    (3) replace <u>flag and</u> with <u>flag. And</u>
    (4) change <u>have</u> to <u>having</u>
    (5) insert <u>they</u> before <u>have</u>

24. Sentences 8 and 9: **They take a <u>moment. To think</u> about war and peace and enjoy their summer activities too.**

Which of the following is the best way to write the underlined portion of these sentences? If you think the original is the best way, choose option (1).

(1) moment. To think
(2) moment. And to think
(3) moment. For thinking
(4) moment to think
(5) moment to. Think

<u>Items 25 to 27</u> refer to the following paragraph.

(1) AIDS is a devastating disease that the medical profession has trouble. (2) Understanding or treating. (3) The name is an abbreviation for acquired immunodeficiency syndrome. (4) People with AIDS suffer a breakdown. (5) In their bodies' immune systems. (6) In a healthy body, a certain type of white blood cell attacks foreign substances that enter it. (7) That type of cell protects us from disease. (8) Scientists believe that AIDS is caused by a virus that kills this particular type of blood cell. (9) Leaving the AIDS victim defenseless against infection and tumors. (10) Researchers hope to produce a vaccine against AIDS.

25. Sentences 1 and 2: **AIDS is a devastating disease that the medical profession has <u>trouble. Understanding or</u> treating.**

Which of the following is the best way to write the underlined portion of these sentences? If you think the original is the best way, choose option (1).

(1) trouble. Understanding or
(2) trouble. To understand or
(3) trouble understanding or
(4) trouble understanding. Or
(5) trouble. With understanding or

26. Sentences 4 and 5: **People with AIDS suffer a <u>breakdown. In their</u> bodies' immune systems.**

Which of the following is the best way to write the underlined portion of these sentences? If you think the original is the best way, choose option (1).

(1) breakdown. In their
(2) breakdown in their
(3) breakdown in. Their
(4) breakdown. That's in
(5) breakdown that's also in

27. Sentence 9: **Leaving the AIDS victim defenseless against infection and tumors.**

What correction should be made to this sentence?

(1) change <u>Leaving</u> to <u>Leaves</u>
(2) replace <u>Leaving</u> with <u>This leaves</u>
(3) replace <u>victim defenseless</u> with <u>victim. Defenseless</u>
(4) insert <u>is</u> after <u>victim</u>
(5) replace <u>defenseless against</u> with <u>defenseless. Against</u>

To check your answers, turn to page 154.

Word Groups That Lack Subjects

With a capital letter at the beginning and a period at the end, the following words look like a sentence:

Fell off the horse.

But the words make no sense because we can't tell who or what fell off the horse. There's no subject. The **subject** of a sentence tells us who or what the sentence is about.

To correct this fragment, let's add a subject: *The jockey*. Now we have a complete sentence:

The *jockey* fell off the horse.

Subjects tell us who or what the sentence is about. A **simple subject** tells us in just one or two words. The sentence above has a simple subject: *jockey*.

When we speak of the **complete subject**, we mean the simple subject with some descriptive words attached to it: If we add some descriptive words to the subject above, the complete subject might be something like this: *The confident jockey with the winning streak*.

Sometimes the subject occurs after the verb in a sentence. This is typical of questions:

Why are *jockeys* small?

Subjects also follow verbs in *there are* or *there is* constructions:

There are *eight horses* in the first race.

Sentences that tell someone to do something (commands) don't appear to have a subject at all because it's not stated. We understand the subject to be *You*.

Sit down immediately. (*You* sit down immediately.)

We understand the subject to be *You* even though it is not stated.

Some commands consist of single word:

Run!

Again, the unspoken but understood subject is *You. (You run!)*

EXERCISE 2

Directions: Identify the *simple subject* in each of the following sentences. If the subject is understood, write *You*.

1. Even the host ate too much at the party.
2. The service station across from the sandwich shop is closed.
3. Gathering all his courage, John invited her to the dance.
4. Everyone, no matter how tired or hungry, continued to work.
5. Always helpful, the butcher suggested a different cut of meat.
6. Stop that car!
7. The dogs bark all night long.
8. Meaningless conversation bores Shelley.
9. No one could understand the computer manual.
10. Too many people wanted to get on the crowded bus.

Directions: Choose the <u>one best answer</u> to each item.

<u>Items 11 to 13</u> refer to the following paragraph.

(1) To gain an extra hour of daylight in the summer, many states institute daylight savings time. (2) This involves moving the clock forward one hour in the spring and back one hour in the fall. (3) Confuses a lot of people. (4) Once they've set their clocks correctly, they have to get used to the new time. (5) Falling asleep and waking up at the right time. (6) These are big problems for a while. (7) Farmers dislike daylight savings time because their animals don't change habits just because human beings change the clock. (8) Not every state. (9) Practices daylight savings time.

11. Sentence 3: **Confuses a lot of people.**

    What correction should be made to this sentence?

    (1) replace <u>Confuses</u> with <u>This procedure confuses</u>
    (2) insert <u>and annoys</u> after <u>Confuses</u>
    (3) replace <u>lot of</u> with <u>lot. Of</u>
    (4) remove the period after <u>people</u>
    (5) no correction is necessary

12. Sentences 5 and 6: **Falling asleep and <u>waking up at the right time. These are</u> big problems for a while.**

    Which of the following is the best way to write the underlined portion of these sentences? If you think the original is the best way, choose option (1).

    (1) waking up at the right time. These are
    (2) waking up at the right time these are
    (3) waking up at the right time. Are
    (4) Waking up at the right time are
    (5) waking up at the right time are

13. Sentences 8 and 9: **Not every <u>state. Practices daylight</u> savings time.**

    Which of the following is the best way to write the underlined portion of these sentences? If you think the original is the best way, choose option (1).

    (1) state. Practices daylight
    (2) state practices daylight
    (3) state practices. Daylight
    (4) state, Practices daylight
    (5) State practices daylight.

To check your answers, turn to page 154.

Word Groups That Lack Verbs or Parts of Verbs

Here's another word group that looks like a sentence but isn't:

Five dogs in our neighborhood.

These words don't make sense because you don't know anything about the five dogs. You don't know who they are or what they are doing because there's no **verb.** The verb in a sentence tells what the subject *does* or what it *is*.

Action verbs show that the subject is *doing* something. To correct this fragment, let's add a verb, *growled*. Now you have a complete sentence:

Five dogs in our neighborhood growled.

Here are some more sentences with action verbs:

The military leaders met to discuss the Russian incident.

Reporters waited all night for the results of the meeting.

Tension increased among the worried citizens.

TEST-TAKING TIP

When you're looking for the verb in a sentence, ask yourself what the subject *does* or *is*.

Linking verbs show no action but still tell something about the subject. They link the subject to another word so that you know what the subject *seems like*, what it *is*, or how it *feels*.

Example: The five dogs in our neighborhood *seem* ferocious.
Actually, they *are* harmless unless they *feel* threatened.

Here are three more sentences with linking verbs. The fourth sentence has an action verb because it tells us something the people are doing:

The people in line for movie tickets feel cold.

They seem restless.

They are impatient.

They shiver in the night air.

Sometimes fragments occur because the verb is not complete. Consider the following word group:

Music blaring outside my window.

Because *blaring* expresses an action, you may see it as a verb. But it really is only part of a verb, and without the other part, the word group doesn't make sense. To correct this fragment, let's complete the verb by adding *is*.

Music is blaring outside my window.

Another way to correct the fragment would be to change the form of the verb:

Music blares outside my window.

A third way to correct the fragment would be to add a comma and attach the word group to a complete thought:

> Blaring outside my window, that music keeps me awake all night.

Finally, we can correct the fragment if we use the entire word group as the subject of the sentence and add a verb to it:

> Music blaring outside my window annoys me.

EXERCISE 3

Directions: Identify the verbs in the following sentences. Some of the sentences may contain more than one verb.

1. Helicopters flew over our house.
2. The laughing toddlers ran through the park and seemed happy.
3. The local team didn't have a chance.
4. The dues increase angered the club members.

Directions: Complete the verbs or change their forms to make the following sentence fragments into complete sentences.

5. Tires screeching around the corner.
6. The sirens alarming everyone.
7. Locusts threatening the crops.

Directions: Choose the <u>one best answer</u> to each item.

<u>Items 8 and 9</u> refer to the following paragraph.

(1) After becoming concerned about the environment, many people have decided to try recycling. (2) Most commonly, newspapers, glass, and aluminum cans. (3) However, automotive oil, cardboard, and plastic can be recycled too. (4) In most communities, several recycling centers taking these materials. (5) Some are private operations, and others are public. (6) Some local governments hire collectors to pick up the recycled material in front of people's houses. (7) Organic material, like vegetable peelings, combined with lawn clippings, leaves, and other organic material can form a mulch that enriches the soil and promotes new growth. (8) Some dedicated environmentalists creating these compost piles in their yards and gardens.

8. Sentence 2: **Most commonly, newspapers, glass, and aluminum cans.**

   What correction should be made to this sentence?

   (1) insert <u>they</u> before <u>newspapers</u>
   (2) insert <u>collect</u> before newspapers
   (3) insert <u>they collect</u> before <u>newspapers</u>
   (4) insert <u>collecting</u> before <u>newspapers</u>
   (5) insert <u>collected</u> before <u>newspapers</u>

9. Sentence 4: **In most communities, several recycling centers taking these materials.**

   What correction should be made to this sentence?

   (1) replace <u>communities several</u> with <u>communities. Several</u>
   (2) replace <u>centers taking</u> with <u>centers. Taking</u>
   (3) remove <u>taking</u>
   (4) change <u>taking</u> to <u>take</u>
   (5) no correction is necessary

   To check your answers, turn to page 154.

Word Groups That Do Not Express a Complete Thought

Although the following word group contains a subject and a verb, it is not a sentence because it doesn't express a complete thought:

> Whenever I drink milk.

I drink milk makes sense. But when we precede that sentence with *whenever,* we raise a question: What happens whenever I drink milk? Do I still feel thirsty? Do I get an upset stomach? To correct this fragment and complete the thought, we need to add some words:

> Whenever I drink milk, I get a headache.

Now we're looking at a complete sentence with two clauses. A **clause** is a group of words containing a subject and a verb. Some clauses are *independent.* That means they can stand alone and be understood.

> **Example:**   I get a headache.

Independent clauses are just like sentences, and they can be combined with other clauses to make longer sentences.

Some clauses have no meaning by themselves.

> **Example:**   Whenever I drink milk.

They *depend* on another word group for their meaning and, therefore, are called **dependent clauses.**

Here's a sentence with two independent clauses joined by the word *and:*

> The lions entered the circus ring, and the crowd roared with excitement.

Let's see what happens when we make one of the clauses dependent:

> When the lions entered the circus ring.

The dependent clause doesn't make sense by itself. It's a sentence fragment because it doesn't express a complete thought.

There are two easy ways to correct fragments that result from writing dependent clauses. One way is to attach the dependent clause to an independent clause:

> The crowd roared with excitement when the lions entered the circus ring.

The other way is to eliminate the word that makes the clause dependent: if we drop the *when* from the word group, we create an independent clause or a sentence:

> The lions entered the circus ring.

Here's another example. *Even though I ate a big breakfast* is a dependent clause or sentence fragment. *I am hungry* is an independent clause or complete sentence. When we link them, we create a new sentence:

Even though I ate a big breakfast, I am hungry.

A dependent clause can appear at the beginning or at the end of a sentence. If it appears at the beginning, it is followed by a comma:

When I climb stairs, I become tired.

If it appears at the end, there is no need for a comma:

I become tired when I climb stairs.

Let's look at another dependent clause:

Wherever flowers bloom.

To have meaning, this clause must be attached to an independent clause. Any number of independent clauses could give meaning to our dependent one. Adding it to the end of each of the clauses below, we create new sentences:

- I get an allergic reaction and begin to sneeze
- Expect splashes of color
- You'll find insects
- Hiking is especially pleasant
- They like to take a walk

Let's look at one more dependent clause:

Unless it rains.

By putting this one at the beginning of each clause below, we create new sentences:

- we'll lose our crops.
- the city will have to ration water.
- food prices will increase.
- the air pollution will get worse.
- we're leaving the area.

When the following words appear at the beginning of a sentence, they signal a dependent clause.

after	even though	until
although	if	when
as	since	whenever
because	though	where
before	unless	wherever

Remember, a clause that begins with one of these words must be attached to an independent clause, or it will be a sentence fragment.

TEST-TAKING TIP

Sometimes the words *who, that,* and *which* also signal a dependent clause but not always. You must check the entire word group between the capital letter and the end punctuation to be sure it expresses a complete thought:

Dependent clause: That you gave me.

Independent clause: That gift is my favorite.

EXERCISE 4

Directions: Identify the dependent clauses in the following sentences. Not all the sentences contain one.

1. All the ticket holders can get a good seat if they wait patiently.

2. Whenever their grandparents visit, the children become excited.

3. Who wants to go to the ball game?

4. Since you fixed the latch, the door closes more easily.

5. We won't know what to order until we see the menu.

6. That book was really funny.

Directions: Identify the cause of each sentence fragment below with an *S* if it's missing a subject, a *V* if it's missing a verb, a *P* if it's missing part of a verb, and a *D* if the fragment is a dependent clause. Not all the word groups are fragments. Use a *C* to identify complete sentences.

 If you are working in a group, you should discuss what questions the fragments raise.

7. All the parents in the neighborhood.

8. Unless you get permission first.

9. The performers backstage.

10. The messenger waiting in line at the bank.

11. Where you can go right up to the animals and pet them.

12. The train was on time.

13. The poodle standing patiently.

14. Paid for the shoes and wore them out of the store.

15. Before spreading the parts all over the floor, they read the instructions.

16. The singers and the entire orchestra.

WRITE ON TARGET

Using four of the sentence fragments in items 7–16, write complete sentences. Discuss your sentences with others if you are working in a group.

Directions: Choose the one best answer to each item.

Items 17 to 20 refer to the following paragraph.

(1) While she prepares to become an American citizen. (2) Kimiko attends a class once a week. (3) In the class, students from all over the world. (4) Studying U.S. government. (5) They examine each of the three branches of government, discussing real issues to see how the system works. (6) The instructor quizzes the students each week to help them remember what they've learned. (7) Kimiko will be ready to pass the naturalization examination after completing the class. (8) It will be a proud day for her and the others when they receive their U.S. citizenship.

17. Sentences 1 and 2: **While she prepares to become an American citizen. Kimiko attends a class once a week.**

    Which of the following is the best way to rewrite the underlined portion of these sentences? If you think the original is the best way, choose option (1).

    (1) American citizen. Kimiko
    (2) American citizen, Kimiko
    (3) American citizen: Kimiko
    (4) American citizen Kimikoi
    (5) American citizen; Kimiko

18. Sentences 3 and 4: **In the class, students from all over the <u>world. Studying</u> U.S. government.**

Which of the following is the best way to write the underlined portion of these sentences? If you think the original is the best way, choose option (1).

(1) world. Studying
(2) world studying
(3) world that studying
(4) world are studying
(5) world have studying

19. Sentence 7: **Kimiko will be ready to pass the naturalization examination after completing the class.**

If you rewrote sentence 7 beginning with

<u>After she completes the class,</u>

the next word should be

(1) they
(2) everyone
(3) Kimiko
(4) students
(5) citizens

20. Sentence 8: **It will be a proud day for her and the others when they receive their U.S. citizenship.**

What correction should be made to this sentence?
(1) replace <u>day for</u> with <u>day. For</u>
(2) replace <u>others when</u> with <u>others. When</u>
(3) replace <u>others when</u> with <u>others, when</u>
(4) change <u>receive</u> to <u>receiving</u>
(5) no correction is necessary

CONNECTIONS

American families have undergone radical changes since the 1960s. The **CONNECTIONS** Family Life theme pages (at the back of the book) show some of these changes. Write one paragraph describing the change in the number of families maintained by women from 1960 to 1991. You may want to include income level information. Proofread your work and correct any sentence fragments when you've finished.

To check your answers, turn to page 155.

G E D T EST P REVIEW

Directions: Choose the <u>one best answer</u> to each item.

<u>Items 1 to 5</u> refer to the following paragraph.

(1) Pet owners can hire someone to take care of their pets. (2) While they go on vacation. (3) It might be a neighbor or a professional pet sitter. (4) The sitters will come to your house, feed your pet, and take it for walks. (5) They'll take the animal to the vet. (6) If there's a medical problem. (7) Keeping the animals company and playing with them. (8) The pet sitters make sure the animals have some fun. (9) Many people prefer this to putting their pets in the unfamiliar setting of an expensive kennel. (10) Because they know their pets are well cared for at home. (11) They enjoy their vacations more.

1. Sentences 1 and 2: **Pet owners can hire someone to take care of their <u>pets. While they</u> go on vacation.**

   Which of the following is the best way to write the underlined portion of these sentences? If you think the original is the best way, choose option (1).

   (1) pets. While they
   (2) pets, while they
   (3) pets while they
   (4) pets while, they
   (5) pets while. They

2. Sentence 4: **The sitters will come to your house, feed your pet, and take it for walks.**

   What correction should be made to this sentence?

   (1) change <u>will come</u> to <u>coming</u>
   (2) replace <u>house, feed</u> with <u>house. Feed</u>
   (3) insert <u>to</u> before <u>feed</u>
   (4) replace <u>pet, and</u> with <u>pet. And</u>
   (5) no correction is necessary

3. Sentences 5 and 6: **They'll take the animal to the <u>vet. If</u> there's a medical problem.**

   Which of the following is the best way to write the underlined portion of these sentences? If you think the original is the best way, choose option (1).

   (1) vet. If
   (2) vet; if
   (3) vet, so if
   (4) vet if
   (5) vet, and if

4. Sentences 7 and 8: **Keeping the animals company and playing with <u>them. The pet sitters make</u> sure the animals have some fun.**

   Which of the following is the best way to write the underlined portion of these sentences? If you think the original is the best way, choose option (1)

   (1) them. The pet sitters make
   (2) them, the pet sitters make
   (3) them the pet sitters. Make
   (4) them, and the pet sitters make
   (5) them. The pet sitters making

5. Sentences 10 and 11: **Because they know their pets are well cared for at <u>home. They enjoy</u> their vacations more.**

   Which of the following is the best way to write the underlined portion of these sentences? If you think the original is the best way, choose option (1).

   (1) home. They enjoy
   (2) home. They enjoying
   (3) home, they enjoy
   (4) home they enjoy
   (5) home, and they

Items 6 to 10 refer to the following paragraph.

(1) About 40,000 letters arrive at the White House. (2) Every day. (3) A staff of volunteers reads and answers this mail. (3) The presidential correspondence office uses the services of about 450 people. (4) Ranging from Girl Scouts to retirees. (5) These workers cleared by the Secret Service. (6) The letter writers send the president their ideas about economic problems, health care, and other important issues. (7) Sometimes they ask for help with their personal problems. (8) Like illnesses or job searches. (9) Some of the letters sources of future presidential speeches.

6. Sentences 1 and 2: **About 40,000 letters arrive at <u>the White House. Every</u> day.**

Which of the following is the best way to write the underlined portion of these sentences? If you think the original is the best way, choose option (1).

(1) the White House. Every
(2) the White House, and every
(3) the White House: Every
(4) the White House every
(5) the White House; every

7. Sentences 3 and 4: **The presidential correspondence office uses the services of about 450 <u>people. Ranging</u> from Girl Scouts to retirees.**

Which of the following is the best way to write the underlined portion of these sentences? If you think the original is the best way, choose option (1).

(1) people. Ranging
(2) people. Who range
(3) people. Ranged
(4) people, who ranging
(5) people ranging

8. Sentence 5: **These workers cleared by the Secret Service.**

What correction should be made to this sentence?

(1) insert a comma after <u>workers</u>
(2) insert <u>being</u> before <u>cleared</u>
(3) insert <u>must be</u> before <u>cleared</u>
(4) change <u>cleared</u> to <u>clearing</u>
(5) insert a comma after <u>cleared</u>

9. Sentences 7 and 8: **Sometimes they ask for help for their personal <u>problems. Like</u> illnesses or job searches.**

Which of the following is the best way to write the underlined portion of these sentences? If you think the original is the best way, choose option (1).

(1) problems. Like
(2) problems like
(3) problems. Such as
(4) problems. Being
(5) problems. Including

10. Sentence 9: **Some of the letters sources of future presidential speeches.**

What correction should be made to this sentence?

(1) insert <u>being</u> before <u>sources</u>
(2) insert <u>become</u> before <u>sources</u>
(3) insert <u>becoming</u> before <u>sources</u>
(4) insert a comma after <u>letters</u>
(5) change <u>letters sources</u> to <u>letters. Sources</u>

To check your answers, turn to page 155.

2 Avoiding Run-on Sentences

**ACHIEVEMENT GOALS
In this lesson, you will learn how to**

- correctly link two or more ideas in a single sentence using punctuation

- recognize compound subjects and compound verbs

- link two or more ideas into one sentence using connecting words

Describing the scene of an accident to the police, an excited witness pours out details so fast that the police can barely understand. Eager to report what happened, the witness strings all the events together, almost forgetting to breathe.

"Slow down," the police officer says. "I can't understand you. Tell me one thing at a time."

Of course, the witness is just talking, not thinking about sentences. Thoughts come out in a jumble, often making little sense.

When you write, you don't have someone there to slow you down or to ask you to explain. If you have more than one thought to express, you must take care to separate the thoughts with proper punctuation and connecting words.

Recognizing Run-on Sentences

A **run-on sentence** is simply a string of two or more sentences written as a single sentence.

> Charles worked late last night he didn't get enough sleep he fell asleep in class today.

Sometimes a question and answer are run together into a single sentence. This is still a run-on sentence.

> Are you hungry let's get some pizza I like just about anything on pizza what kind do you want to order?

As you can see, whether it's a series of statements or a series of questions and answers, a run-on sentence can go on and on and on.

EXERCISE 1

Directions: Identify the run-on sentences below with an *R* for each run-on and a *C* for each complete sentence. Then correct the run-ons by placing a period at the end of each complete thought. Start the next thought with a capital letter.

1. A generation ago, people went for rides in the car they wanted something to do on a Sunday or a summer evening.

2. They would drive into the country and look at scenery.

3. Gasoline was inexpensive no one worried about using too much because it was plentiful.

4. There was much less traffic then there also was less danger because people didn't drive as fast as they do now.

5. Going for a ride was a nice family activity those were the days before people just sat around watching television.

Directions: Choose the <u>one best answer</u> to each item.

<u>Items 6 to 7</u> refer to the following paragraph.

(1) A temporary employment agency is a good place to get job experience. (2) These agencies match people's skills with companies that are seeking temporary help. (3) Working as a temp gives you an opportunity to sharpen skills you can also learn about different kinds of businesses. (4) Temp work helps both employers and employees.

6. Sentence 1: **A temporary employment agency is a good place to get job experience.**

What correction should be made to this sentence?

(1) replace <u>agency is</u> with <u>agency. Is</u>
(2) remove <u>is</u>
(3) remove <u>good</u>
(4) replace <u>place to</u> with <u>place. To</u>
(5) no correction is necessary

7. Sentence 3: **Working as a temp gives you an opportunity to sharpen skills you can also learn about different kinds of businesses.**

What correction should be made to this sentence?

(1) replace <u>temp gives</u> with <u>temp. Gives</u>
(2) replace <u>opportunity to</u> with <u>opportunity. To</u>
(3) replace <u>skills you</u> with <u>skills. You</u>
(4) replace <u>learn about</u> with <u>learn. About</u>
(5) remove the period after <u>businesses</u>

To check your answers, turn to page 156.

Recognizing Run-ons with Commas

Sometimes writers try to avoid run-ons by inserting commas after each complete thought. However, even if you separate the ideas with commas, you still have a run-on sentence. It becomes a list of ideas rather than a sentence:

The lawn mower made too much noise in the early morning, it annoyed Dorothy, she asked the neighbor to mow the lawn later in the day, the neighbor agreed, Dorothy felt better, it was quiet for a while.

A series of thoughts separated by commas is called a **comma splice.** A comma splice, then, is one kind of a run-on sentence.

If you suspect a group of words is a run-on, you can check by reading it slowly. Put a period, not a comma, at the end of the first complete thought. Then check the following words to be sure you haven't left any fragments standing. For example, in the run-on above, you might put a period after *The lawn mower made too much noise.* But when you read *in the early morning,* you should see that those words do not form a complete thought. You need to place the period after *morning,* not *noise.*

You can often identify a run-on sentence by reading it out loud. You'll find yourself running out of breath because you don't get the natural stop indicated by a period at the end of each thought. Try it with the run-on sentence above.

TEST-TAKING TIP

When you're looking for a run-on, ask yourself how many separate ideas there are. Look for word groups that can stand by themselves and make sense. In other words, look for independent clauses.

EXERCISE 2

Directions: Identify the run-on sentences below with an *R* for each run-on and a *C* for each complete sentence. Then correct the run-ons.

Read aloud if you have to. If you have a partner or are working in a group, read to another person or have someone read to you. Try to hear the difference between the complete sentences and the run-ons.

1. Sometimes on family outings, everyone would stop for ice cream cones, everybody would choose a favorite flavor they could have two scoops if they were lucky.

2. It's sad that we have lost those simple pleasures.

3. It's important that we take time to relax, it's not good for our mental or physical health to be running all the time, we need time for recreation.

4. Some people think a shorter work week would help.

5. Some companies give their workers four-day weeks the employees have to work longer hours each day though.

Directions: Choose the <u>one best answer</u> to each item.

<u>Items 6 to 9</u> refer to the following paragraph.

(1) Local governments fund a variety of services, including libraries. (2) Libraries are much more than just places to check out entertaining books they offer information on all kinds of subjects. (3) Trained librarians help people find all kinds of information. (4) Educators depend on libraries to enrich their classroom teaching writers use libraries to research articles. (5) And students use library resources to help them with their classes. (6) Libraries collect large varieties of newspapers and magazines they're great places to find current reading material that would be quite expensive to purchase. (7) In addition to books and information, libraries often sponsor lectures and films. (8) Story hours and summer reading contests instill a love of books even in young children. (9) Along with reading material, some libraries lend records and films to the public. (10) The only fee is a fine if the material isn't returned on time. (11) When governments have to trim their budgets, it is unfortunate that libraries are often among the first things cut back. (12) As sources of culture, knowledge, and recreation, they are valuable social institutions.

6. Sentence 1: **Local governments fund a variety of services, including libraries.**

What correction should be made to this sentence?

(1) replace <u>governments fund</u> with <u>governments. Fund</u>
(2) remove the comma after <u>services</u>
(3) replace the comma after <u>services</u> with a period
(4) remove the period after <u>libraries</u>
(5) no correction is necessary

7. Sentence 2: **Libraries are much more than just places to check out entertaining books they offer information on all kinds of subjects.**

What correction should be made to this sentence?

(1) replace <u>out entertaining</u> with <u>out. Entertaining</u>
(2) replace <u>books they</u> with <u>books. They</u>
(3) replace <u>offer information</u> with <u>offer. Information</u>
(4) remove the period after <u>subjects</u>
(5) no correction is necessary

8. Sentence 4: **Educators depend on libraries to enrich their classroom teaching writers use libraries to research articles.**

What correction should be made to this sentence?

(1) replace <u>libraries to</u> with <u>libraries. To</u>
(2) replace <u>enrich their</u> with <u>enrich. Their</u>
(3) replace <u>classroom teaching</u> with <u>classroom. Teaching</u>
(4) replace <u>teaching writers</u> with <u>teaching. Writers</u>
(5) replace <u>research articles</u> with <u>research. Articles</u>

9. Sentence 6: **Libraries collect large varieties of newspapers and magazines they're great places to find current reading material that would be quite expensive to purchase.**

What correction should be made to this sentence?

(1) replace <u>magazines they're</u> with <u>magazines. They're</u>
(2) replace <u>material that</u> with <u>material. That</u>
(3) replace <u>that would</u> with <u>so it would</u>
(4) replace <u>expensive to</u> with <u>expensive. To</u>
(5) no correction is necessary

To check your answers, turn to page 156.

Using Punctuation to Correct Run-ons

Here's a word group that looks like a sentence because it begins with a capital letter, ends with a period, and even contains several subjects and verbs.

We went to the movie the line was very long we didn't get in.

Even though it looks like a sentence, it is a run-on sentence because it contains three complete thoughts, each with its own subject/verb pair. One way to correct this run-on is to separate the three thoughts with periods.

We went to the movie. The line was very long. We didn't get in.

Another tool to correct run-on sentences is the semicolon. If you have two separate ideas that are closely related, you can include them in one sentence by using a semicolon to punctuate the two thoughts.

Emilio and Akira went fishing at sunrise; they caught many fish.

The two complete thoughts could have been written as two separate sentences. However, the writer wanted to emphasize the connection between the early hour and the large catch by writing the two thoughts as one sentence. As a writer, it's up to you to decide whether to use semicolons or periods.

TEST-TAKING TIP

You can use periods or semicolons to separate independent clauses. Both correct run-on sentences.

EXERCISE 3

Directions: Using either a period or a semicolon, correct each of the following run-ons. If you're working in a group, you may discuss reasons to choose one punctuation mark instead of the other. You'll see that sometimes one person sees a close connection between ideas while another doesn't.

1. It rained all day yesterday I was sorry I hadn't taken an umbrella.

2. There were several items on the menu we all chose something different.

3. Dan and Therese have to get up early I'm glad I don't have to be at work until noon.

4. Passing the test improved Ai-Ling's chance for a promotion I think I'd like a different job, too.

Directions: Choose the one best answer to each item.

Items 5 to 7 refer to the following paragraph.

(1) Sometimes you can find great bargains when a store has a going-out-of-business sale. (2) The neighborhood appliance store had that kind of a sale, it was a great opportunity to buy a coffeemaker at a low price. (3) Marie decided to look for one there she also thought she'd shop for a couple of other items. (4) She found a coffeemaker she liked; she liked the low price too. (5) She saw a food processor on sale she bought that also. (6) Her shopping trip was so successful that Marie resolved to watch for more going-out-of-business sales.

5. Sentence 2: **The neighborhood appliance store had that kind of a sale, it was a great opportunity to buy a coffeemaker at a low price.**

Which of the following is the best way to write the underlined portion of this sentence? If you think the original is the best way, choose option (1).

(1) sale, it
(2) sale it
(3) sale; it
(4) sale but it
(5) sale, but it

6. Sentence 3: **Marie decided to look for <u>one there she also</u> thought she'd shop for a couple of other items.**

Which of the following is the best way to write the underlined portion of this sentence? If you think the original is the best way, choose option (1).

(1) one there she also
(2) one there she; also
(3) one there, she also
(4) one there. She also
(5) one there she. Also

7. Sentence 5: **She saw a food <u>processor on sale she bought</u> that also.**

Which of the following is the best way to write the underlined portion of this sentence? If you think the original is the best way, choose option (1).

(1) processor on sale she bought
(2) processor. On sale she bought
(3) processor was on sale she bought
(4) processor on sale. She bought
(5) processor on sale, she bought

<u>Items 8 to 10</u> refer to the following paragraph.

(1) Although the reunification of Germany and the breakdown of the Soviet Union held out hope for a more peaceful world, the ending of the Cold War has had a serious economic impact on Americans. (2) As the defense industry cut back, many people found themselves unemployed highly skilled workers suddenly faced an uncertain future. (3) Military personnel no longer felt secure about their career choice. (4) The government closed bases at home and abroad this affected service people and also hurt the civilians who worked on these bases. (5) We must find ways to turn defense industries to peaceful endeavors it's tragic to waste the skills of former defense workers.

8. Sentence 2: **As the defense industry cut back, many people found themselves unemployed highly skilled workers suddenly faced an uncertain future.**

What correction should be made to this sentence?

(1) replace <u>back, many</u> with <u>back. Many</u>
(2) replace <u>people found</u> with <u>people. Found</u>
(3) remove <u>many</u>
(4) insert a semicolon after <u>unemployed</u>
(5) insert a semicolon after <u>workers</u>

9. Sentence 4: **The government closed bases at <u>home and abroad this affected</u> service people and also hurt the civilians who worked on these bases.**

Which of the following is the best way to write the underlined portion of this sentence? If you think the original is the best way, choose option (1).

(1) home and abroad this affected
(2) home and abroad. This affected
(3) home. And abroad this affected
(4) home and abroad this affecting
(5) home and abroad affected

10. Sentence 5: **We must find ways to turn defense industries to peaceful endeavors it's tragic to waste the skills of former defense workers.**

If you rewrote sentence 5 beginning with

<u>Because it's tragic to waste the skills of former defense workers,</u>

the next word would be

(1) skills
(2) peaceful
(3) endeavors
(4) we
(5) there

To check your answers, turn to page 156.

Is It Really a Run-on? Recognizing Compound Subjects and Verbs

Some sentences contain more than one subject or more than one verb but still express only one complete thought. If you see a **compound subject** or a **compound verb,** don't assume you're looking at a run-on sentence. A run-on sentence has *two subject and verb pairs.*

Let's compare two sentences to see the difference:

(1)   *The car and the house* needed repairs at the same time.

(2)   *The car needed* repairs *the house needed* repairs at the same time.

The first sentence has a compound subject and is written correctly. The second sentence has two subject and verb pairs. Therefore, it's a run-on. Putting a period or semicolon after *The car needed repairs* will correct the run-on sentence. (Of course, if you use a period, the second sentence must begin with a capital letter.)

Let's look at two more examples:

(1)   The architect *designed* the building *and drew* the plans.

(2)   One architect designed *the building* another drew *the plans.*

The first sentence has a compound verb. Although the architect did two things, this is only one sentence because there is only one subject. The second sentence has two subjects and two verbs, so it's a run-on. Writing the ideas as two separate sentences or using a semicolon after *One architect designed the building* would correct the run-on.

Some sentences contain a compound subject and a compound verb:

The motorist and the truck driver swerved quickly and avoided a collision.

Chou and Tsia felt sick and went home.

TEST-TAKING TIP

Remember there are two kinds of verbs—action verbs and linking verbs. When you are looking for compound subjects and verbs as well as complete thoughts, don't forget to consider both types of verbs.

EXERCISE 4

Directions: In the following passage, correct the run-on sentences with a period or semicolon and find any compound subjects and verbs.

1. Rush-hour traffic is a huge problem everyone goes to work or comes home at the same time the streets and freeways fill up with cars people sometimes daydream and don't concentrate on their driving this can cause accidents and arouse tempers cautious drivers and commuters know how to drive and pay attention in rush-hour traffic the problem is made worse by the many people who aren't used to driving in rush-hour traffic these inexperienced drivers are surprised that cars stop and go every few seconds.

Directions: Choose the <u>one best answer</u> to each item.

<u>Items 2 to 5</u> refer to the following paragraph.

(1) Mr. Herrera had an appointment at the medical clinic he was supposed to be there at 1:30. (2) He arrived on time but had to wait for the doctor. (3) Mr. Herrera's doctor was attending to an emergency and was behind in her appointments. (4) The receptionist told Mr. Herrera that the doctor had been delayed and was sorry. (5) He sat quietly. (6) And read magazines for nearly half an hour. (7) When Mr. Herrera was finally called, the receptionist, and the doctor apologized again for keeping him waiting.

2. Sentence 1: **Mr. Herrera had an appointment at the medical <u>clinic he was</u> supposed to be there at 1:30.**

Which of the following is the best way to write the underlined portion of this sentence? If you think the original is the best way, choose option (1).

(1) clinic he was
(2) clinic, he was
(3) clinic but he was
(4) clinic. He was
(5) clinic; He was

3. Sentence 3: **Mr. Herrera's doctor was attending to an emergency and was behind in her appointments.**

What correction should be made to this sentence?

(1) change <u>emergency and</u> to <u>emergency. And</u>
(2) insert a comma after <u>emergency</u>
(3) remove <u>and</u>
(4) change <u>and was</u> to <u>and. Was</u>
(5) no correction is necessary

4. Sentences 5 and 6: **He sat quietly. And read magazines for nearly half an hour.**

What correction should be made to these sentences?

(1) remove <u>And</u>
(2) replace <u>quietly. And</u> with <u>quietly; and</u>
(3) insert <u>the doctor</u> before <u>read</u>
(4) replace <u>quietly. And</u> with <u>quietly and</u>
(5) insert a semicolon after <u>magazines</u>

5. Sentence 7: **When Mr. Herrera was finally called, the receptionist, and the doctor apologized again for keeping him waiting.**

What correction should be made to this sentence?

(1) remove the comma after <u>called</u>
(2) replace <u>called, the</u> with <u>called. The</u>
(3) remove the comma after <u>receptionist</u>
(4) replace <u>doctor apologized</u> with <u>doctor. Apologized</u>
(5) replace <u>again for</u> with <u>again. For</u>

WRITE ON TARGET

Write a four-sentence paragraph about sports. Be sure there are no run-on sentences in your paragraph. Include at least one compound subject and one compound verb.

To check your answers, turn to page 156.

Using Connecting Words to Correct Run-on Sentences

You've seen that run-on sentences can be corrected by writing two sentences or by separating related ideas with a semicolon. Another way to correct a run-on is to use a comma and a connecting word such as *and, or, but, for, yet,* and *so.* These words are also called **conjunctions.** When choosing a connecting word, be sure it accurately expresses the relationship between the two ideas in the sentence.

For example, it makes sense to say *Akemi and Maria enjoyed the movie, but Sumio didn't like it.* You're expressing a contrast between the ways people reacted to the movie, and the word *but* suggests the contrast. The sentence has a very different meaning if you say *Akemi and Maria enjoyed the movie, so Sumio didn't like it.*

If either of the independent clauses in a run-on already contains commas, you should always use a semicolon to separate the independent clauses.

Akemi, Maria, Lucas, and Tom enjoyed the movie; but Sumio, Mario, and Irene didn't like it.

EXERCISE 5

Directions: Use a comma and a connecting word (or a semicolon) to correct each of the following run-on sentences.

1. Terry and I went shopping we found nothing to buy.

2. Margaret ran into the store Loretta, Krista, and the poodles waited in the car.

3. The audience gave a standing ovation the performers played two more songs.

4. He arrived at the meeting place at 4 p.m. there was no one waiting.

5. The fans wouldn't quiet down the basketball player missed his shot.

6. Chih and Gabriel liked different food, sports, and television programs they were good friends.

7. Mrs. McCall carefully tended her vegetable garden she had fresh vegetables every day during the summer.

Directions: Choose the <u>one best answer</u> to each item.

<u>Items 8 to 10</u> refer to the following paragraph.

(1) Balloons and flags announced the grand opening of the new supermarket. (2) The store opened at eight o'clock crowds already were lined up at the doors. (3) It would be a great day to find special prices, free samples, and prizes. (4) Inside, tables were set up with samples of frozen pizza, yogurt, fruit juice, sausage, and other kinds of food you could easily eat a meal even if you didn't buy a thing. (5) The crowded store was noisy, but children were running up and down the aisles.

8. Sentence 2: **The store opened at <u>eight o'clock crowds</u> already were lined up at the doors.**

Which of the following is the best way to write the underlined portion of this sentence? If you think the original is the best way, choose option (1).
(1) eight o'clock crowds
(2) eight o'clock, crowds
(3) eight o'clock, and crowds
(4) eight o'clock and crowds
(5) eight o'clock; and crowds

9. Sentence 4: **Inside, tables were set up with samples of frozen pizza, yogurt, fruit juice, sausage, and other kinds of food you could easily eat a meal even if you didn't buy a thing.**

Which of the following is the best way to write the underlined portion of this sentence? If you think the original is the best way, choose option (1).

(1) food you
(2) food; you
(3) food, you
(4) food and you
(5) food but you

10. Sentence 5: **The crowded store was noisy, but children were running up and down the aisles.**

What correction should be made to this sentence?

(1) replace but with and
(2) remove but
(3) replace the comma with a semicolon
(4) replace but with so
(5) no correction is necessary

Items 11 to 13 refer to the following paragraph.

(1) "Doves" and "hawks" are terms that came into use during the Vietnam War. (2) Doves are birds that symbolize peace, but that became the name applied to people who opposed the war. (3) They wanted the United States to negotiate peace. (4) Hawks are more aggressive birds their name was applied to those who wanted to step up the fighting. (5) The terms continue to be used to identify people according to their attitudes toward global conflict. (6) For example, the media refer to those who advocate negotiated settlements as doves those who believe military force is the answer are called hawks.

11. Sentence 2: **Doves are birds that symbolize peace, but that became the name applied to people who opposed the war.**

What correction should be made to this sentence?

(1) remove the comma
(2) replace peace, but with peace. But
(3) replace the comma with a semicolon
(4) replace but with yet
(5) replace but with so

12. Sentence 4: **Hawks are more aggressive birds their name was applied to those who wanted to step up the fighting.**

Which of the following is the best way to write the underlined portion of this sentence? If you think the original is the best way, choose option (1).

(1) birds their
(2) birds, but their
(3) birds, so their
(4) birds; and their
(5) birds, their

13. Sentence 6: **For example, the media refer to those who advocate negotiated settlements as doves those who believe military force is the answer are called hawks.**

Which of the following is the best way to write the underlined portion of this sentence? If you think the original is the best way, choose option (1).

(1) doves those
(2) doves, because those
(3) doves, or those
(4) doves, those
(5) doves; those

C O N N E C T I O N S

How have communications satellites changed our lives? The Technology theme in **CONNECTIONS** (at the back of the book) gives an idea. Write one or more complete sentences to answer these questions: (1) Which two years are important in communications satellite history? (2) If you placed a long-distance call, how would a satellite transmit it? Proofread your answers and correct any run-on sentences.

To check your answers, turn to page 157.

Directions: Choose the <u>one best answer</u> to each item.

<u>Items 1 to 5</u> refer to the following paragraph.

(1) Fear of public speaking is a common problem ninety-five percent of the adult population considers public speaking to be its number one fear. (2) Many people never have to worry about speaking in public, but for others, this fear can be a real obstacle. (3) It can keep people from following certain career paths, teaching, law, and sales require people to speak in front of others. (4) It's unfortunate when a talented person who could help others gives up a particular kind of job because of this fear because there are ways to get help. (5) Books, classes, and counseling can help a person overcome a fear of public speaking classes give them opportunities to speak in front of a small and nonthreatening group. (6) Books may have helpful tips but, counseling may be the most valuable help for many. (7) Many people once feared public speaking they are now professional speakers.

1. Sentence 1: **Fear of public speaking is a common <u>problem ninety-five</u> percent of the adult population considers public speaking to be its number one fear.**

Which of the following is the best way to write the underlined portion of this sentence? If you think the original is the best way, choose option (1).

(1) problem ninety-five
(2) problem. Ninety-five
(3) problem, ninety-five
(4) problem, but ninety-five
(5) problem, yet ninety-five

2. Sentence 3: **It can keep people from following certain career <u>paths, teaching,</u> law, and sales require people to speak in front of others.**

Which of the following is the best way to write the underlined portion of this sentence? If you think the original is the best way, choose option (1).

(1) paths, teaching
(2) paths, and teaching
(3) paths, but teaching
(4) paths, so teaching
(5) paths. Teaching

3. Sentence 5: **Books, classes, and counseling can help a person overcome a fear of public <u>speaking classes</u> give them opportunities to speak in front of a small and nonthreatening group.**

Which of the following is the best way to write the underlined portion of this sentence? If you think the original is the best way, choose option (1).

(1) speaking classes
(2) speaking, but classes
(3) speaking. Classes
(4) speaking and, classes
(5) speaking, classes

4. Sentence 6: **Books may have helpful <u>tips but, counseling</u> may be the most valuable help for many.**

Which of the following is the best way to write the underlined portion of this sentence? If you think the original is the best way, choose option (1).

(1) tips but, counseling
(2) tips, but counseling
(3) tips, so Counseling
(4) tips, but, counseling
(5) tips but. Counseling

5. Sentence 7: **Many people once feared public <u>speaking they are</u> now professional speakers.**

Which of the following is the best way to write the underlined portion of this sentence? If you think the original is the best way, choose option (1).

(1) speaking they are
(2) speaking, they are
(3) speaking; and they are
(4) speaking, yet they
(5) speaking, or they

<u>Items 6 to 8</u> refer to the following paragraph.

(1) A few generations ago, cities built rapid electric transit systems to move people about. (2) Automobiles were new, few people owned one. (3) Tracks to carry streetcars or trolleys were built along major streets. (4) Electric poles on the tops of streetcars attached to wires overhead that's how the cars got their power. (5) The streetcars, like today's buses, could carry large numbers of people to and from work, shopping, or wherever they needed to go. (6) Although electric streetcar lines provided clean transportation, people began to dislike the unsightly tracks. (7) The tracks were removed, and the streets were cemented over. (8) Trackless trolleys still depended on overhead wires for power. (9) However, they could now cover much more territory they didn't have to go only where the tracks went. (10) Eventually people came to dislike the wires and poles too, so cities turned to diesel-powered buses for public transportation. (11) Mounting concern over air pollution caused people to yearn for the clean transportation of the old streetcar systems. (12) Today, many communities are once again building tracks and running electric streetcars.

6. Sentence 2: **Automobiles were <u>new, few</u> people owned one.**

Which of the following is the best way to write the underlined portion of this sentence? If you think the original is the best way, choose option (1).

(1) new, few
(2) new, not many
(3) new not many
(4) new. Few
(5) new few

7. Sentence 4: **Electric poles on the tops of streetcars attached to wires overhead that's how the cars got their power.**

What correction should be made to this sentence?

(1) replace <u>streetcars attached</u> with <u>streetcars. Attached</u>
(2) replace <u>overhead that's</u> with <u>overhead. That's</u>
(3) insert a comma after <u>overhead</u>
(4) remove <u>that's</u>
(5) replace <u>cars got</u> with <u>cars. Got</u>

8. Sentence 9: **However, they could now cover much more territory they didn't have to go only where the tracks went.**

What correction should be made to this sentence?

(1) replace <u>cover much</u> with <u>cover. Much</u>
(2) replace <u>more territory</u> with <u>more. Territory</u>
(3) replace <u>territory they</u> with <u>territory. They</u>
(4) replace <u>to go</u> with <u>to. Go</u>
(5) replace <u>go only</u> with <u>go. Only</u>

To check your answers, turn to page 157.

Linking Ideas of Equal Importance

ACHIEVEMENT GOALS
In this lesson, you will
learn how to

- recognize compound sentences

- connect only ideas that relate closely

- understand the relationship between equal ideas and to choose appropriate connecting words

A **simple sentence** contains one subject and one verb and expresses a complete thought, but a string of simple sentences is not very interesting to read. To make your writing more appealing, you should occasionally combine two or more ideas into one sentence.

Let's compare the following two examples:

Charles was thirsty. He poured a glass of juice.

Charles was thirsty, so he poured a glass of juice.

Both examples express the same ideas, but the second flows more smoothly than the first.

When you combine independent clauses into single sentences, you're writing compound sentences. A compound sentence links ideas of equal importance. That is, each idea could stand by itself and make sense. You've already learned how to punctuate compound sentences using semicolons or commas with connecting words.

You can also join two independent clauses using a semicolon and a connecting word or phrase to smooth the transition from one idea to the next. The connecting word or phrase is followed by a comma.

Thomas ate three sandwiches; nevertheless, he was still hungry.

Identifying Compound Sentences

In Lesson 2 you learned how to use proper punctuation and connecting words to combine two or more independent clauses into a single sentence.

106 **Unit 1** Building Sentences

Remember, an independent clause contains a subject and a verb, and it must be a complete thought.

Even though a **compound sentence** is a combination of two or more simple sentences, you cannot always identify a compound sentence by its length. A simple sentence (a sentence with just one complete thought) can be quite long, and a compound sentence can be short.

The long sentence below is a *simple sentence:*

The gusty northerly wind, filling the billowing blue and white sails of the boat, carries the sailors swiftly through the waters and across the lake.

If you search, you'll find the one subject, *wind*, and the one verb, *carries*, that make this a simple sentence.

The short sentence below is a *compound sentence:*

The boat sails by, and the swimmers wave.

It's easy to spot the two subject-verb sets that make this a compound sentence: *boat sails* and *swimmers wave.*

Compare the lengths of the following simple and compound sentences:

Simple sentence: The telephone rang.

Compound sentence: The telephone rang, and Mrs. Sheng answered it.

Clearly, the subject and verb in the first sentence are *telephone rang.* It's just as easy to spot the two subject-verb sets in the second sentence: *telephone rang* and *Mrs. Sheng answered.*

Simple sentence: The faraway sound of cheerful voices and lively music suggested a big, happy crowd at the county fair across the freeway from the Delgado ranch.

Compound sentence: They added a ferris wheel this year, and the fairgoers love it.

Can you find the single subject-verb set in the first sentence? (*sound suggested*) Can you find both subject-verb sets in the second sentence? (*They added* and *fairgoers love*)

Simple sentence: Budget-conscious shoppers save money on all kinds of products with coupons from the newspaper and magazines.

Among all those words is a single subject, *shoppers*, and a single verb, *save.*

Compound sentence: Grocery stores display the most expensive items at eye level, and people often buy them without looking around for a better buy.

Do you see the two subject-verb sets: *stores display* and *people buy?*

Directions: Look for the subjects and verbs in the sentences below. If you find two sets of subjects and verbs, place a comma after the first complete thought and mark the sentence *C* for compound.

1. Many consumers worry about unemployment and they don't spend their money.
2. Many bicycle riders resist helmets and thousands of head injuries result every year from bike accidents.
3. Rivers and lakes offer countless recreational possibilities.
4. Water activities are inexpensive and many, like fishing and swimming, are free.
5. The stamped seal of a notary public gives authenticity to certain documents.

Directions: Identify the compound and the simple sentences in the group below using a *C* for compound and an *S* for simple. Remember, compound sentences contain more than one complete thought.

 If you think a sentence is compound, ask your partner or a member of your group to identify both subjects and verbs.

6. Julie bought a new purse, and Elaine bought shoes.
7. Ralph and Arturo went bungee jumping, but James thought it was too dangerous.
8. Marsha travels around the country for her job.
9. Backpacking is a popular outdoor activity, but Suzanne and Tony don't like it.
10. Working in the driveway, Ben adjusted his car's brakes.
11. Libraries offer free books and hours of pleasure.
12. Michelle faithfully attends aerobics class or plays racquetball every day, including Saturday and Sunday.
13. No one understood the directions, and the instructor had to repeat them twice.
14. Charlotte drove the truck, and four people rode in the back.

15. The broken traffic light at the corner of one of the city's busiest intersections caused a huge traffic jam at the height of the rush hour last Wednesday.

Directions: Choose the one best answer to each item.

Items 16 to 18 refer to the following paragraph.

(1) Some states charge a sales tax on food. (2) It seems like a fair tax because everyone has to buy food everyone pays the tax. (3) There are those, however, who think this kind of tax is unfair. (4) They point out that people with little money have to buy just as much food as people with lots of money. (5) These people spend a larger portion of their income on food, so they also pay a larger portion of their income on the taxes. (6) Taxes that cost some people a higher proportion of their income than others are called regressive taxes. (7) Income taxes are called progressive taxes they increase proportionately as the taxpayer's income goes up. (8) Thus, a person earning $60,000 a year pays a higher tax than someone earning $18,000. (9) Because sales tax is regressive, many states do not apply it to food. (10) On the other hand, some states collect no state income tax they rely instead on other taxes, including sales tax on food.

16. Sentence 2: **It seems like a fair tax because everyone has to buy <u>food everyone</u> pays the tax.**

   Which of the following is the best way to write the underlined portion of this sentence? If you think the original is the best way, choose option (1).

   (1) food everyone
   (2) food, everyone
   (3) food but everyone
   (4) food and everyone
   (5) food. Everyone

17. Sentence 7: **Income taxes are called progressive taxes they increase proportionately as the taxpayer's income goes up.**

What correction should be made to this sentence?

(1) replace <u>progressive taxes</u> with <u>progressive.</u> <u>Taxes</u>
(2) insert a comma after <u>taxes</u>
(3) insert a semicolon after <u>taxes</u>
(4) replace <u>proportionately as</u> with <u>proportionately. As</u>
(5) remove <u>as</u>

18. Sentence 10: **On the other hand, some states collect no state income tax they rely instead on other taxes, including sales tax on food.**

What correction should be made to this sentence?

(1) replace <u>hand, some</u> with <u>hand. Some</u>
(2) replace <u>income tax they</u> with <u>income tax. They</u>
(3) insert a comma after <u>income tax</u>
(4) remove <u>they</u>
(5) replace <u>taxes, including</u> with <u>taxes. Including</u>

<u>Items 19 to 21</u> refer to the following paragraph.

(1) One of the most painful judicial issues is that of child custody. (2) Custody cases have always been difficult, but they have become increasingly complicated today. (3) These cases once dealt with divorce the question was which parent should have custody of the children after the dissolution of a marriage. (4) Now judges must consider the custody rights of adoptive parents as well as those of birth parents. (5) Cases have come to court because one or both birth parents change their minds months or even years after releasing their offspring for adoption. (6) Adoptive parents fight to keep the children they have raised since birth biological parents fight to get custody of the children they conceived. (7) It seems unlikely the children can benefit from these legal battles.

19. Sentence 2: **Custody cases have always been difficult, but they have become increasingly complicated today.**

What correction should be made to this sentence?

(1) remove the comma after <u>difficult</u>
(2) replace the comma with a semicolon
(3) remove <u>but</u>
(4) replace <u>but they</u> with <u>but. They</u>
(5) no correction is necessary

20. Sentence 3: **These cases once dealt with divorce the question was which parent should have custody of the children after the dissolution of a marriage.**

What correction should be made to this sentence?

(1) replace <u>divorce the</u> with <u>divorce. The</u>
(2) insert a comma after <u>divorce</u>
(3) replace <u>was which</u> with <u>was. Which</u>
(4) replace <u>children after</u> with <u>children. After</u>
(5) no correction is necessary

21. Sentence 6: **Adoptive parents fight to keep the children they have raised since birth biological parents fight to get custody of the children they conceived.**

What correction should be made to this sentence?

(1) replace <u>children they have</u> with <u>children. They have</u>
(2) replace <u>raised since</u> with <u>raised. Since</u>
(3) replace <u>birth biological</u> with <u>birth. Biological</u>
(4) replace <u>custody of</u> with <u>custody. Of</u>
(5) insert a semicolon after <u>custody</u>

To check your answers, turn to page 158.

Connecting Ideas That Are Closely Related

Not all independent clauses can be combined effectively into compound sentences. Be sure to link only those ideas that are closely related.

The following two ideas, for example, would not make an effective compound sentence:

Armando borrowed three books from the library. Leah has always enjoyed browsing in libraries.

But the following two ideas are so closely related that it does make sense to link them into one sentence:

Armando borrowed three books from the library, but Leah was unable to find the books she wanted.

Let's look at two more pairs of sentences to see whether they would make effective compound sentences:

Tickets were available for the championship football game.

Chuck didn't really enjoy sports.

David and Nellie were big football fans.

They rushed to buy tickets to the championship game.

The first pair contains two completely separate ideas. The subject of one is *tickets*, and the subject of the other is *Chuck*, who doesn't like sports. These unrelated subjects would not make an effective compound sentence.

In the second pair, however, both sentences talk about David and Nellie. Furthermore, they both talk about David and Nellie in relation to football. It makes sense to join the second pair into a compound sentence:

David and Nellie were big football fans, so they rushed to buy tickets to the championship game.

EXERCISE 2

Directions: Read the following pairs of sentences. Use semicolons to connect ideas that are closely related.

1. At last the snow fell in the mountains. The skiers were thrilled.

2. Joaquin wanted Diana to go skiing with him. His brother went to a movie.

3. Diana had never skied. She was afraid to go.

4. Diana said no. Her best friend loves to ski.

5. Joaquin went without Diana. He didn't have much fun.

Directions: Choose the one best answer to each item.

Items 6 to 8 refer to the following paragraph.

(1) Thirty-seven million people in America have little or no medical coverage. (2) For several years, to publicize this problem and to help those people, concerned health providers in California have put together a huge health fair. (3) Volunteer doctors, nurses, dentists, optometrists, and others examine and treat people for free they have access to high-tech computers that screen blood samples. (4) In addition to treatment, participants at the fair can get counseling on nutrition, poison and accident prevention, tobacco use, and parenting skills. (5) Some uninsured people are found to need further medical attention they receive appointments with private physicians who will see them for no charge. (6) The fair is only a temporary solution to health care problems, a big help for thousands of people who show up each year.

6. Sentence 3: **Volunteer doctors, nurses, dentists, optometrists, and others examine and treat people for free they have access to high-tech computers that screen blood samples.**

What correction should be made to this sentence?

(1) insert <u>because</u> after <u>free</u>
(2) insert <u>so</u> after <u>free</u>
(3) insert a comma after <u>free</u>
(4) insert a semicolon after <u>free</u>
(5) change <u>free they</u> to <u>free. They</u>

7. Sentence 5: **Some uninsured people are found to need further medical <u>attention they</u> receive appointments with private physicians who will see them for no charge.**

Which of the following is the best way to write the underlined portion of this sentence? If you think the original is the best way, choose option (1).

(1) attention they
(2) attention; they
(3) attention; nevertheless, they
(4) attention, but they
(5) attention, or they

8. Sentence 6: **The fair is only a temporary solution to health care <u>problems, a big</u> help for the thousands of people who show up each year.**

Which of the following is the best way to write the underlined portion of this sentence? If you think the original is the best way, choose option (1).

(1) problems, a big
(2) problems. A big
(3) problems, but it is a big
(4) problems, so it is a big
(5) problems, and is a big

To check your answers, turn to page 158.

Understanding the Relationship Between Equal Ideas

When you use only a semicolon to link two independent clauses, you show that that the ideas are closely related, but you don't explain what the relationship is.

To clarify the relationship between the ideas, you must use connecting words. Some connecting words follow a semicolon and then are followed by a comma:

Robin likes action *movies; however,* her husband Art prefers romances.

Other connecting words simply follow a comma:

Robin likes action *movies, but* her husband Art prefers romances.

The line was *long, but* they decided to wait.

The line was *long; however,* they decided to wait.

The line was *long; they* decided, however, to wait.

To choose the proper connecting words, you must understand the relationship between the ideas in the two independent clauses. For example, it would be senseless to say

Milton was ill; however, he had to stay home from work.

The writer really means

Milton was ill; consequently, he had to stay home from work.

In this case, *however* is an inappropriate connector because it shows contrast between ideas. *Consequently* makes more sense because it shows that the second idea is the result of the first.

Let's look at another compound sentence to see whether the connecting word is appropriate.

The building inspector came yesterday; otherwise, the building is now ready for occupancy.

You could spend a lot of time trying to figure out what that sentence means. The connecting word, *otherwise*, suggests contrast; however, the two ideas are related by cause and effect.

The building inspector came yesterday; therefore, the building is now ready for occupancy.

There are several kinds of relationships between clauses in a compound sentence. One has to do with *cause and effect*:

Miguel and Claudia couldn't find a parking place, so they drove around the block two or three times.

TEST-TAKING TIP

If the connecting word can be moved to another part of the sentence without changing the meaning, you should use a semicolon; otherwise, you should use a comma after the first complete idea. Remember, a connecting word after a semicolon should be followed by a comma.

Another relationship shows *contrast* between two ideas:

> They looked for a parking spot for fifteen minutes, but they weren't late for the movie.

A third relationship involves *choices:*

> They could spend time looking for a parking place near the theater, or they could park far away and walk.

A fourth relationship involves *time,* or the *order of events:*

> It rained for several days; then the flowers bloomed.

A fifth relationship involves showing an *illustration* of one idea.

> The heavy rain caused problems; for example, several streets flooded.

Sometimes the relationship is simply the *addition of similar information.*

> Some of the streets were flooded; furthermore, traffic was congested for miles.

Table 3-1 Be sure to choose connecting words that express an accurate relationship among the ideas you combine into compound sentences.

CONNECTING WORDS	RELATIONSHIP BETWEEN CLAUSES
as a result consequently so therefore thus	**cause and effect**
but however instead nevertheless otherwise still yet	**contrast**
nor or	**choice**
finally then	**time, or order of events**
for example for instance	**illustration**
and besides furthermore in addition likewise moreover	**additional similar information**

EXERCISE 3

Directions: Read the following compound sentences and change the inappropriate connecting words.

1. Gloria was late for work almost every day, but she lost her job.

2. Carmen had never used a cash register; furthermore, she was willing to learn how.

3. The cab driver knew every street in town; however, he never got lost.

4. The doctor examined Richard immediately, or he discovered a broken bone.

5. Marilyn was rarely cheerful or upbeat, so she managed to laugh when things went wrong.

WRITE ON TARGET

Write three compound sentences about how advertising influences your shopping habits. Be sure combined ideas are closely related and that you use the proper connecting words and punctuation.

Directions: Choose the one best answer to each item.

Items 6 to 8 refer to the following paragraph.

(1) Advertising is an essential feature of our economy. (2) Clever ads can entertain the public as they introduce them to goods and services. (3) Advertising gives consumers useful information on new products, so it also makes consumers want things they don't need. (4) Ads are everywhere; however, they appear on television, on the radio, in magazines, and in newspapers. (5) Some ads are misleading, so they cause people to spend money unwisely. (6) The wise consumer approaches advertising claims carefully.

6. Sentence 3: **Advertising gives consumers useful information on new products, so it also makes consumers want things they don't need.**

What correction should be made to this sentence?

(1) remove the comma after products
(2) replace so with but
(3) change products, so to products. So
(4) replace so with then
(5) no correction is necessary

7. Sentence 4: **Ads are everywhere; however, they appear on television, on the radio, in magazines, and in newspapers.**

What correction should be made to this sentence?

(1) replace however with for example
(2) replace however with nevertheless
(3) replace the comma after however with a semicolon
(4) remove the comma after however
(5) no correction is necessary

8. Sentence 5: **Some ads are misleading, so they cause people to spend money unwisely.**

If you rewrote sentence 4 beginning with

Misleading ads

The next word should be

(1) and
(2) people
(3) cause
(4) prevent
(5) help

Items 9 to 11 refer to the following paragraph.

(1) For many years, the motion picture industry has used a rating code for movies. (2) The ratings indicate the degree of sex, violence, and profanity in a movie; however, some parents use the ratings to decide what movies to let their children see. (3) Supporters of the rating system hoped the result would be more wholesome movies, but that isn't what happened instead, many people look for the movies with restricted ratings and avoid those that are rated appropriate for family viewing. (4) There have been indications that moviemakers use sex or violence to get an R rating, hoping that more people will come to their movies. (5) Now the television industry is under similar pressure to rate television shows because the public feels violence in society reflects violence on television. (6) Warnings about objectionable material in television programs could make the programs more enticing to people; otherwise, more viewers than ever would tune in to violent programs.

9. Sentence 2: **The ratings indicate the degree of sex, violence, and profanity in a <u>movie; however, some parents</u> use the ratings to decide what movies to let their children see.**

Which of the following is the best way to write the underlined portion of this sentence? If you think the original is the best way, choose option (1).

(1) movie; however, some parents
(2) movie, however some parents
(3) movie; even though some parents
(4) movie; and some parents
(5) movie; but some parents

10. Sentence 3: **Supporters of the rating system hoped the result would be more wholesome movies, but <u>that isn't what happened instead, many</u> people look for the movies with restricted ratings and avoid those that are rated appropriate for family viewing.**

Which of the following is the best way to write the underlined portion of this sentence? If you think the original is the best way, choose option (1).

(1) that isn't what happened instead, many
(2) that isn't what happened instead. Many
(3) that isn't what happened, instead many
(4) that isn't what happened instead; many
(5) that isn't what happened; instead, many

11. Sentence 6: **Warnings about objectionable material in television programs could make the programs more enticing to people; otherwise, more viewers than ever would tune in to violent programs.**

What correction should be made to this sentence?

(1) remove the semicolon
(2) replace the semicolon with a comma
(3) replace <u>otherwise</u> with <u>then</u>
(4) replace <u>otherwise</u> with <u>nevertheless</u>
(5) no correction is necessary

CONNECTIONS

To explore the job outlook for different industries, turn to the Employment theme pages in **CONNECTIONS**. Compare the job outlook to service-producing industries in general and to retail industries specifically. Write the same comparison in three different ways: as two simple sentences, as a compound sentence, and as a compound sentence with a connecting word or words and a comma.

To check your answers, turn to page 159.

GED TEST PREVIEW

Directions: Choose the <u>one best answer</u> to each item.

<u>Items 1 to 5</u> refer to the following paragraph.

(1) Americans seem to be obsessed with dieting, so not everyone who diets is overweight. (2) There are many opportunities to lose weight health clubs, commercial diet programs, even grocery stores offer help to people who think they're too fat. (3) It's been shown that crash diets don't work. (4) Studies show that people who lose weight on quick-loss fad diets usually gain most or all of it back within a year. (5) This intense concern with dieting worries health experts; however, they are troubled by increasing numbers of people with eating disorders. (6) Some people are truly obese, or many others just think they are overweight. (7) This is especially true among women and girls. (8) Both physical and mental health professionals would like to see people become less image conscious. (9) They say we should take care of our health then we would worry less about our image.

1. Sentence 1: **Americans seem to be obsessed with dieting, so not everyone who diets is overweight.**

What correction should be made to this sentence?

(1) remove the comma after <u>dieting</u>
(2) replace <u>so</u> with <u>therefore</u>
(3) replace <u>so</u> with <u>for example</u>
(4) replace <u>so</u> with <u>but</u>
(5) no correction is necessary

2. Sentence 2: **There are many opportunities to lose <u>weight health</u> clubs, commercial diet programs, even grocery stores offer help to people who think they're too fat.**

Which of the following is the best way to write the underlined portion of this sentence? If you think the original is the best way, choose option (1).

(1) weight health
(2) weight. Health
(3) weight, health
(4) weight; nevertheless, health
(5) weight, but health

3. Sentence 5: **This intense concern with dieting worries health experts; however, they are troubled by increasing numbers of people with eating disorders.**

What correction should be made to this sentence?

(1) replace <u>however,</u> with <u>but</u>
(2) replace <u>however,</u> with <u>or</u>
(3) remove <u>however,</u>
(4) replace <u>however</u> with <u>on the other hand</u>
(5) no correction is necessary

4. Sentence 6: **Some people are truly <u>obese, or</u> many others just think they are overweight.**

Which of the following is the best way to write the underlined portion of this sentence? If you think the original is the best way, choose option (1).

(1) obese, or
(2) obese, but
(3) obese, so
(4) obese or
(5) obese. Or

5. Sentence 9: **They say we should take care of our health then we would worry less about our image.**

What correction should be made to this sentence?

(1) insert a comma after <u>health</u>
(2) insert a semicolon after <u>health</u>
(3) replace <u>then</u> with <u>but</u>
(4) replace <u>then</u> with <u>yet</u>
(5) no correction is necessary

Items 6 to 9 refer to the following paragraph.

(1) The first cities in civilization arose around five and a half thousand years ago. (2) In the part of the world we know as the Middle East. (3) Because of new advances in agriculture, food became plentiful enough that many people were able to give up farming. (4) These people moved away from the farms they pursued other kinds of jobs. (5) At first, many of them became craftspeople who made and sold items like tools and pottery. (6) Eventually there emerged a class of merchants who sold the goods other people made. (7) With improvements in transportation, the merchant class flourished. (8) Around 3000 B.C., the Egyptians established trade routes by water their ships were primitive and had to be rowed by teams of oarsmen. (9) Nevertheless, they did serve to increase trading opportunities for people in ancient times.

6. Sentences 1 and 2: **The first cities in civilization arose around five and a half thousand year ago. In the part of the world we know as the Middle East.**

   Which of the following is the best way to write the underlined portion of these sentences? If you think the original is the best way, choose option (1).

   (1) ago. In
   (2) ago in
   (3) ago; in
   (4) ago, in
   (5) ago; however, in

7. Sentence 4: **These people moved away from the farms they pursued other kinds of jobs.**

What correction should be made to this sentence?

(1) replace <u>people moved</u> with <u>people. Moved</u>
(2) replace <u>away from</u> with <u>away. From</u>
(3) insert a comma after <u>away</u>
(4) replace <u>farms they</u> with <u>farms. They</u>
(5) insert a comma after <u>farms</u>

8. Sentence 5: **At first, many of them became craftspeople who made and sold items like tools and pottery.**

   What correction should be made to this sentence?

   (1) change <u>craftspeople who</u> to <u>craftspeople. Who</u>
   (2) insert a comma after <u>craftspeople</u>
   (3) insert a comma after <u>made</u>
   (4) insert a semicolon after <u>made</u>
   (5) no correction is necessary

9. Sentence 8: **Around 3000 B.C., the Egyptians established trade routes by <u>water their</u> ships were primitive and had to be rowed by teams of oarsmen.**

   Which of the following is the best way to write the underlined portion of this sentence? If you think the original is the best way, select option (1).

   (1) water their
   (2) water, so their
   (3) water, but their
   (4) water, and their
   (5) water, or their

   To check your answers, turn to page 159.

4 Linking Ideas of Unequal Importance

Besides combining two equally important ideas into one sentence, you can vary your sentence structure and make your writing more interesting with complex sentences.

Like a compound sentence, a **complex sentence** links two ideas into one sentence. However, in a complex sentence, one of the ideas is less important than the other and depends on the main idea for its meaning. The main idea appears in the independent clause, whereas the less important idea appears in the dependent one. Here's an example:

> Because he was late, Jeff decided not to stop at the cleaners on the way to work.

You see that, by itself, *Because he was late* doesn't make sense. When it's added to the independent clause, *Jeff decided not to stop at the cleaners on the way to work,* we understand it.

Identifying Complex Sentences

You may remember from Lesson 1, Avoiding Sentence Fragments, that an *independent clause* is the same as a complete sentence. It can stand alone and make sense. A *dependent clause,* on the other hand, doesn't make sense unless it's attached to another idea, the sentence's main idea.

Complex sentences combine dependent clauses with independent clauses. This is one way to combine ideas and make your writing more interesting. When you write a complex sentence, you need to keep in mind the relationship between the two ideas so that you know which one logically depends on the other.

Consider the following two simple sentences:

It was Sunday. There was no mail delivery.

To vary the writing, you might combine those ideas into a compound sentence:

It was Sunday, so there was no mail delivery.

A third way to express the two ideas is with a *complex sentence:*

Because it was Sunday, there was no mail delivery.

In the third sentence, you have made one idea *(it was Sunday)* less important by making it dependent for its meaning on the other idea *(there was no mail delivery)*. You've done this with the connecting word *because*.

The important information in the sentence is that there is no mail delivery. The dependent clause tells us why there is no mail, but the reason is less important than the fact itself.

The way ideas are combined gives them different meanings. Look at the following pair of sentences:

They met for coffee. They finished their work.

TEST-TAKING TIP

Both sentences are complete, with a subject and a verb. But we don't know the relationship between the two ideas. Did they finish work and drink coffee at the same time? Did they do one first and then the other? If so, which one came first? A complex sentence answers such questions. Notice how the meaning changes in the sentences below because of the various combinations and connecting words.

To find a dependent clause, first seek the main clause in a sentence. Determine which group of words makes sense on its own. Then look at the remaining words to identify the dependent clause.

After they finished their work, they met for coffee.

While they met for coffee, they finished their work.

Before they finished their work, they met for coffee.

Because they finished their work early, they met for coffee.

Dependent clauses may precede the main clause or they may follow it. If the dependent clause comes first, it is followed by a comma. If the dependent clause appears at the end of the sentence, a comma is not needed.

Because it was 102 degrees in the shade, they stayed in the house all day.

They stayed in the house all day because it was 102 degrees in the shade.

EXERCISE 1

Directions: Write five complete sentences by matching each dependent clause from List A with an appropriate independent clause from the List B. Be sure to punctuate and capitalize the sentences correctly.

List A

1. as if they had all the time in the world
2. so that everyone could hear
3. until the neighbors complained
4. whether it needed it or not
5. unless you're sure of the answer

List B

a. don't volunteer to explain the problem
b. Rebecca washed her kitchen floor every day
c. they adjusted the microphone
d. they ate their lunch slowly
e. they collected car parts in their front yard

Directions: Identify the dependent clauses in the complex sentences below. Not all the sentences are complex.

6. Because the owner was ill, the shop's opening was postponed.
7. Victoria and Monica enjoyed the soccer game, but their team didn't win.
8. The group rented a boat for the afternoon even though there were clouds in the sky.
9. As long as they had enough participants, they could start the building project.
10. William sneezes whenever a cat enters the room.
11. No one told Bernice about the change in time, so she arrived late.
12. While he waited for the exam to begin, Keith became more and more confident.
13. They'll cancel the picnic if it rains.

14. Some people want to stop smoking, but they don't know how.
15. Wherever they looked, they saw mountains.

Directions: Choose the one best answer to each item.

Items 16 to 18 refer to the following paragraph.

(1) One of our constitutional guarantees is the right to a trial by jury. (2) With the right to a trial by jury goes the responsibility to serve on a jury. (3) If we are called. (4) After Dolores served on a jury. (5) She felt proud. (6) The judge had instructed the jurors carefully, and they followed her instructions with equal care. (7) When the trial was over, Dolores felt satisfied with the verdict because of the intense jury room discussions. (8) Furthermore, she had learned some important lessons in civics while she worked closely with new and interesting people.

16. Sentences 2 and 3: **With the right to a trial by jury goes the responsibility to serve on a jury. If we are called.**

    What correction should be made to these sentences?

    (1) insert a comma after trial by jury
    (2) replace responsibility to with responsibility. To
    (3) change jury. If to jury if
    (4) change If we to if. We
    (5) no correction is necessary

17. Sentences 4 and 5: **After Dolores served on a jury. She felt proud.**

    Which of the following is the best way to write the underlined portion of these sentences? If you think the original is the best way, choose option (1).

    (1) jury. She
    (2) jury, so she
    (3) jury because she
    (4) jury, she
    (5) jury; therefore, she

18. Sentence 7: **When the trial was over, Dolores felt satisfied with the verdict because of the intense jury room discussions.**

What correction should be made to this sentence?

(1) replace <u>over, Dolores</u> with <u>over. Dolores</u>
(2) replace <u>satisfied with</u> with <u>satisfied. With</u>
(3) insert a comma after <u>verdict</u>
(4) replace <u>verdict because</u> with <u>verdict. Because</u>
(5) no correction is necessary

<u>Items 19 to 21</u> refer to the following paragraph.

(1) The history of ice cream, perhaps America's favorite dessert, goes back to colonial times. (2) It was enjoyed by people like George Washington and Dolly Madison. (3) Although ice cream is delicious by itself. (4) It also forms the basis for other wonderful treats. (5) According to legend, in 1874 a businessman in Philadelphia combined ice cream with a carbonated beverage to create the ice cream soda.(6) Laws were passed prohibiting the sale of ice cream sodas on Sundays. (7) Because the drink was so sinfully delicious. (8) This led to a new creation. (9) A druggist in Illinois put noncarbonated syrup over ice cream and called it a Sunday. (10) The spelling changed over the years, and the ice cream sundae became a favorite dessert.

19. Sentences 3 and 4: **Although ice cream is delicious by <u>itself. It</u> also forms the basis for other wonderful treats.**

Which of the following is the best way to write the underlined portion of these sentences? If you think the original is the best way, choose option (1).

(1) itself. It
(2) itself, it
(3) itself, and it
(4) itself, so it
(5) itself because it

20. Sentence 5: **According to legend, in 1874 a businessman in Philadelphia combined ice cream with a carbonated beverage to create the ice cream soda.**

What correction should be made to this sentence?

(1) insert a period after <u>legend</u>
(2) insert a comma after <u>Philadelphia</u>
(3) insert a period after <u>beverage</u>
(4) insert a comma after <u>create</u>
(5) no correction is necessary

21. Sentences 6 and 7: **Laws were passed prohibiting the sale of ice cream sodas on Sundays. Because the drink was so sinfully delicious.**

What correction should be made to these sentences?

(1) insert a semicolon after <u>passed</u>
(2) replace <u>sodas on Sundays</u> with <u>sodas. On Sundays</u>
(3) replace <u>Sundays. Because</u> with <u>Sundays, but</u>
(4) replace <u>Sundays. Because</u> with <u>Sundays because</u>
(5) insert a comma after <u>drink</u>

To check your answers, turn to page 160.

Choosing Appropriate Connecting Words

Whether you're writing compound sentences or complex sentences, you must not combine ideas into one sentence unless they have a logical relationship. In a complex sentence, the main idea is the important one and appears in an independent clause. The secondary (less important) idea appears in a dependent clause.

For example, look at the following sentence.

Eugene was afraid he'd lose his apartment because his rent was late.

The relationship between the two ideas is cause and effect. Eugene was afraid of losing his apartment *because* his rent was late. The late rent is the reason he's afraid, but it's secondary to the main idea. If the ideas held equal importance, we could write them as two sentences or as a compound sentence: *Eugene's rent was late; he was afraid he would lose his apartment.*

Consider this sentence.

Charles could buy the radio if he borrowed some money from his best friend.

The relationship between these ideas is one of condition. Charles could do one thing *(buy a camera)* on the condition that he do another *(borrow the money)*. If these two ideas were written as a pair of sentences, the meaning would be different: *Charles could buy the radio. He borrowed money from his best friend.* You see how important it is to use proper connecting words.

In Lesson 3, you learned to choose appropriate connectors to combine independent clauses into compound sentences. The connectors in complex sentences also must accurately express the relationship between the ideas in the two clauses. Complex sentences relate ideas in several different ways.

- cause and effect

In order to meet the train, they had to postpone dinner.

Since the house was dark, they didn't ring the doorbell.

- contrast

Although it was a holiday, most of the stores were open.

Leona turned down the invitation *despite the fact that* she loved parties.

- time

One of their parents reads them a story *before* the children go to bed.

They screamed *until* their throats hurt.

- place

Sharon was happy *wherever* she could play tennis.

They put the key *where* no one would see it.

• condition

If you work hard, you'll get good grades.

Enrique didn't know *whether* his brother would be home that week.

• similarity between the ideas in the two clauses

Terry felt *as if* he could eat a horse.

Carrie ran the race *as though* she'd been running all her life.

Table 4-1 Be sure to choose words that express an accurate relationship among the ideas you combine into complex sentences.

CONNECTING WORDS	RELATIONSHIP BETWEEN CLAUSES
because in order that since so that	**cause and effect**
although despite the fact that even though in spite of the fact that though	**contrast**
after as long as as soon as before until when whenever while	**time**
where wherever	**place**
if unless whether	**condition**
as if as though	**similarity**

EXERCISE 2

Directions: Some of the word groups below are complete sentences, and some are dependent clauses. Find the dependent clauses and the connecting words that make them dependent. With your partner or a member of your group, write down the relationship suggested by each connecting word. Use the table on page 123 to help you identify the relationships.

1. Even though she loved parties.
2. Mr. and Mrs. Rodriguez opened their own florist shop.
3. Running a restaurant seemed appealing.
4. Because Hal loved to cook.
5. The Mackenzie family had visitors all summer.
6. Wherever there was a job to do.
7. Whenever there was a full moon.
8. Unless the meeting ends early.
9. Jane didn't finish the project.
10. As if she were bored with the conversation.

WRITE ON TARGET

Write three complex sentences about recycling.

Directions: Choose the one best answer to each item.

Items 11 to 13 refer to the following paragraph.

(1) Owning a car can be more expensive than you think. (2) Because you find a car for a reasonable price, there are other costs to consider. (3) Whether the car is new or used, it will take money to service it. (4) New cars require scheduled maintenance checks to keep the warranty valid. (5) Each time you service the car, you spend money. (6) Since a used car is not under warranty, it must have periodic servicing or it will be likely to develop mechanical problems. (7) You might have to buy some expensive new parts to keep the car running. (8) Insurance costs are another large expense for car owners. (9) In fact, many people drive without insurance, even though they may be breaking a law. (10) Just keeping gas and oil in the car becomes costly, and those are just the everyday expenses.

11. Sentence 2: **Because you find a car for a reasonable price, there are other costs to consider.**

    Which of the following is the best way to write the underlined portion of this sentence? If you think the original is the best way, choose option (1).

    (1) Because you find
    (2) As though you find
    (3) So that you find
    (4) Although you find
    (5) In order that you find

12. Sentence 6: **Since a used car is not under warranty, it must have periodic servicing or it will be likely to develop mechanical problems.**

    What correction should be made to this sentence?

    (1) replace Since with Even though
    (2) replace Since with Because
    (3) replace the comma with a semicolon
    (4) replace servicing or with servicing. Or
    (5) no correction is necessary

13. Sentence 9: **In fact, many people drive without insurance, even though they may be breaking a law.**

What correction should be made to this sentence?

(1) replace <u>insurance, even</u> with <u>insurance. Even</u>
(2) remove the comma after <u>insurance</u>
(3) replace <u>even though</u> with <u>because</u>
(4) replace <u>even though</u> with <u>whenever</u>
(5) replace <u>even though</u> with <u>wherever</u>

<u>Items 14 to 16</u> refer to the following paragraph.

(1) We can remember things more easily if we write them down. (2) Some people use calendars or appointment books, although others just use a piece of paper. (3) Then we have to remember to look at the reminder we wrote. (4) Jean forgot to look at her calendar. (5) She missed her dental appointment. (6) When Jean made the appointment, she had a toothache. (7) She was sorry she missed the appointment. (8) In order that her tooth no longer hurt.

14. Sentence 2: **Some people use calendars or appointment books, although others just use a piece of paper.**

What correction should be made to this sentence?

(1) replace <u>books, although</u> with <u>books. Although</u>
(2) replace the comma with a semicolon
(3) remove the comma after <u>books</u>
(4) replace <u>although</u> with <u>in order that</u>
(5) replace <u>although</u> with <u>whenever</u>

15. Sentences 4 and 5: **Jean forgot to look at her calendar. She missed her dental appointment.**

The most effective combination of sentences 4 and 5 would begin with which of the following words?

(1) Unless
(2) As soon as
(3) Until
(4) Because
(5) Although

16. Sentences 7 and 8: **She was sorry she missed the appointment. In order that her tooth no longer hurt.**

The most effective combination of sentences 7 and 8 would include which of the following groups of words?

(1) Because Jean's tooth no longer hurt,
(2) Although Jean's tooth no longer hurt,
(3) Unless Jean had a toothache,
(4) Since Jean never had a toothache,
(5) So that she missed her appointment,

CONNECTIONS

Americans rely on the media for important news. Facts about the media are given on the News Media theme pages in **CONNECTIONS**. Determine the main idea of the excerpt, graph, diagram, and chart. Write a complex sentence for each, expressing one of the following relationships: contrast, cause/effect, or time. Be sure to use commas correctly as you write.

To check your answers, turn to page 160.

GED TEST PREVIEW

Directions: Choose the <u>one best answer</u> to each item.

<u>Items 1 to 5</u> refer to the following paragraph.

(1) Families feel the impact, as more women join the workforce. (2) Some women seek jobs outside the home voluntarily. (3) Others seek jobs out of financial necessity. (4) Whatever the reasons are more and more women are away from home during the day. (5) This means more children are left home alone or spend large amounts of time at day care facilities. (6) Because they lack adult supervision. (7) Children at home alone may be more inclined than others to get into trouble or may become injured. (8) On the other hand, these same children may develop a strong sense of responsibility and independence that can serve them well as adults. (9) As they keep an eye on the house these kids learn to cook, clean, and watch younger children. (10) It's important for working parents to establish rules since children who are left alone need definite limits. (11) Although they know their parents care, kids will talk freely about their own problems and concerns. (12) Parents and children can solve their problems if they discuss concerns and establish rules together.

1. Sentence 1: **Families feel the impact, as more women join the workforce.**

What correction should be made to this sentence?

(1) remove the comma after <u>impact</u>
(2) change <u>impact, as</u> to <u>impact. As</u>
(3) insert <u>because</u> after the comma
(4) replace <u>as</u> with <u>even though</u>
(5) no correction is necessary

2. Sentence 4: **Whatever the reasons are more and more women are away from home during the day.**

What correction should be made to this sentence?

(1) insert a comma after <u>reason</u>
(2) insert a semicolon after <u>are</u>
(3) insert a comma after <u>are</u>
(4) insert a semicolon after <u>away</u>
(5) insert a comma after <u>home</u>

3. Sentences 6 and 7: **Because they lack adult <u>supervision. Children</u> at home alone may be more inclined than others to get into trouble or may become injured.**

Which of the following is the best way to write the underlined portion of these sentences? If you think the original is the best way, choose option (1).

(1) supervision. Children
(2) supervision, and children
(3) supervision whenever children
(4) supervision, children
(5) supervision children

4. Sentence 9: **As they keep an eye on the house these kids learn to cook, clean, and watch younger children.**

What correction should be made to this sentence?

(1) insert a comma after <u>eye</u>
(2) insert a semicolon after <u>house</u>
(3) insert a comma after <u>house</u>
(4) replace <u>house these</u> with <u>house. These</u>
(5) insert a semicolon after <u>clean</u>

5. Sentence 10: **It's important for working parents to establish rules since children who are left alone need definite limits.**

If you rewrote sentence 10 beginning with

<u>Working parents should establish rules because</u>

The next word should be

(1) parents
(2) they
(3) rules
(4) limits
(5) children

6. Sentence 11: **Although they know their parents care, kids will talk freely about their own problems and concerns.**

What correction should be made to this sentence?

(1) replace <u>Although</u> with <u>If</u>
(2) remove the comma
(3) change <u>care, kids</u> to <u>care. Kids</u>
(4) change the comma to a semicolon
(5) insert a comma after <u>freely</u>

<u>Items 7 to 9</u> refer to the following paragraph.

(1) Some natural disasters, like earthquakes and hurricanes, do their damage in a matter of minutes or days and move on. (2) Floods, however, cause ongoing devastation, as well as immediate suffering. (3) Because of flooding in America's midwestern states, the entire nation notices food shortages and high prices. (4) Mosquitoes and flies multiply because they breed in water. (5) River channels fill with tons of silt and bring further damage to flooded areas. (6) Birds stray from their usual migratory paths although they can't find food. (7) The water carries poisonous snakes into people's homes. (8) The rivers themselves change because debris alters shorelines and strong currents reshape river bottoms. (9) Since destruction, drownings, food and water shortages, and disease, flood victims work hard to fight the raging waters.

7. Sentence 2: **Floods, however, cause ongoing devastation, as well as immediate suffering.**

What correction should be made to this sentence?

(1) remove <u>however</u>
(2) remove the comma after <u>devastation</u>
(3) insert a comma after <u>as well as</u>
(4) replace <u>as well as</u> with <u>or</u>
(5) no correction is necessary

8. Sentence 6: **Birds stray from their usual migratory <u>paths although</u> they can't find food.**

Which of the following is the best way to write the underlined portion of this sentence? If you think the original is the best way, choose option (1).

(1) paths although
(2) paths, although
(3) paths, because
(4) paths because
(5) paths, and

9. Sentence 9: **Since destruction, drownings, food and water shortages, and disease, flood victims work hard to fight the raging waters.**

What correction should be made to this sentence?

(1) replace <u>Since</u> with <u>In spite of</u>
(2) remove the comma after disease
(3) insert a semicolon after <u>hard</u>
(4) change <u>to fight</u> to <u>fighting</u>
(5) insert <u>while</u> before <u>the</u>

To check your answers, turn to page 161.

5 Using Modifiers to Add Information

ACHIEVEMENT GOALS

In this lesson, you will learn how to

- recognize different kinds of modifiers

- place modifiers properly in a sentence

- punctuate sentences with modifiers

You have learned that complete sentences must have at least a subject and a verb. Most sentences, of course, contain much more information than a simple subject and verb. *Citizens meet* is a complete sentence, but it's not very interesting or very informative. A sentence about citizens meeting probably would contain additional descriptive information about the subject and the verb.

To illustrate, let's add information to the sentence:

Angry citizens from several small communities meet regularly to discuss taxes and unemployment while nervous politicians listen.

We call word groups that add information modifiers.

Recognizing Modifiers

A **modifier** is a word or word group that describes another word or word group in a sentence. Let's look at our sample sentence with the modifiers italicized:

Angry citizens *from several small communities* meet *regularly to discuss taxes and unemployment while nervous politicians listen.*

Within that sentence, we have both single-word modifiers and word-group modifiers. In other words, even some of the modifiers contain modifiers! For example, *from several small communities* modifies *citizens*, but within that modifier, *several* and *small* modify *communities*.

Let's examine this concept with a shorter sentence:

The local basketball coach recruited several players.

The subject and verb in this sentence are *coach recruited.* The modifiers tell us something about the coach. We know, from only two words, *local* and *basketball,* where this coach works and what the sport is. Another single word, *several,* tells us that the coach is looking for more than one player. All of these words are modifiers that tell us something about other words in the sentence.

One-word modifiers (adjectives and adverbs) don't usually cause many problems with sentence structure, but it's important to be able to recognize them.

Adjectives describe **nouns,** which are words that often represent persons, places, or things (*angry* citizens). **Adverbs** describe verbs (meet *regularly*), adjectives (*very* angry), and other adverbs (*quite* regularly).

Prepositional phrases and verb phrases are the modifiers most likely to cause problems in writing. Unlike clauses, **phrases** are word groups that do not contain a subject and verb. They play the same role in a sentence that a single word might play.

Prepositions are words that show the relationship of a noun to some other word in the sentence. For example, the athlete ran *with* the ball. Other prepositions include *of, in, to, at, across, above, through, over,* and *under.*

Prepositional phrases are word groups that begin with a preposition and answer questions about the words they modify, like when? where? and why? Look at the examples below:

Before class, the students discussed their homework.

The phrase in this sentence tells us *when* the discussion took place.

Lee found the book *on the desk.*

The phrase tells us *where* the book was found.

James brought balloons *for the children.*

Here we learn for *whom* the balloons were brought.

Verb phrases also answer questions about other words in the sentence, but they begin with some form of a verb. Look at the examples below:

Swerving across the lanes, the car skidded *into the snow bank.*

The verb phrase tells us *how* the car was moving; the prepositional phrase tells us *where* it skidded.

Martha gave the puppy a toy *to calm him down.*

The verb phrase explains *why* she gave the puppy a toy.

Notice that modifiers do not make sense on their own. They must be attached to an independent clause to have meaning. In that sense, they are like dependent clauses.

Like dependent clauses, modifiers can appear before or after the independent clause in a sentence. If they precede the clause, they must be followed by a comma. If they follow the clause, there is no need for a comma.

To feel better, Jill took a nap.

Jill took a nap to feel better.

EXERCISE 1

Directions: Write five complete sentences by matching each modifier from List A with an appropriate independent clause from List B. Be sure to punctuate with the necessary commas and capital letters.

List A

1. around the corner

2. to see better

3. under the table

4. searching all day

5. feeling hot and tired

List B

a. Marshall cleaned his glasses

b. everyone jumped into the river

c. they finally found the leak

d. the motorcycle disappeared

e. he found his socks

Directions: Identify the modifiers in the following sentences. Some of the modifiers are just one word; others are phrases.

 With your partner or a member of your group, add another modifier to each sentence.

6. Concerned about local events, Dorothy watched the news.

7. Their new car needed repairs.

8. Consuelo lifted the weights with little effort.

9. The severely damaged bicycle was useless.

10. Angered by the article, Matthew stopped reading.

11. During the snowstorm, the tires of the car gripped the road.

12. Rereading the instructions, Meredith felt more confident.

13. A loud explosion silenced everyone.

14. Imitating the announcer, the comedian made everyone laugh.

15. Babe Ruth hit the ball over the fence, and the excited fans cheered.

Directions: Choose the one best answer to each item.

Items 16 to 20 refer to the following paragraphs.

(1) According to the U.S. Census Bureau. (2) Today's young Americans are marrying later than past generations did. (3) This is because they have many other demands. (4) On their lives. (5) They're concerned about school and career, for example. (6) Because many good jobs require higher education, one out of two high school graduates goes on to college. (7) A hundred years ago, more people lived on farms. (8) Couples postponed marriage. (9) Until they could afford a house. (10) Now couples postpone marriage for a variety of reasons.

(11) Fear joblessness, young adults also move out of their parents' homes at a later age than in the past. (12) Experts think this is because of the uncertain economic picture young people face. (13) After graduation. (14) Many continue to live with their parents for years.

16. Sentences 1 and 2: **According to the U.S. Census Bureau. Today's young Americans are marrying later than past generations did.**

Which of the following is the best way to write the underlined portion of these sentences? If you think the original is the best way, choose option (1).

(1) Bureau. Today's young
(2) Bureau today's young
(3) Bureau, today's young
(4) Bureau; today's young
(5) Bureau because today's young

17. Sentences 3 and 4: **This is because they have many other demands. On their lives.**

What correction should be made to these sentences?

(1) insert a comma after <u>because</u>
(2) replace <u>they have</u> with <u>having</u>
(3) replace <u>demands. On</u> with <u>demands on</u>
(4) replace <u>demands. On</u> with <u>demands, on</u>
(5) no correction is necessary

18. Sentences 8 and 9: **Couples postponed marriage. Until they could afford a house.**

Which of the following is the best way to write the underlined portion of these sentences? If you think the original is the best way, choose option (1).

(1) marriage. Until
(2) marriage. While
(3) marriage. So
(4) marriage until
(5) marriage while

19. Sentence 11: **Fear joblessness, young adults also move out of their parents' homes at a later age than in the past.**

What correction should be made to this sentence?

(1) change <u>Fear</u> to <u>Fear of</u>
(2) change <u>Fear</u> to <u>Fearing</u>
(3) change <u>Fear</u> to <u>Until they fear</u>
(4) replace <u>homes at</u> with <u>homes. At</u>
(5) insert a comma after <u>age</u>

20. Sentences 12 and 13: **Experts think this is because of the uncertain economic picture young people face. After graduation.**

If you rewrote sentences 12 and 13 beginning with

<u>Experts believe young people stay home longer after graduation</u>

the next word(s) should be

(1) although
(2) as if
(3) unless
(4) after
(5) because

To check your answers, turn to page 161.

Putting Modifiers in the Right Place

When writers are careless about where they put modifiers, they confuse readers with unclear sentences. Some misplaced modifiers appear to describe two different things. The reader can't tell what the writer really means.

For example, imagine that a representative from the police department gave a talk at a local high school. He talked about heroic crimestoppers. Here's what one reporter wrote about the event:

> The police officer spoke about heroic crimestoppers at the local high school.

The sentence suggests that the crimestoppers were from the local high school. Perhaps some of the students heroically stopped crimes, but it was the talk, not the crimestopping, that took place at the high school. The modifier *at the local high school* seems to be modifying *crimestoppers* because it appears next to it.

Here's what the writer meant to say:

> The police officer spoke at the local high school about heroic crimestoppers.

This time the modifier is next to *spoke,* the word it modifies.

Place modifiers carefully. If they appear too far from the word they modify, they confuse readers and often make sentences sound ridiculous.

> Crawling up the wall, the exterminator poisoned all the ants.

It doesn't seem likely that the exterminator would be crawling up the wall, but that's what the sentence says. Probably the writer means:

> The exterminator poisoned all the ants crawling up the wall.

Again, the sentence becomes clear when the modifier appears closer to the word it modifies.

noun = ants

modifier = crawling up the wall

Another way to correct misplaced modifiers is to turn the phrase into a dependent clause.

> *While the ants were crawling up the wall,* the exterminator poisoned them.

EXERCISE 2

Directions: Rewrite the sentences below to correct the misplaced modifiers.

1. While moving through the maze, Dr. Jones observed the rats.
2. Bill finished chopping the onions wiping his eyes.
3. Being too loud, Jeff hated the music.
4. Dean was clearly surprised by the expression on his face.
5. The cook explained how the participants could cut fat from their recipes, including the beginners.

Directions: Choose the one best answer to each item.

Items 6 to 8 refer to the following paragraph.

(1) Breakthroughs in disease prevention and cure often result from years of careful scientific study. (2) Much of this research relies on help from the public. (3) Medical researchers depend on volunteers, needing a variety of subjects. (4) Some studies require thousands of volunteers and take many years to complete. (5) Researchers must be precise about their data, testing heredity and environment. (6) They must also enjoy working with people, conducting experiments. (7) Along with volunteers, the studies involve scientists, physicians, lab technicians, statisticians, and others skilled in collecting and analyzing research data. (8) Without the dedication and expertise of all these people, Americans would have a much lower standard of health.

6. Sentence 3: **Medical researchers depend on volunteers, needing a variety of subjects.**

   If you rewrote sentence 3 beginning with

   Needing a variety of subjects,

   the next word should be

   (1) volunteers
   (2) researchers
   (3) people
   (4) depending
   (5) variety

7. Sentence 5: **Researchers must be precise about their data, testing heredity and environment.**

   If you rewrote sentence 5 beginning with

   Testing heredity and environment,

   the next word should be

   (1) researchers
   (2) must
   (3) precise
   (4) data
   (5) volunteers

8. Sentence 6: **They must also enjoy working with people, conducting experiments.**

   If you rewrote sentence 6 beginning with

   Because researchers conduct experiments on human subjects,

   the next word should be

   (1) enjoy
   (2) work
   (3) they
   (4) subjects
   (5) must

Items 9 to 11 refer to the following paragraph.

(1) Companies that offer their employees flexible workplace arrangements find a remarkable increase in productivity. (2) Workers are able to do much of their work from their homes rather than going into the company's offices under a flexible system. (3) Employers aren't sure why productivity increases under these conditions, but there are several possibilities. (4) Employees who are ill or disabled working at home have less of a burden. (5) They can continue to be valuable contributors to the company even if they are confined to their homes. (6) It's also possible that people do better work when they are relieved of long commutes, complex child care arrangements, and the need to dress up for work every day. (7) Workplace flexibility benefits society, decreasing pollution and traffic.

9. Sentence 2: **Workers are able to do much of their work from their homes rather than going into the company's offices under a flexible system.**

If you rewrote sentence 2 beginning with

Under a flexible system,

the next word should be

(1) workers
(2) much
(3) home
(4) company's
(5) offices

10. Sentence 4: **Employees who are ill or disabled working at home have less of a burden.**

Which of the following is the best way to write the underlined portion of this sentence? If you think the original is the best way, choose option (1).

(1) Employees who are ill or disabled working at home
(2) Employees, working at home, who are ill or disabled
(3) Working at home, employees who are ill or disabled
(4) Employees working at home and ill or disabled
(5) Ill or disabled, working at home

11. Sentence 7: **Workplace flexibility benefits society, decreasing pollution and traffic.**

Which of the following is the best way to write the underlined portion of this sentence? If you think the original is the best way, choose option (1).

(1) society, decreasing
(2) society. Decreasing
(3) society because it decreases
(4) society, although decreasing
(5) society which decreases

Items 12 to 14 refer to the following paragraph.

(1) Most Americans who were alive at the time remember where they were when President John F. Kennedy was assassinated. (2) The date was November 22, 1963, and although it was a sunny day in Dallas, the nation was covered in gloom after the shooting. (3) People were glued to their television sets, watching again and again the recorded images of the motorcade, the shooting of the president, and the shooting of Lee Harvey Oswald. (4) The nation watched as Lyndon Johnson took the oath of office, saddened and frightened about the future. (5) At the time, despair gripped the American people. (6) People walked around cities, college campuses, schoolyards, and rural towns in a daze. (7) Thousands paraded through the capitol rotunda in Washington to view the president's casket, and on television millions watched the funeral. (8) That was a painful November in America's history.

12. Sentence 4: **The nation watched as Lyndon Johnson took the oath of office, saddened and frightened about the future.**

If you rewrote sentence 4 beginning with

Saddened and frightened, the

the next word should be

(1) oath
(2) nation
(3) office
(4) president
(5) future

13. Sentence 6: **People walked around cities, college campuses, schoolyards, and rural towns in a daze.**

If you rewrote sentence 6 beginning with

Feeling dazed,

the next word should be

(1) walked
(2) schoolyards
(3) campuses
(4) people
(5) shock

14. Sentence 7: **Thousands paraded through the capitol rotunda in Washington to view the president's casket, and <u>on television millions watched the funeral</u>.**

Which of the following is the best way to write the underlined portion of this sentence? If you think the original is the best way, choose option (1).

(1) on television millions watched the funeral
(2) millions on television watched the funeral
(3) millions watched the funeral on television
(4) millions of televisions watched the funeral
(5) the funeral was watched by millions on television

WRITE ON TARGET

Write three sentences, each with only a simple subject and a verb, like *Hunger hurts*. Then add a modifying phrase to each sentence, placing it carefully to keep the meaning of the sentence clear.

To check your answers, turn to page 162.

Making Sure There's Something to Modify

Some sentences are unclear because of dangling modifiers. These phrases are confusing because there is nothing in the sentence they could logically modify.

Diving into the pool, the tension was extreme.

Who was diving into the pool? Who was feeling the tension?

To correct dangling modifiers, you must change the main part of the sentence so that it includes something for the modifier to describe:

Diving into the pool, *the athlete* felt extreme tension.

TEST-TAKING TIP

If you're unsure whether a modifier is dangling, ask yourself what or whom it modifies. If you can't find an answer, you're probably dealing with a dangling modifier.

You may turn the modifier into a prepositional phrase:

Before diving into the pool, the athlete felt extreme tension.

You may also turn the modifier into a dependent clause:

The athlete felt extreme tension *before she dove into the pool.*

Notice where to put the commas. When a modifying phrase appears at the beginning of a sentence, place a comma after it. When it appears at the end of the sentence, there is seldom a need for a comma.

EXERCISE 3

Directions: Find the sentences below that contain dangling or misplaced modifiers and correct them. Not all the sentences are incorrect.

1. Sitting in the sun, the picnic was great.

2. Being cold, the fire was inviting.

3. Wanting dinner, the food looked wonderful.

4. Pacing back and forth, Marilyn waited for the phone to ring.

5. Sitting in the middle of the street, a car just missed the cat.

6. Jumping up and down, the show finally started.

7. The judge dismissed me after I paid my fine.

8. Before shooting, the ducks disappeared.

9. Chirping cheerfully, Carol could hear the birds.

10. Having waited all day, the line moved quickly.

Directions: Choose the <u>one best answer</u> to each item.

<u>Items 11 to 13</u> refer to the following paragraph.

(1) Counting on public transportation, schedules are very important. (2) People who ride buses count on them to be on time. (3) Most buses and commuter trains do stick closely to the advertised schedule. (4) Missing a bus is often the fault of the rider. (5) Carmela often gets last minute phone calls at work that force her to miss her bus. (6) Tired from working late, missing the bus can be extremely annoying. (7) Carmela wonders whether it's any worse to be stuck in a traffic jam in her car. (8) Out of patience, another bus is seen coming down the street. (9) Once she boards the bus, she settles down and reads or naps.

11. Sentence 1: **Counting on public transportation, schedules are very important.**

If you rewrote sentence 1 beginning with

<u>For people who count on</u>

the next word(s) should be

(1) schedules
(2) public transportation
(3) work
(4) importance
(5) the time

12. Sentence 6: **Tired from working late, missing the bus can be extremely annoying.**

If you rewrote sentence 6 beginning with

<u>Because Carmela is tired from working late,</u>

the next word should be

(1) missing
(2) annoying
(3) working
(4) the
(5) while

13. Sentence 8: **Out of patience, <u>another bus is seen coming</u> down the street.**

Which of the following is the best way to write the underlined portion of this sentence? If you think the original is the best way, choose option (1).

(1) another bus is seen coming
(2) the bus is coming
(3) the bus sees
(4) Carmela sees another bus coming
(5) Carmela is seen coming

CONNECTIONS

Architectural remains give us a fascinating look at life in another place and time. For example, look at the photograph in the Cultures theme pages in **CONNECTIONS**. Write one paragraph describing the photograph. Make your paragraph as descriptive as possible by adding appropriate modifiers. Proofread to ensure that your modifiers are neither dangling nor misplaced.

To check your answers, turn to page 162.

G E D TEST PREVIEW

Directions: Choose the <u>one best answer</u> to each item.

<u>Items 1 to 5</u> refer to the following paragraphs.

(1) Increasingly working at home, business is booming for many men and women. (2) These entrepreneurs are applying their job skills to their own businesses and are operating from home. (3) Tired of long hours commuting to offices and working for someone else, some men and women enjoy having a home office. (4) The problem is making family members understand every day that Mom or Dad has to work. (5) Having an office right in the house, interruptions abound. (6) Errands must be run; children must be attended to; meals must be prepared. (7) Distracted, the telephone and doorbell could ring all day.

(8) Working at home doesn't work for everybody. (9) Some people can't discipline themselves to work when the television, refrigerator, and freedom beckon. (10) Unable to stop working and relax, home offices can turn people into workaholics. (11) Still, more and more people seem to be trying to make a living while they maintain the convenience of being at home all day. (12) Many, but not all, succeed.

1. Sentence 1: **Increasingly working at home, business is booming for many men and women.**

If you rewrote sentence 1 beginning with

<u>For the increasing number of men and women who work at home,</u>

the next word should be

(1) entrepreneurs
(2) business
(3) booming
(4) people
(5) whenever

2. Sentence 4: **The problem is making family members understand <u>every day that Mom or Dad has to work.</u>**

Which of the following is the best way to write the underlined portion of this sentence? If you think the original is the best way, choose option (1).

(1) every day that Mom or Dad has to work.
(2) every day. That Mom or Dad has to work.
(3) every day, that Mom or Dad has to work.
(4) every day that Mom, or Dad has to work.
(5) that Mom or Dad has to work every day.

3. Sentence 5: **Having an office right in the house, interruptions abound.**

If you rewrote sentence 5 beginning with

<u>For people who have an office at home,</u>

the next word should be

(1) they
(2) abound
(3) interruptions
(4) house
(5) in

4. Sentence 7: **Distracted, the telephone and doorbell could ring all day.**

What correction should be made to this sentence?

(1) replace <u>Distracted,</u> with <u>Being distracted,</u>
(2) replace <u>Distracted,</u> with <u>Because they are distracted,</u>
(3) replace <u>Distracted,</u> with <u>Distracting the worker,</u>
(4) replace <u>could ring</u> with <u>ringing</u>
(5) no correction is necessary

5. Sentence 10: **Unable to stop working and relax, home offices can turn people into workaholics.**

If you rewrote sentence 10 beginning with

<u>Because they can't stop working and relax,</u>

the next word should be

(1) workaholics
(2) people
(3) at
(4) work
(5) home offices

Items 6 to 9 refer to the following paragraph.

(1) Concerned about the environment. (2) Researchers are seeking alternatives to the gasoline-powered automobile. (3) Electric cars are one answer. (4) Running on both batteries and solar energy, people can save money with an electric car. (5) A 1985-model car, priced at $22,500, runs on eighteen batteries and a solar energy collector. (6) The drawbacks to electric vehicles are that they accelerate slowly and their batteries must be recharged every forty to sixty miles. (7) Other alternatives to gasoline are cars that run on alcohol fuels, propane, and natural gas. (8) Burning cleaner than gasoline, people can use them in a modified internal combustion engine. (9) On the other hand, they produce less energy than gasoline, so cars have to be filled up more often. (10) A compromise in the same tank may be "fuel-flexible" cars that burn a combination of methanol and unleaded gasoline. (11) By experimenting with this type of fuel in some of its state-operated cars, California is trying to curb pollution.

6. Sentences 1 and 2: **Concerned about the environment. Researchers are** seeking alternatives to the gasoline-powered automobile.

Which of the following is the best way to write the underlined portion of these sentences? If you think the original is the best way, choose option (1).

(1) Concerned about the environment. Researchers are
(2) Concerned about the environment, researchers are
(3) Concern for the environment researchers are
(4) Concerned, about the environment researchers are
(5) Researchers are concerned about the environment

7. Sentence 4: **Running on both batteries and solar energy, people can save money with an electric car.**

Which of the following is the best way to write the underlined portion of this sentence? If you think the original is the best way, choose option (1).

(1) people can save money with an electric car
(2) people and electric cars can save money
(3) money is saved with an electric car
(4) savings come with electric cars
(5) electric cars can save people money

8. Sentence 8: **Burning cleaner than gasoline, people can use them in a modified internal combustion engine.**

What correction should be made to this sentence?

(1) change Burning to They burn
(2) change Burning to Because these fuels burn
(3) replace gasoline, people with gasoline. People
(4) replace people with fuels
(5) replace them in with them. In

9. Sentence 10: **A compromise in the same tank may be "fuel-flexible" cars that burn a combination of methanol and unleaded gasoline.**

If you rewrote sentence 10 beginning with

Burning a combination of methanol and unleaded gasoline in the same tank,

the next word(s) should be

(1) gasoline
(2) compromise
(3) efficiency
(4) "fuel-flexible" cars
(5) people

To check your answers, turn to page 163.

6 Understanding Parallel Structure

LESSON

ACHIEVEMENT GOALS
In this lesson, you will learn to use parallel structure

• with single words

• with groups of words

Y ou've already learned about compound sentences, which contain two or more complete thoughts. Many sentences also contain compound elements. This means parts within the sentence are linked with connecting words, such as *and, but,* and *or.* To maintain clarity in your writing, it's important to put elements that play similar roles within a sentence into the same form. Consider the following sentence:

JoAnn does billing for a dental office, a law firm, and a medical office.

The sentence names three businesses JoAnn does billing for, so all three play the same role in the sentence. They should be written in the same form, which we call **parallel structure**.

Parallel structure makes your writing smooth and easy to read. Compare a sentence about JoAnn and her work that does not have parallel structure:

JoAnn does billing for a dentist, a law firm, and one doctor's office also employs her.

As you can see, a sentence that lacks parallel structure does not flow smoothly.

Compare two more sentences to see the importance of parallel structure:

Nonparallel: His boss asked him to sweep the floors, wipe the tables, and the trash had to be taken out.

Parallel: His boss asked him to sweep the floors, wipe the tables, and take out the trash.

Notice how much clearer the second sentence is. We know that taking out the trash is one of three things to be done by the same person. The nonparallel sentence suggests that a different person has to take out the trash.

Keeping the Meaning Clear with Parallel Structure

Parallel structure not only makes sentences smoother to read but keeps meaning clear as well.

Let's look again at the two sentences about JoAnn and her billing jobs:

(1) JoAnn does billing for a dental office, a law firm, and a medical office.

(2) JoAnn does billing for a dentist, a law firm, and one doctor's office also employs her.

Sentence 1 shows that she does the same work for all her employers. At least the sentence doesn't suggest otherwise. Sentence 2 is not only harder to read but also harder to understand. Its meaning is questionable. Does she do billing for the doctor's office or does she do some other kind of work?

The part of the sentence that tells us she works for a doctor is written in a different form, so it could be different in meaning as well.

These sentences also illustrate the importance of parallel structure:

(1) Scott's car is sporty, powerful, and easy to handle.

(2) Scott's car is sporty, powerful, and he can handle it easily.

Sentence 1 tells us three things about Scott's car. Sentence 2 tells us two things about his car and one thing about Scott (he handles his car easily).

It's easier to maintain parallel structure if you repeat the small words, such as *a, the, an, that, for,* and other prepositions, within a series. Compare the following examples:

Words missing: In the confusion, someone lost a book, hat, and keys.

Words repeated: In the confusion, someone lost **a** book, **a** hat, and **a** set of keys.

Words missing: The chef explained that the ingredients should be fresh, temperature exact, and measurements accurate.

Words repeated: The chef explained that **the** ingredients should be fresh, **the** temperature exact, and **the** measurements accurate.

NOTE: *It's never incorrect to repeat words to achieve parallel structure, but there are times when you may decide not to. Repetition of the word* to, *for example, might seem awkward. Compare the two sentences below.*

Words missing: I have to mail a letter, eat dinner, and study for tomorrow's test.

Words repeated: I have to mail a letter, to eat dinner, and to study for tomorrow's test.

EXERCISE 1

Directions: Correct the faulty (nonparallel) structure in the sentences below. Some of the sentences already have parallel structure.

1. Chad's hobbies include photography, music, and he enjoys computers.

2. Dwight and Dorothy travelled to London, to Paris, and they visited Italy too.

3. The amusement park had rides, games, and a petting zoo.

4. Laurie liked to garden, Al liked to build things, and painting pleased Marnie.

5. It's difficult for teachers to help children learn, to teach them values, and discipline is hard to maintain.

Directions: Add the small words that would improve parallelism in the following sentences.

6. Preschool teaches children to play with others, take turns, and to share toys.

7. Nuclear energy can be used to destroy things or make life easier.

8. Tutors help students improve their knowledge, confidence, and their test scores.

9. The speaker explained that they could save energy by turning off lights, keeping the refrigerator door closed, and by lowering the thermostat.

10. The youths were admired for their honesty and their heroism.

Directions: Choose the <u>one best answer</u> to each item.

<u>Items 11 to 13</u> refer to the following paragraphs.

(1) The glory days of American railroading are over. (2) America has superhighways, numerous airlines, and has to cover long distances. (3) Few Americans take the train. (4) Rail travel in the United States is also expensive, so most people choose a faster, an easier, and a cheaper way to go places. (5) However, train travel is more popular on the compact East Coast than on the spacious West Coast.

(6) European train travel is better than ours in America. (7) Trains in Europe are fast, convenient, and you can depend on them. (8) With government support, European railroads can afford to build high-speed rail lines. (9) Trains are a convenient way to move from one European country to another.

11. Sentence 2: **America has superhighways, numerous airlines, and has to cover long distances.**

What correction should be made to this sentence?

(1) insert <u>to travel</u> before <u>superhighways</u>
(2) insert <u>and</u> before <u>numerous</u>
(3) replace <u>airlines, and</u> with <u>airlines. And</u>
(4) replace <u>has to cover long distances</u> with <u>it's a big country</u>
(5) replace <u>has to cover long distances</u> with <u>long distances to cover</u>

12. Sentence 6: **European train travel is better than ours in America.**

What correction should be made to this sentence?

(1) Replace <u>European train travel</u> with <u>Travel by train in Europe</u>
(2) replace <u>ours</u> with <u>our travel systems</u>
(3) replace <u>ours in America</u> with <u>American train travel</u>
(4) remove <u>ours</u>
(5) no correction is necessary

13. Sentence 7: **Trains in Europe are fast, convenient, and you can depend on them.**

Which of the following is the best way to write the underlined portion of this sentence? If you think the original is the best, choose option (1).

(1) you can depend on them
(2) they can be depended on
(3) people depend on them
(4) they're dependable
(5) dependable

Items 14 to 16 refer to the following paragraph.

(1) The Peace Corps was established in 1961, during President John F. Kennedy's administration. (2) That year, about three thousand volunteers worked in Asia, in Africa, and countries in Latin America to help the natives improve their standard of living. (3) Peace Corps workers live among the natives, learn their language, and their standard of living is just like that of the natives. (4) Their pay, about $75 a month, is deposited for them in the United States, and they receive travel and living expenses. (5) Although most Peace Corps volunteers are young men and women, the age range is from eighteen to sixty. (6) Not only has this program developed good will between the United States and underdeveloped countries, it has taught people in hundreds of communities to help themselves improve their lives. (7) Some people believe all Americans, when they reach the age of eighteen, should be required to serve for two years either at home or go to foreign countries.

14. Sentence 2: **That year, about three thousand volunteers worked in Asia, in Africa, and countries in Latin America to help the natives improve their standard of living.**

Which of the following is the best way to write the underlined portion of this sentence? If you think the original is the best way, choose option (1).

(1) and countries in Latin America
(2) and other countries in Latin America
(3) and in Latin America
(4) and the many countries of Latin America
(5) and countries that are in Latin America

15. Sentence 3: **Peace Corps workers live among the natives, learn their language, and their standard of living is just like that of the natives.**

Which of the following is the best way to write the underlined portion of this sentence? If you think the original is the best, choose option (1).

(1) their standard of living is just like that of the natives
(2) share their standard of living
(3) their standard of living is the same
(4) their standard of living matches that of the natives
(5) standard of living goes down

16. Sentence 7: **Some people believe all Americans, when they reach the age of eighteen, should be required to serve for two years either at home or go to foreign countries.**

What correction should be made to this sentence?

(1) replace of eighteen, should with of eighteen. Should
(2) replace years either with years. Either
(3) remove at
(4) replace go to with in
(5) no correction is necessary

WRITE ON TARGET

Write one sentence in which you maintain parallel structure with single words. Write another in which you maintain parallel structure with word groups (phrases or clauses).

To check your answers, turn to page 163.

Balancing Your Writing with Parallel Structure

Sometimes sentences lack parallel structure because the writer adds an entire clause when a single word is better. For example:

> Dogs require food, shelter, and you have to bathe them.

The sentence above tells us three things about dogs. Two of those things are expressed as nouns (*food* and *shelter*), but the third is expressed as a clause, with a subject (*you*) and a verb (*have*).

Parallel structure expresses each requirement as a noun and changes the sentence:

> Dogs require food, shelter, and baths.

Sometimes sentences lack parallel structure because the writer switches subjects in midsentence. Think about this example:

> At parks, people play baseball, toss Frisbees, and parks are good places to talk to friends.

This sentence has three word groups, but the third one changes subjects from *people* to *parks*, which spoils the parallel structure. A better sentence would be:

> At parks, people play baseball, toss Frisbees, and talk to friends.

TEST-TAKING TIP

Whenever you link items in a sentence with *and, or, but,* or *not*, check for parallel structure.

EXERCISE 2

Directions: Identify the nonparallel elements in the following sentences and rewrite the sentences using parallel structure.

1. Larry was a soccer player, a baseball player, and he could swim.

2. A good baby-sitter must be patient, mature, and like to play with children.

3. Children sleep better if they go to bed relaxed, calm, and their parents read them a story.

4. Most parents try to teach their children to be respectful, to be obedient, and want them to do well in school.

5. Evelyn is talented at sports, academics, and she plays the flute.

Directions: Choose the one best answer to each item.

Items 6 to 8 refer to the following paragraph.

(1) Harriet Tubman was born a slave in 1821. (2) For twenty-five years, she did heavy fieldwork. (3) A slaver bought two of her sisters, and they were taken by him into the Deep South to work. (3) Harriet set off on her own, determined to escape. (4) She followed the North Star at night, made her way to Philadelphia, and it turned out there were homes where people helped escaped slaves hide as they made their way north. (5) Taking advantage of this "underground railroad," she returned to the south, determined to help her sisters and other slaves escape. (6) In nineteen trips, she managed to free three hundred slaves, including many members of her own family. (7) Although rewards of $12,000 were offered for her capture, she was never caught. (8) She served the Union as a nurse and as a spy during the Civil War.

6. Sentence 3: **A slaver bought two of her sisters, and they were taken by him into the Deep South to work.**

Which of the following is the best way to write the underlined portion of this sentence? If you think the original is the best way, choose option (1).

(1) sisters, and they were taken by him
(2) sisters. And they were taken by him
(3) sisters, but they were taken by him
(4) sisters and took them
(5) sisters, and took them

7. Sentence 4: **She followed the North Star at night, made her way to Philadelphia, and it turned out there were homes where people helped escaped slaves hide as they made their way north.**

Which of the following is the best way to write the underlined portion of this sentence? If you think the original is the best way, choose option (1).

(1) it turned out there were
(2) discovered there were
(3) people were there who
(4) slaves found help
(5) escaped slaves stayed in homes

8. Sentence 8: **She served the Union as a nurse and as a spy during the Civil War.**

What correction should be made to this sentence?

(1) replace as a nurse with being a nurse
(2) replace as a nurse with nursing
(3) replace as a spy to being a spy
(4) change as a spy to spying
(5) no correction is necessary

CONNECTIONS

Do vacations always go as planned? The Leisure theme pages in **CONNECTIONS** tell some of the story. On your own or in a small group, read the selection from *Travels with Charley*. Look closely at the second paragraph. Which sentences demonstrate parallel structure? Which words or word phrases are involved?

To check your answers, turn to page 163.

G E D T EST P REVIEW

Directions: Choose the <u>one best answer</u> to each item.

<u>Items 1 to 6</u> refer to the following paragraph.

(1) One way to give children a sense of family history is to share memories with them. (2) Through memories, children can learn about relatives they may not see often, such as aunts, uncles, cousins, or even grandparents. (3) It can be fun for parents to share family memories with their children. (4) They can do this through photographs, scrapbooks, and the children ask questions. (5) Modern technology makes it easier than ever to capture the past. (6) Many types of cameras help people record family events, capture vacation highlights, and remembering all kinds of things. (7) Cameras come in a wide range of prices and sophistication, from video cameras that record sound to disposable cameras that are used once and turned in with the film. (8) With the help of cameras, tape recorders, and by keeping diaries, parents can easily look back on their children's growing up. (9) Adults are often amused by their own childhood photos, drawings, report cards, and to remember special times from years back. (10) To record your children's growing up is giving them a precious gift for their later years.

1. Sentence 2: **Through memories, children can learn about relatives they may not see often, such as aunts, uncles, cousins, or even grandparents.**

What correction should be made to this sentence?

(1) replace <u>relatives they</u> with <u>relatives. They</u>
(2) replace <u>often, such as</u> with <u>often. Such as</u>
(3) insert <u>including</u> before <u>cousins</u>
(4) insert <u>their</u> before <u>grandparents</u>
(5) no correction is necessary

2. Sentence 4: **They can do this through photographs, scrapbooks, and <u>the children ask questions.</u>**

Which of the following is the best way to write the underlined portion of this sentence? If you think the original is the best way, choose option (1).

(1) the children ask questions
(2) when the children ask questions
(3) children's questions
(4) whenever the children ask questions
(5) the parents answer questions

3. Sentence 6: **Many types of cameras help people record family events, capture vacation highlights, and remembering all kinds of things.**

What correction should be made to this sentence?

(1) change <u>record</u> to <u>recording</u>
(2) insert <u>to</u> before <u>capture</u>
(3) change <u>remembering</u> to <u>to remember</u>
(4) change <u>remembering</u> to <u>remember</u>
(5) no correction is necessary

4. Sentence 8: **With the help of cameras, tape recorders, and by keeping diaries, parents can easily look back on their children's growing up.**

What correction should be made to this sentence?

(1) replace <u>by keeping diaries</u> with <u>diaries</u>
(2) replace <u>With the help of</u> with <u>By</u>
(3) remove <u>can easily</u>
(4) replace <u>can easily look</u> with <u>by looking</u>
(5) no correction is necessary

5. Sentence 9: **Adults are often amused by their own childhood photos, drawings, report cards, and to remember special times from years back.**

What correction should be made to this sentence?

(1) replace <u>photos</u> with <u>pictures</u>
(2) replace <u>drawings</u> with <u>they drew pictures</u>
(3) replace <u>to remember</u> with <u>memories of</u>
(4) remove <u>report cards</u>
(5) remove <u>from years back</u>

6. Sentence 10: **To record your children's growing up is giving them a precious gift for their later years.**

What correction should be made to this sentence?

(1) replace <u>To</u> with <u>Parents who</u>
(2) replace <u>To record</u> with <u>When you record</u>
(3) insert <u>like</u> before <u>giving</u>
(4) change <u>giving</u> to <u>to give</u>
(5) remove <u>their</u>

<u>Items 7 to 9</u> refer to the following paragraph.

(1) From the time of the Industrial Revolution, injury in the workplace has been a problem. (2) Workers in America's sweatshops had no protection against poorly ventilated rooms, fire hazards, overcrowded workspace, and some of the equipment was dangerous. (3) Low-hanging uncovered light bulbs could start fires. (4) It wasn't uncommon for a sewing machine needle to pierce someone's finger. (5) Labor unions have helped change all that. (6) Now employers must provide insurance to pay their workers if they need medical care because of injury on the job or illness. (7) Physical injuries and illness, such as broken bones, strained backs, reactions to toxic chemicals, and radiation exposure have been around as long as factories. (8) Now, however, many workers blame their jobs for emotional stress and if they become mentally ill. (9) They cite such things as too much work for too little pay. (10) They complain of feeling powerless because they're not allowed to make decisions. (11) They accuse employers of discriminating on the basis of race, gender, age, and if they don't like a person's looks. (12) The physical and mental toll of the workplace contributes to America's serious health care problems.

7. Sentence 2: **Workers in America's sweatshops had no protection against poorly ventilated rooms, fire hazards, overcrowded workspace, and some of the equipment was dangerous.**

What correction should be made to this sentence?

(1) replace <u>Workers</u> with <u>People who worked</u>
(2) replace <u>poorly ventilated rooms</u> with <u>rooms had poor ventilation</u>
(3) replace <u>fire hazards</u> with <u>if there was a fire</u>
(4) replace <u>some of the equipment was dangerous</u> with <u>dangerous equipment</u>
(5) remove <u>was</u>

8. Sentence 8: **Now, however, many workers blame their jobs for emotional stress and if they become mentally ill.**

What correction should be made to this sentence?

(1) replace <u>jobs for emotional stress</u> with <u>emotional stress on their jobs</u>
(2) replace <u>jobs for emotional stress</u> with <u>stressful jobs</u>
(3) change <u>emotional</u> to <u>emotionally</u>
(4) replace <u>if they become mentally ill</u> with <u>mental illness</u>
(5) no correction is necessary

9. Sentence 11: **They accuse employers of discriminating on the basis or race, gender, age, and <u>if they don't like a person's looks.</u>**

Which of the following is the best way to write the underlined portion of this sentence? If you think the original is the best way, choose option (1).

(1) if they don't like a person's looks
(2) if they don't like a person's appearance
(3) the way a person looks
(4) whether someone looks good
(5) appearance

To check your answers, turn to page 164.

1 **Building Sentences**
R E V I E W

By now you should have a clear understanding of what a sentence is and how to write a good one.

Key Terms to Review

action verb	a verb that shows the subject doing something
adjective	a word that modifies a noun
adverb	a word that modifies a verb, adjective, or another adverb
clause	a word group that contains a subject and a verb but is not necessarily a complete thought
comma splice	two or more complete sentences separated only by commas
complete sentence	a sentence that contains a subject and a complete verb and that expresses a complete thought
complete subject	a simple subject, along with any modifiers
complex sentence	a sentence containing an independent clause and a dependent clause
compound sentence	a sentence that contains two or more independent clauses
compound subject	two subjects using the same verb
compound verb	two verbs for the same subject
conjunction	a word used to connect other words, phrases, or clauses
dependent clause	a clause that depends on the rest of a sentence for its meaning
fragment	a word group that looks like a sentence but lacks a subject, a verb, part of a verb, or is not a complete thought
independent clause	a clause that has meaning on its own (a complete sentence)
linking verb	a verb that shows what the subject is, seems, or feels
modifier	a word or group of words that describes another word or word group in a sentence
noun	a word that names a person, place, or thing
parallel structure	putting similar elements in a sentence into the same form
phrase	a group of related words that lacks a subject and a verb
preposition	a word that links a noun to another word in a sentence
prepositional phrase	a modifying word group that begins with a preposition and tells where, when, and why
run-on sentence	two or more complete sentences not separated by punctuation
simple sentence	a sentence containing one complete thought
simple subject	a single subject, without any modifiers
subject	the person or thing that performs the action in a sentence and tells who or what the sentence is about
verb	the word in a sentence that shows what the subject is or what it does
verb phrase	a modifying word group that tells why and begins with some form of a verb

You know that a complete sentence must contain a subject and a verb and express a complete thought. When a word group lacks any of these components, it is a sentence fragment. You can correct it by determining which component is missing and adding it to the fragment.

Joining two or more complete thoughts without punctuation causes a run-on sentence. You've seen how to correct run-on sentences by using correct punctuation and appropriate connecting words to link the separate ideas.

You've learned how to write compound sentences that join ideas of equal importance. You've also learned to write complex sentences that combine ideas when one idea is less important than the other. You've learned the importance of correctly expressing the relationship between ideas through the use of appropriate connecting words and proper punctuation.

Finally, you've seen how to write clear sentences by placing modifiers correctly and using parallel structure for words or word groups that play the same role within a sentence.

EXERCISES

Directions: Choose the one best answer to each item.

Items 1 to 5 refer to the following paragraph.

(1) With all the talk about weight loss, diets, exercise, cholesterol, and calories, one thing seems clear. (2) More and more people must cut fat from their diets. (3) To improve their health. (4) Grocery shelves are stocked with products labeled "light," "low-fat," and "cholesterol-free." (5) Government officials and health professionals are concerned about what these labels really mean, and for consumers, the prices are high. (6) It's not necessary to spend a lot of money to reduce fat in your diet. (7) In fact, low-fat eating is relatively inexpensive because it involves lots of fruit and vegetables rather than expensive red meat. (8) You can cut fat from your diet by eating more salads, using low-fat sauces, and don't use fat when you cook. (9) If you eliminate mayonnaise from sandwiches, you can get rid of a major source of fat. (10) For dessert, you can substitute ice milk for ice cream although milk has less fat than cream.

1. Sentences 2 and 3: **More and more people must cut fat from their diets. To improve their health.**

   Which of the following is the best way to write the underlined portion of these sentences? If you think the original is the best way, choose option (1).
   (1) diets. To
   (2) diets To
   (3) diets; to
   (4) diets, to
   (5) diets to

2. Sentence 5: **Government officials and health professionals are concerned about what these labels really mean, and for consumers, the prices are high.**

   Which of the following is the best way to write the underlined portion of this sentence? If you think the original is the best way, choose option (1).

   (1) and for consumers, the prices are high
   (2) and for consumers, high prices
   (3) and consumers are concerned about the high prices
   (4) and for consumers, price is the issue
   (5) and high prices worry consumers

3. Sentence 8: **You can cut fat from your diet by eating more salads, using low-fat sauces, and don't use fat when you cook.**

Which of the following is the best way to write the underlined portion of this sentence? If you think the original is the best way, choose option (1).

(1) don't use fat when you cook
(2) cooking without fat
(3) to cook without fat
(4) don't cook with fat
(5) watch fat in cooking

4. Sentence 9: **If you eliminate mayonnaise from sandwiches, you can get rid of a major source of fat.**

What correction should be made to this sentence?

(1) remove the comma
(2) change the comma to a period
(3) insert a period after source
(4) insert a comma after source
(5) no correction is necessary

5. Sentence 10: **For dessert, you can substitute ice milk for ice cream although milk has less fat than cream.**

What correction should be made to this sentence?

(1) remove the comma after dessert
(2) change substitute ice to substitute. Ice
(3) change ice cream although to ice cream. Although
(4) replace although with since
(5) replace although with and

Items 6 to 14 refer to the following paragraphs.

(1) The Great Depression of the 1930s. (2) One of the most devastating periods in American history. (3) It was a time many people still remember filled with pain. (4) Not everyone was devastated by the Depression, but most people were at least touched by it. (5) Whether it was unemployment, food shortages, or the landlord kicked them out, people remember the anguish of those years. (6) This period of economic crisis began with the Stock Market Crash of 1929 and continued until World War II created a demand for new goods and services. (7) Which put people back to work.

(8) During the Depression, more than five thousand banks closed. (9) Causing people to lose all their savings. (10) Wealthy people who had made fortunes in the stock market lost everything, even though many of them committed suicide. (11) Unemployment reached 25 percent, with 15 million people out of jobs. (12) Many young people who were ready to go to work for the first time had no hope of employment so they wandered around the country. (13) Aimlessly riding freight trains, many of these hobos were injured or killed. (14) The railroads added empty car to help them. (15) Years of drought in the part of the country known as the Great Plains drove people west. (16) Families abandoned their unproductive farms, loaded their possessions on their beat-up cars, and California seemed to promise a better life. (17) They found little relief when they got there unless things were bad all over. (18) A famous book by John Steinbeck, called *The Grapes of Wrath*, tells the story of some of these people.

6. **The Great Depression of the 1930s. One of the most devastating periods in American history.**

What correction should be made to these sentences?

(1) change 1930s. One to 1930s, one
(2) change 1930s. One to 1930s was one
(3) change 1930s. One to 1930s, being one
(4) replace one of the with a
(5) change periods in to periods. In

7. Sentence 3: **It was a <u>time many people still remember filled with pain</u>.**

Which of the following is the best way to write the underlined portion of this sentence? If you think the original is the best way, choose option (1).

(1) time many people still remember filled with pain
(2) time filled with pain many people still remember
(3) painful time many people still remember
(4) time many people fill with pain
(5) painful memory to many people most of the time

8. Sentence 5: **Whether it was unemployment, food shortages, or the landlord kicked them out, people remember the anguish of those years.**

What correction should be made to this sentence?

(1) remove <u>Whether</u>
(2) replace <u>it was</u> with <u>people faced</u>
(3) replace <u>the landlord kicked them out</u> with <u>eviction from their homes</u>
(4) replace <u>the landlord kicked them</u> out with <u>they had no place to live</u>
(5) change <u>anguish of</u> to <u>anguish. Of</u>

9. Sentence 7: **Which put people back to work.**

What correction should be made to this sentence?

(1) replace <u>Which</u> with <u>The war</u>
(2) insert <u>finally</u> before <u>put</u>
(3) replace <u>put people</u> with <u>saw people go</u>
(4) insert <u>again</u> after <u>work</u>
(5) no correction is necessary

10. Sentences 8 and 9: **During the Depression, more than five thousand banks closed. Causing people to lose all their savings.**

If you rewrote sentences 8 and 9 beginning with

The closing of the banks

the next word should be

(1) people
(2) lost
(3) savings
(4) Depression
(5) caused

11. Sentence 10: **Wealthy people who had made fortunes in the stock market lost <u>everything, even though many</u> of them committed suicide.**

Which of the following is the best way to write the underlined portion of this sentence? If you think the original is the best way, choose option (1).

(1) everything, even though many
(2) everything even though many
(3) everything. Even though many
(4) everything, and many
(5) everything because many

12. Sentence 12: **Many young people who were ready to go to work for the first time had no hope of employment so they wandered around the country.**

What correction should be made to this sentence?

(1) change <u>work for</u> to <u>work. For</u>
(2) change <u>time had</u> to <u>time. Had</u>
(3) insert a comma after <u>employment</u>
(4) replace <u>so</u> with <u>or</u>
(5) change <u>wandered around</u> to <u>wandered. Around</u>

13. Sentence 16: **Families abandoned their unproductive farms, loaded their possessions on their beat-up cars, and <u>California seemed to promise a better life</u>.**

Which of the following is the best way to write the underlined portion of this sentence? If you think the original is the best way, choose option (1).

(1) California seemed to promise a better life
(2) headed to California for a better life
(3) California looked better to them
(4) better things awaited them in California
(5) life would improve in California

14. Sentence 17: **They found little relief when they got there unless things were bad all over.**

What correction should be made to this sentence?

(1) change <u>relief when</u> to <u>relief. When</u>
(2) insert a comma after <u>there</u>
(3) change <u>there unless</u> with <u>there. Unless</u>
(4) replace <u>unless</u> with <u>although</u>
(5) replace <u>unless</u> with <u>since</u>

<u>Items 15 to 23</u> refer to the following paragraphs.

(1) For several years, public knowledge about the hazards of cigarette smoking has increased, so one in four Americans smokes cigarettes. (2) Public health officials now express a growing concern for nonsmokers who are exposed involuntarily to the secondhand smoke of others. (3) They see a need to publicize the injurious effects of passively inhaling smoke, and are especially worried about children. (4) Because of diseases from passive smoke inhalation under eighteen months of age, between 7,500 and 15,000 children are hospitalized each year. (5) Becoming ill, our country faces a serious problem. (6) Even though they aren't all hospitalized. (7) Between 7,500 and 150,000 children get sick from secondhand smoke. (8) Exposed to cigarette smoke, children are likely to contract ear infections, pneumonia, bronchitis, and their lungs will get other diseases. (9) The Environmental Protection Agency (EPA) also estimates that every year 3,000 lung cancer deaths result from secondhand smoke.

(10) The EPA would like citizens to discourage smoking in their houses, legislators to pass antismoking laws, and steps taken to protect workers. (11) Government guidelines suggest ways to reduce illness from secondhand smoke. (12) They say bars and restaurants should check a building's ventilation capabilities before they allow smoking. (13) Air from designated smoking areas should be directed outside.

(14) Instead of being recycled. (15) Employers should support programs that help their workers quit smoking. (16) People should not allow smoking in their homes, and the public should go only to restaurants and bars that ban smoking.

15. Sentence 1: **For several years, public knowledge about the hazards of cigarette smoking has increased, so one in four Americans smokes cigarettes.**

What correction should be made to this sentence?

(1) change <u>years, public</u> to <u>years. Public</u>
(2) change <u>public knowledge</u> to <u>knowing about</u>
(3) change <u>increased, so</u> to <u>increased so</u>
(4) replace <u>so</u> with <u>yet</u>
(5) no correction is necessary

16. Sentence 3: **They see a need to publicize the injurious effects of passively inhaling smoke, and are especially worried about children.**

What correction should be made to this sentence?

(1) change <u>effects of</u> to <u>effects. Of</u>
(2) replace <u>smoke, and</u> with <u>smoke. And</u>
(3) replace <u>and</u> with <u>although they</u>
(4) replace <u>and</u> with <u>so</u>
(5) remove the comma before <u>and</u>

17. Sentence 4: **Because of diseases from passive smoke inhalation under eighteen months of age, between 7,500 and 15,000 children are hospitalized each year.**

If you rewrote sentence 4 beginning with

<u>Between 7,500 and 15,000 children</u>

the next word should be

(1) smoke
(2) under
(3) passive
(4) hospitalized
(5) age

18. Sentence 5: **<u>Becoming ill</u>, our country faces a serious problem.**

Which of the following is the best way to write the underlined portion of this sentence? If you think the original is the best way, choose option (1).

(1) Becoming ill
(2) To become ill
(3) Children being ill
(4) When children become ill
(5) Being ill

19. Sentences 6 and 7: **Even though they aren't all <u>hospitalized. Between</u> 7,500 and 150,000 children get sick from secondhand smoke.**

Which of the following is the best way to write the underlined portion of these sentences? If you think the original is the best way, choose option (1).

(1) hospitalized. Between
(2) hospitalized between
(3) hospitalized, between
(4) in the hospital. Between
(5) in the hospital between

20. Sentence 8: **Exposed to cigarette smoke, children are likely to contract ear infections, pneumonia, bronchitis, and their lungs will get other diseases.**

What correction should be made to this sentence?

(1) change <u>smoke, children</u> to <u>smoke. Children</u>
(2) change <u>infections, pneumonia</u> to <u>infections. Pneumonia</u>
(3) change <u>bronchitis, and</u> to <u>bronchitis. And</u>
(4) change <u>their lungs will get other diseases</u> to <u>other lung diseases</u>
(5) change <u>their lungs will get other diseases</u> to <u>they'll have other lung diseases</u>

21. Sentence 10: **The EPA would like citizens to discourage smoking in their houses, legislators to pass antismoking laws, and <u>steps taken to protect workers.</u>**

Which of the following is the best way to write the underlined portion of this sentence? If you think the original is the best way, choose option (1).

(1) steps taken to protect workers
(2) steps to protect workers
(3) employers to take steps to protect workers
(4) workers take steps to protect themselves
(5) workers to be protected

22. Sentence 14: **Instead of being recycyled.**

What correction should be made to this sentence?

(1) replace <u>Instead of being</u> with <u>It shouldn't be</u>
(2) replace <u>Instead of</u> with <u>Air is</u>
(3) replace <u>of</u> with a comma
(4) replace <u>of being</u> with <u>it should be</u>
(5) replace <u>being recycled</u> with <u>recycling it</u>

23. Sentence 16: **People should not allow smoking in their homes, and the public should go only to restaurants and bars that ban smoking.**

What correction should be made to this sentence?

(1) change <u>allow smoking</u> to <u>allow. Smoking</u>
(2) change <u>homes, and</u> to <u>homes. And</u>
(3) replace <u>and</u> with <u>but</u>
(4) replace <u>and</u> with <u>so</u>
(5) no correction is necessary

To check your answers, turn to page 164.

Answers and Explanations

Lesson 1: Recognizing Sentence Fragments

Exercise 1 (page 82)

1. F
2. C
3. C
4. F
5. C
6. F
7. F
8. C
9. F
10. C
11. What about it?
12. Who?
13. Who?
14. What?
15. Who?
16. Who?
17. What?
18. What? or Who?
19. What about it?
20. Did what? Is what?

21. **(2) replace <u>To recognize</u> with <u>It recognizes</u>** The word *It* tells us what the sentence is about. The other options still create fragments that leave us with questions about the sentence.

22. **(1) replace <u>Because</u> with <u>This is because</u>** Option (1) creates a complete sentence that makes sense. The other options are fragments.

23. **(2) replace <u>Displaying</u> with <u>They display</u>** Option (2) lets us know whom the sentence is talking about. The other options create different fragments.

24. **(4) moment to think** Removing the period corrects the fragment by linking the two parts of the sentence to form a complete thought. The other options create different sentence fragments.

25. **(3) trouble understanding or** Removing the period corrects the fragment by attaching it to the rest of a complete sentence. The other options create different fragments.

26. **(2) breakdown in their** Removing the period corrects the fragment by attaching it to the rest of a complete sentence. Options (2) and (3) create different fragments. Options (4) and (5) change the meaning of the sentence.

27. **(2) change <u>Leaving</u> to <u>This leaves</u>** Option (2) creates a sentence that makes sense. The other options create more fragments.

Exercise 2 (page 85)

1. host
2. service station
3. John
4. Everyone
5. butcher
6. You (understood, not stated)
7. dogs
8. conversation
9. No one
10. people

11. **(1) replace <u>Confuses</u> with <u>This procedure confuses</u>** Option (1) gives the sentence a subject. The other options do not correct the fragment, which lacks a subject.

12. **(5) waking up at the right time are** The fragment, when attached to the next sentence, becomes the subject of a complete sentence. Option (2) adds an unnecessary word *(these)* to the subject, and the other options do not correct the sentence fragment.

13. **(2) state practices daylight** Removing the period completes the sentence by linking the subject to the rest of the sentence. The other options create different sentence fragments.

Exercise 3 (page 87)

1. Flew
2. ran, seemed
3. did have (The word *not* is a modifier.)
4. angered

Answers may vary for items 5 to 9.

5. *Are screeching* completes the verb; *screech* changes its form.
6. *are alarming* completes the verb; *alarm* changes its form.
7. *are threatening* completes the verb; *threaten* changes its form.

8. **(3) insert <u>they collect</u> before <u>newspapers</u>** Option (3) gives the sentence a subject and a verb. The other options do not correct the fragment.

9. **(4) change <u>taking</u> to <u>take</u>** The verb must be complete to complete the sentence. The other options create different fragments.

1. **if they wait patiently**   *If* at the beginning of this clause makes it dependent on the rest of the sentence for its meaning.

2. **Whenever their grandparents visit**   *Whenever* makes this clause dependent on the rest of the sentence for its meaning.

3. There is no dependent clause in this sentence. *Who* is the subject of the sentence.

4. **Since you fixed the latch**   *Since* makes this clause dependent on the rest of the sentence for its meaning.

5. **Until we see the menu**   *Until* makes this clause dependent on the rest of the sentence for its meaning.

6. There is no dependent clause in this sentence. *That* specifies a particular book, but does not introduce a dependent clause.

7. V
8. D
9. V
10. P
11. D
12. C
13. P
14. S
15. C
16. V

Write on Target

Answers may vary. Here are some sample sentences:

1. All the parents in the neighborhood take their children for walks in the evening.

2. You may not cut down a tree unless you get permission first.

3. The performers backstage were nervous.

4. The messenger waiting in line at the bank became impatient.

5. There's a petting zoo where you can go right up to the animals and pet them.

6. The poodle was standing patiently.

7. The customer paid for the shoes and wore them out of the store.

8. The singers and the entire orchestra gave an outstanding performance.

17. **(2) American citizen, Kimiko**   When a dependent clause precedes the main clause, it takes a comma. The other options use incorrect punctuation.

18. **(4) world are studying**   Option (4) completes the verb. The other options do not complete the verb.

19. **(3) Kimiko**   Kimiko is the subject of the sentence. The other options don't make sense.

20. **(5) no correction is necessary**

Connections

Paragraphs will vary. Here is a sample paragraph:

Today, more American families are maintained by women than in the past. In 1960, for example, about 4.5 million families were headed by women with no husband present. Only about 500,000 of these 4.5 million families were maintained by women who had never been married. Over the next thirty years, these numbers rose dramatically. By 1991, more than 11 million families were maintained by women; nearly 3 million of these included women who had never been married.

GED Test Preview (page 92)

1. **(3) pets while they**   Option (3) is correct because there is no punctuation between clauses when a dependent clause follows the main clause. The other options incorrectly use punctuation marks.

2. **(5) no correction is necessary**

3. **(4) vet if**   There is no comma before a dependent clause that follows an independent clause. The other options incorrectly use punctuation marks.

4. **(2) them, the pet sitters make**   Option (2) corrects the fragment by attaching it to an independent clause. The other options do not correct the fragment.

5. **(3) home, they enjoy**   When a dependent clause comes before the main clause, it takes a comma. The other options use incorrect punctuation.

6. **(4) the White House every**   Option (4) corrects the fragment by attaching it to the complete sentence that precedes it. The other options create different fragments.

7. **(5) people ranging**   Option (5) corrects the fragment by attaching it to the complete sentence that precedes it. Options (1), (2), and (3) create different fragments. Option (4) uses an incomplete verb.

8. **(3) insert must be before cleared**   Option (3) completes the verb to complete the sentence. The other options do not correct the fragment.

9. **(2) problems like**   Option (2) corrects the fragment by attaching it to the complete sentence that precedes it. The other options create different fragments.

10. (2) insert <u>become</u> before <u>sources</u> The sentence must have a verb. Options (1) and (3) use incomplete verbs, and options (4) and (5) create different fragments.

Lesson 2: Avoiding Run-on Sentences

Exercise 1 (page 95)

1. R A generation ago, people went for rides in the car. They wanted something to do on a Sunday or a summer evening.

2. C

3. R Gasoline was inexpensive. No one worried about using too much because it was plentiful.

4. R There was much less traffic then. There also was less danger because people didn't drive as fast as they do now.

5. R Going for a ride was a nice family activity. Those were the days before people just sat around watching television.

6. (5) no correction is necessary Sentence (1) is a complete sentence.

7. (3) replace <u>skills you</u> with <u>skills. You</u> *Skills* marks the end of the first complete thought. Options (1), (2), and (3) create fragments. Option (5) creates a longer run-on sentence.

Exercise 2 (page 96)

1. R Sometimes on family outings, everyone would stop for ice cream cones. Everybody would choose a favorite flavor. They could have two scoops if they were lucky.

2. C

3. R It's important that we take time to relax. It's not good for our mental or physical health to be running all the time. We need time for recreation.

4. C

5. R Some companies give their workers four-day weeks. The employees have to work longer hours each day though.

6. (5) no correction is necessary

7. (2) replace <u>books they</u> with <u>books. They</u> Option (2) indicates the end of the first complete thought. Options (1) and (3) create fragments, and option (4) would create a longer run-on sentence.

8. (4) replace <u>teaching writers</u> with <u>teaching. Writers</u> Option (4) indicates the end of the first complete thought. Although it forms two complete sentences, the second sentence formed by option (1) alters the intended meaning and is not correctly punctuated. The other options create fragments.

9. (1) replace <u>magazines they're</u> with <u>magazines. They're</u> Option (1) indicates the end of the first complete thought. Options (2) and (4) create fragments, and option (3) changes the meaning of the sentence.

Exercise 3 (page 98)

Punctuating the two thoughts as two sentences is always correct, but a semicolon is best used when there is a strong relationship between the ideas. Answers may vary.

1. yesterday; I There's a close relationship between the rain and the regret about not having an umbrella.

2. menu; we Both sentences refer to the menu, so there's a compelling reason to use the semicolon, but it's not necessary.

3. early. I'm There are two different thoughts, so a period is the preferred punctuation.

4. promotion. I The first sentence is about Ai-ling, and the second is about someone else. A period is a good choice.

5. (3) sale; it A semicolon is one of two punctuation marks that are appropriate to separate independent clauses (the other is a period). The other options use incorrect punctuation or no punctuation.

6. (4) one there. She also Putting the ideas in separate sentences is appropriate since the ideas are not closely related. The other options use punctuation incorrectly.

7. (4) processor on sale. She bought The first complete thought ends with the word *sale*. A period or semicolon is the appropriate punctuation. Option (2) places the period after the wrong word. The other options do not correct the run-on.

8. (4) insert a semicolon after <u>unemployed</u> *Unemployed* marks the end of the first complete thought. A semicolon is the appropriate punctuation. Options (1), (2), and (5) create fragments. Option (3) doesn't correct the run-on.

9. (2) home and abroad. This affected *Abroad* marks the end of the first complete thought. A period or semicolon is the appropriate punctuation. Option (3) forms two complete sentences but the intended meaning is changed in the second sentence. The other options do not correct the run-on.

10. (4) we The other options don't make sense in this sentence.

Exercise 4 (page 100)

1. Rush-hour traffic is a huge problem. Everyone <u>goes</u> to work <u>or comes</u> home at the same time. The <u>streets and freeways</u> fill up with cars; people sometimes <u>daydream and don't concentrate</u> on their driving. This can <u>cause</u>

accidents <u>and</u> <u>arouse</u> tempers. Cautious <u>drivers and</u> <u>commuters</u> know how to <u>drive and pay</u> attention in rush-hour traffic. The problem is made worse by the many people who aren't used to driving in rush-hour traffic. These inexperienced drivers are surprised that cars <u>stop and go</u> every few seconds.

2. (4) clinic. He was   Option (4) places a period after the first complete thought. Options (1), (2), and (3) are run-ons. Option (5) incorrectly capitalizes the word *He*.

3. (5) no correction is necessary   This sentence contains one complete thought and a compound verb: *was attending* and *was*.

4. (4) replace <u>quietly. And</u> with <u>quietly and</u>   This sentence contains a compound verb, *sat and read,* so there is no need for any punctuation between the verbs. Option (3) changes the intended meaning. The other options either ignore the original error or interfere with the compound verb.

5. (3) remove the comma after receptionist   Option 3 removes a comma that incorrectly separates parts of a compound subject. Option (1) removes a comma after a dependent clause; the other options create sentence fragments.

Write on Target

Answers may vary. Here is a sample paragraph:

<u>Vincente and Antonio</u> love baseball. They <u>watch</u> games on television <u>and go</u> to the ballpark whenever possible. They also play softball in their spare time. This is their favorite summer activity.

Exercise 5 (page 102)

1. Terry and I went shopping, but we found nothing to buy.   With no other commas in the clauses, it's appropriate to use a comma to separate the two thoughts. *And* would be another appropriate connecting word.

2. Margaret ran into the store; but Loretta, Krista, and the poodles waited in the car.   The semicolon is necessary because the second clause contains commas.

3. The audience gave a standing ovation, and the performers played two more songs.   *So* would be another appropriate connecting word.

4. He arrived at the meeting place at 4 p.m., but there was no one waiting.   *And* would be another appropriate connecting word.

5. The fans wouldn't quiet down, so the basketball player missed his shot.   You could use different connecting words, like "and." The comma is appropriate because there are no other commas in the sentence.

6. Chih and Gabriel liked different food, sports, and television programs; nevertheless, they were good friends.

7. Mrs. McCall carefully tended her vegetable garden, so she had fresh vegetables every day during the summer.

8. (3) eight o'clock, and crowds   It is correct to use a comma and a connecting word to separate two independent clauses in a single sentence. Option (1) is a run-on, option (2) leaves out a connecting word, option (4) leaves out the comma, and option (5) incorrectly uses a semicolon instead of a comma.

9. (2) food; you   A semicolon is an appropriate way to separate two independent clauses that are closely related in meaning. Option (1) is a run-on, option (3) uses incorrect punctuation, and options (4) and (5) leave out the needed punctuation.

10. (1) replace <u>but</u> with <u>and</u>   This option uses a more appropriate connecting word than option (4). The other options would not result in a correctly punctuated sentence.

11. (5) replace <u>but</u> with <u>so</u>   *So* is a more appropriate connecting word than either the original *but* or *yet,* which is given in option (4). The other options incorrectly punctuate.

12. (3) birds, so their   Option (3) uses the best connecting word and punctuates correctly.

13. (5) doves; those   Option (5) uses a semicolon to separate two independent clauses. Option (1) is a run-on sentence. Options (2) and (3) link the two independent clauses with a comma and a connecting word, but the connecting words are inappropriate. Option (4) is punctuated incorrectly.

Connections

Sentences will vary. Here are some sample sentences:

1. The years 1962 and 1965 were very important in communications satellite history. In 1962, the first communications satellite was launched into orbit. In 1965, telephone calls between the United States and Europe were first transmitted by satellite.

2. When I place a long-distance telephone call, the call is picked up by a ground station that transmits my call through radio waves to a communications satellite. The satellite retransmits the radio waves to a different ground station that connects the call for me.

GED Test Preview (page 104)

1. (2) problem. Ninety-five   It's best here to use a period to separate these independent clauses so that the first sentence can stand alone to introduce the paragraph. The original sentence is a run-on, and the other options use incorrect punctuation or an inappropriate connecting word.

2. (5) paths. Teaching Because the two independent clauses are long, it's best to separate them by making two complete sentences. Option (1) is a run-on. Options (2), (3), and (4) use inappropriate connecting words.

3. (3) speaking. Classes A period separates the clauses into two complete sentences. The two clauses are too long for a semicolon if you want to emphasize a strong relationship between the two clauses, but do not capitalize the word that follows the semicolon. The original sentence is a run-on, and the other options incorrectly punctuate. Option (2) also uses an inappropriate connecting word.

4. (2) tips, but counseling When a comma and a connecting word separate independent clauses, the comma comes before the connecting word. Option (1) misplaces the comma, option (3) uses an inappropriate connecting word, option (4) uses an extra comma, and option (5) separates the clauses at the wrong place.

5. (4) speaking, yet they *Yet* is the most appropriate connecting word. Options (3) and (5) use the wrong connectors, option (1) is a run-on, and option (2) lacks a connecting word or should change its comma to a semicolon.

6. (4) new. Few Option (4) indicates the end of the first complete thought. The other options do not correct the run-on.

7. (2) replace <u>overhead that's</u> with <u>overhead. That's</u> Option (2) indicates the end of the first complete thought. Options (1) and (5) create fragments, option (3) doesn't correct the original run-on sentence, and option (4) doesn't make sense.

8. (3) replace <u>territory they</u> with <u>territory. They</u> Option (3) indicates the end of the first complete thought. The other options create fragments.

Lesson 3: Linking Ideas of Equal Importance

Exercise 1 (page 108)

1. C Many *consumers worry* about unemployment, and *they do*n't *spend* their money.

2. C Many bicycle *riders resist* helmets, and *thousands* of head injuries *result* every year from bike accidents.

3. *Rivers and lakes offer* countless recreational possibilities.

4. C Water *activities are* inexpensive, and *many,* like fishing and swimming, *are* free.

5. The stamped *seal* of a notary public *gives* authenticity to certain documents.

6. C The first idea has to do with Julie, and the second is about Elaine.

7. C One idea deals with Ralph and Arturo; the other deals with James.

8. S There is only one subject and one verb.

9. C One idea is about the popularity of backpacking. The other is about Suzanne and Tony.

10. S There is only one subject and one verb.

11. S There is only one subject and one verb.

12. S There are two verbs but only one subject.

13. C The first idea says no one understood, and the second tells what the instructor did.

14. C The first clause is about Charlotte, and the second is about the four people in the back of the truck.

15. S There is one subject, *light,* and one verb, *caused.*

16. (5) food. Everyone The first independent clause ends with *food.* The two clauses are not closely connected, so a period should be used to separate them. The other options do not correct the run-on.

17. (3) insert a semicolon after <u>taxes</u> Because of the close connection between the clauses, a semicolon is the best way to link them into one sentence. However, making two separate sentences would also work. Option (1) creates two complete sentences, but the second one contains an extra word. Option (4) creates a fragment. Options (2) and (5) don't correct the run-on.

18. (2) replace <u>income tax they</u> with <u>income tax. They</u> *Income tax* marks the end of the first complete thought. The other options either create fragments or do not correct the run-on.

19. (5) no correction is necessary The comma and the connecting word *but* correctly join the two clauses.

20. (1) replace <u>divorce the</u> with <u>divorce. The</u> *Divorce* marks the end of the first complete thought. The other options create fragments or do not correct the run-on.

21. (3) replace <u>birth biological</u> with <u>birth. Biological</u> *Birth* marks the end of the first complete thought. The other options create fragments or sentences that don't make sense.

Exercise 2 (page 111)

1. At last the snow fell in the mountains; the skiers were thrilled.

2. Do not combine. The ideas in the two sentences are not closely related.

3. Diana had never skied; she was afraid to go.

4. Do not combine.

5. Joaquin went without Diana; he didn't have much fun.

6. (5) change <u>free they</u> to <u>free. They</u> *Free* indicates the end of the first complete thought. Options (1) and (2) change the meaning of the sentence. Option (3) doesn't correct the run-on, and option (4) is not a good choice because the two ideas are not related closely enough to justify a semicolon.

7. (2) attention; they *Attention* indicates the end of the first complete thought, and the semicolon is appropriate for these closely related ideas. Option (1) is a run-on. The other options change the meaning of the sentence.

8. (3) problems, but it is a big Option (3) adds the words necessary for the sentence to make sense. Option (1) is not clear, option (2) is a fragment, and options (4) and (5) change the meaning of the sentence.

Exercise 3 (page 114)

1. Change <u>but</u> to <u>so</u> The word *but* implies contrast with the idea in the first clause. A better connector would be *so* to show cause and effect.

2. Change <u>furthermore</u> to <u>but</u> The word *furthermore* implies addition of similar information. A better connector would be *but* to show contrast.

3. Change <u>however</u> to <u>therefore</u> The word *however* implies contrast. A better connector would be *therefore* to show cause and effect.

4. Change <u>or</u> to <u>and</u> The word *or* implies contrast. A better connector would be *and* to show additional similar information.

5. Change <u>so</u> to <u>yet</u> (or <u>but</u>) The word *so* implies the addition of similar information. A better connector would be *yet* or *but* to show the contrast.

Write on Target

Sentences will vary. Here are three sample sentences:

1. My sister uses manufacturer's coupons, and she saves a great deal of money at the store.

2. I look for good values; I'm not fooled by the advertiser's claims about a product.

3. Fancy packaging is attractive, but it doesn't make food taste better.

6. (2) replace <u>so</u> with <u>but</u> The connector *but* shows the correct relationship between the two ideas. Option (1) creates a run-on. Options (3) and (4) show the wrong relationship between the ideas.

7. (1) replace <u>however</u> with <u>for example</u> Option (1) provides the proper connecting word. Option (2) uses the wrong connecting word. Options (3) and (4) incorrectly punctuate a compound sentence.

8. (3) cause Option (3) provides an appropriate verb for the sentence. Options (1) and (2) don't make sense, and options (4) and (5) change the meaning of the sentence.

9. (4) movie; and some parents Option (4) uses the proper connecting word to show that similar information is being added to the sentence. The other options use inappropriate connecting words. Option (2) is also incorrectly punctuated.

10. (5) that isn't what happened; instead, many Option (5) correctly uses a semicolon before a connecting word that is followed by a comma. The other options incorrectly punctuate a compound sentence.

11. (3) replace <u>otherwise</u> with <u>then</u> Option (3) uses a connecting word that shows the order of events. Options (1) and (2) incorrectly punctuate a compound sentence, and option (4) uses an inappropriate connecting word.

Connections

Sentences will vary. Here are three sample answers:

1. (two simple sentences) The service-producing industries have an excellent employment outlook. Retail trade, a service-producing industry, is expected to have a 26 percent growth in jobs by 2005.

2. (compound sentence with semicolon) The service-producing industries have an excellent employment outlook; for example, retail trade, a service-producing industry, is expected to have a 26 percent growth in jobs by 2005.

3. (compound sentence with connecting word and comma) The service-producing industries have an excellent employment outlook, and retail trade is expected to have a 26 percent growth in jobs by 2005.

GED Test Preview (page 116)

1. (4) replace <u>so</u> with <u>but</u> Option (4) shows that the relationship between the two ideas is contrast, not cause and effect. Option (1) deletes the comma required before a connecting word in a compound sentence. The other options do not use the appropriate connecting word.

2. (2) weight. Health Option (2) separates these two independent clauses into two sentences. Options (1) and (3) are run-ons. Options (4) and (5) suggest the wrong relationship between the clauses.

3. (3) remove <u>however,</u> Option (3) removes the unnecessary connecting word. *However* is an inappropriate word to express the relationship between the two ideas. All the other options use inappropriate connecting words.

4. (2) obese, but Option (2) is correct because the relationship between the two ideas is contrast. Options (1), (3), and (4) show the wrong relationship. Option (4) also removes a needed comma. Option (5) creates a fragment.

5. (2) insert a semicolon after health The two ideas are related enough to justify a semicolon. Option (1) uses incorrect punctuation, and options (3) and (4) suggest the wrong relationship between the ideas.

6. (2) ago in This is a simple sentence. Option (1) is a fragment, options (3), (4), and (5) insert unnecessary punctuation.

7. (4) replace farms they with farms. They The period separates two independent clauses into two sentences. The other options do not correct the run-on.

8. (5) no correction is necessary

9. (3) water, but their Option (3) uses the only appropriate connecting word to express the relationship between the two ideas in this compound sentence.

Lesson 4: Linking Ideas of Unequal Importance

Exercise 1 (page 120)

Dependent clauses may appear either before or after the independent clause. Remember, when the dependent clause appears at the end, it is not separated from the main clause by a comma.

1. As if they had all the time in the world, they ate their lunch slowly.

2. So that everyone could hear, they adjusted the microphone.

3. They collected car parts in their front yard until the neighbors complained.

4. Rebecca washed her kitchen floor every day whether it needed it or not.

5. Don't volunteer to explain the problem unless you're sure of the answer.

These sentences contain dependent clauses:

6. Because the owner was ill
8. even though there were clouds in the sky
9. As long as they had enough participants
10. whenever a cat enters the room
12. While he waited for the exam to begin
13. if it rains
15. Wherever they looked

16. (3) change jury. If to jury if This is a complex sentence with the dependent clause following the main clause. Option (1) inserts a comma incorrectly. Options (2) and (4) create sentence fragments.

17. (4) jury, she To correct the fragment, separate the dependent clause from the main clause with a comma. Option (1) creates a fragment. The other options don't make sense.

18. (5) no correction is necessary

19. (2) itself, it A dependent clause at the beginning of the sentence should be followed by a comma. Option (1) creates a fragment. The other options don't make sense.

20. (5) no correction is necessary

21. (4) replace Sundays. Because with Sundays because A dependent clause that follows the main clause should not be separated from the main clause by a comma. The other options don't make sense.

Exercise 2 (page 124)

1. (Even though) she loved parties: contrast
4. (Because) Hal loved to cook: cause and effect
6. (Wherever) there was a job to do: place
7. (Whenever) there was a full moon: time
8. (Unless) the meeting ends early: condition
10. (As if) she were bored with the conversation: similarity

Write on Target

Sentences will vary. Here are some sample sentences:

1. Because our environment is endangered, it's important to recycle.

2. It's easy to recycle if the city provides containers.

3. Whenever we recycle, we save landfill space.

11. (4) Although you find The relationship between the clauses is contrast. The other options don't make sense.

12. (1) replace Since with Even though The connector *even though* shows the correct relationship of the dependent clause to the main clause. Option (2) expresses an incorrect relationship. Option (3) incorrectly punctuates the sentence. Option (4) creates a fragment.

13. (2) remove the comma after insurance The dependent clause follows the main clause, so there is no comma. Option (1) creates a fragment, and the other options use inappropriate connecting words.

14. (3) remove the comma after books When the dependent clause follows the main clause, there is no need for a comma. Option (1) creates a fragment, option (2) uses incorrect punctuation, and options (4) and (5) use inappropriate connecting words.

15. (4) Because The relationship is cause and effect. The other options use inappropriate connecting words.

16. (2) Although Jean's tooth no longer hurt, The relationship between the two ideas is contrast. The other options use inappropriate connecting words.

Connections

Sentences will vary. Here are some sample sentences:

1. ("Citizen Kane" excerpt) This sentence shows a **time relationship: After** changing the paper four times, Charles Kane adds his Declaration of Principles to the New York "Inquirer."

2. (Circulation of Morning and Evening Newspapers graph) This sentence shows a **contrasting relationship: Although** the circulation of evening newspapers declined over twenty years, the circulation of morning papers rose.

3. (What Can You Do with Old News? diagram) This sentence shows a **cause/effect relationship:** Paper must be de-inked and immersed in a chemical bath **in order to** be recycled.

4. (Who's Watching the News? chart) This sentence shows a **contrasting relationship: Even though** news programs have a large audience, situation comedies have more viewers among all age groups than news programs do.

Ged Test Preview (page 126)

1. **(1) remove the comma after impact** There is no need for a comma when the dependent clause follows the main clause. Option (2) would create a fragment. Options (3) and (4) use incorrect connecting words.

2. **(3) insert a comma after are** When the dependent clause precedes the main clause, it should be followed by a comma. The other options don't correctly punctuate this complex sentence.

3. **(4) supervision, children** When the dependent clause precedes the main clause, it must be followed by a comma. Option (1) creates a fragment, and the other options don't correctly punctuate this complex sentence. Options (2) and (3) also insert unneeded connecting words.

4. **(3) insert a comma after house** When the dependent clause precedes the main clause, it must be followed by a comma. The other options use incorrect punctuation.

5. **(5) children** The dependent clause must state the idea that children need limits. The word *because* begins the dependent clause, and it should be followed by the subject *children*.

6. **(1) replace Although with If** The relationship between the clauses is one of condition. The other options don't correct the connecting word error.

7. **(2) remove the comma after devastation** When the dependent clause follows the main clause, there is no need for a comma. The other options do not correct the complex sentence.

8. **(4) paths because** The relationship between the two ideas is cause and effect. The other options use inappropriate connecting words or punctuation.

9. **(1) replace Since with In spite of** The relationship between the two ideas is contrast. The other options do not change the connecting word in the complex sentence to express contrast.

Lesson 5: Using Modifiers to Add Information

Exercise 1 (page 130)

Modifiers may appear before or after the independent clause. Additional modifiers will vary.

1. The motorcycle disappeared around the corner.
2. To see better, Marshall cleaned his glasses.
3. He found his socks under the table.
4. Searching all day, they finally found the leak.
5. Feeling hot and tired, everyone jumped into the river.
6. *Concerned about local events*, Dorothy watched the (evening) news.
7. Their *new* car needed (minor) repairs.
8. Consuelo lifted the (heavy) weights *with little effort.*
9. The *severely damaged* bicycle was (almost) *useless.*
10. *Angered by the article*, Matthew stopped reading (altogether).
11. *During the fierce snowstorm*, the tires *of the car* gripped the road.
12. *Rereading the instructions*, Meredith felt (somewhat) more confident.
13. A *loud* explosion (immediately) silenced everyone.
14. *Imitating the* (radio) *announcer*, the comedian made everyone laugh.
15. Babe Ruth hit the ball *over the fence*, and the *excited* fans cheered (wildly).

16. **(3) Bureau, today's young** To correct the fragment, you need to attach the modifier to the main clause. Option (2) omits the comma that is required when a modifier precedes the independent clause. Options (3) and (4) punctuate incorrectly, and option (5) creates a fragment.

17. **(3) replace demands. On with demands on** To correct the fragment, you need to attach the modifier to the main clause. Option (4) attaches the modifier to the main clause but inserts an unneeded comma. The other options don't correct the fragment.

18. **(4) marriage until** To correct the fragment, you need to attach the modifier to the main clause. The other options use inappropriate connecting words and options (1), (2), and (3) also create fragments.

19. (2) change <u>Fear</u> to <u>Fearing</u>   Option (2) creates a verb phrase to modify the main part of the sentence. Options (1) and (3) don't correct the modifier; option (4) creates a fragment; option (5) inserts an unneeded comma.

20. (5) because   The reason that young people stay home can be given in a dependent clause beginning with the word *because*. None of the other connecting words show cause and effect.

Exercise 2 (page 133)

1. Dr. Jones observed the rats moving through the maze.

2. Wiping his eyes, Bill finished chopping the onions.

3. Because it was too loud, Jeff hated the music.

4. By the expression on his face, it was clear that Dean was surprised.

5. The cook explained how the participants, including the beginners, could cut fat from their recipes.

6. (2) researchers   Option (2) places the modifier close to the word it modifies. Options (1) and (3) change the meaning of the sentence, and options (4) and (5) don't make sense.

7. (1) researchers   Option (1) places the modifier close to the word it modifies. Option (5) changes the meaning of the sentence, and the other options don't make sense.

8. (3) they   Option (3) places the modifier close to the word it modifies. Option (4) changes the meaning of the sentence, and the other options don't make sense.

9. (1) workers   It is workers who will operate under the flexible system. The other options change the meaning.

10. (3) Working at home, employees who are ill or disabled   Option (3) places the modifier close to *employees*, the word it modifies. The remaining options change the meaning of the sentence.

11. (3) society because it decreases   Option (3) corrects the misplaced modifier by changing it to a dependent clause and creating a complex sentence. The other options don't correct the misplaced modifier.

12. (2) nation   Option (2) is the word modified, so it must be closest to the modifier. The other options change the meaning of the sentence.

13. (4) people   Option (4) is the logical noun to be modified by the verb phrase *feeling dazed*. Option (1) doesn't make sense, and the other options are inappropriate for the modifier.

14. (3) millions watched the funeral on television
Option (3) correctly places the modifier *on television* next to *funeral,* the word it modifies. Options (1), (2), and (5) suggest the people who watched the funeral were on television, and option (4) changes the meaning.

Write on Target
Sentences will vary. Here are three samples:

1. The alarm rings. The alarm rings at six o'clock in the morning.

2. Exercise invigorates. Exercise after work invigorates.

3. Friends understand. Listening to our problems, friends understand.

Exercise 3 (page 136)
Answers will vary.

1. Sitting in the sun, Marge and Craig thought the picnic was great. Because Marge and Craig were sitting in the sun, the picnic was great.

2. Being cold, Mark found the fire inviting. Mark found the fire inviting because he was cold.

3. Because they wanted dinner, the food looked wonderful. When they were ready for dinner, the food looked wonderful.

4. Correct

5. Because the cat was sitting in the middle of the street, a car just missed it. A car just missed a cat sitting in the middle of the street.

6. Jumping up and down, the children were glad the show finally started.

7. Correct

8. Before the shooting began, the ducks disappeared.

9. Carol could hear the birds chirping cheerfully.

10. After having waited all day, everyone was pleased that the line moved quickly.

11. (2) public transportation   Option (2) doesn't change the sentence's meaning and it clarifies the modifier. The other options change the meaning of the sentence.

12. (1) missing   The main part of the sentence doesn't need to change. The other options change the meaning of the sentence.

13. (4) Carmela sees another bus coming   Option (4) puts the modifier next to the word it modifies. Option (5) changes the meaning of the sentence, and the other options do not correct the dangling modifier.

Connections
Paragraphs will vary. Here is a sample paragraph:

In an open green field in Mexico, the Castillo at Chichen Itza stands proud and tall. This ancient temple is a stone temple with a square base. Each of the four sides is leveled like a massive stairstep with nine large steps on each side. The huge steps are etched with geometric carvings and topped with what looks like green grass or short moss. Moving up the middle of each side of the building is a dramatic staircase leading to the top of the magnificent temple. This impressive staircase looks as if it were built for humans to climb. Topping the temple is an enclosed square room with at least one door on each side. Although the temple is very old, the parts visible in the photograph are remarkably well preserved.

GED Test Preview (page 138)

1. **(2) business** Option (2) is the only option that makes sense as the subject of the main part of the sentence.

2. **(5) that Mom or Dad has to work every day.** Option (5) puts the modifier as close as possible to *work*, the word it modifies. The other options don't correct the misplaced modifier.

3. **(3) interruptions** Option (3) is the only option that makes sense as the subject of the sentence's main part.

4. **(3) replace <u>Distracted</u> with <u>Distracting the worker,</u>** Option (3) creates a possible modifier for the subject of the sentence. The other options do not correct the dangling modifier.

5. **(2) people** Option (2) is the only option that makes sense as the subject of the main part of the sentence.

6. **(2) Concerned about the environment, researchers are** Option (2) correctly uses a verb phrase to modify *researchers*. Option (1) is a fragment; option (3) changes the verb phrase to a noun phrase; option (4) inserts a comma in the wrong place; option (5) changes the meaning of the sentence.

7. **(5) electric cars can save people money** Option (5) is correct because the modifier is close to the word it modifies: *electric cars*. The other options do not correct the problem with the modifier.

8. **(2) change <u>Burning</u> to <u>Because these fuels burn</u>** Option (2) corrects the misplaced modifier. Option (1) creates a run-on, and options (3) and (5) create fragments. Option (4) doesn't make sense.

9. **(4) "fuel-flexible" cars** Option (4) is correct because the modifier should logically modify *cars*. The other options don't make sense.

Lesson 6: Understanding Parallel Structure

Exercise 1 (page 142)

1. Chad's hobbies include photography, music, and computers.
2. Dwight and Dorothy travelled to London, to Paris, and to Italy. (You may choose not to repeat *to* in this sentence.)
3. Correct

4. Laurie liked to garden, Al liked to build things, and Marnie liked to paint.
5. It's difficult for teachers to help children learn, to teach them values, and to maintain discipline.
6. *to* take turns
7. *to* make life easier
8. *their* confidence
9. *by* keeping the refrigerator door closed
10. *for* their heroism

11. **(5) replace <u>has to cover long distances</u> with <u>long distances to cover</u>** Option (5) is the only option that maintains parallel structure.

12. **(3) replace <u>ours in America</u> with <u>American train travel</u>** Option (3) is the only option that maintains parallel structure.

13. **(5) dependable** Option (5) is the only option that maintains parallel structure.

14. **(3) and Latin America** Option (3) is the only option that maintains parallel structure.

15. **(2) share their standard of living** Option (2) is the only option that maintains parallel structure.

16. **(4) replace <u>go to</u> with <u>in</u>** Option (4) is the only option that maintains parallel structure.

Write on Target

Single-word parallelism: Andy had a cough, a sore throat, and a headache.

Word-group parallelism: Andy felt miserable, looked terrible, and lacked energy.

Exercise 2 (page 144)

1. **he could swim** Larry was a soccer player, a baseball player, and a swimmer.

2. **like to play with children** A good baby-sitter must be patient, mature, and playful with children.

3. **their parents read them a story** Children sleep better if they go to bed relaxed, calm, and soothed by a bedtime story.

4. **want them to do well in school** Most parents try to teach their children to be respectful, to be obedient, and to do well in school.

5. **she plays the flute** Evelyn is talented at sports, academics, and music.

6. **(4) sisters and took them** Option (4) is the only option that maintains parallel structure.

7. **(2) discovered there were** Option (2) is the only option that maintains parallel structure.

8. **(5) no correction is necessary**

Connections

The following sentences demonstrate parallel structure (words or phrases involved in parallel structure are highlighted in **bold** type):

- Once a journey is **designed, equipped, and put in process,** a new factor enters and takes over.

- **A trip, a safari, an exploration,** is an entity, different from all other journeys.

- It has **personality, temperament, individuality, uniqueness.**

- And all **plans, safeguards, policing, and coercion** are fruitless.

- **Tour masters, schedules, reservations,** brass-bound inevitable, dash themselves to wreckage on the personality of the trip.

GED Test Preview (page 146)

1. **(5) no correction is necessary**

2. **(3) children's questions**   Option (3) is the only option that maintains parallel structure.

3. **(4) change <u>remembering</u> to <u>remember</u>**   Option (4) is the only option that maintains parallel structure.

4. **(1) replace <u>by keeping diaries</u> with <u>diaries</u>**   Option (1) is the only option that maintains parallel structure.

5. **(3) replace <u>to remember</u> with <u>memories of</u>**   Option (3) is the only option that maintains parallel structure.

6. **(4) change <u>giving</u> to <u>to give</u>**   Option (4) is the only option that maintains parallel structure.

7. **(4) replace <u>some of the equipment was dangerous</u> with <u>dangerous equipment</u>**   Option (4) is the only option that maintains parallel structure.

8. **(4) replace <u>if they become mentally ill</u> with <u>mental illness</u>**   Option (4) is the only option that maintains parallel structure

9. **(5) appearance**   Option (5) is the only option that maintains parallel structure.

Unit Review

1. **(5) diets to**   When the modifier follows the main clause, there is no comma. The other options use incorrect punctuation.

2. **(3) and consumers are concerned about the high prices**   Option (3) is the only option that corrects the faulty parallel structure.

3. **(2) cooking without fat**   Option (2) is the only option that corrects the faulty parallel structure.

4. **(5) no correction is necessary**

5. **(4) replace <u>although</u> with <u>since</u>**   The error is an inappropriate connecting word. Option (1) doesn't correct the error in word choice, options (2) and (3) ignore the error in word choice and create fragments, and option (5) doesn't correct the word.

6. **(2) change <u>1930s. One</u> to <u>1930s was one</u>**   Option (2) connects the two fragments with a verb and creates a complete sentence. The other options do not correct the fragments.

7. **(3) painful time many people still remember**   Option (3) places the modifier *painful* next to the word it modifies. Options (1) and (2) misplace the modifier. Options (4) and (5) change the meaning of the sentence.

8. **(3) replace <u>the landlord kicked them out</u> with <u>eviction from their homes</u>**   Option (3) is the only option that corrects the faulty parallel structure. Option (5) creates a fragment.

9. **(1) replace <u>Which</u> with <u>The war</u>**   Option (1) gives the fragment a subject to make a complete sentence. The other options don't correct the fragment.

10. **(5) caused**   Option (5) provides a verb to follow the subject. *Lost,* in option (2), changes the meaning of the sentence. The other options are nouns.

11. **(4) everything, and many**   Option (4) uses the appropriate connecting word to link the two clauses. The other options use incorrect connecting words, and option (3) creates a fragment as well.

12. **(3) insert a comma after <u>employment</u>**   Option (3) uses a comma and a connecting word together to separate the two clauses in a compound sentence. Options (1), (2), and (5) create fragments. Option (4) uses an inappropriate connecting word.

13. **(2) headed to California for a better life**   Option (2) is the only option that corrects for parallel structure.

14. **(5) replace <u>unless</u> with <u>since</u>**   Option (5) supplies the appropriate connecting word for the two clauses in this sentence. Option (4) is not an appropriate connector. Options (1) and (3) create fragments, and option (2) inserts an unneeded comma.

15. **(4) replace <u>so</u> with <u>yet</u>**   Option (4) supplies the appropriate connecting word. Option (1) creates a fragment. The other options don't correct the connector.

16. **(5) remove the comma before <u>and</u>**   Option (5) removes the incorrect separation of a compound verb (*see* and *are*). Options (1) and (2) create fragments. Options (3) and (4) use inappropriate connecting words.

17. **(2) under**   Option (2) rightly places the modifier next to the word it modifies. The other options make no sense.

18. **(4) When children become ill**   Option (4) turns the modifier into a dependent clause and clarifies the sentence. The other options don't correct the dangling modifier.

19. **(3) hospitalized, between**   Option (3) connects the dependent clause to the main clause with a comma to correct the fragment. The other options don't correct the fragment or are not correctly punctuated.

20. **(4) change their lungs will get other diseases to other lung diseases**   Option (4) maintains parallel structure, unlike option (5). Option (1) creates a fragment. Options (2) and (3) don't make sense.

21. **(3) employers to take steps to protect workers**   Option (3) maintains parallel structure. Options (1), (2), and (5) don't. Option (4) changes the meaning of the sentence.

22. **(1) replace Instead of being with It shouldn't be**   Option (1) provides a subject and verb to turn the fragment into a complete sentence. Options (2) and (4) change the meaning of the sentence. Options (3) and (5) don't correct the fragment.

23. **(5) no correction is necessary**

SKILLS ANALYSIS CHART

You may use this chart to determine your strengths and weaknesses in using language. The numbers in the boxes represent the items in the GED test previews and the unit review exercises. The column on the left shows you where to find more information about the items you missed.

LESSONS	EXERCISES	SENTENCE CORRECTION	SENTENCE REVISION	CONSTRUCTION SHIFT	SCORE
Fragments	Test Preview	2, 8, 10	1, 3, 4, 5, 6, 7, 9		
(Lesson 1, pp. 80–93)	Unit Review	6, 9, 22	1	10	_____ of 14
Run-ons	Test Preview	7, 8	1, 2, 3, 4, 5, 6		
(Lesson 2, pp. 94–105)	Unit Review	23, 16			_____ of 10
Linking equal ideas	Test Preview	1, 3, 5, 7, 8	2, 4, 6, 9		
(Lesson 3, pp. 106–117)	Unit Review	12			_____ of 10
Linking unequal ideas	Test Preview	1, 2, 4, 6, 7, 9	3, 8	5	
(Lesson 4, pp. 118–127)	Unit Review	4, 5, 14, 15	11, 19		_____ of 15
Using modifiers	Test Preview	4, 8	2, 6, 7	1, 3, 5, 9	
(Lesson 5, pp. 128–139)	Unit Review		7, 18	17	_____ of 13
Parallel structure	Test Preview	1, 3, 4, 5, 6, 7, 8	2, 9		
(Lesson 6, pp. 140–147)	Unit Review	8, 20	2, 3, 13, 21		_____ of 15
SCORE		_____ of 37	_____ of 33	_____ of 7	_____ of 77

For further practice, see:

⬜ *GED Writing Skills Exercises,* Unit 1, pages 1–32

💾 *GED ADVANTAGE—Writing Skills Software*

2 Using Language

OVERVIEW		**168**
Lesson 1	**Does the Verb Match the Subject?**	**170**
	Is There More Than One Subject? 171 • When It's Hard to Tell Whether the Subject Is Singular or Plural, 174 • Special Case Subjects, 176	
Lesson 2	**Placing Verbs in Sentences**	**180**
	When Subjects Are Separated from Their Verbs, 180 • When the Verb Comes Before the Subject, 184	
Lesson 3	**Recognizing Parts of Verbs**	**188**
	Using Verb Phrases, 188 • Using the Correct Verb Form, 192	
Lesson 4	**When Does the Action Take Place?**	**198**
	Keeping Verb Tense Consistent Within a Sentence, 198 • Keeping Verb Tense Consistent Throughout a Paragraph, 202	
Lesson 5	**Looking at Noun Substitutes**	**206**
	Recognizing Pronouns, 207 • Choosing the Proper Noun Substitute, 210	
Lesson 6	**Does the Pronoun Fit the Rest of the Sentence?**	**216**
	What Does the Pronoun Refer To? 216 • Pronouns That Relate Two Parts of a Sentence, 218	

See page 238 for SKILLS ANALYSIS CHART

REVIEW	**222**
ANSWERS AND EXPLANATIONS	**228**

2 Using Language
O V E R V I E W

To produce a truly effective essay, it's important that you have a command of the language as you write. In the Foundation Skills and Unit 1 you learned how to structure an essay, develop paragraphs, and write clear, complete sentences. Unit 2 focuses on the *words* that make up all those sentences and paragraphs.

Lessons 1 and 2 look closely at the way subjects and verbs work together. You've seen how subjects and verbs form complete sentences. Now you will see how to use them properly within each sentence. Subjects and verbs don't always appear next to each other in a sentence, so writers can become confused and make language mistakes that detract from the overall effect of their essay.

The verbs in a sentence are usually more complicated than the subjects, so they can cause problems on their own. While subjects tell *who* the actor is in the sentence, verbs tell *what* the action is and *when* it takes place.

Lesson 3 talks about verb structures and helps you deal with the irregularities in English verbs.

Lesson 4 deals particularly with time in sentences. It shows you how to stay with the appropriate **verb tense** within sentences and among the paragraphs in your essay. It also looks at the correct form of the verb for the different tenses.

Lesson 5 shows you how to use **pronouns** without confusing your reader. Pronouns often cause problems for writers, but in this lesson, you'll learn how to avoid those pitfalls. You'll learn how to use pronouns consistently throughout a sentence or paragraph, making clear to your reader what noun the pronoun stands for.

In Lesson 6, you'll see how to use pronouns to add ideas to sentences.

These language skills will help you use the best words in the proper manner to build the sentences and paragraphs that make up your essay.

verb tense: form of the verb that indicates the time of the action

pronoun: a word that substitutes for or refers to a noun

1 Does the Verb Match the Subject?

ACHIEVEMENT GOALS
In this lesson, you will learn how to

- determine whether the subject is singular or plural

- make sure the verb agrees with the subject

You already know that subjects and verbs are the basic components of a complete sentence. You must also understand how to write those subjects and verbs in their correct forms if your writing is to be clear.

Can you tell that something is wrong with the following sentence?

Lee and Melva lives in a mountain community sixty-five miles from the nearest city.

The problem is that the verb *lives* doesn't match the subject *Lee and Melva*. If the sentence mentioned Lee *or* Melva instead of both of them, the verb would be correct:

Melva *lives* in a mountain community sixty-five miles from the nearest city.

Lee *lives* in a mountain community sixty-five miles from the nearest city.

But when there are two subjects, making the subject plural, the verb must also be plural.

Sometimes it's difficult to tell whether the subject is singular or plural. Which verb form would you use for the following sentence?

The jury (is/are) still undecided.

Even though a jury is made up of twelve people, the word *jury* is a single unit and takes a singular verb:

The jury is still undecided.

Is There More Than One Subject?

In discussing language, when we talk about one thing, we call it **singular.** Look at the following sentence:

A tree grows in the park.

It contains two singular nouns: *tree* and *park.* One of those nouns, *tree,* is the subject of the sentence. We can say this sentence has a singular subject. But if there is more than one tree in the park, the subject would be **plural:**

Several trees grow in the park.

Here's another example:

The quarterback threw a thirty-five yard pass.

This sentence has a singular subject because there is only one actor, *the quarterback.*

A plural subject would look like this:

Both quarterbacks relied on passing during the game's second half.

There are two quarterbacks performing the action in this sentence.

Subject-verb agreement means that when we change the subject from singular to plural, we also have to change the verb. In English, we usually make a noun plural by adding *s* or *es* to it: *tree* becomes *trees.* (For more information on plural nouns, refer to page 280.) But a plural verb never ends in *s.*

Here are some sentences with *singular* subjects and verbs:

- *He goes* to night school.
- *Cheryl is* angry.
- *Babette watches* wrestling more than bowling.
- My *truck has* new paint.

These sentences have *plural* subjects and verbs:

- The *skates are* too tight.
- All the *tires wore* out.
- Several *members quit* the organization.
- Those *people behave* rudely.

You learned about compound subjects in Unit 1 (refer to page 100).

TEST-TAKING TIP

If a sentence has a plural subject and a verb that ends in s, you know the verb doesn't agree with the subject.

Remember that compound subjects are two words linked by *and*. They always take plural verbs:

- *Naomi and Judson* sell hot dogs from a corner stand.
- *The copy machine and the stapler* break about once a week.
- *Skateboards and bicycles* are hazards in congested areas.

If the sentence has one subject and two verbs, be sure both verbs agree with the subject:

- Every month, a *firefighter speaks* to our club and *shows* slides.
- The *soup smells* wonderful and *looks* delicious.
- *Tourists visit* the museums during the day and *enjoy* the clubs at night.

EXERCISE 1

Directions: Choose the correct verb from the pair in each of the following sentences.

1. Bruce Lee (was/were) a good actor.
2. They (cheer/cheers) for different teams.
3. Flashing yellow lights (warn/warns) drivers of road hazards.
4. Four-way stops (confuse/confuses) some drivers.
5. Elsa (take/takes) the bus everywhere.
6. Television news programs (entertain/entertains) viewers.
7. Weather reports (help/helps) with the next day's planning.
8. Truck drivers often (intimidate/intimidates) car drivers.
9. Some local governments (ban/bans) smoking in all public buildings.
10. High winds (make/makes) some people angry.

Directions: Correct the following sentences for subject-verb agreement. Not all the sentences have errors.

11. Charles play card games with his friends and sometimes he win.
12. Michelle seem to win every time she play.
13. Carla enjoys her job at the hardware store.
14. Computers scare my mother.
15. Mr. Chan hate long lines and becomes impatient in them.
16. The students studies together for every exam.
17. Those cars get low mileage and use too much oil.
18. Lectures bores me.
19. Mr. and Mrs. Jen loves school and is the first people in class every day.
20. The account clerk hand out the paychecks and makes everyone happy.

Items 21 to 24 refer to the following paragraph.

(1) Strikes is the most powerful weapon workers have against unfair treatment by employers. (2) Strikes usually occur over wages, but working conditions can also be a source of dissatisfaction for laborers. (3) When all negotiation attempts fails, labor union members may vote to strike. (4) This means they stops work so that the employer will lose money. (5) The hope are that this tactic will force the employer to meet their demands. (6) They gamble that the employer would rather give in to them than risk the financial ruin of the company. (7) Strikes can last for weeks or even months and can be a severe hardship on the striking workers as well as the company they work for. (8) The economic impact of these battles of will between labor and management can be felt in communities or across the nation for a long time.

21. Sentence 1: **Strikes is the most powerful weapon workers have against unfair treatment by employers.**

What correction should be made to this sentence?

(1) change is to are
(2) change weapon to weapons
(3) change have to has
(4) replace have against with have. Against
(5) replace treatment by with treatment. By

22. Sentence 3: **When all negotiation attempts fails, labor union members may vote to strike.**

Which of the following is the best way to write the underlined portion of this sentence? If you think the original is the best way, choose option (1).

(1) negotiation attempts fails
(2) negotiation attempts fail
(3) negotiation attempt fail
(4) negotiations attempt to fail
(5) negotiation fails to attempt

23. Sentence 4: **This means they stops work so that the employer will lose money.**

What correction should be made to this sentence?

(1) change means to mean
(2) change stops to stop
(3) replace work so with work. So
(4) remove will
(5) no correction is necessary

24. Sentence 5: **The hope are that this tactic will force the employer to meet their demands.**

What correction should be made to this sentence?

(1) replace The with They
(2) replace The with Their
(3) change hope are to hopes is
(4) change are to is
(5) no correction is necessary

WRITE ON TARGET

Write five sentences. Use singular subjects in some and plural subjects in others. Be sure the verbs agree with the subjects.

To check your answers, turn to page 228.

When It's Hard to Tell Whether the Subject Is Singular or Plural

You've seen that two singular words linked by *and* take a plural verb: *A tree and a rose bush grow in our front yard.*

When two subjects are connected by *either/or* or *neither/nor*, the verb must agree with the subject closest to it. Compare the following two sentences:

Either the doctor or the *nurses answer* questions.

Either the nurses or the *doctor answers* questions.

There are some nouns that seem to be plural because they refer to groups of individuals. However, these words usually take a singular verb:

- The *team practices* daily.
- The *staff goes* home early.
- That insurance *company has* low rates.

Here are some other nouns that take a singular verb:

group	congress	choir	orchestra
council	class	family	band
crowd	audience	public	army

There are also nouns that appear to be plural because they end in *s,* but they are actually singular and require a singular verb:

- No *news is* good news.
- *Civics is* not my favorite subject.

Here are some other nouns that appear to be plural but take a singular verb:

mumps	measles	athletics	economics	United States
physics	politics	genetics	series	mathematics

EXERCISE 2

Directions: Determine whether the subjects in the following sentences are singular or plural and choose the correct verb from each pair.

1. Congress (vote/votes) on every tax law.
2. You (go/goes) first.

3. Today's news (look/looks) good.
4. The city council (choose/chooses) the site for games.
5. They (ask/asks) too many questions.
6. That roller coaster (scare/scares) me.

Directions: Correct any errors in subject-verb agreement in the following sentences. Not all the sentences have errors. Exchange papers with your partner or a member of your group and correct any errors you find. Explain to the other person why the subject and verb did not agree.

7. Either my brothers or my sister wash the car.

8. Ellen and Donald trade dessert recipes.

9. We prefers movies to books.

10. Shawn and Cherie solves problems easily.

11. Connie and Larry know how to program computers.

12. Neither my grandparents nor my uncle drive a car.

13. The entire company receive a yearly bonus.

14. The jury have to listen carefully to the evidence.

15. They rents their house.

16. She don't like broccoli, but he does.

Directions: Choose the one best answer to each item.

Items 17 to 19 refer to the following paragraph.

(1) A large dental group has set up business in a new shopping mall. (2) As a gesture of good will, the dental group use several promotional gimmicks. (3) The dentists give everyone a free toothbrush and dental floss. (4) They hopes to attract new patients. (5) The members also wants to promote good dental health habits.

17. Sentence 2: **As a gesture of good will, the dental group use several promotional gimmicks.**

Which of the following is the best way to write the underlined portion of this sentence? If you think the original is the best way, choose option (1).

(1) the dental group use
(2) the dental groups uses
(3) the dental group uses
(4) the dental groups use
(5) the dental group. Use

18. Sentence 4: **They hopes to attract new patients.**

What correction should be made to this sentence?

(1) replace They with Their
(2) change hopes to hope
(3) insert very much before hopes
(4) replace to with it will
(5) insert many before new

19. Sentence 5: **The members also wants to promote good dental health habits.**

Which of the following is the best way to write the underlined portion of this sentence? If you think the original is the best way, choose option (1).

(1) also wants to promote
(2) also does promote
(3) also want to promote
(4) also promotes
(5) also promote

To check your answers, turn to page 228.

Special Case Subjects

Personal pronouns (*I, we, you, he, she, they,* and *it*) have their own set of subject-verb agreement rules. *He, she,* and *it* take a singular verb, while all the others (including the singular *I* and the singular *you*) take a plural verb:

- He/she/it (singular) goes.
- They (plural) go.
- I (singular) go.
- We (plural) go.
- You (singular or plural) go.

Look at the following table to see how pronouns agree with verbs.

SUBJECT	VERB		
I	go	eat	read
we	go	eat	read
you	go	eat	read
they	go	eat	read
he	goes	eats	reads
she	goes	eats	reads

Sometimes beginning writers have trouble with subject-verb agreement when they work with the verb *to be.* You must learn the correct forms of that verb to avoid problems.

Notice the word *be* is not one of the forms and must not be used by itself as the verb in a sentence. Compare the following two sentences:

They be late again. (incorrect)

They are late again. (correct)

Here are the correct forms for the verb *to be*:

I am	you are	he/she/it is	we/they are
I was	you were	he/she/it was	we/they are

To learn other tricky singular and plural subjects, study the lists below. These words always take singular verbs:

another	either	one	nothing
anyone	everybody	other	somebody
anybody	everyone	either	someone
anything	everything	nobody	something
each	much	no one	

Everything costs too much these days.

These words always take plural verbs:

both	few	many	several

Few put forth their best effort.

These words take either singular or plural verbs, depending on how they are used in the sentence:

all	half	part	some
any	most	none	

Half of the room *is* empty.

Half of the dancers *are* exhausted.

E X E R C I S E 3

Directions: Choose the correct verb form for the following sentences.

1. She (say/says) to hurry back from the store.

2. No one (know/knows) the park rules.

3. I (am/be) too tired for a movie tonight.

4. Most (run/runs) on regular gasoline.

5. Everybody (was/were) excited about the job offer.

Directions: Choose the <u>one best answer</u> to each item.

<u>Items 6 and 7</u> refer to the following paragraph.

(1) A three-day weekend is coming up. (2) No one wants to waste a weekend, but Holly and Kent has no particular plans. (3) Kent thinks about going to the beach for at least one day. (4) Holly fears bad weather, so she suggest staying home instead. (5) Kent doesn't mind, as long as they find something relaxing to do.

6. Sentence 2: **No one wants to waste a weekend, but Holly and Kent has no particular plans.**

What correction should be made to this sentence?

(1) change <u>wants</u> to <u>want</u>

(2) remove the comma

(3) replace <u>has</u> with <u>be without</u>

(4) change <u>has</u> to <u>have</u>

(5) change <u>Kent has</u> to <u>Kent. Has</u>

7. Sentence 4: **Holly fears bad weather, so she suggest staying home instead.**

What correction should be made to this sentence?

(1) change <u>fears</u> to <u>fear</u>

(2) remove the comma

(3) change <u>weather, so</u> to <u>weather. She</u>

(4) change <u>suggest</u> to <u>suggests</u>

(5) replace <u>staying</u> with <u>they stays</u>

C O N N E C T I O N S

The Leisure theme pages in the **CONNECTIONS** section (at the back of the book) describe the nature of some American vacations. Using any or all of this information, write three sentences describing these vacations. In each sentence, use a "tricky" singular or plural subject such as *everyone, no one, each,* or *many.* Have a partner check to see that you chose the correct verb form for each subject.

To check your answers, turn to page 229.

GED TEST PREVIEW

Directions: Choose the <u>one best answer</u> to each item.

<u>Items 1 to 5</u> refer to the following paragraph.

(1) It is becoming more and more difficult to find an old-fashioned barber shop with a red and white barber pole in front. (2) The days when men and women went to separate establishments for haircuts is gone. (3) Barber shops, once havens for men only, were so named because the barber trimmed men's beards. (4) Today men and women gets their hair cut by stylists, male and female, in the same shop or salon. (5) Many shops is available for budget-conscious individuals who want a good, fast haircut at a reasonable price. (6) Like barber shops, these places requires no appointment. (7) But they offer more services than the traditional barber's shave and a haircut. (8) If they wants, both men and women can get their hair cut, washed, permed, colored, and styled in a single sitting.

1. Sentence 2: **The days when men and women went to separate establishments for haircuts is gone.**

What correction should be made to this sentence?

(1) replace <u>went to</u> with <u>went. To</u>
(2) change <u>went</u> to <u>goes</u>
(3) replace <u>establishment for</u> with <u>establishments. For</u>
(4) change <u>is</u> to <u>are</u>
(5) no correction is necessary

2. Sentence 4: **Today men and women <u>gets their hair cut</u> by stylists, male and female, in the same shop or salon.**

Which of the following is the best way to write the underlined portion of this sentence? If you think the original is the best way, choose option (1).

(1) gets their hair cut
(2) gets haircuts
(3) get their hair cuts
(4) gets their haircuts
(5) get their hair cut

3. Sentence 5: **Many shops is available for budget-conscious individuals who want a good, fast haircut at a reasonable price.**

What correction should be made to this sentence?

(1) change <u>shops</u> to <u>shop</u>
(2) change <u>is</u> to <u>are</u>
(3) replace <u>individuals who</u> with <u>individuals. Who</u>
(4) replace <u>individuals who want</u> with <u>individuals wants</u>
(5) insert <u>to have</u> before <u>a</u>

4. Sentence 6: **Like barber shops, these places requires no appointment.**

What correction should be made to this sentence?

(1) replace <u>shops, these</u> with <u>shops. These</u>
(2) replace <u>these</u> with <u>such</u>
(3) change <u>places</u> to <u>place</u>
(4) insert <u>doesn't</u> before <u>requires</u>
(5) change <u>requires</u> to <u>require</u>

5. Sentence 8: **<u>If they wants</u>, both men and women can get their hair cut, washed, permed, colored, and styled in a single sitting.**

Which of the following is the best way to write the underlined portion of this sentence? If you think the original is the best way, choose option (1).

(1) If they wants
(2) If they want
(3) If they wishes
(4) When they wants
(5) Whenever they wants

Items 6 to 10 refer to the following paragraphs.

(1) Whether your need are for groceries, household items, clothing, or tools, chances are there is a discount store that sells it. (2) Manufacturers sometimes overproduces a particular item. (3) These products, in perfect condition, are available at discount prices. (4) Discounters buy these extra goods and sell them for low prices. (5) Some discounted goods are slightly damaged, but the damage often is minor and don't harm the product.

(6) The damage could be in the packaging or on a label. (7) Perhaps there's a nearly invisible flaw in the fabric of a piece of clothing. (8) These goods, called seconds, also are sold at discount prices. (9) Some discounters simply negotiates prices with manufacturers and buy enough volume to get a low price that they then pass on to consumers. (10) The only problem with discount shopping is that the stores change their merchandise frequently and never know what they will be getting next. (11) Some people finds discount shopping a bit like hunting for treasure.

6. Sentence 1: **Whether your need are for groceries, household items, clothing, or tools, chances are there is a discount store that sells it.**

What correction should be made to this sentence?

(1) replace <u>need are</u> with <u>need is</u>
(2) replace <u>tools, chances</u> with <u>tools. Chances</u>
(3) replace <u>chances are</u> with <u>chances is</u>
(4) replace <u>there is</u> with <u>there are</u>
(5) change <u>sells</u> to <u>sell</u>

7. Sentence 2: <u>**Manufacturers sometimes overproduces**</u> **a particular item.**

Which of the following is the best way to write the underlined portion of this sentence? If you think the original is the best way, choose option (1).

(1) Manufacturers sometimes overproduces
(2) Manufacturers overproduces
(3) Sometimes manufacturers overproduces
(4) Manufacturers sometimes overproduce
(5) Manufacturers sometimes. Overproduce

8. Sentence 5: **Some discounted goods are slightly damaged, but the damage often is minor and don't harm the product.**

What correction should be made to this sentence?

(1) change <u>are</u> to <u>is</u>
(2) remove <u>often</u>
(3) change <u>is</u> to <u>are</u>
(4) replace <u>minor and</u> with <u>minor. And</u>
(5) change <u>don't</u> to <u>doesn't</u>

9. Sentence 9: **Some discounters simply negotiates prices with manufacturers and buy enough volume to get a low price that they then pass on to consumers.**

What correction should be made to this sentence?

(1) remove <u>simply</u>
(2) change <u>negotiates</u> to <u>negotiate</u>
(3) change <u>buy</u> to <u>buys</u>
(4) change <u>pass</u> to <u>passes</u>
(5) no correction is necessary

10. Sentence 11: **Some people finds discount shopping a bit like hunting for treasure.**

If you rewrote sentence 11 beginning with

<u>For some people, discount shopping</u>

the next word should be

(1) finds
(2) is
(3) be
(4) are
(5) hunts

To check your answers, turn to page 229.

2 Placing Verbs in Sentences

ACHIEVEMENT GOALS
In this lesson, you will learn how to

- match subjects and verbs that are separated by other words

- work with subjects that appear after verbs

Y ou've learned that your essay will be more interesting if you write different kinds of sentences by varying the length and mixing dependent clauses with independent clauses and phrases.

However, when you vary your sentence structure to add interest, you do increase the chances of losing subject-verb agreement. In a simple sentence, like *The fish swims*, you probably won't have a subject-verb problem, but such a simple statement isn't very interesting either.

A reader might be more compelled by the following sentence:

The black and yellow striped neon tetra, darting among dozens of fish in my tropical fish tank, swims back and forth all day long, shooting sparks of light throughout the water.

It might take you a minute or so to locate the subject and verb of that sentence. The verb is particularly hard to find because it appears far from the subject. Simply, *neon tetra* is the subject and *swims* is the verb.

In compound and complex sentences especially, writers can have trouble making subjects and verbs agree grammatically when they don't appear right next to each other.

When Subjects Are Separated from Their Verbs

Matching a verb to a plural or a singular subject isn't difficult if you know what the subject is. Occasionally, however, you may be confused by phrases that appear between the subject and the verb. For example, can you select the correct verb in the following sentence?

Millie, like her sisters and her mother, (has/have) small feet.

To choose the correct verb, you must first determine who or what the subject is. Is *Millie* the subject in this sentence? Or is it *Millie and her mother and sisters?*

Remember: Two or more words *must be joined by* "and" to be a plural subject. In the sentence above, only *Millie* is the subject. The verb must be the singular *has*.

To take a plural verb, the subjects would have to be linked by "and": Millie, her sisters, *and* her mother have small feet.

Notice that in the original sentence, the interrupting words *like her sisters and her mother* are set off by commas. Sometimes, however, words that separate the subject and verb are not set apart by commas, so it's easier to mistake them for the subject. These interrupters are the prepositional phrases you learned about in Lesson 5 of Unit 1. For example, can you identify the subject and then select the correct verb in the following sentence?

The anger between the two groups (grow/grows) more intense every day.

You might look first at the verb. If you ask who or what is growing, you'll identify the subject as *The anger*. Because *anger* is singular, you'll know that the correct verb form must be the singular *grows*.

Another way to locate the subject is to identify the prepositional phrase and eliminate it. Try this sentence:

One of the dancers (is/are) especially graceful.

If you set aside *of the dancers*, you can see the subject next to the verb: *One. . . is.*

Verb phrases, which you also worked with in Lesson 5 of Unit 1, can sometimes be subjects of sentences and cause confusion:

Studying for three straight hours (make/makes) me tired.

Again, to identify the subject of this sentence you might look at the verb and ask *who* or *what makes* me tired. You'll see that *studying*, not *hours*, is the subject of the sentence.

TEST-TAKING TIP

Look for the actor in a sentence when you try to identify subjects. Remember: The word right next to the verb is not necessarily the subject.

EXERCISE 1

Directions: Identify the subject in each of the following sentences and then choose the correct verb form. Compare answers with your partner or members of your group. Resolve any differences by referring back to the preceding discussion.

1. Nancy, along with her husband and children, (enjoy/enjoys) hiking.

2. One of the most troubling social problems (is/are) homelessness.

3. Not knowing the whereabouts of her children (worry/worries) Stephanie.

4. Tim and the dog (exercise/exercises) every morning at dawn.

5. Usually, each of the players (score/scores) points during a game.

6. Taking notes, as well as listening, (help/helps) you learn the material.

7. The representatives from the bank (explain/explains) the new interest rates very clearly.

Directions: Choose the one best answer to each item.

Items 8 to 10 refer to the following paragraph.

(1) Mario and Jaime, skilled wallpaper hangers, have started a small business. (2) Unfortunately, they have many problems running their business. (3) One of their problems arise because Mario doesn't want to include painting among their services. (4) He feels hanging paper, especially because they do it well, keep them busy enough. (5) A potential for more jobs make Jaime want to expand their services. (6) It would be a shame if they had to split up because most of the time they make a good, hard-working team.

8. Sentence 3: **One of their problems arise because Mario doesn't want to include painting among their services.**

What correction should be made to this sentence?

(1) remove of their problems
(2) change arise to arises
(3) change doesn't to don't
(4) replace painting among with painting. Among
(5) no correction is necessary

9. Sentence 4: **He feels hanging paper, especially because they do it well, keep them busy enough.**

What correction should be made to this sentence?

(1) change feels to feel
(2) change paper, especially to paper. Especially
(3) remove the commas
(4) change do to does
(5) change keep to keeps

10. Sentence 5: **A potential for more jobs make Jaime want to expand their services.**

Which of the following is the best way to write the underlined portion of this sentence? If you think the original is the best way, choose option (1).

(1) A potential for more jobs make Jaime want
(2) A potential for more jobs make Jaime wants
(3) A potential for more jobs makes Jaime want
(4) A potential for more jobs makes Jaime wants
(5) More job potential make Jaime want

Items 11 to 13 refer to the following paragraphs.

(1) Mr. Brewer wants his adult education students to learn math in the context of real life. (2) He feels it's not enough for them just to work problems from a math book. (3) To show his class how math really can help them, he holds or has them enter several contests during the year. (4) The contests allow his students to have fun while they practice math and raises money.

(5) Once they filled a fishbowl with marbles, asked people to guess how many marbles there was, and awarded a free lunch to the winner. (6) Another time they entered and won a contest to guess how many soda cans the back of a pickup truck held. (7) To win, they had to practice their skills at estimating, multiplying, dividing, and measuring. (8) They used most of the prize money for an end-of-the-year field trip. (9) The class thinks the best thing about entering contests are winning.

11. Sentence 4: **The contests allow his students to have fun while they practice math and raises money.**

What correction should be made to this sentence?

(1) change <u>allow</u> to <u>allows</u>
(2) change <u>fun while</u> to <u>fun. While</u>
(3) change <u>fun while</u> to <u>fun, while</u>
(4) change <u>practice</u> to <u>practices</u>
(5) change <u>raises</u> to <u>raise</u>

12. Sentence 5: **Once they filled a fishbowl with marbles, <u>asked people to guess how many marbles there was</u>, and awarded a free lunch to the winner.**

Which of the following is the best way to write the underlined portion of this sentence? If you think the original is the best way, choose option (1).

(1) asked people to guess how many marbles there was
(2) asked people to guess how many marbles was there
(3) asked how many could guess the right number
(4) asked people to guess how many marbles there were
(5) asked people how many marbles there was

13. Sentence 9: **The class thinks the best thing about entering contests are winning.**

What correction should be made to this sentence?

(1) change <u>thinks</u> to <u>think</u>
(2) remove <u>entering</u>
(3) change <u>are</u> to <u>is</u>
(4) change <u>contests are</u> to <u>contests. Are</u>
(5) no correction is necessary

To check your answers, turn to page 229.

When the Verb Comes Before the Subject

Sometimes the structure of the sentence makes it difficult to spot errors in subject-verb agreement.

In sentences that begin with *There* or *Here*, the verb comes before the subject: *Here come the clowns.* The verb in the preceding sentence is *come*, but when we ask who or what comes, we see the subject is *the clowns*, which appears after the verb. As always, the subject must agree with the verb. It would be incorrect to write *Here comes the clowns* because that would put a singular verb with a plural subject.

Questions pose a particular problem for subject-verb agreement because they often split the verb into two parts with the subject in between: *Does Judith have her shoes?* The singular subject *Judith* must take a singular verb *does.* It would be incorrect to write: *Do Judith have her shoes?*

Both the subject and the verb sometimes appear at the ends of sentences, which can cause some confusion:

In the backyard are two peach trees.

The subject of the sentence above is *peach trees,* so it must take a plural verb: *are.* If you think *backyard* is the subject, you will use a singular verb, which would be incorrect.

To ensure subject-verb agreement:

- find the verb
- ask who or what is performing the action
- make the verb agree in number (singular or plural) with the subject.

EXERCISE 2

Directions: Choose the correct verb from the pairs in the sentences below.

1. There (is/are) too many leaves to rake in one afternoon.
2. (Does/Do) both of them want to go to the game?
3. In the cupboard (is/are) all the things you need to bake a cake.
4. Upstairs (is/are) two more bedrooms.
5. Here (is/are) the information you asked for.

> **WRITE ON TARGET**
>
> **W**rite the following: (1) a sentence that begins with *Here,* (2) a sentence that begins with *There,* (3) a question, and (4) a sentence with the subject and verb at the end. Be sure the verbs agree with the subjects.

Directions: Choose the <u>one best answer</u> to each item.

<u>Items 6 to 8</u> refer to the following paragraph.

(1) In the summer, mountain trails fill with hikers. (2) But is hiking a good idea at other times of the year? (3) In snowy mountains lurk potential danger. (4) Winter hiking demands special skills and care because of the weather. (5) There is many weather hazards to endanger inexperienced hikers. (6) These include blizzards, fog, and rainstorms that can cause mudslides. (7) It's probably a good idea to learn to hike well in summer before tackling a winter excursion.

6. Sentence 3: **In snowy mountains lurk potential danger.**

What correction should be made to this sentence?

(1) remove <u>In</u>
(2) change <u>lurk</u> to <u>lurks</u>
(3) change <u>lurk</u> to <u>lurked</u>
(4) change <u>lurk</u> to <u>lurking</u>
(5) replace <u>lurk</u> with <u>are</u>

7. Sentence 5: **There is many weather hazards to endanger inexperienced hikers.**

What correction should be made to this sentence?

(1) change <u>is</u> to <u>are</u>
(2) insert a comma after <u>hazards</u>
(3) change <u>endanger</u> to <u>endangers</u>
(4) replace the period with a question mark
(5) no correction is necessary

8. Sentence 6: **These include blizzards, fog, and rainstorms that can cause mudslides.**

What correction should be made to this sentence?

(1) change <u>include</u> to <u>includes</u>
(2) replace <u>include</u> with <u>be</u>
(3) change <u>rainstorms that</u> to <u>rainstorms. That</u>
(4) replace <u>can cause</u> with <u>causes</u>
(5) no correction is necessary

C O N N E C T I O N S

The Family Life theme pages in **CONNECTIONS** (at the back of the book) display information about life expectancy in the United States. Find the correct data to answer or complete items 1–3 below. Choose the correct verb as well.

1. How long (are/is) women born in 1970 expected to live?
2. Women born in 1980 (have/has) a life expectancy of _____ .
3. How many years (are/is) a man born in 1970 expected to live?

To check your answers, turn to page 230.

Directions: Choose the <u>one best answer</u> to each item.

<u>Items 1 to 6</u> refer to the following paragraph.

(1) Many people hate to cook, but others find cooking is a good way to relax. (2) There is many ways to learn to cook. (3) One of the best ways are watching other people do it. (4) This can be done in an actual kitchen, in a cooking class, or by watching cooking programs on television. (5) There are all kinds of cooks. (6) Some people follow recipes carefully, measuring and counting with precision. (7) Others prefers to create as they go, tasting and testing along the way. (8) Cooks, especially when modifying recipes, has to use some basic math skills, such as estimating amounts. (9) In a well-stocked kitchen is many kinds of ingredients. (10) A creative cook must also be familiar with them all. (11) Otherwise, it would be difficult to know which herbs and spices goes best with different foods. (12) The kitchen is a place where creative people can experiment and expand their talents.

1. Sentence 2: **There is many ways to learn to cook.**

What correction should be made to this sentence?

(1) replace <u>There</u> with <u>Here</u>
(2) change <u>is</u> to <u>are</u>
(3) replace <u>to learn</u> with <u>for learn</u>
(4) change <u>learn</u> to <u>learning</u>
(5) change <u>cook</u> to <u>cooking</u>

2. Sentence 3: **One of the best ways are watching other people do it.**

What correction should be made to this sentence?

(1) change <u>are</u> to <u>is</u>
(2) change <u>are</u> to <u>be</u>
(3) insert <u>to</u> before <u>watching</u>
(4) change <u>watching</u> to <u>to watch</u>
(5) change <u>do</u> to <u>did</u>

3. Sentence 7: **Others prefers to create as they go, tasting and testing along the way.**

What correction should be made to this sentence?

(1) replace <u>Others</u> with <u>Other people</u>
(2) change <u>prefers</u> to <u>prefer</u>
(3) replace <u>to create</u> with <u>creating</u>
(4) insert <u>they are</u> before <u>tasting</u>
(5) insert <u>everything</u> before <u>along</u>

4. Sentence 8: **Cooks, especially when modifying recipes, has to use some basic math skills, such as estimating amounts.**

If you rewrote sentence 8 beginning with

<u>When modifying recipes, cooks</u>

the next word should be

(1) has
(2) uses
(3) use
(4) estimates
(5) modify

5. Sentence 9: <u>**In a well-stocked kitchen is many kinds**</u> of ingredients.

Which of the following is the best way to write the underlined portion of this sentence? If you think the original is the best way, choose option (1).

(1) In a well-stocked kitchen is many kinds
(2) In a well-stocked kitchen many kinds
(3) A well-stocked kitchen have many kinds
(4) A well-stocked kitchen has many kinds
(5) Many kinds of well-stocked kitchens

6. Sentence 11: **Otherwise, it would be difficult to know which herbs and spices goes best with different foods.**

What correction should be made to this sentence?

(1) remove <u>would</u>

(2) change <u>to know</u> to <u>knowing</u>

(3) replace <u>know which</u> with <u>know. Which</u>

(4) change <u>goes</u> to <u>go</u>

(5) insert <u>kinds of</u> after <u>different</u>

<u>Items 7 to 10</u> refer to the following paragraph.

(1) Bubonic plague is the most common form of an infectious epidemic disease transmitted to humans by the fleas from infected rats. (2) History refer to this plague as the Black Death. (3) Although epidemics occurred during Greek and Roman times, the most famous epidemic of the Black Death occurred in Europe in the fourteenth century. (4) The disease killed up to three quarters of the populations of Europe and Asia in just twenty years. (5) The symptoms includes high fever, chills, delirium, and enlarged lymph nodes. (6) Some variations also affects the lungs and blood. (7) Officials used quarantine to try to stop the spread of the disease in the fourteenth century, but it was only mildly effective. (8) By the twentieth century, antibiotics became available to treat the disease. (9) Rat-proofing ships and carefully controlling cargo at ports helped cut down its spread. (10) Variations of the plague afflicts parts of Asia even today.

7. Sentence 2: **History refer to this plague as the Black Death.**

What correction should be made to this sentence?

(1) change <u>refer</u> to <u>refers</u>

(2) insert <u>do</u> before <u>refer</u>

(3) replace <u>refer to</u> with <u>call</u>

(4) replace <u>plague as</u> with <u>plague. As</u>

(5) insert <u>known</u> before <u>Black</u>

8. Sentence 5: <u>**The symptoms includes high fever, chills, delirium, and enlarged lymph nodes.**</u>

Which of the following is the best way to write the underlined portion of this sentence? If you think the original is the best way, choose option (1).

(1) The symptoms includes high fever

(2) The symptom include high fever

(3) High fever are among the symptoms

(4) Among the symptoms be high fever

(5) The symptoms include high fever

9. Sentence 6: **Some variations also affects the lungs and blood.**

What correction should be made to this sentence?

(1) remove <u>Some</u>

(2) remove <u>also</u>

(3) change <u>affects</u> to <u>affect</u>

(4) replace <u>affects</u> with <u>injures</u>

(5) change <u>lungs</u> to <u>lung</u>

10. Sentence 10: **Variations of the plague afflicts parts of Asia even today.**

What correction should be made to this sentence?

(1) insert <u>Many</u> before <u>variations</u>

(2) insert a comma after <u>plague</u>

(3) change <u>afflicts</u> to <u>affects</u>

(4) change <u>afflicts</u> to <u>afflict</u>

(5) no correction is necessary

To check your answers, turn to page 230.

3 Recognizing Parts of Verbs

ACHIEVEMENT GOALS
In this lesson, you will learn how to

- form verb phrases
- use the correct verb form
- use irregular verbs correctly

Understanding subject-verb agreement is important for clear writing and for getting a high score on the GED examination, but there's something more to learn about verbs. Verbs tell us not only *what* the subject does or is, but also *when*.

The form of the verb changes to show an action's place in time. Those forms indicate **verb tense.** You must change the forms of verbs to show the reader whether something happened in the past, will happen in the future, or is happening right now.

Notice that some tenses require more than one word in the verb form:

The relatives *have arrived* for the wedding.

A verb form with more than one word is called a **verb phrase,** containing a helper *(have)* and some form of the main verb *(arrive).*

There are rules to help you learn many of the verb forms in English, but the language also contains a number of commonly used **irregular verbs,** verbs that do not obey the rules.

Using Verb Phrases

To see how verb phrases affect meaning, look at the two sentences below:

Jake and Brigitte have gone to the store.

Jake and Brigitte went to the store.

From the first sentence we learn that the action (going to the store) happened at some unclear time in the past, but not too long ago. They are probably still at the store. That is, the action began in the past and continues into the present. Notice that the verb form includes two words, or a *verb phrase*.

The second sentence tells us something slightly different. We learn from that sentence that Jake and Brigitte went to the store at a particular time in the past, perhaps *this morning*, and the action is complete. Presumably, they are back. This verb form is in the simple past tense and uses only one word *(went)*.

In the first sentence, the word *gone* is a participle. Because the action started in the past, it a past participle. **Participles** must not be used alone as verbs. They must appear with a helping verb, like *have*. If you wrote *Jake and Brigitte gone to the store,* you would be using only the past participle form of the verb, and the sentence would be incorrect. Either Jake and Brigitte *went* to the store (simple past tense) or they *have gone* to the store (verb phrase).

Sometimes a verb phrase will have more than two words:

The crew *should have arrived* at the site earlier in the day.

We also use participles to show action that is taking place in the present:

Ruth *is mowing* the lawn.

When we add *ing* to a verb to show action that is occurring in the present, we form a present participle. This form of the verb also requires a helper, like *is*. A present participle can also show ongoing action in both future and past tenses:

Ruth *will be mowing* the lawn after school. (future)

Ruth *was mowing* the lawn when I last saw her. (past)

Gerunds are present participles that are used in sentences as nouns rather than as parts of verb phrases.

Her *dancing* on the table shocked everyone.

Compare the following sentences to see the difference between gerunds and participles:

Their *working* extra hours impressed the boss.

Because of the new project, they are *working* extra hours this month.

In the first sentence, *working* is a gerund that is the subject of the sentence. The verb is *impressed*. In the second sentence *working* is part of a verb phrase. *They* is the subject of the sentence; *are working* is the verb.

There are differences in meaning between simple tenses and those that use a participle. Consider the following two sentences:

The team *was running* when it began to rain.

The team *ran* when it began to rain.

The first sentence tells us that the team was in the process of running when the rain came, but the second sentence suggests that the rain made the team run away.

Here's another example of the difference between the simple tense and a verb phrase:

Mr. Eberhart *was* a musician.

Mr. Eberhart *has been* a musician for most of his life.

The first sentence tells us that Mr. Eberhart once was a musician, but from the second sentence we understand that he began being a musician some time in the past and continues to be one today.

EXERCISE 1

Directions: Identify the participles in the following sentences, paying attention to the meaning of the sentence, and determine whether the participle is past or present.

1. The rain had persisted for three days.

2. Jill and Evan are planning a party for next week.

3. Maurice had helped with the presentation .

4. They have completed everything on the list.

5. Everyone was beginning to wonder about the food.

6. Marcus has been to that park several times.

7. Everyone has gone to see the fire.

8. The boss will be sitting at Eva's table.

9. The car had entered the intersection before the light changed.

10. Mr. and Mrs. Walters will be returning right after the movie.

Directions: Choose the one best answer to each item.

Items 11 and 12 refer to the following paragraph.

(1) After three unsuccessful job interviews, Jessica had learned that employers look at more than just job skills when they conduct employment interviews. (2) One thing they take into account is the applicant's appearance. (3) To feel comfortable, Jessica worn her favorite jeans to three job interviews. (4) Although she had prepared well for the interviews, the employers asked her only two or three questions. (5) Each time she was dismissed quickly. (6) Finally, a job counselor told her she should not gone to a job interview in jeans.

11. Sentence 3: **To feel comfortable, Jessica worn her favorite jeans to three job interviews.**

   What correction should be made to this sentence?

   (1) insert Wanting before to feel
   (2) replace To feel with Feeling
   (3) remove worn
   (4) insert had before worn
   (5) replace worn with wearing

12. Sentence 6: **Finally, a job counselor told her she should not gone to a job interview in jeans.**

Which of the following is the best way to write the underlined portion of this sentence? If you think the original is the best way, choose option (1).

(1) she should not gone
(2) she should gone
(3) she should have gone
(4) she should not have gone
(5) she have gone

Items 13 to 15 refer to the following paragraph.

(1) Although much of the country suffers from crippling snowstorms, Californians usually have to drive to the mountains to see snow. (2) The California Highway Patrol knows that many people will be plan trips to the snow during wet winters. (3) The authorities warn people to prepare well for trips to the mountains. (4) A sudden storm could close roads and tie up traffic for hours. (5) Travelling without tire chains, good windshield wipers, plenty of gasoline, and antifreeze in your radiator is foolish. (6) Start out on a mountain drive without blankets and extra food and water could also be regrettable. (7) If you get stuck in the snow, you'll know you should have pay attention to the highway patrol's advice.

13. Sentence 2: **The California Highway Patrol knows that many people will be plan trips to the snow during wet winters.**

What correction should be made to this sentence?

(1) change knows that to knows. That
(2) change plan to planning
(3) change plan to planned
(4) change snow during to snow. During
(5) no correction is necessary

14. Sentence 6: **Start out on a mountain drive without blankets and extra food and water could also be regrettable.**

What correction should be made to this sentence?

(1) change Start to Starting
(2) change drive to driven
(3) insert take before blankets
(4) change be to been
(5) change regrettable to regretting

15. Sentence 7: **If you get stuck in the snow, you'll know you should have pay attention to the highway patrol's advice.**

Which of the following is the best way to write the underlined portion of this sentence? If you think the original is the best way, choose option (1).

(1) you should have pay attention
(2) you should have paying attention
(3) you should have been pay attention
(4) you should have attention
(5) you should have paid attention

To check your answers, turn to page 231.

Using the Correct Verb Form

For most verbs in English, the past participle looks exactly like the simple past tense form of the verb. We merely place a helper in front of it:

The ponies *trotted* around the track.

The ponies *have trotted* around the track many times before.

They *heard* the music yesterday.

They *have heard* the music many times.

Look at the past participles of regular verbs in the chart below.

The past participle for regular verbs is the same as the past tense.

PRESENT TENSE (TODAY I...)	PAST TENSE (YESTERDAY I...)	PAST PARTICIPLE (MANY TIMES I HAVE...)
sit	sat	sat
walk	walked	walked
play	played	played

Unfortunately, English contains numerous *irregular verbs* that have past participles that differ from their past tense forms. There is, for example, the *I, A, U* group of verbs:

sing, sang, sung

ring, rang, rung

drink, drank, drunk

swim, swam, swum

But watch out for these groupings:

bring, brought, brought

swing, swung, swung.

Because there are so many irregular verbs in English, you must listen and read carefully to become alert to them. You can't assume that verbs with similar present tense forms will make the same changes to form their past tense and past participle forms.

Look at the following example. The words *arrive* and *drive* rhyme, but they have very different past tense and past participle forms.

present tense	arrive	drive
past tense	arrived	drove
past participle	have arrived	have driven

The chart below shows you the forms of some frequently used irregular verbs.

Some irregular verbs that rhyme (e.g., *tear* and *wear, take* and *shake*) work the same way. It may help you to learn these forms in groups or pairs.

PRESENT (TODAY I...)	PAST TENSE (YESTERDAY I...)	PAST PARTICIPLE (MANY TIMES I HAVE...)
am	was	been
become	became	become
bite	bit	bitten
blow	blew	blown
break	broke	broken
bring	brought	brought
burst	burst	burst
buy	bought	bought
choose	chose	chosen
come	came	come
do	did	done
draw	drew	drawn
eat	ate	eaten
fall	fell	fallen
fly	flew	flown
forget	forgot	forgotten
freeze	froze	frozen
get	got	gotten
give	gave	given
go	went	gone
grow	grew	grown
hide	hid	hidden
know	knew	known
lay (put)	laid	laid
lie (recline)	lay	lain
ride	rode	ridden
rise (up)	rose	risen
run	ran	run
see	saw	seen
shake	shook	shaken
speak	spoke	spoken
steal	stole	stolen
take	took	taken
tear	tore	torn
throw	threw	thrown
wake	woke	waked
wear	wore	worn
write	wrote	written

Be careful not to use participles alone, as if they were complete verbs: I *seen* you at the restaurant is incorrect. The writer means either I *saw* you at the restaurant (past tense) or I *have seen* you at the restaurant (verb phrase).

Also be careful not to use the past tense form of irregular verbs as the participle. He *had ate* everything by noon is incorrect. The writer means either He *ate* everything by noon (past tense) or He *had eaten* everything by noon (verb phrase).

There is one other verb form to consider. A verb form with *to* in front of it is called an **infinitive:** *to go, to stare, to study.* Infinitives are written with the word *to* in front of the same present tense form of the verb that you would use with the pronoun "I."

PRESENT TENSE	INFINITIVE
I go	to go
I stare	to stare
I study	to study

EXERCISE 2

Directions: Select the correct verb from the pairs in the following sentences.

1. James (saw/seen) Dana across the street.
2. Harry (had rode/had ridden) that bus in the past.
3. Marianne and Rita (have gave/have given) hours to the project.
4. Have you (done/did) your homework yet?
5. The hamsters had (ate/eaten) all their food.
6. Had they (drunk/drank) the water, too?
7. Stan (run/ran) all the way to the river.
8. That family (was/been) out of town.
9. Ms. Rogers' class has (travelled/travel) all over town.
10. He had (ask/asked) for jelly beans.

Directions: Complete the chart below by filling in the missing verb forms.

PRESENT TENSE	PAST TENSE	PAST PARTICIPLE
11. get	got	
12. swim	swam	
13. bring		brought
14. listen	listened	
15. ride		ridden
16. eat	ate	
17. am		been
18. see		seen
19. laugh		laughed
20. do		done

Directions: Choose the <u>one best answer</u> to each item.

<u>Items 21 to 24</u> refer to the following paragraph.

(1) Coffee houses have became popular places for people to meet. (2) These gathering places begun in England and Europe in the seventeenth century. (3) There never was a time when people just drunk coffee there; they discussed ideas and ate food, too. (4) Even people who have never liked coffee enjoy coffee houses.

21. Sentence 1: **Coffee houses have became popular places for people to meet.**

What correction should be made to this sentence?

(1) insert <u>would</u> before <u>have</u>
(2) change <u>became</u> to <u>become</u>
(3) change <u>became</u> to <u>becamed</u>
(4) remove <u>to</u>
(5) change <u>meet</u> to <u>meeting</u>

22. Sentence 2: **These gathering places begun in England and Europe in the seventeenth century.**

What correction should be made to this sentence?

(1) change <u>begun</u> to <u>began</u>
(2) change <u>begun</u> to <u>beginned</u>
(3) change <u>begun</u> to <u>were began</u>
(4) insert <u>will</u> before <u>begun</u>
(5) no correction is necessary

23. Sentence 3: **There never was a time when people just drunk coffee there; they discussed ideas and ate food, too.**

What correction should be made to this sentence?

(1) change <u>drunk</u> to <u>drinked</u>
(2) change <u>drunk</u> to <u>drank</u>
(3) insert <u>had</u> before <u>ate</u>
(4) change <u>ate</u> to <u>eaten</u>
(5) no correction is necessary

24. Sentence 4: **Even people who have never liked coffee enjoy coffee houses.**

What correction should be made to this sentence?

(1) change <u>liked</u> to <u>like</u>
(2) change <u>liked</u> to <u>liken</u>
(3) remove <u>never</u>
(4) change <u>enjoy</u> to <u>enjoys</u>
(5) no correction is necessary

C O N N E C T I O N S

Who uses communications technology? The Technology theme pages in **CONNECTIONS** will show you. Using the information given, write five sentences to describe U.S. households' use of communications technology. Each sentence should contain one of the following verbs or verb phrases: *have bought; to buy; are using; had* and *to use.*

To check your answers, turn to page 231.

Directions: Choose the <u>one best answer</u> to each item.

<u>Items 1 to 5</u> refer to the following paragraph.

(1) The Central Intelligence Agency, which is known as the CIA, established by Congress in 1947. (2) The formation of this government agency was a direct result of the bombing of Pearl Harbor in 1941. (3) The government was determined that the United States would never again be surprise by such an attack. (4) To make sure, the people felt that the federal government should have an agency to gather intelligence information from around the world. (5) Much of the CIA's funding, personnel, and operations are secret, but it is a matter of public record that the agency is not allow to spy on American citizens at home. (6) Nevertheless, in 1975 President Ford appoint a committee to investigate CIA operations. (7) The committee found that the CIA violate the civil rights of American citizens through illegal domestic spying.

1. Sentence 1: **The Central Intelligence Agency, which is known as the CIA, established by Congress in 1947.**

What correction should be made to this sentence?

(1) change <u>known</u> to <u>knowed</u>
(2) change <u>known</u> to <u>knew</u>
(3) change <u>is</u> to <u>be</u>
(4) insert <u>was</u> before <u>established</u>
(5) change <u>established</u> to <u>establishing</u>

2. Sentence 3: **The government was determined that the United States would never again be surprise by such an attack.**

What correction should be made to this sentence?

(1) change <u>was determined</u> to <u>determine</u>
(2) change <u>was determined</u> to <u>determining</u>
(3) change <u>determined</u> to <u>determine</u>
(4) change <u>surprise</u> to <u>surprising</u>
(5) change <u>surprise</u> to <u>surprised</u>

3. Sentence 5: **Much of the CIA's funding, personnel, and operations are secret, but it is a matter of public record that <u>the agency is not allow to spy</u> on American citizens at home.**

Which of the following is the best way to write the underlined portion of this sentence? If you think the original is the best way, choose option (1).

(1) the agency is not allow to spy
(2) the agency is not allowed to spy
(3) the agency is not allowed to spying
(4) the agency is not spying
(5) the agency does not spy

4. Sentence 6: **Nevertheless, in 1975 President Ford appoint a committee to investigate CIA operations.**

What correction should be made to this sentence?

(1) replace <u>appoint a</u> with <u>appoint. A</u>
(2) replace <u>appoint</u> with <u>appointment</u>
(3) change <u>appoint</u> to <u>appointed</u>
(4) insert <u>didn't</u> before <u>appoint</u>
(5) change <u>investigate</u> to <u>investigated</u>

5. Sentence 7: **The committee found that the CIA violate the civil rights of American citizens through illegal domestic spying.**

If you rewrote sentence 7 beginning with

<u>Committee findings showed American citizens' civil rights had been</u>

the next word should be

(1) domestic
(2) illegal
(3) violated
(4) spied
(5) violation

Items 6 to 10 refer to the following paragraph.

(1) Not long ago, people thought the way to lose extra pounds was to cutting out starchy foods like potatoes, pasta, and bread. (2) Believing that protein was better for them than carbohydrates, weight-conscious individuals ate extra meat. (3) High protein diets made the dieters feel hungry and frustrated with their failed efforts to lose weight. (4) They would give up counting calories and go on eating binges, which caused them to gain back whatever pounds they had lose. (5) Nutritionists now understand that the best way to lose excess pounds and maintain a healthful weight is to cut fat rather than carbohydrates out of the diet. (6) It had not be the bread, potatoes, and pasta that caused weight problems. (7) It actually had been the butter, sour cream, and rich sauces that people were put on them. (8) Pasta with fresh vegetables has became one of the most popular meals among health-conscious people. (9) Of course, they combine exercise with their low-fat diets too.

6. Sentence 1: **Not long ago, people thought the way to lose extra pounds was to cutting out starchy foods like potatoes, pasta, and bread.**

What correction should be made to this sentence?

(1) change thought to thinked
(2) change thought to thinking
(3) change lose to losing
(4) change lose to lost
(5) change cutting to cut

7. Sentence 4: **They would give up counting calories and go on eating binges, which caused them to gain back whatever pounds they had lose.**

If you rewrote sentence 4 beginning with

Any weight they had

the next word should be

(1) lose
(2) losing
(3) lost
(4) gained
(5) eaten

8. Sentence 6: **It had not be the bread, potatoes, and pasta that caused weight problems.**

What correction should be made to this sentence?

(1) change had to have
(2) change be to been
(3) change be to being
(4) insert had before caused
(5) change caused to causing

9. Sentence 7: **It actually had been the butter, sour cream, and rich sauces that people were put on them.**

What correction should be made to this sentence?

(1) change been to being
(2) replace had been with be
(3) remove had
(4) change put to putting
(5) change put to putten

10. Sentence 8: **Pasta with fresh vegetables has became one of the most popular meals among health-conscious people.**

Which of the following is the best way to write the underlined portion of this sentence? If you think the original is the best way, choose option (1).

(1) Pasta with fresh vegetables has became one
(2) Pasta with fresh vegetables have became one
(3) Pasta with fresh vegetables have become one
(4) Pasta with fresh vegetables has become one
(5) Pasta with fresh vegetables now be one

To check your answers, turn to page 232.

4 When Does the Action Take Place?

ACHIEVEMENT GOALS
In this lesson, you will learn how to

• keep verb tense consistent within a sentence

• keep verb tense consistent throughout a paragraph

Verb tense tells your reader when the action in sentences and paragraphs takes place. Whether an event happened in the past, is happening right now, happens all the time, or will happen in the future is important. *When* the action takes place affects people's reactions to information.

Suppose, for example, you must compile survey data for a report at work. Your deadline is in three days and you feel rushed and anxious about your ability to meet it. Imagine how your feelings would change if you received a memo beginning with the following sentence:

Our survey report *will be postponed* for at least the next three weeks.

That would be quite a relief, right?

Whether something is completed, ongoing, about to happen, or going to happen sometime in the future comes across through verb tense, so it's important that you use the proper verb forms and that you not change tenses carelessly.

Keeping Verb Tense Consistent Within a Sentence

When you write, you must be careful not to change tenses in midsentence or midparagraph. The following sentence is incorrect because it changes from past to future tense:

The crowd *went* wild when the team *will enter* the stadium.

Does the writer mean the crowd *will go* wild or that the team *entered* the stadium?

Here's another example of inappropriate tense change:

During her childhood, Mrs. Connelly likes to play with dolls.

The correct sentence reads *During her childhood, Mrs. Connelly liked to play with dolls.*

Both examples contain clues to tell us which tense is correct. In the first example, the clue is another verb: *went.* If that verb is in past tense, it follows that the next verb should also be in past tense.

In the second example, the clue is *During her childhood.* Those words suggest that the action in the sentence took place in the past, so past tense is needed.

In addition to other verbs, you can determine the correct verb tense if you watch for word clues like *now, currently, twenty-five years ago, last week, next summer,* or *after the test.*

The verb tense that uses a present tense helping verb with a past participle *(has gone)* is called present perfect. It may mean the action occurred over a period of time in the past, or that it occurred in the past but continues into the present.

For example, *Josiah has gone swimming* could mean he went this morning and hasn't yet returned. It could also mean that in the past he has gone swimming many times.

A past tense helping verb with a past participle is called past perfect, and it indicates that an action was completed in the past after another past action occurred:

By the time the sun came up, the street cleaners had finished their work.

Passive verbs use a past participle with the verb *to be* rather than *to have.* They occur in sentences where the subject doesn't perform action but has something done to it:

The ladder was placed against the fence.

In the sentence above, we don't see the actor—whoever placed the ladder against the fence. We see only the ladder that someone has placed against the fence. In passive sentences, the subject doesn't perform action; it receives it. Compare the two sentences below to see the difference between passive and active verbs:

The telephone pole was hit hard.

No actor is apparent. Instead, the subject *(the telephone pole)* receives action.

The truck hit the telephone pole hard.

Here the subject *(the truck)* appears and performs an action *(hits the telephone pole).*

TEST-TAKING TIP

When you can't quickly find the subject of a sentence, chances are the sentence is using a passive verb.

EXERCISE 1

Directions: Identify the time clues in the following sentences and then choose the correct verb tense.

1. When she heard thunder, the kitten (will crawl/crawled) under the chair.

2. Whenever it rains, I (felt/feel) cold all over.

3. By the time his roommate arrived, Guy (walks/had walked) home.

4. Now Jonathan loves cross-country skiing, but last year he (will refuse/refused) to try it.

5. Currently, we (receive/received) only one newspaper, but next fall we will subscribe to two.

6. Now that school has started, I (am/was) ready to study.

7. Last year, Ken and Lucille (will have/had) a long vacation.

8. After the game ended, everyone (cheers/cheered).

9. Next winter, I (plan/planned) to try ice skating.

10. For the past three months, Chad (works/worked) on his car.

Directions: Choose the <u>one best answer</u> to each item.

<u>Items 11 to 13</u> refer to the following passage.

(1) Mr. and Mrs. Nozaki wanted to explore the mountains surrounding their new home, so they will go on a camping trip. (2) First they bought maps and read wilderness guidebooks. (3) Then they listed the clothing, supplies, and food they would take. (4) They knew they wouldn't get far if their packs was overloaded, so they cut down their list. (5) When they were well prepared, they began their trip. (6) Once they began to hike, they were glad they had lightened their packs.

11. Sentence 1: **Mr. and Mrs. Nozaki wanted to explore the mountains surrounding their new home, so they will go backpacking.**

    What correction should be made to this sentence?

    (1) replace <u>mountains that</u> with <u>mountains. That</u>
    (2) change <u>surrounding</u> to <u>surrounded</u>
    (3) change <u>will go</u> to <u>goes</u>
    (4) change <u>will go</u> to <u>went</u>
    (5) change <u>will go</u> to <u>gone</u>

12. Sentence 4: **They knew they wouldn't get far if their packs was overloaded, so they cut down their list.**

    What correction should be made to this sentence?

    (1) change <u>knew</u> to <u>know</u>
    (2) change <u>was</u> to <u>is</u>
    (3) change <u>was</u> to <u>were</u>
    (4) change <u>cut</u> to <u>will cut</u>
    (5) no correction is necessary

13. Sentence 6: **Once they began to hike, they were glad they had lightened their packs.**

    What correction should be made to this sentence?

    (1) change <u>began</u> to <u>begin</u>
    (2) change <u>were</u> to <u>was</u>
    (3) change <u>had</u> to <u>have</u>
    (4) change <u>lightened</u> to <u>lighten</u>
    (5) no correction is necessary

Items 14 to 16 refer to the following paragraph.

(1) Schools are frequently under attack for not teaching basic reading, writing, and math skills. (2) But even those children who do acquire basic skills in school may be ill educated for the world of work. (3) Included among workplace skills are being able to listen, speak, and work well with others. (4) Workplace success also calls for critical thinking skills. (5) Knowing how to handle information and modern technology also will help in the workplace. (6) Equally important were a sense of personal responsibility. (7) Business and labor are working with educators to close the skills gap between the classroom and the job.

14. Sentence 3: **Included among workplace skills are being able to listen, speak, and work well with others.**

If you rewrote sentence 3 beginning with

Workplace skills

the next word should be

(1) will
(2) had
(3) meant
(4) include
(5) were

15. Sentence 5: **Knowing how to handle information and modern technology also will help in the workplace.**

What correction should be made to this sentence?

(1) change Knowing to Know
(2) change handle to handling
(3) change will help to helps
(4) change will help to helped
(5) change help in to help. In

16. Sentence 6: **Equally important were a sense of personal responsibility.**

What correction should be made to this sentence?

(1) change important were to important. Were
(2) change were to is
(3) change were to are
(4) change were to was
(5) no correction is necessary

To check your answers, turn to page 232.

Keeping Verb Tense Consistent Throughout a Paragraph

Within paragraphs, the clue for tense in one sentence often comes from the other sentences. For example, if the first three sentences in a paragraph are written in present tense, the fourth sentence should also be in present tense. Look at the paragraph below to see what happens when tense changes unnecessarily.

> Kim's parents watch the news every evening. They like to keep up with current events. Kim watches with them, but she preferred game shows.

The sudden shift to past tense in the last sentence is incorrect and confusing to the reader. The writer should say she *prefers* game shows.

There are times, however, when one sentence in a paragraph could require a different tense from the others. When this is the case, there will be a clue, as in the following example:

> *Last year* the school parking lot *was* a disaster. Cars *parked* in no parking zones, blocked driveways, and *hemmed* in other cars. No one paid attention to signs or directions. People *came* in and *went* out the same driveways, and there *were* several accidents. Finally, the police *were called* in to direct traffic and *give* tickets to illegally parked cars. *This year,* our parking lot *is* easy to use.

All the italicized clues call for past tense verbs except for the last one, which calls for a present tense verb.

EXERCISE 2

Directions: Write the word, <u>present</u>, <u>past</u>, or <u>future</u> to indicate which verb tense would follow each of the clues below.

1. yesterday

2. when I get old

3. the other day

4. next summer

5. right now

6. when I was at my brother's house

7. whenever I hear loud noises

8. at this time tomorrow

9. for the next three months

10. last time

WRITE ON TARGET

With your partner or a member of your group, use the time clues in items 1–10 to create sentences. Write one sentence for each clue.

Directions: Correct the following paragraph for appropriate verb tense. Not all the verbs are incorrect.

11. Last summer, the Orangerie Produce Co. *had* an employee picnic. The picnic *is* a great success, thanks to the Planning Committee. The committee members *will work* for weeks by the time picnic day *arrived*. The employees *had played* games, *danced, swam,* and *ate* hot dogs and apple pie by the end of the day. Everyone *will hope* there *was* another picnic next year.

Directions: Choose the <u>one best answer</u> to each item.

<u>Items 12 to 14</u> refer to the following paragraph.

(1) When Ana Maria went to get her driver's license, there was much confusion at the Motor Vehicles Department. (2) The office was so crowded people couldn't find the right lines to wait in. (3) Ana Maria looked for signs about driving tests. (4) When she found the right line, she had to wait twenty minutes for her turn. (5) After she fills out the papers, she takes her test. (6) Because she had been so nervous, she was surprised that she passed the test and received her license. (7) Next time she makes an appointment.

12. Sentence 1: **When Ana Maria went to get her driver's license, there was much confusion at the Motor Vehicles Department.**

What correction should be made to this sentence?

(1) insert <u>had</u> before <u>went</u>
(2) change <u>went</u> to <u>gone</u>
(3) change <u>was</u> to <u>be</u>
(4) change <u>was</u> to <u>will be</u>
(5) no correction is necessary

13. Sentence 5: **After she fills out the papers, she takes her test.**

If you rewrote sentence 5 beginning with

<u>After she filled out the papers, she</u>

the next word should be

(1) takes
(2) took
(3) taken
(4) will take
(5) take

14. Sentence 7: **Next time she makes an appointment.**

What correction should be made to this sentence?

(1) change <u>makes</u> to <u>make</u>
(2) change <u>makes</u> to <u>making</u>
(3) change <u>makes</u> to <u>will make</u>
(4) change <u>makes</u> to <u>had maken</u>
(5) change <u>makes</u> to <u>made</u>

C O N N E C T I O N S

Have Americans changed their spending habits in the last twenty-five years? The Lifestyles theme pages in **CONNECTIONS** discuss U.S. Spending on entertainment. Using this information, write one paragraph comparing the difference in spending between 1980 and 1990. What reasons can you give for the change? As you write, check to be sure that your verb tenses are correct.

To check your answers, turn to page 232.

GED TEST PREVIEW

Directions: Choose the one best answer to each item.

Items 1 to 5 refer to the following paragraph.

(1) Sudden changes in the weather are not uncommon in the Midwest. (2) Last night, without warning, the weather will turn cold. (3) The Carver family sleeps through the change. (4) Nevertheless, it was cold inside their house as well as outside. (5) The temperature dropped twelve degrees because the furnace had broke during the night. (6) In the morning, when they discovered the broken furnace, they called a repairman. (7) They learned no one could come to check their furnace before the afternoon. (8) The family huddles around their fireplace until help came. (9) They done what they could to stay warm. (10) They drank hot tea, ate soup, and wore coats, hats, and gloves inside the house. (11) By the time the repairman arrived, they thought they were used to the cold. (12) However, after the repairman finished his work and the house warmed up, they realized how uncomfortable they been.

1. Sentence 2: **Last night, without warning, the weather will turn cold.**

What correction should be made to this sentence?

(1) change <u>turn</u> to <u>turning</u>
(2) change <u>will turn</u> to <u>turns</u>
(3) change <u>will turn</u> to <u>turned</u>
(4) change <u>will turn</u> to <u>has turned</u>
(5) no correction is necessary

2. Sentence 3: **The Carver family sleeps through the change.**

What correction should be made to this sentence?

(1) change <u>sleeps</u> to <u>slept</u>
(2) change <u>sleeps</u> to <u>will sleep</u>
(3) change <u>sleeps</u> to <u>is sleeping</u>
(4) change <u>sleeps</u> to <u>sleep</u>
(5) no correction is necessary

3. Sentence 5: **The temperature dropped twelve degrees because the furnace had broke during the night.**

What correction should be made to this sentence?

(1) change <u>dropped</u> to <u>drops</u>
(2) change <u>dropped</u> to <u>dropping</u>
(3) change <u>broke</u> to <u>broken</u>
(4) change <u>broke</u> to <u>breaked</u>
(5) change <u>had broke</u> to <u>will break</u>

4. Sentence 8: **The family huddles around their fireplace until help came.**

What correction should be made to this sentence?

(1) change <u>huddles</u> to <u>huddled</u>
(2) change <u>huddles</u> to <u>will huddle</u>
(3) change <u>came</u> to <u>comes</u>
(4) change <u>came</u> to <u>will come</u>
(5) no correction is necessary

5. Sentence 9: **They done what they could to stay warm.**

What correction should be made to this sentence?

(1) change <u>done</u> to <u>do</u>
(2) change <u>done</u> to <u>will do</u>
(3) change <u>done</u> to <u>did</u>
(4) change <u>done</u> to <u>would have done</u>
(5) change <u>stay</u> to <u>stayed</u>

6. Sentence 12: **However, after the repairman finished his work and the house warmed up, they realized how uncomfortable they been.**

If you rewrote sentence 6 beginning with

<u>By the time the repairman finished his work, they realized they</u>

the next word should be

(1) been
(2) worked
(3) was
(4) had
(5) be

Items 7 to 10 refer to the following paragraphs.

(1) For generations, the United States has been a haven for people from vastly different cultures. (2) The first wave of immigrants, who came primarily from Europe, poured into the country, learned American ways, and become part of the huge American "melting pot." (3) The idea of a melting pot suggests that everyone became the same, adopting the same attitudes, language, and customs.

(4) A new wave of immigration in the 1970s and 1980s has change this view of America. (5) While people continue to seek freedom and opportunity in the United States, they clung with pride to the culture of their homelands. (6) No longer wanting to be like everyone else, American citizens are taking renewed pride in their heritage. (7) It's common to hear a variety of languages in American schools. (8) Restaurants and food stores offer numerous kinds of ethnic foods. (9) Cultural fairs and festivals gave Americans an opportunity to learn about the music, stories, and costumes of each other's native countries.

7. Sentence 2: **The first wave of immigrants, who came primarily from Europe, poured into the country, learned American ways, and become part of the huge American "melting pot."**

Which of the following is the best way to write the underlined portion of this sentence? If you think the original is the best way, choose option (1).

(1) poured into the country, learned American ways, and become part of
(2) pour into the country, learn American ways, and become part of
(3) poured into the country, learned American ways, and became part of
(4) poured into the country, learn American ways, and become part of
(5) pour into the country, learn American ways, and became part of

8. Sentence 4: **A new wave of immigration in the 1970s and 1980s has change this view of America.**

What correction should be made to this sentence?

(1) replace has change with is changing
(2) replace has change with has changed
(3) change has to had
(4) remove has
(5) no correction is necessary

9. Sentence 5: **While people continue to seek freedom and opportunity in the United States, they clung with pride to the culture of their homelands.**

Which of the following is the best way to write the underlined portion of this sentence? If you think the original is the best way, choose option (1).

(1) they clung with pride to
(2) they clinged with pride to
(3) they clang with pride to
(4) they cling with pride to
(5) they were proud of

10. Sentence 9: **Cultural fairs and festivals gave Americans an opportunity to learn about the music, stories, and costumes of each other's native countries.**

What correction should be made to this sentence?

(1) change gave to give
(2) change gave to had given
(3) replace to with for
(4) remove to
(5) replace to with and

To check your answers, turn to page 233.

5 Looking at Noun Substitutes

Writing stays both interesting and clear when we use pronouns. **Pronouns** substitute for or refer to nouns, and we use them all the time. Without them, both speech and writing would not only sound ridiculous but would be difficult to understand.

ACHIEVEMENT GOALS
In this lesson, you will learn how to

- recognize pronouns

- choose appropriate pronouns

Look at what happens when we eliminate pronouns from our writing:

Jason and Peter were long-time friends, Jason and Peter worked together in construction, and Jason and Peter shared Jason and Peter's tools.

Three repetitions of the subjects' names confuse the reader and sound very strange.

Here's how pronouns improve writing:

Jason and Peter were long-time friends who worked together in construction and shared their tools.

In this sentence, we name Jason and Peter only once. We refer to them the second and third times with the pronouns *who* and *their*. Not only is the sentence shorter, it's clearer and certainly more natural. We could also break the sentence into two sentences:

Jason and Peter were long-time friends. They worked together in construction and shared their tools.

This time we used the pronouns *they* and *their* to make the writing sound more natural.

Recognizing Pronouns

English has a variety of pronouns for several different purposes. The most common group of pronouns refers to specific people:

I	you	he	she
it	me	him	her
we	they	us	them

Example: The lifeguard said *we* can swim today.

Another group of pronouns refers to indefinite people (or things); that is, nouns that are not specified elsewhere in the sentence:

anyone	everybody	no one
each	one	both
many	others	one

Example: *Many* disagreed.

Some pronouns suggest ownership:

yours	his	hers
mine	theirs	ours

Example: Joel said to keep *your* hands off *his* car.

Others are used for emphasis or to reflect back on the noun:

myself	ourselves	yourself
himself	herself	themselves

Examples: The children can tie their shoes by *themselves*.
I, *myself*, wouldn't do that.

(Be sure not to say Give it to *myself*. What you should say is Give it to *me*.)

E X E R C I S E 1

Directions: Identify the pronouns in the following sentences.

With your partner or a member of your group, determine what the pronoun does. Does it refer to specific people? Does it refer to indefinite people? Does it show ownership? Does it show emphasis? Does it reflect back?

1. All the campers lost their backpacks.

2. Without a job, one can't obtain credit.

3. Melinda said she would be home late today.

4. Don't try to do that work yourself.

5. Everyone was late for the performance.

6. Our dinner was cold by the time Charlene arrived.

7. Mr. and Mrs. Okano said they can't come to the open house.

8. No one should have to do such hard work.

Directions: Choose the one best answer to each item.

Items 9 to 11 refer to the following paragraph.

(1) In an age of terrorism, it's good to remember that protest can be powerful and also nonviolent. (2) The symbol of nonviolent protest during India's movement for independence is Mohandas Karamchand Gandhi and Gandhi died in 1948. (3) He is known as Mahatma, which means "great soul," because he believed in nonviolence as a means of protest. (4) To gain concessions from India's British rulers in the 1930s, Gandhi used hunger strikes and led masses of people in peaceful protest. (5) Following Gandhi's example in America was Martin Luther King, Jr. (6) King preached nonviolent civil disobedience as a means to end racial segregation. (7) His successful bus boycott in Alabama in 1956 proved the effectiveness of his methods, although, like Gandhi, King was jailed many times for his nonviolent activities. (8) These men were heroes to these men's people and admired throughout the world. (9) Both died at the hands of assassins.

9. Sentence 2: **The symbol of nonviolent protest during India's movement for independence is Mohandas Karamchand Gandhi and Gandhi died in 1948.**

Which of the following is the best way to write the underlined portion of this sentence? If you think the original is the best way, choose option (1).

(1) Gandhi and Gandhi died
(2) Gandhi. He was dead
(3) Gandhi; he died
(4) Gandhi and Gandhi dead
(5) Gandhi and Gandhi dying

10. Sentence 8: **These men were heroes to these men's people and admired throughout the world.**

What correction should be made to this sentence?

(1) replace heroes to with heroes. To
(2) replace these men's with Gandhi's and King's
(3) replace these men's with their
(4) remove These men
(5) change admired to admiring

11. Sentence 9: **Both died at the hands of assassins.**

What correction should be made to this sentence?

(1) insert They before both
(2) insert Gandhi and King before both
(3) replace Both with They
(4) replace the with their
(5) no correction is necessary

Items 12 to 15 refer to the following paragraph.

(1) About 35 million Americans suffer from an illness called Seasonal Affective Disorder. (2) These 35 million Americans lack energy and feel sad and hopeless during the long nights and dreary days of winter. (3) Victims of SAD, as the disorder is called by psychiatrists, often overeat, gain weight, loses interest in their jobs, and have trouble with their relationships. (4) Children and adolescents who suffer from SAD along with adults exhibit disruptive behavior in school, have short attention spans, and lack interest in learning. (5) The illness affects more women than men. (6) Researchers think the dim light of winter causes a reduction in certain brain chemicals and that people who are sensitive to this deprivation feel the symptoms of SAD. (7) It's possible to buy special lights that are twenty times brighter than ordinary indoor lights. (8) To control the symptoms for many people. (9) Anyone who suffers from SAD should consult a physician for advice and treatment.

12. Sentence 2: **These 35 million Americans lack energy and feel sad and hopeless during the long nights and dreary days of winter.**

What correction should be made to this sentence?

(1) replace These 35 million Americans with They
(2) change lack to lacks
(3) change lack to lacked
(4) replace the with their
(5) no correction is necessary

13. Sentence 3: **Victims of SAD, as the disorder is called by psychiatrists, often overeat, gain weight, loses interest in their jobs, and have trouble with their relationships.**

What correction should be made to this sentence?

(1) change called to call
(2) change psychiatrists, often to psychiatrists. Often
(3) change overeat to overeats
(4) change gains to gained
(5) change loses to lose

14. Sentence 8: <u>**To control the symptoms**</u> **for many people.**

Which of the following is the best way to write the underlined portion of this sentence? If you think the original is the best way, choose option (1).

(1) To control the symptoms
(2) They control the symptoms
(3) Their control the symptoms
(4) Its control of the symptoms
(5) They themselves control the symptoms

15. Sentence 9: **Anyone who suffers from SAD should consult a physician for advice and treatment.**

What correction should be made to this sentence?

(1) replace Anyone with They
(2) change suffers to suffer
(3) change consult to consulted
(4) change physician for to physician. For
(5) no correction is necessary

To check your answers, turn to page 234.

Choosing the Proper Noun Substitute

The form of personal pronouns, those that substitute for specific people, is determined by the role the pronoun plays in the clause it appears in. That means if the pronoun is the actor in the clause, it must be in the subject form *(we, he, her, they)*. If it's the receiver of the action, it must be in the object form *(us, him, her, them)*.

For example, how would we choose the correct pronoun in the following sentence?

The coach gave the equipment to Anne and (she/her).

Because the pronoun is the receiver of the action, the correct choice is *her*.

Just as verbs must agree with the nouns they go with in a sentence, pronouns must agree with the nouns they replace. The noun that is replaced by a pronoun is called an **antecedent,** and pronouns must agree with their antecedents in two ways.

First, the pronoun and antecedent must agree in number. That is, if the noun is plural, the pronoun must be plural, and if the noun is singular, the pronoun must be singular. Consider the following sentences:

Brad and Norma wanted their money back because they weren't satisfied with the meal.

Mary Jo was satisfied with hers.

In the first sentence, the pronoun *their* must be plural because the antecedent, *Brad and Norma*, is plural. In the second sentence, the antecedent *Mary Jo* is singular, so the pronoun *hers* is also singular.

The most common mistake with pronoun agreement in number confuses *their* with *his or her* and *them* with *him or her*.

Each applicant must turn in their cards.

This sentence is incorrect because the antecedent, *applicant*, is singular, but the pronoun, *their*, is plural. The correct sentence would be: *Each applicant must turn in his or her card*.

You can also make the pronoun and antecedent agree in number by changing the antecedent:

All applicants must turn in their cards.

This construction actually is preferable because it avoids the awkwardness of using *his or her*.

TEST-TAKING TIP

In a sentence like the one on the right, you can tell which pronoun to use by reading the sentence to yourself, leaving out the noun *(Anne)*.
Here are your choices:
- The coach gave the equipment to *she*.
- The coach gave the equipment to *her*.

Clearly, the second sentence has the correct pronoun.

Pronouns and antecedents must also agree by person.

- First person pronouns refer to me: *I, we, me, us, my, mine, our, ours, myself,* and *ourselves.*

- Second person pronouns refer to you: *you, your, yourself,* and *yourselves.*

- Third person pronouns refer to everyone and everything other than me or you: *he, she, it, they, him, her, them, his, hers, its, theirs, himself, herself,* and *themselves.*

Agreement by person means if you write a sentence or a paragraph in third person, it would be incorrect to suddenly shift to first or second person pronouns. For example, if you're talking about *Marjorie* (third person), do not shift to *you* for the pronoun:

Incorrect: Marjorie knows that if she wants to win, *you* must practice every day.

Correct: Marjorie knows that if she wants to win, *she* must practice every day.

Incorrect: Mr. Ximenez says we should try to solve *your* own problems.

Correct: Mr. Ximenez says we should try to solve *our* own problems.

Incorrect: A person can't do that by *myself.*

Correct: A person can't do that by *himself.*

If your sentence is written in first person, do not switch to second or third person pronouns:

Incorrect: We will do it yourself.

Correct: We will do it ourselves.

Sometimes the antecedent appears in an earlier sentence:

Trang enrolled in an English as a Second Language class after arriving in America. *She* learned English and made many friends in the class.

EXERCISE 2

Directions: Correct the following sentences. Make sure the pronouns agree with their nouns and are in the proper form.

1. Manuel and Umeki agreed to share one's study notes with each other.

2. A baby seal can swim by themselves right away.

3. The basketball team lost their third game in a row.

4. Give the paper to myself when you finish.

5. This piece of cake is just for Larry and I.

WRITE ON TARGET

Write a five-sentence paragraph about an animal or a person. After the first sentence, use pronouns to substitute for or refer to nouns whenever possible.

Directions: Choose the one best answer to each item.

Items 6 to 9 refer to the following paragraph.

(1) If you're looking for a bargain, many people love to shop in consignment stores. (2) For low prices, these stores sell used clothing and other items that are in good condition. (3) It's possible to find wonderful bargains and hidden treasures. (4) One might find great clothing for yourself and gifts for your friends. (5) Consignment items might come from people who need new clothes because they have gained or lost weight. (6) Some people just get tired of their perfectly good clothes and want to sell it. (7) After selling an item, the owner of the store gives a portion of the money to the original owner and keeps the rest. (8) They make money, and you get our bargain.

6. Sentence 1: **If you're looking for a bargain, many people love to shop in consignment stores.**

Which of the following is the best way to write the underlined portion of this sentence? If you think the original is the best way, choose option (1).

(1) many people love to shop
(2) they love to shop
(3) you might like to shop
(4) everyone loves to shop
(5) I would prefer to shop

7. Sentence 4: **One might find great clothing for yourself and gifts for your friends.**

What correction should be made to this sentence?

(1) replace <u>One</u> with <u>I</u>
(2) replace <u>One</u> with <u>We</u>
(3) replace <u>One</u> with <u>They</u>
(4) replace <u>One</u> with <u>You</u>
(5) replace <u>One</u> with <u>It</u>

8. Sentence 6: **Some people just get tired of their perfectly good clothes and want to sell it.**

What correction should be made to this sentence?

(1) replace <u>Some people</u> with <u>We</u>
(2) replace <u>their</u> with <u>your</u>
(3) replace <u>their</u> with <u>our</u>
(4) replace <u>it</u> with <u>them</u>
(5) replace <u>it</u> with <u>him</u>

9. Sentence 8: **They make money, and you get our bargain.**

What correction should be made to this sentence?

(1) replace <u>They</u> with <u>We</u>
(2) replace <u>They</u> with <u>You</u>
(3) replace <u>you</u> with <u>we</u>
(4) replace <u>you</u> with <u>they</u>
(5) replace <u>our</u> with <u>your</u>

Items 10 to 12 refer to the following paragraphs.

(1) Seneca Falls, New York, is the home of the National Women's Hall of Fame. (2) For about a quarter of a century, the hall has existed to honor women who have made important contributions to our society. (3) The women inducted into the hall of fame are risk takers. (4) She's been courageous enough to challenge and improve society on many fronts. (5) Rosa Parks, for example, is known as the mother of the civil rights movement because she dared to defy segregation laws on public buses. (6) The inductees include contemporary feminist Gloria Steinem; politician Shirley Chisholm, the first African-American woman elected to Congress; Annie Oakley, who was famous for her skill with a rifle; Wilma Mankiller, principal chief of the Cherokee Nation; and Rosalyn Yalow, the first American woman to win a Nobel Prize in medicine.

(7) Original rules for induction into this hall of fame allowed only two living women and two deceased women to be inducted each year. (8) However, the rules were changed because it put women into competition with each other. (9) Now, it's possible to have as many as thirty-five inductees at one time. (10) This hall of fame is important, many feel, because women's accomplishments have gone unrecognized in this country. (11) The inductees serve as inspiration and models for her daughters, granddaughters, and women of future generations.

10. Sentence 4: **She's been courageous enough to challenge and improve society on many fronts.**

What correction should be made to this sentence?

(1) replace <u>She's</u> with <u>It's</u>
(2) replace <u>She's</u> with <u>They've</u>
(3) change <u>enough to</u> to <u>enough. To</u>
(4) change <u>challenge</u> to <u>challenged</u>
(5) change <u>challenge</u> to <u>challenging</u>

11. Sentence 8: **However, the rules were changed because it put women into competition with each other.**

What correction should be made to this sentence?

(1) change <u>changed</u> to <u>change</u>
(2) insert a comma after <u>changed</u>
(3) replace <u>it</u> with <u>they</u>
(4) replace <u>women</u> with <u>them</u>
(5) no correction is necessary

12. Sentence 11: **The inductees <u>serve as inspiration and models for her daughters</u>, granddaughters, and women of future generations.**

Which of the following is the best way to write the underlined portion of this sentence? If you think the original is the best way, choose option (1).

(1) serve as inspiration and models for her daughters
(2) serve as inspiration and models. For her daughters
(3) served as inspiration and models for her daughters
(4) serve her daughter's inspiration and models
(5) serve as inspiration and models for their daughters

CONNECTIONS

Most people agree that parenthood has its ups and downs. The Family Life theme pages in **CONNECTIONS** present one man's experiences with fatherhood. Analyze the poet's word choices. Who is "I"? Who is "you"? Write one paragraph comparing or contrasting the poem's message with your own observations about the relationship between parents and children. Use noun substitutes when appropriate.

To check your answers, turn to page 234.

GED TEST PREVIEW

Directions: Choose the <u>one best answer</u> to each item.

<u>Items 1 to 5</u> refer to the following paragraph.

(1) As a result of sophisticated medical care and readily available information on healthful living, people are living longer than you ever have before. (2) A growing population of aging citizens has spurred the growth of an entire field of study called gerontology. (3) Gerontologists look at trends in health care, housing, and recreation for the aged. (4) Our concerns include financial stability, independent living, and community resources to aid the elderly. (5) Unfortunately, another area of concern is abuse of the elderly. (6) A generation caught between raising one's own children and caring for aging parents often experiences severe stress that leads to abuse. (7) Most of us don't like to talk about this growing problem, but we must face them. (8) Like child abuse, it won't go away if they ignore it.

1. Sentence 1: **As a result of sophisticated medical care and readily available information on healthful living, people are living longer than you ever have before.**

What correction should be made to this sentence?

(1) replace <u>information on</u> with <u>information. On</u>
(2) replace <u>people</u> with <u>no one</u>
(3) replace <u>you</u> with <u>he or she</u>
(4) replace <u>you</u> with <u>they</u>
(5) remove <u>ever</u>

2. Sentence 4: <u>**Our concerns include**</u> **financial stability, independent living, and community resources to aid the elderly.**

Which of the following is the best way to write the underlined portion of this sentence? If you think the original is the best way, choose option (1).

(1) Our concerns include
(2) We are concerned about
(3) His concerns include
(4) Their concerns include
(5) You see concern about

3. Sentence 6: **A generation caught between raising one's own children and caring for aging parents often experiences severe stress that leads to abuse.**

What correction should be made to this sentence?

(1) change <u>A generation</u> to <u>Generations</u>
(2) replace <u>one's</u> with <u>its</u>
(3) replace <u>one's</u> with <u>their</u>
(4) replace <u>one's</u> with <u>your</u>
(5) change <u>experiences</u> to <u>experience</u>

4. Sentence 7: **Most of us don't like to talk about this growing problem, <u>but we must face them.</u>**

Which of the following is the best way to write the underlined portion of this sentence? If you think the original is the best way, choose option (1).

(1) but we must face them
(2) but you must face them
(3) but they must be faced
(4) but you must face it
(5) but we must face it

5. Sentence 8: **Like child abuse, it won't go away if they ignore it.**

What correction should be made to this sentence?

(1) replace <u>it won't</u> with <u>they won't</u>
(2) replace <u>it won't</u> with <u>we won't</u>
(3) replace <u>they</u> with <u>it</u>
(4) replace <u>they</u> with <u>we</u>
(5) replace <u>ignore it</u> with <u>ignore them</u>

Items 6 to 10 refer to the following paragraph.

(1) A usually dependable cure for a sagging economy is low interest rates. (2) They enable consumers to borrow money more easily to making large purchases such as houses and cars. (3) The resulting demand for products means more people have to be hired to manufacture it. (4) Those people, in turn, earn money that he or she use to buy things, thus creating even more demand for goods and services. (5) As the demand rises, so does employment. (6) As employment rises, so does demand. (7) But none of this works if people lack confidence in the economy. (8) After a long period of economic recession, consumers are wary, even with low interest rates, increased employment, and more money to spend. (9) You're afraid their jobs may not last, so they hesitate to make large purchases. (10) If consumers hold back on its spending, manufacturing decreases, and unemployment begins to rise again. (11) It's a stubborn cycle.

6. Sentence 2: **They enable consumers to borrow money more easily to making large purchases such as houses and cars.**

If you rewrote sentence 2 beginning with

With low interest rates, consumers are better able to

the next word should be

(1) had
(2) borrow
(3) driven
(4) made
(5) purchasing

7. Sentence 3: **The resulting demand for products means more people have to be hired to manufacture it.**

What correction should be made to this sentence?

(1) change means to mean
(2) change have to has
(3) replace more people with everyone
(4) replace it with them
(5) no correction is necessary

8. Sentence 4: **Those people, in turn, earn money that he or she use to buy things, thus creating even more demand for goods and services.**

Which of the following is the best way to write the underlined portion of this sentence? If you think the original is the best answer, choose option (1).

(1) earn money that he or she use to buy things
(2) earn money that they use to buy things
(3) earn money that you use to buy things
(4) earn money that we use to buy things
(5) earn money that those people use to buy things

9. Sentence 9: **You're afraid their jobs may not last, so they hesitate to make large purchases.**

What correction should be made to this sentence?

(1) change You're to We're
(2) change You're to I'm
(3) change You're to They're
(4) change their to his or her
(5) change their to its

10. Sentence 10: **If consumers hold back on its spending, manufacturing decreases, and unemployment begins to rise again.**

What correction should be made to this sentence?

(1) replace its with your
(2) replace its with our
(3) replace its with their
(4) replace its with his or her
(5) no correction is necessary

To check your answers, turn to page 235.

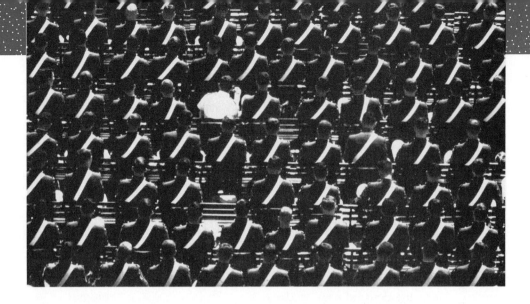

6 Does the Pronoun Fit the Rest of the Sentence?

ACHIEVEMENT GOALS
In this lesson, you will learn how to

- keep pronoun references clear

- use relative pronouns to link parts of sentences

You've seen how confusing writing is when pronouns do not agree with their antecedents in number and person. In some writing, antecedents are so unclear that readers can't tell whether the pronouns agree with them or not. Can you tell what all the pronouns refer to in the following passage?

> A group of us had hoped to go fishing over the weekend. We had gathered several times at one person's house to plan the trip. We agreed that some of us would have to go to the store to purchase supplies, while the others would get the boat and fishing gear ready. The day before the trip, when it was time to buy the food, they were so tired that we decided to forget it.

The last sentence raises a few questions: Who are *they?* Are they the people who were going on the trip? Are they the people who sold supplies? What is *it* they decided to forget? Is it shopping for supplies or it is the entire fishing trip?

When you use pronouns, you must make sure the antecedents are clear. Otherwise, the reader can't tell what the pronoun refers to and probably won't be able to understand what you're writing.

What Does the Pronoun Refer To?

Unclear pronoun references usually occur for one of three reasons:

1. There are two possible antecedents for a single pronoun.
Mario told Albert he was wrong.

Because there are two possible antecedents (*Mario* and *Albert*) for the pronoun *he* the reader can't tell who was wrong.

2. The antecedent is placed too far away from the pronoun.

At the bottom of the hill was a huge forest. Hundreds of trees crowded together to hide the sky. Pine needles covered up the paths, and overgrown shrubs and vines blocked the view. Hiking to the other side was difficult. The campers were frightened by it.

The pronoun *it* is so far from its antecedent *forest* that a reader might be unsure what *it* is.

3. There is no antecedent.

Patricia always loved school which made her want to become a teacher.

The pronoun *which* doesn't refer to any particular noun.

EXERCISE 1

Directions: Rewrite the following sentences to make the pronoun references clear. Compare your sentences with those of your partner or members of your group to see that there is more than one way to solve each problem of unclear pronoun reference.

1. Everyone saluted the flag which is a sign of patriotism.
2. Peggy invited Linda to visit as soon as she felt better.

Directions: Choose the <u>one best answer</u> for each item.

<u>Items 3 and 4</u> refer to the following paragraph.

(1) Historians and sociologists study periods of time and attach labels to them. (2) Some decades, for example, carry names that suggest their main characteristics. (3) We refer to the last decade of the 1800s as the Gay Nineties because of general prosperity. (4) These were years when people had jobs. (5) They were industrially productive. (6) The Roaring Twenties suggests a time of wild behavior, when women cut their hair short and smoked cigarettes. (7) Wild dances like the Charleston were popular, and young people drove fast cars and partied a great deal. (8) Student protest, the sexual revolution, and feminism characterize the radical 60s and 70s. (9) The 1980s are seen as a time of greed, when selfish pursuit of money is what drove them.

3. Sentences 4 and 5: **These were years when people had jobs. They were industrially productive.**

The most effective combination of sentences 4 and 5 would include which of the following groups of words?

(1) Although people had jobs
(2) Although they were industrially productive
(3) During these industrially productive years
(4) Despite their productivity
(5) Even though most people had jobs

4. Sentence 9: **The 1980s are seen as a time of greed, when <u>selfish pursuit of money is what drove them.</u>**

Which of the following is the best way to write the underlined portion of this sentence? If you think the original is the best way, choose option (1).

(1) selfish pursuit of money is what drove them
(2) they were driven by selfish pursuit of money
(3) selfish pursuit of money motivated them
(4) people selfishly pursued money
(5) they were selfish and drove big cars

To check your answers, turn to page 235.

Pronouns That Relate Two Parts of a Sentence

Relative pronouns are special kinds of pronouns that don't actually replace a noun but refer to it.

who	whom	which
whoever	whomever	that

Like compound and complex sentences, relative pronouns give you another way to combine ideas into a single sentence. Compare the examples below.

Compound sentence: Some people want muscular bodies, so they work out regularly.

Complex sentence: Because some people want muscular bodies, they work out regularly.

Simple sentence with a relative pronoun clause: People *who want muscular bodies* work out regularly.

When we refer to animals or things, we use *that* or *which*, but when we refer to people, we use *who* or *whom*.

The birds *that* sing all morning have built a nest in our tree.

The people *who* sing in the choir have nice voices.

Many people are troubled by *who* and *whom* because they can't figure out which one to use. You can solve this problem by remembering that *who* is used in the subject or actor position in a sentence or clause, and *whom* is used in the object or receiver position.

In the sentence below, the relative pronoun *who* is used as the subject of a clause. The verb in the clause is *is going*.

Give a ticket to everyone *who* is going.

In the following sentence, the relative pronoun *whom* is used as an object:

The man *whom* the police suspected was proved innocent.

Sometimes it helps to turn the words in the clause around (the police suspected *whom*) to be sure of the correct relative pronoun.

TEST-TAKING TIP

When you're not sure whether to use *who* or *whom*, look only at the words in the clause. Mentally substitute *he* or *him* for the pronoun, and if *he* fits, use *who*; if *him* fits, use *whom*. **Example:** The officer told the jury *(who/whom)* was at the scene of the crime. Make the *he/him* substitution, and you find that only *he* makes sense. The officer told the jury *(he/who)* was at the scene of the crime.

EXERCISE 2

Directions: Choose the correct relative pronouns in the following sentences.

1. All the dogs (who/that) went to obedience school can perform tricks.

2. Everyone (who/that) asked received an announcement.

3. Mrs. Doak, (who/which) lives next door, travels every summer.

4. (Who/whom) shall I ask to help?

5. They finally fixed the car (who/that) had broken down four times.

6. (Whoever/whomever) wants to come is welcome.

7. Jennifer gave her bus seat to an elderly woman (who/that) thanked her.

8. Jack is the one (who/whom) will do the best job.

WRITE ON TARGET

Choose three of the six relative pronouns listed at the top of page 218 and write a sentence using each one.

Directions: Choose the <u>one best answer</u> to each item.

<u>Items 9 to 11</u> refer to the following paragraph.

(1) People that feel helpless trying to solve personal problems in their lives needn't be alone. (2) Support groups exist for countless human needs. (3) Recovering drug abusers, compulsive gamblers, parents of difficult children, people in the process of divorce, and victims of abuse can find a group to help them deal with their problems. (4) A group leader whom is an expert in family relationships is able to suggest solutions that have worked for other people. (5) We all have problems. (6) That seem impossible to solve by ourselves.

9. Sentence 1: **People that feel helpless trying to solve personal problems in their lives needn't be alone.**

What correction should be made to this sentence?

(1) replace <u>that</u> with <u>whom</u>
(2) replace <u>that</u> with <u>who</u>
(3) replace <u>that</u> with <u>which</u>
(4) replace <u>their</u> with <u>your</u>
(5) replace <u>their</u> with <u>our</u>

10. Sentence 4: **A group leader whom is an expert in family relationships is able to suggest solutions that have worked for other people.**

What correction should be made to this sentence?

(1) remove <u>whom</u>
(2) replace <u>whom</u> with <u>which</u>
(3) change <u>whom</u> to <u>who</u>
(4) replace <u>whom</u> with <u>that</u>
(5) no correction is necessary

11. Sentences 5 and 6: **We all have <u>problems.</u> <u>That seem</u> impossible to solve by ourselves.**

Which of the following is the best way to write the underlined portion of these sentences? If you think the original is the best way, choose option (1).

(1) problems. That seem
(2) problems. Which seem
(3) problems. Who seem
(4) problems that seem
(5) problems who seem

CONNECTIONS

How do most Americans tune into the news? The News Media theme pages in **CONNECTIONS** let you know. On your own or with a partner, analyze the chart and graph to discover more about Americans' use of the news media. Write four sentences comparing the information. In each sentence, use a relative pronoun such as *who, which,* or *that.* Be sure your pronoun references are clear.

To check your answers, turn to page 236.

GED TEST PREVIEW

Directions: Choose the <u>one best answer</u> to each item.

<u>Items 1 to 5</u> refer to the following paragraph.

(1) Because of their convenience, more and more people are running businesses out of their homes. (2) A home-based business is good for anyone who can discipline themselves. (3) Some companies allow employees to work at home, so they can have a home office without being responsible for owning their own business. (4) People that work at home might miss the company of other workers and become lonely. (5) However, some people do very well on your own. (6) Working at home means one must be careful not to get caught up in the distractions of family, housework, or watching television instead of working; it can be a problem. (7) Some people who work at home find they snack all day long and gain weight. (8) Some home-based workers work late into the night and fail to get enough sleep, but others find the quiet of night hours the most appealing part of working in a home office.

1. Sentence 1: **Because of their convenience, more and more people are running businesses out of their homes.**

   Which of the following is the best way to write the underlined portion of this sentence? If you think the original is the best way, choose option (1).

   (1) Because of their convenience,
   (2) Because they find it convenient,
   (3) Being convenient,
   (4) For your convenience,
   (5) Because of your convenience,

2. Sentence 2: **A home-based business is good for anyone who can discipline themselves.**

   What correction should be made to this sentence?

   (1) replace <u>anyone</u> with <u>someone</u>
   (2) replace <u>anyone</u> with <u>people</u>
   (3) replace <u>anyone</u> with <u>a person</u>
   (4) change <u>themselves</u> to <u>themself</u>
   (5) no correction is necessary

3. Sentence 4: **People that work at home might miss the company of other workers and become lonely.**

   What correction should be made to this sentence?

   (1) replace <u>People</u> with <u>Someone</u>
   (2) replace <u>People</u> with <u>Anyone</u>
   (3) replace <u>that</u> with <u>whom</u>
   (4) replace <u>that</u> with <u>who</u>
   (5) replace <u>that</u> with <u>which</u>

4. Sentence 5: **However, some people do very well on your own.**

   What correction should be made to this sentence?

   (1) replace <u>your</u> with <u>his or her</u>
   (2) replace <u>your</u> with <u>our</u>
   (3) replace <u>your</u> with <u>their</u>
   (4) replace <u>your</u> with <u>one's</u>
   (5) no correction is necessary

5. Sentence 6: **Working at home means one must be careful not to get caught up in the distractions of family, housework, or watching television instead of working; it can be a problem.**

   If you rewrote sentence 6 beginning with

   <u>Home-based workers must beware of</u>

   the next word should be

   (1) working
   (2) them
   (3) it
   (4) him or her
   (5) distractions

Items 6 to 9 refer to the following paragraph.

(1) In terms of costs, depression in America is as serious an illness as heart disease. (2) Every year approximately 11 million people suffers from depression. (3) As many as two-thirds of them are undiagnose and untreated. (4) The high cost of depression comes partly from the number of missed workdays and days patients spend in the hospital or at home. (5) Job productivity decrease by about 20 percent because of depression. (6) Their coworkers also feel the effects. (7) Indirectly related to depression are costs associated with programs for treatment of substance abuse, unnecessary medical tests, and even suicide. (8) The few people with depression which do seek medical advice go to physicians who are not psychiatrists. (9) These doctors incorrectly diagnose one out of every four patients. (10) And most health plans do not provide adequate coverage for mental health treatment.

6. Sentence 2: **Every year approximately 11 million people suffers from depression.**

What correction should be made to this sentence?

(1) change year approximately to year. Approximately
(2) replace people with of them
(3) change suffers to suffer
(4) change suffers to suffered
(5) no correction is necessary

7. Sentence 3: **As many as two-thirds of them are undiagnose and untreated.**

Which of the following is the best way to write the underlined portion of this sentence? If you think the original is the best way, choose option (1).

(1) are undiagnose and untreated
(2) were undiagnose and untreated
(3) be undiagnose and untreated
(4) are undiagnose and untreating
(5) are undiagnosed and untreated

8. Sentence 5: **Job productivity decrease by about 20 percent because of depression.**

What correction should be made to this sentence?

(1) insert is before decrease
(2) change decrease to decreased
(3) change decrease to decreases
(4) change decrease to will decrease
(5) replace decrease with rises

9. Sentence 8: **The few people with depression which do seek medical advice go to physicians who are not psychiatrists.**

What correction should be made to this sentence?

(1) replace which with who
(2) replace which with whom
(3) replace which with that
(4) change are to were
(5) change are to is

To check your answers, turn to page 236.

2 Using Language
R E V I E W

You've seen there's more to writing an essay than organizing, planning, and developing a good idea. You've learned the importance of using proper English to help your reader understand your essay and to recognize you as a writer who is in control of the language.

You now know that subjects must agree with verbs, and how to make sure they do. You've learned how to make subjects and verbs agree even when they appear in unusual positions in the sentence. That is, you can ensure subject and verb agreement when the verb precedes the subject or when many words appear in between subject and verb.

You've learned how to use verb phrases and how to maintain the correct verb tense throughout a sentence or a paragraph.

You also know about different kinds of pronouns or noun substitutes. You can choose the proper one for your sentence, making sure it agrees with the noun it replaces both in number and in person. That is, you know how to write plural pronouns to substitute for plural antecedents, and you know not to switch among first, second, and third person in midsentence or in the middle of paragraphs.

Finally, you know how to make sure your pronouns have clear antecedents that are easy for the reader to identify.

All of these points make your writing more clear and effective.

Key Terms to Review

antecedent	the noun that a pronoun substitutes for or refers to
gerund	present participle used in a sentence as a noun
infinitive	form of the verb that consists of the word *to* followed by the present tense form of the verb
irregular verb	verb that does not follow the normal pattern of English verbs
participle	a form of the main verb that follows a helping verb in a verb phrase
plural	more than one
pronoun	a word that substitutes for or refers to a noun
relative pronoun	does not replace a noun but refers to it
singular	one
subject-verb agreement	singular subjects take singular verbs, and plural subjects take plural verbs
verb phrase	a verb form with more than one word: a helping verb and some form of the main verb
verb tense	form of the verb that indicates the time of the action

EXERCISES

Directions: Choose the one best answer to each item.

Items 1 to 10 refer to the following paragraph.

(1) Nutritionists and doctors tell us that breakfast may be the most important meal of the day, yet many people skips this meal. (2) They say breakfast is too time-consuming or food is unappealing early in the morning. (3) They find many reasons skipping breakfast. (4) Nevertheless, studies show that people perform better at work and at school if you have eaten a nutritious breakfast. (5) Breakfast didn't have to take a lot of time. (6) In fact, we're now told not to eat the huge bacon-and-egg breakfasts of the past. (7) Those meals, who do take time to prepare, contain too much fat and cholesterol. (8) Lighter breakfasts is better. (9) A bowl of cereal with milk, a piece of toast, fruit, juice, and perhaps a cup of coffee provide a wholesome breakfast in very little time. (10) People who skip breakfast often experience a sudden attack of hunger midmorning. (11) He or she may satisfy this hunger quickly with something like donuts, potato chips, and canned soda. (12) It's high in calories and fat but low in nutritional value. (13) Even if it seem hard at first, it's important to try to eat a good breakfast.

1. Sentence 1: **Nutritionists and doctors tell us that breakfast may be the most important meal of the day, yet many people skips this meal.**

   What correction should be made to this sentence?

   (1) replace <u>us</u> with <u>you</u>
   (2) replace <u>meal</u> with <u>one</u>
   (3) change <u>skips</u> to <u>skip</u>
   (4) change <u>skips</u> to <u>skipping</u>
   (5) change <u>skips</u> to <u>skipped</u>

2. Sentence 2: **<u>They say</u> breakfast is too time-consuming or food is unappealing early in the morning.**

   Which of the following is the best way to write the underlined portion of this sentence? If you think the original is the best way, choose option (1).

   (1) They say
   (2) It says
   (3) He or she says
   (4) These experts
   (5) These people

3. Sentence 3: **They find many reasons skipping breakfast.**

   What correction should be made to this sentence?

   (1) replace <u>They</u> with <u>He or she</u>
   (2) replace <u>find</u> with <u>finds</u>
   (3) change <u>skipping</u> to <u>skipped</u>
   (4) change <u>skipping</u> to <u>to skip</u>
   (5) no correction is necessary

4. Sentence 4: **Nevertheless, studies show that people perform better at work and at school if you have eaten a nutritious breakfast.**

   If you rewrote sentence 4 beginning with
   <u>Nevertheless, studies show better performance at work and school from people</u>
   the next word should be

   (1) which
   (2) whom
   (3) who
   (4) that
   (5) skipping

5. Sentence 5: **Breakfast didn't have to take a lot of time.**

What correction should be made to this sentence?

(1) change <u>didn't</u> to <u>don't</u>
(2) change <u>didn't</u> to <u>doesn't</u>
(3) replace <u>didn't</u> with <u>won't</u>
(4) replace <u>didn't</u> with <u>does</u>
(5) replace <u>didn't</u> with <u>will</u>

6. Sentence 7: **Those meals, <u>who do take time to prepare</u>, contain too much fat and cholesterol.**

Which of the following is the best way to write the underlined portion of this sentence? If you think the original is the best way, choose option (1).

(1) who do take time to prepare
(2) which do take time to prepare
(3) who spend a lot of time preparing
(4) who prepare for a long time
(5) which are quick

7. Sentence 8: **Lighter breakfasts is better.**

What correction should be made to this sentence?

(1) insert <u>A</u> before <u>lighter</u>
(2) change <u>Lighter</u> to <u>Light</u>
(3) change <u>is</u> to <u>were</u>
(4) change <u>is</u> to <u>are</u>
(5) no correction is necessary

8. Sentence 11: **He or she may satisfy this hunger quickly with something like donuts, potato chips, and canned soda.**

What correction should be made to this sentence?

(1) replace <u>He or she</u> with <u>It</u>
(2) replace <u>He or she</u> with <u>One</u>
(3) replace <u>He or She</u> with <u>They</u>
(4) replace <u>He or She</u> with <u>We</u>
(5) replace <u>He or She</u> with <u>You</u>

9. Sentence 12: **It's high in calories and fat but low in nutritional value.**

What correction should be made to this sentence?

(1) replace <u>It's</u> with <u>This is</u>
(2) replace <u>It's</u> with <u>These foods are</u>
(3) replace <u>It's</u> with <u>Donuts, potato chips, and canned soda are</u>
(4) replace <u>It's</u> with <u>Which are</u>
(5) no correction is necessary

10. Sentence 13: **Even if it seem hard at first, it's important to try to eat a good breakfast.**

What correction should be made to this sentence?

(1) replace <u>it</u> with <u>they</u>
(2) replace <u>it</u> with <u>you</u>
(3) change <u>seem</u> to <u>seemed</u>
(4) change <u>seem</u> to <u>seeming</u>
(5) change <u>seem</u> to <u>seems</u>

<u>Items 11 to 18</u> refer to the following paragraph.

(1) Teenagers need ways to assert their independence. (2) One way was to drive a car. (3) Unfortunately, you don't always realize how powerful and dangerous a car is. (4) They see a car as a source of power and freedom who can get them places fast. (5) They forgot cars are like weapons that can cause serious injury or even kill. (6) Insurance companies charge high rates for teenage drivers. (7) Which suggests they are a high risk. (8) It might help if driver's licenses showed how much a person will understand the hazards of driving a car. (9) Then states could issue licenses only to those kids whom understand how serious driving is. (10) Teenagers must remember that you and your car are not the only ones on the road.

11. Sentence 2: **One way was to drive a car.**

What correction should be made to this sentence?

(1) change <u>was</u> to <u>will be</u>
(2) change <u>was</u> to <u>be</u>
(3) change <u>was</u> to <u>being</u>
(4) change <u>was</u> to <u>is</u>
(5) change <u>was</u> to <u>are</u>

12. Sentence 3: **Unfortunately, you don't always realize how powerful and dangerous a car is.**

What correction should be made to this sentence?

(1) replace <u>you</u> with <u>we</u>
(2) replace <u>you</u> with <u>they</u>
(3) replace <u>a car</u> with <u>it</u>
(4) replace <u>a car is</u> with <u>they are</u>
(5) no correction is necessary

13. Sentence 4: **They see a car as a source of power and freedom who can get them places fast.**

What correction should be made to this sentence?

(1) replace <u>They</u> with <u>He or she</u>
(2) replace <u>They</u> with <u>We</u>
(3) replace <u>who</u> with <u>whom</u>
(4) replace <u>who</u> with <u>that</u>
(5) replace <u>freedom who</u> with <u>freedom. Who</u>

14. Sentence 5: **They forgot cars are like weapons that can cause serious injury or even kill.**

What correction should be made to this sentence?

(1) replace <u>They</u> with <u>He</u>
(2) replace <u>They</u> with <u>Someone</u>
(3) change <u>forgot</u> to <u>forget</u>
(4) change <u>forgot</u> to <u>forgetting</u>
(5) change <u>forgot</u> to <u>forgotten</u>

15. Sentences 6 and 7: **Insurance companies charge high rates for teenage drivers. Which suggests they are a high risk.**

If you rewrote sentences 6 and 7 beginning with

<u>Because insurance companies believe teenage drivers are a high risk,</u>

the next word(s) should be

(1) charging
(2) you
(3) they
(4) the companies
(5) charges

16. Sentence 8: **It might help if driver's licenses showed how much a person will understand the hazards of driving a car.**

What correction should be made to this sentence?

(1) replace <u>It</u> with <u>They</u>
(2) replace <u>driver's licenses</u> with <u>they</u>
(3) replace <u>a person</u> with <u>they</u>
(4) change <u>will understand</u> to <u>understand</u>
(5) change <u>will understand</u> to <u>understands</u>

17. Sentence 9: **Then states could issue licenses only to those kids whom understand how serious driving is.**

What correction should be made to this sentence?

(1) replace <u>states</u> with <u>they</u>
(2) replace <u>states</u> with <u>it</u>
(3) change <u>whom</u> to <u>who</u>
(4) replace <u>whom</u> with <u>that</u>
(5) replace <u>whom</u> with <u>which</u>

18. Sentence 10: **Teenagers must remember that <u>you and your car</u> are not the only ones on the road.**

Which of the following is the best way to write the underlined portion of this sentence? If you think the original is the best way, choose option (1).

(1) you and your car
(2) they and their cars
(3) other cars
(4) anyone else's car
(5) many cars

(1) The advent of railroads goes hand in hand with the Industrial Revolution in England in the 19th century. (2) Although England had good transportation systems on water and roads, the Industrial Revolution increases the need to transport raw materials and manufactured goods. (3) The steam engine, a new power source that powered industrial machinery and ships, will help solve the transportation problem. (4) In 1825, George Stephenson will build a steam locomotive that could carry heavy loads long distances by rail. (5) Rail transport was not new. (6) Horse-drawn cars that moved along rails had been use in British coal mines for a long time. (7) Stephenson's accomplishment was to combine the concept of rail transport with the steam engine. (8) The first railroad linked two English mining towns, but by 1845 rail lines linked every large city and industrial region in Britain. (9) Its expansion enhanced the expansion of the Industrial Revolution.

19. Sentence 2: **Although England had good transportation systems on water and roads, the Industrial Revolution increases the need to transport raw materials and manufactured goods.**

What correction should be made to this sentence?

(1) change <u>had</u> to <u>will have</u>
(2) insert <u>has</u> before <u>had</u>
(3) change <u>increases</u> to <u>increase</u>
(4) change <u>increases</u> to <u>increased</u>
(5) change <u>increases</u> to <u>increasing</u>

20. Sentence 3: **The steam engine, a new power source that powered industrial machinery and ships, will help solve the transportation problem.**

If you rewrote sentence 3 beginning with

<u>The steam engine was a new power source that</u>

the next word should be

(1) helps
(2) helped
(3) will
(4) powerful
(5) powering

21. Sentence 4: **In 1825, George <u>Stephenson will build</u> a steam locomotive that could carry heavy loads long distances by rail.**

Which of the following is the best way to write the underlined portion of this sentence? If you think the original is the best way, choose option (1).

(1) Stephenson will build
(2) Stephenson building
(3) Stephenson builded
(4) Stephenson was building
(5) Stephenson built

22. Sentence 6: **Horse-drawn cars that moved along rails had been use in British coal mines for a long time.**

What correction should be made to this sentence?

(1) replace <u>that</u> with <u>who</u>
(2) change <u>moved</u> to <u>will move</u>
(3) change <u>been</u> to <u>be</u>
(4) change <u>use</u> to <u>used</u>
(5) change <u>use</u> to <u>using</u>

23. Sentence 9: **<u>Its expansion</u> enhanced the expansion of the Industrial Revolution.**

Which of the following is the best way to write the underlined portion of this sentence? If you think the original is the best way, choose option (1).

(1) Its expansion
(2) Expanding this
(3) Expansion of rail lines
(4) To expand it
(5) Their expansion

To check your answers, turn to page 236.

Answers and Explanations

Lesson 1: Does the Verb Match the Subject?

Exercise 1 (page 172)

1. was
2. cheer
3. warn
4. confuse
5. takes
6. entertain
7. help
8. intimidate
9. ban
10. make

11. Charles *plays* cards with his friends and sometimes he *wins.* Charles is singular, so the verbs must be singular.

12. Michelle *seems* to win every time she *plays. Michelle* is a singular subject and takes singular verbs.

13. Correct

14. Correct

15. Mr. Chan *hates* long lines, and becomes impatient in them. A singular subject *(Mr. Chan)* takes a singular verb.

16. The students *study* together for every exam. The plural subject *(students)* requires a plural verb.

17. Correct

18. Lectures *bore* me. The plural subject *(lectures)* takes a plural verb.

19. Mr. and Mrs. Jen *love* school and *are* the first people in class every day. The plural subject *(Mr. and Mrs. Jen)* takes a plural verb.

20. The account clerk *hands* out the paychecks and makes everyone happy. The singular subject *(account clerk)* takes a singular verb.

21. **(1) change is to are** Option (1) has a plural subject *(strikes)* that requires a plural verb. Options (2) and (3) do not correct for subject-verb agreement. Options (4) and (5) create fragments.

22. **(2) negotiation attempts fail** Option (2) has a plural subject *(attempts)* that requires a plural verb. Options (1) and (3) do not correct for subject-verb agreement; options (4) and (5) change the meaning of the sentence.

23. **(2) change stops to stop** Option (2) has a plural subject *(they)* that requires a plural verb. Options (1) and (4) don't correct for subject-verb agreement, and option (3) creates a fragment.

24. **(4) change are to is** Option (4) has a singular subject *(hope)* that requires a singular verb. The other options don't correct for subject-verb agreement.

Write on Target
Sentences will vary. Here are five samples:

1. Three riders handle their horses expertly.
2. They answer every question on the form.
3. Mike and Jeff dive from the highest board.
4. Sally competes with other bowlers.
5. I don't like vegetables, but I do eat them.

Exercise 2 (page 174)

1. Congress votes
2. You go
3. news looks
4. council chooses
5. They ask
6. roller coaster scares

7. Either my brothers or my sister *washes* the car. When sentences contain either/or, the verb matches the subject closest to it (in this case *sister,* which is singular).

8. Correct

9. We *prefer* movies to books. A plural subject requires a plural verb.

10. Shawn and Cherie *solve* problems easily. A compound subject is plural and takes a plural verb.

11. Correct

12. Neither my grandparents nor my uncle *drives* a car. With neither/nor, make the verb match the subject closest to the *nor. Uncle* is singular.

13. The entire company *receives* a yearly bonus. Although several people may be involved, the word *company* is singular and takes a singular verb.

14. The jury *has* to listen carefully to the evidence. *Jury* is also a singular subject, even though it is made up of twelve people.

15. They *rent* their house. A plural subject takes a plural verb.

16. She *doesn't* like broccoli, but he does. A singular subject *(she)* takes a singular verb *(does not).*

17. **(3) the dental group uses** Option (3) is correct because *group* is a singular noun that takes a singular verb. Options (1) and (2) don't correct for subject-verb agreement. Option (4) changes the meaning of the sentence. Option (5) creates fragments.

18. (2) change <u>hopes</u> to <u>hope</u>   Option (2) uses a plural verb form with the plural subject *(they)*. The other options don't correct subject-verb agreement.

19. (3) also want to promote   Option (3) uses a plural verb *(wants)* to match a plural subject *(members)*. Options (1), (2), and (4) do not correct for subject-verb agreement; and option (5) changes the meaning of the sentence.

Exercise 3 (page 177)

1. She says
2. No one knows
3. I am
4. Most run
5. Everybody was
6. **(4) change <u>has</u> to <u>have</u>**   Option (4) matches a plural verb *(have)* with a plural subject *(Holly and Kent)*. Option (1) does not correct for subject-verb agreement. Option (2) is incorrect punctuation for a compound sentence. Option (3) is an incorrect verb form, and option (5) creates sentence fragments.
7. **(4) change <u>suggest</u> to <u>suggests</u>**   Option (4) matches the singular verb *(suggests)* with a singular subject *(Holly)*. Option (2) is incorrect punctuation for a compound sentence. Options (1), (3), and (5) don't correct for subject-verb agreement.

Connections

Sentences will vary. Here are some sample sentences:

1. Nearly **everyone** (that is, 77 percent) **travels** primarily by motor vehicle on vacation.
2. **Each** vacation **lasts** an average of 4.4 nights.
3. **Few** Americans **travel** outside the United States for vacation.
4. **Many** Americans **travel** to the South, which is in the Eastern time zone.

GED Test Preview (page 178)

1. **(4) change <u>is</u> to <u>are</u>**   Option (4) matches a plural verb, *are,* with a plural subject, *days*. Options (1) and (3) create fragments. Option (2) doesn't correct for subject-verb agreement.
2. **(5) get their hair cut**   Option (5) matches a compound subject *(men and women)* with a plural verb *(get)*. The other options do not correct for subject-verb agreement.
3. **(2) change <u>is</u> to <u>are</u>**   Option (2) matches a plural verb *(are)* with a plural subject *(shops)*. Options (1), (4), and (5) don't correct for subject-verb agreement. Option (3) creates fragments.

4. (5) change <u>requires</u> to <u>require</u>   Option (5) matches a plural verb *(require)* with a plural subject *(places)*. Option (1) creates a fragment. Options (2) and (4) don't correct for subject-verb agreement. Option (3) is incorrect because *these* suggests more than one place.

5. (2) If they want   Option (2) matches a plural verb *(want)* with a plural subject *(they)*. The other options do not correct for subject-verb agreement.

6. (1) replace <u>need are</u> with <u>need is</u>   Option (1) matches the singular subject with the singular verb. Option (2) creates a fragment, and the other options do not correct for subject-verb agreement.

7. (4) Manufacturers sometimes overproduce   Option (4) matches the plural verb with the plural subject. Option (5) creates fragments. The other options do not correct for subject-verb agreement.

8. (5) change <u>don't</u> to <u>doesn't</u>   Option (5) matches a singular verb *(does not)* with a singular subject *(damage)*. Option (4) creates a fragment, and the other options do not correct for subject-verb agreement.

9. (2) change <u>negotiates</u> to <u>negotiate</u>   Option (2) matches a plural subject *(discounters)* with a plural verb *(negotiate)*. The other options do not correct for subject-verb agreement.

10. (2) is   Option (2) is the correct form of the verb *to be* for this sentence. Options (1) and (5) change the meaning of the sentence, option (3) uses *be* alone as a verb, and option (4) doesn't agree with the singular subject.

Lesson 2: Placing Verbs in Sentences

Exercise 1 (page 182)

1. *Nancy,* along with her husband and children, *enjoys* hiking.
2. *One* of the most troubling social problems *is* homelessness.
3. *Not knowing* the whereabouts of her children *worries* Stephanie.
4. *Tim and the dog exercise* every morning at dawn.
5. Usually, *each* of the players *scores* points during a game.
6. *Taking notes,* as well as listening, *helps* you learn the material.
7. The *representatives* from the bank *explain* the new interest rates very clearly.

8. (2) change arise to arises Option (2) matches a singular verb with a singular subject, *one*. Options (1), (3), and (5) don't correct for subject-verb agreement. Option (4) creates a fragment.

9. (5) change keep to keeps Option (5) matches a singular verb to a singular subject *(hanging paper)*. Options (1), (3), and (4) do not correct for subject-verb agreement. Option (2) creates a fragment.

10. (3) A potential for more jobs makes Jaime want Option (3) matches a singular verb *(makes)* with a singular subject *(potential)*. The other options don't correct for subject-verb agreement.

11. (5) change raises to raise Option (5) uses a plural verb *(raise)* to agree with a plural subject *(they)*. Options (1) and (4) lack subject-verb agreement, option (2) creates a fragment, and option (3) inserts a comma before a dependent clause.

12. (4) asked people to guess how many marbles there were Option (4) uses a plural verb *(were)* to agree with a plural subject *(marbles)*. Options (1), (2), and (5) lack subject-verb agreement, and option (3) changes the meaning of the sentence.

13. (3) change are to is Option (3) uses a singular verb *(is)* to agree with a singular subject *(thing)*. Option (1) lacks subject-verb agreement, option (2) doesn't correct for subject-verb agreement, and option (4) creates a fragment.

Exercise 2 (page 184)

1. There *are* too many leaves to rake in one afternoon. (subject = leaves)

2. *Do* both of them want to go to the game? (subject = both)

3. In the cupboard *are* all the things you need to bake a cake. (subject = things)

4. Upstairs *are* two more bedrooms. (subject = bedrooms)

5. Here *is* the information you asked for. (subject = information)

Write on Target

Sentences will vary. Here are four samples:

1. Here comes the drum major.
2. There is no room in the back seat.
3. Does everyone see the Big Dipper in the sky?
4. Across from the gardens is a great basketball court.

6. (2) change lurk to lurks Option (2) matches a singular verb with a singular subject *(danger)*. Option (1) makes *mountains* the subject, and then the sentence doesn't make sense. Option (3) changes the meaning, option (4) uses a participle as a verb, and option (5) doesn't correct for subject-verb agreement.

7. (1) replace is with are Option (1) matches a plural verb with a plural subject, *hazards*. The other options do not correct for subject-verb agreement..

8. (5) no correction is necessary

Connections

1. How long **are** women born in 1970 expected to live? 74.6 years

2. Women born in 1980 **have** a life expectancy of 78.4 years.

3. How many years **is** a man born in 1970 expected to live? 67.0 years

GED Test Preview (page 186)

1. (2) Change is to are Option (2) uses a plural verb to agree with the plural subject *(ways)*. Option (1) changes the meaning of the sentence. Options (3), (4), and (5) do not correct for subject-verb agreement.

2. (1) change are to is Option (1) uses a singular verb to agree with a singular subject *(one)*. Option (2) uses *be* alone as a verb, option (3) is not a correct infinitive form, option (4) doesn't correct for subject-verb agreement, and option (5) shifts to past tense.

3. (2) change prefers to prefer Option (2) matches a plural verb to a plural subject *(others)*. The other options do not affect subject-verb agreement.

4. (3) use Option (3) uses a plural verb form to agree with a plural subject *(cooks)*. Options (1), (2), and (4) do not correct for subject-verb agreement, and option (5) changes the meaning of the sentence.

5. (4) A well-stocked kitchen has many kinds Option (4) restructures the sentence to put the subject and verb closer to the beginning. Options (1) and (3) lack subject-verb agreement, option (2) lacks a verb, and option (5) changes the meaning of the sentence.

6. (4) change goes to go Option (4) matches a plural verb with a plural subject *(herbs and spices)*. Option (1) incorrectly uses *be* by itself, option (3) creates a fragment, and the other options do not affect subject-verb agreement.

7. (1) change refer to refers Option (1) matches a singular verb to a singular subject *(History)*. Options (2) and (3) do not correct for subject-verb agreement. Option (4) creates a fragment, and option (5) doesn't make sense.

8. (5) The symptoms include high fever Option (5) matches a plural verb with a plural subject *(symptoms)*. The other options do not correct for subject-verb agreement.

9. (3) change affects to affect Option (3) matches a plural verb to a plural subject (*variations*). Options (1), (2), and (5) have no effect on subject-verb agreement. Option (4) does not correct for subject-verb agreement.

10. (4) change afflicts to afflict Option (4) matches a plural verb with a plural subject (*variations*). Option (1) doesn't affect subject-verb agreement, option (2) incorrectly inserts a comma, and option (3) doesn't correct for subject-verb agreement.

Lesson 3: Recognizing Parts of Verbs

Exercise 1 (page 190)

1. persisted—past
2. planning—present
3. helped—past
4. completed—past
5. beginning—present
6. been—past
7. gone—past
8. sitting—present
9. entered—past
10. returning—present

11. (4) insert had before worn Option (4) completes a verb phrase by adding a helper to a past participle. Options (1) and (2) don't affect the verb phrase. Option (3) removes the verb from a clause, and option (5) is the wrong participle.

12. (4) she should not have gone Option (4) adds the necessary helpers to a participle to complete a verb phrase. Options (1), (2), and (5) are incomplete verb phrases, and option (3) changes the meaning of the sentence.

13. (2) change plan to planning Option (2) uses a present participle to complete the verb and to show future action. Options (1) and (4) create fragments, and option (3) incorrectly uses a past participle.

14. (1) change Start to Starting Option (1) uses a gerund as the subject of the sentence so that the sentence makes sense. Option (2) changes the meaning of the sentence, options (3) and (4) use incorrect verb forms, and option (5) changes an adjective to a verb.

15. (5) you should have paid attention Option (5) uses a past participle to complete the verb. Options (1), (2), and (3) use incorrect verb forms, and option (4) omits the participle.

Exercise 2 (page 194)

1. saw
2. had ridden
3. have given

4. done
5. eaten
6. drunk
7. ran
8. was
9. travelled
10. asked
11. got (or gotten)
12. swum
13. brought
14. listened
15. rode
16. eaten
17. was
18. saw
19. laughed
20. did

Write on Target

Sentences will vary. Here are some sample sentences:

1. The visitors had run to catch the bus. (regular)
2. Everyone but Cheryl had finished. (regular)
3. The were gone by the afternoon. (irregular)
4. He hadn't seen anything unusual. (irregular)
5. The guests had done all the dishes before they left. (irregular)

21. (2) change became to become Option (2) uses the correct past participle; *became* is the past tense form. Option (1) doesn't correct the past participle, option (3) is the wrong tense, and options (4) and (5) are not complete infinitives.

22. (1) change begun to began Option (1) uses the correct past tense form of the verb *begin*. Option (2) is not a correct past tense verb form, option (3) uses an incorrect past participle, and option (4) changes the meaning of the sentence.

23. (2) change drunk to drank Option (2) uses the correct past tense form of the verb *drink*. Option (1) does not use the correct past tense form of *drink*. Options (3) and (4) use incorrect forms of the verb *eat*.

4. (5) no correction is necessary

Connections

Sentences will vary. Here are some sample sentences:

1. Ninety-eight percent of American households **have bought** televisions.
2. In 1990, 59 percent of U.S. households decided **to buy** cable TV.

3. Based on 1990 data, it's probable that about 93 percent of U.S. households **are using** telephones today.

4. In 1990, almost every household in the U.S. **had** one or more radios.

5. Seventy-two percent of the households in the U.S. were able **to use** VCRs in 1990.

GED Test Preview (page 196)

1. (4) insert <u>was</u> before <u>established</u>   Option (4) adds a helper to a past participle to complete the verb phrase. Options (1) and (2) are not correct participle forms of *to know*. Option (3) is not a correct helping verb form, and option (5) is a present, not a past, participle.

2. (5) change <u>surprise</u> to <u>surprised</u>   Option (5) uses the correct past participle form of *to surprise*. Option (1) doesn't have subject-verb agreement, option (2) uses a participle by itself, and options (3) and (4) are not correct participle forms.

3. (2) the agency is not allowed to spy   Option (2) contains a verb phrase, *is allowed,* with the correct past participle. Option (1) is not a correct participle form, option (3) is not a correct infinitive form, and options (4) and (5) change the meaning of the sentence.

4. (3) change <u>appoint</u> to <u>appointed</u>   Option (3) uses the correct past tense form of *to appoint*. Option (1) creates a fragment. Option (2) uses a noun where a verb belongs. Option (4) changes the meaning of the sentence, and option (5) is not a correct infinitive form.

5. (3) violated   Option (3) is the correct past participle to follow the helping verb *had*. The only other option that is a past participle is option (4), but it changes the meaning of the sentence.

6. (5) change <u>cutting</u> to <u>cut</u>   Option (5) uses the correct infinitive form. Option (1) is an incorrect verb form, option (2) uses a participle by itself, and options (3) and (4) are incorrect infinitive forms.

7. (3) lost   Option (3) is the correct past participle of *to lose*. Options (1) and (2) are not past participle forms, and options (4) and (5) change the meaning of the sentence.

8. (2) change <u>be</u> to <u>been</u>   Option (2) is the correct past participle of *to be*. Option (1) does not have subject-verb agreement; option (3) is a present, not a past, participle; option (4) doesn't correct the faulty participle; and option (5) is not a past tense verb form.

9. (4) change <u>put</u> to <u>putting</u>   Option (4) uses the correct participle. Option (1) is not the correct participle, option (2) is an incorrect verb form, option (3) eliminates the required helper in a verb phrase, and option (5) does not use the correct form of the past participle of *to put*.

10. (4) Pasta with fresh vegetables has become one   Option (4) uses the correct past participle. Option (1) uses a past tense, not a past participle, form. Option (2) does not have subject-verb agreement or a correct participle, option (3) lacks subject-verb agreement, and option (5) uses *be* by itself as a verb.

Lesson 4: When Does the Action Take Place?

Exercise 1 (page 200)

1. <u>she heard</u>/crawled
2. <u>Whenever it rains</u>/feel
3. <u>by the time</u>/had walked
4. <u>last year</u>/refused
5. <u>currently</u>/receive
6. <u>Now</u>/am
7. <u>Last year</u>/had
8. <u>After the game ended</u>/cheered
9. <u>Next winter</u>/plan
10. <u>For the past three months</u>/worked

11. (4) change <u>will go</u> to <u>went</u>   Option (4) maintains the past tense in the sentence. Option (1) creates a fragment, option (2) is the wrong participle, option (3) is the wrong tense and does not have subject-verb agreement, and option (5) uses a participle alone as a verb.

12. (3) change <u>was</u> to <u>were</u>   Option (3) uses a plural verb form to agree with the plural subject, *packs*. Option (1) shifts to present tense, options (2) and (5) lack subject-verb agreement, and option (4) shifts to future tense.

13. (5) no correction is necessary

14. (4) include   Option (4) uses a present tense verb, which is consistent with the rest of the paragraph. The other options use incorrect tenses.

15. (3) change <u>will help</u> to <u>helps</u>   Option (3) uses a present tense verb, which is consistent with the rest of the paragraph. Option (1) removes the gerund that serves as the subject of the sentence, option (2) uses an incorrect infinitive form, option (4) uses the past tense, and option (5) creates a fragment.

16. (2) change <u>were</u> to <u>is</u>   Option (2) uses a present tense singular verb to agree with the singular subject (*sense*). Option (1) creates a fragment, option (3) lacks subject-verb agreement, and option (4) uses the past tense.

Exercise 2 (page 202)

1. past
2. future
3. past
4. future
5. present
6. past
7. present
8. future
9. future
10. past

Write on Target

Sentences will vary. Here are some sample sentences:

1. Yesterday I decided to buy a guitar.

2. When I get old, I will want to be able to play a musical instrument.

3. The other day, my friend started taking piano lessons.

4. Next summer, I will play in a country-western band.

5. Right now, I practice with my brother's guitar.

6. When I was at my brother's house, I asked him if he would sell me his guitar.

7. Whenever I hear loud noises, I think about taking drum lessons.

8. At this time tomorrow, I will be home.

9. For the next three months, I will be very enthusiastic about guitar playing.

10. The last time I started music lessons, I ended up selling my guitar to my brother.

11. Last summer, the Orangerie Produce Co. <u>had</u> an employee picnic. The picnic <u>was</u> a great success, thanks to the Planning Committee. The committee members <u>had worked</u> for weeks by the time picnic day <u>arrived</u>. The employees <u>had played</u> games, <u>danced</u>, <u>swum</u>, and <u>eaten</u> hot dogs and apple pie by the end of the day. Everyone <u>hopes</u> there <u>will be</u> another picnic next year.

12. **(5) no correction is necessary**

13. **(2) took**   Option (2) maintains the past tense in the sentence. Option (1) shifts to present tense. Option (3) uses a participle by itself as a verb. Option (4) shifts to future tense, and option (5) lacks subject-verb agreement.

14. **(3) replace <u>makes</u> with <u>will make</u>**   Option (3) uses the future tense in response to the clue *next time*. Option (1) lacks subject-verb agreement, option (2) uses a participle by itself as a verb, option (4) uses the wrong tense and an inaccurate participle, and option (5) uses the wrong tense.

Connections

Paragraphs will vary. Here is a sample paragraph:

Americans **spent** their money differently in 1990 than they **did** in 1980. In 1980, we **spent** about $18 billion on entertainment technology, which **includes** video and audio products, computer equipment and musical instruments. In 1990, however, the amount spent on these products nearly **tripled** to about $52 billion. One possible reason for this spending change **is** the development of new technology such as VCRs and CD players. Today, people **spend** more on movie videos and compact discs than they **did** in 1980—especially, perhaps, people in the West, who **spend** more money on entertainment than people in any other region of the country. It **seems** that the more that technology **is** available, the more money we **will spend.**

GED Test Preview (page 204)

1. **(3) change <u>will turn</u> to <u>turned</u>**   Option (3) uses the past tense in response to the clue *Last night*. Option (1) uses a participle by itself as a verb, options (2) and (4) use an incorrect tense, and option (5) incorrectly uses a verb phrase for a completed action that does not continue into the present.

2. **(1) change <u>sleeps</u> to <u>slept</u>**   Option (1) maintains the past tense that has been established in the paragraph. Option (2) shifts to future tense, option (3) uses a verb phrase for an action that does not continue into the present, and option (4) lacks subject-verb agreement.

3. **(3) change <u>broke</u> to <u>broken</u>**   Option (3) is the correct past participle for *to break*. Option (1) shifts to present tense, option (2) uses a participle by itself as a verb, option (4) uses an incorrect participle form, and option (5) shifts to future tense.

4. **(1) change <u>huddles</u> to <u>huddled</u>**   Option (1) maintains the past tense that has been used throughout the paragraph. The other options use incorrect tenses.

5. **(3) change <u>done</u> to <u>did</u>**   Option (3) maintains the past tense that has been used throughout the paragraph. Options (1), (2), and (4) switch tenses. Option (5) is the incorrect form for an infinitive.

6. **(4) had**   Option (4) starts with the past perfect form of the verb *to be*. No other option correctly uses the past perfect tense. You need a perfect tense because the action was completed after another action had taken place.

7. **(3) poured into the country, learned American ways, and became part of**   Option (3) maintains past tense throughout the sentence. The tenses of the other options are inconsistent.

8. (2) replace <u>has change</u> with <u>has changed</u> Option (2) uses the correct past participle for *to change*. Options (1) and (3) switch tense, and option (4) lacks subject-verb agreement.

9. (4) they cling with pride to Option (4) maintains the present tense that is used throughout the second paragraph. Options (1) and (5) switch to past tense, and the other options use incorrect verb forms.

10. (1) change <u>gave</u> to <u>give</u> Option (1) maintains the present tense that is used throughout the paragraph. Option (2) shifts tense, and options (3), (4), and (5) are incorrect infinitive forms.

Lesson 5: Looking at Noun Substitutes

Exercise 1 (page 207)

1. their—ownership
2. one—indefinite people
3. she—specific people
4. yourself—reflects back
5. Everyone—indefinite people
6. Our—ownership
7. they—specific people
8. No one—indefinite people
9. **(3) Gandhi; he died** Option (3) uses a pronoun to refer to Gandhi the second time in a compound sentence. The semicolon is correct because the ideas in the two clauses are closely linked. Option (1) awkwardly repeats the noun, option (2) changes the meaning of the clause, and options (4) and (5) incorrectly use participles as verbs in clauses.
10. **(3) replace <u>these men's</u> with <u>their</u>** Option (3) uses a pronoun to avoid repeating the noun. Option (1) creates a fragment, option (2) uses nouns to replace nouns, option (4) removes the subject from the sentence, and option (5) uses a participle as a verb.
11. **(5) no correction is necessary**
12. **(1) replace <u>These 35 million Americans</u> with <u>They</u>** Option (1) uses a pronoun so that the writer doesn't have to repeat the long subject from the preceding sentence. Option (2) lacks subject-verb agreement, option (3) shifts to the past tense, and option (4) is incorrect because it implies ownership of winter nights and days.
13. **(5) change <u>loses</u> to <u>lose</u>** Option (5) uses a plural verb *(lose)* to agree with a plural subject *(victims)*. Option (1) is not a participle, option (2) creates a fragment, option (3) lacks subject-verb agreement, and option (4) shifts to the past tense.

14. (2) They control the symptoms Option (2) corrects the fragment by giving the sentence a subject. Option (1) is a fragment, option (3) doesn't make sense, and options (4) and (5) change the meaning of the sentence.

15. (5) no correction is necessary

Exercise 2 (page 212)

1. Manuel and Umeki agreed to share *their* study notes with each other.
2. A baby seal can swim by *itself* right away.
3. The basketball team lost *its* third game in a row.
4. Give the paper to *me* when you finish.
5. This piece of cake is just for Larry and *me*.

Write on Target

Paragraphs will vary. Here is a sample paragraph:

Ernest was a promising football player. He could run fast and pass the ball well. He could also catch it easily. His large size made him a good blocker too. Ernest practiced hard and was proud of himself.

6. **(3) you might like to shop** Option (3) maintains the pronoun *you* that already has been used in the sentence. Option (1) switches from second person to an indefinite pronoun. Options (2) and (4) switch from second person to third person. Option (5) shifts to first person.
7. **(4) replace <u>One</u> with <u>You</u>** Option (4) maintains second person pronoun consistency in the sentence. The other options shift from second person.
8. **(4) replace <u>it</u> with <u>them</u>** Option (4) uses a plural pronoun *(them)* to match a plural antecedent *(clothes)*. Options (1), (2), and (3) switch pronouns from third person in midsentence. Option (5) uses a personal pronoun *(him)* to match a noun that is not a person *(clothes)*.
9. **(5) replace <u>our</u> with <u>your</u>** Option (5) maintains second person in the sentence. The other options change the meaning of the sentence and do not correct the mismatched pronoun *our*.
10. **(2) replace <u>She's</u> with <u>They've</u>** Option (2) uses the plural pronoun *they* to match the plural antecedent *women*. Option (1) uses the wrong pronoun, option (3) creates a fragment, and options (4) and (5) use participles as verbs.
11. **(3) replace <u>it</u> with <u>they</u>** Option (3) uses the plural pronoun *they* to match the plural antecedent *rules*. Option (1) is not a participle, option (2) incorrectly places a comma before a dependent clause, and option (4) inserts an ambiguous pronoun for *women*.

12. (5) serve as inspiration and models for their daughters Option (5) uses the correct pronoun *(their)* to match the antecedent *inductees.* Option (1) uses an incorrect pronoun, option (2) creates a fragment, option (3) shifts to past tense, and option (4) changes the meaning of the sentence.

Connections

Paragraphs will vary. Here is a sample paragraph:

I am not a parent; however, my experience with my own parents was similar to the one described in the poem, "Yeah, You're Right. I'm Not your 'Real' Father." Like the child in the poem, I did not always recognize the things my parents did for me. My parents fed, clothed, and housed me; they gave me love and support as well. I often felt that I deserved even more than they gave me. Like the child in the poem, I asked for expensive things and got angry when my parents wouldn't buy them for me. Now that I am an adult, I recognize all the sacrifices my parents made for me. I understand how difficult parenthood must be.

GED Test Preview (page 214)

1. (4) replace you with they Option (4) uses the third person pronoun to agree with the antecedent *people.* Option (1) creates a fragment, option (2) changes the meaning of the sentence, option (3) doesn't match the pronoun to the antecedent, and option (5) has no effect on pronoun-antecedent agreement.

2. (4) Their concerns include Option (4) uses a pronoun to agree with the antecedent *gerontologists* in the preceding sentence. Options (1) and (2) switch from third to first person, option (3) shifts from plural to singular, and option (5) shifts to second person in midparagraph.

3. (2) replace one's with its Option (2) uses the pronoun *its* to match the collective noun *generation.* Option (1) doesn't correct for pronoun-antecedent agreement, option (3) uses a plural pronoun for a singular antecedent, option (4) shifts to second person, and option (5) doesn't have subject-verb agreement.

4. (5) but we must face it Option (5) uses the singular pronoun *it* to agree with the singular antecedent *problem.* Option (2) shifts to second person and continues to use a plural pronoun, options (1) and (3) use a plural pronoun, and option (4) shifts to second person.

5. (4) replace they with we Option (4) maintains the first-person pronoun used in the preceding sentence. Option (1) uses a plural pronoun *(they)* for a singular antecedent *(problem).* Option (2) uses a personal pronoun for an nonhuman antecedent, option (3) doesn't agree with the verb or the antecedent, and option (5) uses a plural pronoun with a singular antecedent.

6. (2) borrow Option (2) completes the correct infinitive to maintain the meaning of the original sentence. The other options do not complete infinitives.

7. (4) replace it with them Option (4) uses a plural pronoun for a plural antecedent *(products).* Options (1) and (2) lack subject-verb agreement, and option (3) changes the meaning of the sentence.

8. (2) earn money that they use to buy things Option (2) uses a plural pronoun *(they)* for a plural antecedent *(people).* Option (1) uses a singular pronoun, option (3) shifts to second person, option (4) shifts to first person, and option (5) awkwardly repeats the noun.

9. (3) change You're to They're Option (3) maintains third person that has been used throughout the paragraph. Options (1) and (2) incorrectly shift to first person, option (4) shifts to singular, and option (5) shifts to a singular nonhuman pronoun.

10. (3) replace its with their Option (3) uses a plural pronoun *(their)* for a plural antecedent *(consumers).* Option (1) shifts to second person, option (2) shifts to first person, and option (4) uses a singular pronoun.

Lesson 6: Does the Pronoun Fit the Rest of the Sentence?

Exercise 1 (page 217)

1. Everyone showed patriotism by saluting the flag.

2. As soon as Peggy felt better, she invited Linda to visit.

3. (3) During these industrially productive years Option (3) corrects the pronoun *(they),* which lacks a clear antecedent. The other options change the meaning of the sentence.

4. (4) people selfishly pursued money Option (4) uses a noun *(people)* instead of the pronoun *them,* which has no clear antecedent. The other options lack clear antecedents.

Exercise 2 (page 219)

1. that—The pronoun has a nonhuman antecedent.
2. who—The pronoun has a human antecedent.
3. who—The pronoun has a human antecedent.
4. Whom—The pronoun is used in object position, (substitute *him*).
5. that—The pronoun has a nonhuman antecedent.
6. Whoever—The pronoun is used in actor position (substitute *he*).
7. who—The pronoun has a human antecedent.
8. who—The pronoun is used as the actor in a clause (substitute *he*).

Write on Target

1. I give the message to *whoever* answers the phone.

2. I like sports *that* have a lot of action.

3. Marta ia a person *who* loves cats.

9. (2) replace <u>that</u> with <u>who</u>   Option (2) uses a relative pronoun that matches a human antecedent. Option (1) is incorrect because it uses the object rather than the subject form of the pronoun, option (3) uses a pronoun for a nonhuman antecedent, option (4) shifts to second person, and option (5) shifts to first person.

10. (3) change <u>whom</u> to <u>who</u>   Option (3) recognizes the human antecedent and correctly uses the subject form of the relative pronoun. Option (1) requires *and* later in the sentence (after relationships); options (2) and (4) use pronouns for a nonhuman antecedent.

11. (4) problems that seem   Option (4) is correct because the antecedent *problems* takes the relative pronoun *that*. Options (1), (2), and (3) do not correct the problem with the fragment. Option (5) assumes a human antecedent.

Connections

Sentences will vary. Here are some sample sentences:

1. More women **who** are 18 and over watch news programs than men of the same age group.

2. The number of newspapers **that** are distributed in the morning is greater than the number distributed in the evening.

3. The audience **that** watches situation comedies is larger than the audience **that** watches news programs.

4. Evening newspapers, **which** were more popular in 1970 than morning newspapers, have declined in popularity.

GED Test Preview (page 220)

1. (2) Because they find it convenient,   Option (2) is correct because it clears up the vague pronoun reference. Option (1) is incorrect because the reader can't tell what *their* refers to. Option (3) changes the meaning of the sentence, and options (4) and (5) are incorrect because there is no antecedent for *your*.

2. (2) replace <u>anyone</u> with <u>people</u>   Option (2) provides a plural antecedent to go with a plural pronoun *(themselves)*. Options (1) and (3) do not correct the pronoun problem, and option (4) is incorrect because *themself* is not an accepted English word.

3. (4) replace <u>that</u> with <u>who</u>   Option (4) is correct because *who* is the pronoun to use for people. Options (1) and (2) use singular subjects *(Someone* and *Anyone)* with a plural verb *(work)*. Option (3) uses the object form of the pronoun, and option (5) assumes a nonhuman antecedent.

4. (3) replace <u>your</u> with <u>their</u>   Option (3) is correct because *their* agrees with the antecedent *people*. The other options use pronouns that do not agree with the antecedent.

5. (5) distractions   Option (5) expresses the meaning of the original sentence: workers must be aware of distractions (such as family, housework, etc.). Option (1) changes the meaning of the sentence; options (2), (3), and (4) use pronouns without antecedents.

6. (3) change <u>suffers</u> to <u>suffer</u>   Option (3) uses the plural verb *suffer* to agree with the plural subject *people*. Option (1) creates a fragment, option (2) uses a pronoun without a clear antecedent, and option (4) shifts to the past tense.

7. (5) are undiagnosed and untreated   Option (5) is the only option that correctly uses two past participles.

8. (3) change <u>decrease</u> to <u>decreases</u>   Option (3) uses the singular verb *decreases* to agree with the singular subject *productivity*. Option (1) requires a past participle, option (2) shifts to the past tense, option (4) shifts to the future tense, and option (5) changes the meaning of the sentence.

9. (1) replace <u>which</u> with <u>who</u>   Option (1) uses an appropriate pronoun to refer to people. Option (2) uses the object form of the pronoun, option (3) assumes a nonhuman antecedent, option (4) shifts to the past tense, and option (5) lacks subject-verb agreement.

Unit Review

1. (3) replace <u>skips</u> with <u>skip</u>   Option (3) uses a plural verb *(skip)* to match a plural subject *(people)*. The other options do not correct for subject-verb agreement.

2. (5) These people   Option (5) is a clear and logical subject for the sentence. Options (1), (2), and (3) use pronouns without clear antecedents. Option (4) is incorrect because it is the doctors and nutritionists, not the people who skip breakfast, who are the subject of the sentence.

3. (5) change <u>skipping</u> to <u>to skip</u>   Option (4) uses an infinitive to make the sentence make sense. Option (1) uses a singular pronoun for a plural antecedent, option (2) lacks subject-verb agreement, and option (3) uses a participle instead of an infinitive.

4. (3) who   Option (3) is the required relative pronoun to connect the two parts of the sentence. Options (1) and (4) assume a nonhuman antecedent. Option (2) uses the object form of the pronoun, and option (5) changes the meaning of the sentence.

5. (2) change <u>didn't</u> to <u>doesn't</u>   Option (2) uses the present tense, which is consistent throughout the paragraph. Option (1) uses a verb that doesn't agree with the subject in number. Options (3) and (5) switch to future tense, and option (4) changes the meaning of the sentence.

6. (2) which do take time to prepare   Option (2) uses a pronoun that agrees with a nonhuman antecedent. Options (1), (3), and (4) assume human antecedents; option (5) changes the meaning of the sentence.

7. (4) change <u>is</u> to <u>are</u>   Option (4) uses a plural verb to agree with a plural subject. Options (1) and (2) don't correct for subject-verb agreement, and option (3) shifts to past tense.

8. (3) replace <u>He or she</u> with <u>They</u>   Option (3) uses a plural pronoun to agree with a plural antecedent *(people)*. Options (1) and (2) use singular pronouns, option (4) shifts to first person, and option (5) shifts to second person.

9. (2) replace <u>It's</u> with <u>These foods are</u>   Option (2) provides a clear subject for the sentence instead of a pronoun without a clear antecedent. Option (1) doesn't correct for an unclear antecedent, option (3) awkwardly repeats all the nouns, and option (4) uses a relative pronoun incorrectly as a subject.

10. (5) change <u>seem</u> to <u>seems</u>   Option (5) uses a singular verb to agree with a singular subject. Options (1) and (2) replace the indefinite *it* with second and third person pronouns. Option (3) uses an incorrect tense, and option (4) uses a participle by itself as a verb.

11. (4) change <u>was</u> to <u>is</u>   Option (4) uses the present tense, which is consistent throughout the paragraph. Option (1) shifts to future tense, option (2) uses *be* as a verb, option (3) uses a participle as a verb, and option (5) uses a plural verb with a singular subject.

12. (2) replace <u>you</u> with <u>they</u>   Option (2) uses a third person pronoun to agree with the antecedent *teenagers*. Option (1) shifts to first person, and options (3) and (4) use a pronoun without a clear antecedent.

13. (4) replace <u>who</u> with <u>that</u>   Option (4) uses a pronoun that agrees with a nonhuman antecedent. Option (1) shifts to a singular pronoun, option (2) shifts to first person, option (3) uses a relative pronoun that assumes a human antecedent, and option (5) creates a fragment.

14. (3) change <u>forgot</u> to <u>forget</u>   Option (3) uses present tense, which is consistent throughout the paragraph. Options (1) and (2) use singular pronouns for a plural antecedent. Options (4) and (5) use participles as verbs.

15. (4) the companies   Option (4) corrects the fragment and uses a clear subject. Options (1) and (5) use verb forms inappropriately. Option (2) shifts from third to second person, and option (3) makes an unclear pronoun reference.

16. (5) change <u>will understand</u> to <u>understands</u>   Option (5) uses the present tense, which is consistent throughout the paragraph. Option (1) changes a indefinite pronoun *(it)* to a third-person pronoun *(they)*, option (2) uses a pronoun without an antecedent, option (3) uses a plural pronoun for a singular antecedent, and option (4) lacks subject-verb agreement.

17. (3) change <u>whom</u> to <u>who</u>   Option (3) uses the correct pronoun to serve as the actor in its clause. Options (1) and (2) use pronouns without an antecedent; options (4) and (5) assume a nonhuman antecedent.

18. (2) they and their cars   Option (2) uses third person pronouns to agree with the antecedent *teenagers*. Option (1) shifts to second person; options (3), (4), and (5) change the meaning of the sentence.

19. (4) change <u>increases</u> to <u>increased</u>   Option (4) uses the past tense, which is consistent throughout the paragraph. Option (1) shifts to future tense, option (2) uses a verb phrase to shift tense, option (3) lacks subject-verb agreement, and option (5) uses a participle as a verb.

20. (2) helped   Option (2) uses a past tense verb that is consistent with the rest of the sentence and the paragraph. Option (1) shifts to present tense; option (3) shifts to future tense; option (4) is an adjective, not a verb; and option (5) uses a participle as a verb.

21. (5) Stephenson built   Option (5) uses a past tense verb that is consistent with the rest of the paragraph. Option (1) shifts to the future, option (2) uses a participle as a verb, option (3) uses a nonexistent verb form, and option (4) uses a verb phrase that changes the tense.

22. (4) change <u>use</u> to <u>used</u>   Option (4) uses the correct past participle for *use*. Option (1) uses a pronoun that assumes a human antecedent, option (2) shifts to future tense, option (3) incorrectly uses *be* as a verb, and option (5) uses a present participle as a verb.

23. (3) Expansion of rail lines   Option (3) gives the sentence a clear subject. The other options use pronouns that don't have clear antecedents.

SKILLS ANALYSIS CHART

You may use this chart to determine your strengths and weaknesses in using language. The numbers in the boxes represent the items in the GED test previews and the unit review exercises. The column on the left shows you where to find more information about the items you missed.

LESSONS	EXERCISES	SENTENCE CORRECTION	SENTENCE REVISION	CONSTRUCTION SHIFT	SCORE
Subject-verb agreement (Lesson 1, pp. 170–179)	Test Preview	1, 3, 4, 6, 8, 9	2, 5, 7	10	
	Unit Review	1, 7, 10			_____ of 13
Subject-verb agreement (Lesson 2, pp. 180–187	Test Preview	1, 2, 3, 6, 7, 9, 10	5, 8	4	
	Unit Review				_____ of 10
Parts of verbs (Lesson 3, pp. 188–197	Test Preview	1, 2, 4, 6, 8, 9	3, 10	5, 7	
	Unit Review	3, 22			_____ of 12
Verb tense (Lesson 4, pp. 198–205	Test Preview	1, 2, 3, 4, 5, 8, 10	7, 9	6	
	Unit Review	5, 11, 14, 16, 19	21	20	_____ of 17
Pronoun-antecedent (Lesson 5, pp. 206–215	Test Preview	1, 3, 5, 7, 9, 10	2, 4, 8	6	
	Unit Review	4, 8, 9, 12	2, 18, 23	15	_____ of 18
Relative pronouns (Lesson 6, pp. 216–221	Test Preview	2, 3, 4, 6, 8, 9	1, 7	5	
	Unit Review	13, 17	6	4	_____ of 13
SCORE		_____ of 54	_____ of 19	_____ of 10	_____ of 83

For further practice, see:

📖 *GED Writing Skills Exercises,* Unit 2, pages 33–63

💾 *GED ADVANTAGE—Writing Skills Software*

OVERVIEW		**242**
Lesson 1	**Using Capital Letters**	**244**
	Capitalize the Specific, Not the General, 244 • Certain Words *Always* Begin with a Capital Letter, 248	
Lesson 2	**What About Commas?**	**252**
	Separating Items in a Series, 252 • Linking Ideas into One Sentence, 256	
Lesson 3	**Using Commas to Set Off Parts of Sentences**	**262**
	Using Commas with Introductory Material, 263 • Using Commas to Set Off Interrupting Elements, 266 • Avoiding Overuse of Commas, 270	
Lesson 4	**Overcoming Spelling Problems**	**276**
	Some Helpful Spelling Rules, 277 • Changing Nouns: Singular to Plural, 280	
Lesson 5	**Adding Syllables to Words**	**284**
	Adding Prefixes, 284 • Adding Suffixes, 286	
Lesson 6	**What Is the Apostrophe For?**	**290**
	Using Apostrophes to Combine Words, 290 • Using Apostrophes to Show Possession, 292	
Lesson 7	**Words to Watch Out For**	**296**
	Words That Sound Alike, 296 • GED Master List of Frequently Misspelled Words, 300	

See page 327 for SKILLS ANALYSIS CHART

REVIEW	**308**
ANSWERS AND EXPLANATIONS	**314**

3 Handling Mechanics
O V E R V I E W

In conversation, we do many things to make ourselves understood. We pause, raise and lower our voices, invite and answer questions, and even use our hands for emphasis. Best of all, we can stop talking at any point and ask whether our listeners understand us. But in writing, we must rely on the words themselves, plus a few universal clues that tell the reader what we mean. These clues fall into the area of writing called **mechanics**: the capitalization, punctuation, and spelling details that help keep essays clear and effective.

You're well on your way to passing the GED Writing Skills Test once you understand the concept of a well-structured essay that makes a point and supports it with logical, clear details. You've also learned that it's equally important to compose clear, complete sentences and to use language correctly if your essay is to be effective.

This unit focuses on mechanics. Once you have mastered them, you don't have to worry about errors that distract your reader from your essay's message.

In Lesson 1, you'll learn some rules to help you determine when to use capital letters.

Lessons 2 and 3 feature the many ways to use commas. You've already done some work with commas as well as periods and semicolons in earlier lessons when you learned about complex and compound sentences.

In Lesson 4 you'll find guidelines for correct spelling. Lesson 5 shows you how to expand words and spell them correctly. In Lesson 6 you learn how the apostrophe affects spelling. Finally, Lesson 7 shows you some of the words that many people have trouble spelling. You are encouraged to study these words.

The use of proper mechanics helps your reader understand your essay. When you've learned to apply the rules to your words and sentences, you will be able to write a polished essay that is clear and easy for the reader to follow.

mechanics: rules of capitalization, punctuation, and spelling

1 Using Capital Letters

ACHIEVEMENT GOALS
In this lesson, you will learn how to

- determine when to capitalize a word

- recognize words that *always* begin with a capital letter

Besides people's names and the pronoun *I,* only occasional words appear in the middle of a sentence with an initial capital letter. You must consider a word's role in a sentence to know whether to capitalize it.

How can you tell which of the following words are correct? Is it *Uncle* or *uncle, Country* or *country, Mountain* or *mountain, Main Street* or *main street, Douglas* or *douglas?* Except for *Douglas,* which is a person's name, you can't be sure. You can't tell about the other words because you don't see them in the context of a complete sentence.

Notice how capital letters are used in these sentences:

Your *Uncle* Charles won the game. We're going for a drive in the *country.* California's *Magic Mountain* is a great amusement park. The *main street* in town has twelve shops on it.

Even if your essay meets all the other criteria of good writing, misuse of capital letters will distract your reader and spoil the effect of your essay. Knowing a few simple rules can help you determine when to use capital letters.

Capitalize the Specific, Not the General

When you refer to general items, like *cities,* you don't need to capitalize the word. But if you refer to a specific city, like *Dallas,* you must capitalize that city's name.

The following paragraph, which contains no capitalization errors, shows the distinction between general and specific words:

When Jim decided to open a bank account with some money his aunt had given him, he looked for a bank that was both open on Saturdays and located close to home. Looking in the phone book's yellow pages, he discovered First Continental Bank had a branch near his house on Olive Street. His Aunt Millie's check was large enough for him to open the account and still have some extra cash to buy *A Tale of Two Cities,* the book he needed for his class on the French Revolution. At the bank, he was assisted by Mr. Collier, an account clerk.

We learn that Jim received money from his *aunt,* which could be any of his aunts. Later in the paragraph, we learn that the money came from *Aunt Millie.* In this instance, *Aunt* is part of someone's name. It refers to a specific person, so it must be capitalized.

In the same way, we are told that Jim was assisted by *an account clerk,* which could be any unnamed account clerk. But the writer could have said, "Jim was assisted by Account Clerk Collier." In this case, *Account Clerk* is capitalized because it is someone's title.

You see that words that name specific people or places are capitalized, while more general words are not:

Jim is the name of a specific person.
His aunt could be any one of his aunts.
Aunt Millie is a particular person.
A bank could be any bank.
First Continental Bank is a certain bank.
An account clerk could be any unnamed account clerk.
Account Clerk Collier is a particular person.
The *French Revolution* is the name of a particular historical event.

Additional examples of specific and general names and terms appear in the table below.

Table 3-1

NAMES OF PARTICULAR PEOPLE, PLACES, AND THINGS	PEOPLE, PLACES, AND THINGS IN GENERAL
Governor Cuomo will speak.	The governor will speak.
We live at 2511 Oak Street.	Our street is shady.
I'm reading *War and Peace*	There could be a war.
They went rafting on the Colorado River.	They went rafting on the river.
He lives in the West.	She lives on the west side of the street.
Maple Hill Elementary School is around the corner.	The neighborhood elementary school is around the corner.
They enjoyed *Gone with the Wind.*	They enjoyed last night's movie.

EXERCISE 1

Directions: Some of the specific names in the following sentences lack capitalization. Correct the sentences by capitalizing those words. Not all the sentences contain errors.

1. The notice says dr. Juanita Moreno will speak tonight.

2. We heard a deputy sheriff at the july meeting.

3. The governor answered questions for more than an hour.

4. Ryan likes old movies; his favorite is *casablanca*.

5. Chidori speaks several languages, including japanese, english, and french.

6. You'll find the pet store on fifth avenue.

7. I get my hair cut at mane tamers.

8. President Castilla called the meeting to order.

9. I read *the autobiography of Malcolm X* a couple of years ago.

10. The commodore county animal protection society presents a free lecture every month.

Directions: Choose the <u>one best answer</u> to each item.

<u>Items 11 to 13</u> refer to the following paragraph.

(1) Our legislator is senator Sperling. (2) He shows a genuine interest in his constituents. (3) Every month he sends out a newsletter and a questionnaire to survey voters' opinions on several issues. (4) He occasionally holds meetings at a Public Library. (5) Last month he spoke about health care at the Brownsville public library. (6) This is one politician who understands the need for voters to be informed. (7) He wants to keep in touch with the people.

11. Sentence 1: **Our legislator is senator Sperling.**

What correction should be made to this sentence?

(1) change <u>Our</u> to <u>our</u>
(2) change <u>legislator</u> to <u>Legislator</u>
(3) change <u>senator</u> to <u>Senator</u>
(4) change <u>Sperling</u> to <u>sperling</u>
(5) no correction is necessary

12. Sentence 4: **He occasionally holds <u>meetings at a Public Library.</u>**

Which of the following is the best way to write the underlined portion of this sentence? If you think the original is the best way, choose option (1).

(1) meetings at a Public Library
(2) Meetings at a Public Library
(3) meetings at a public Library
(4) meetings at a Public library
(5) meetings at a public library

13. Sentence 5: **Last month he spoke about health care at the Brownsville public library.**

What correction should be made to this sentence?

(1) change <u>month</u> to <u>Month</u>
(2) change <u>health</u> to <u>Health</u>
(3) change <u>Brownsville</u> to <u>brownsville</u>
(4) change <u>public library</u> to <u>Public Library</u>
(5) no correction is necessary

Items 14 to 17 refer to the following paragraphs.

(1) Wind power is a multimillion-dollar industry that could have a profound impact on the environment. (2) In the United States, there are 17,000 wind turbines generating electricity. (3) Ninety-five percent of them are found in california. (4) Wind turbines are modern-day windmills that generate electricity. (5) The American Wind Energy Association says it's possible to use wind to generate enough electricity to power residential use by nearly five and one-half million people for one year.

(6) The appeal of wind as a source of energy is that it is clean, it lessens dependence on foreign oil, and would lower utility rates for consumers. (7) However, there are some problems. (8) Wind turbines can kill birds that fly into their blades or electrocute birds whose wings tamper with Electric Circuits. (9) Twisted cables on turbines can start fires. (10) Advocates of wind energy believe technology can solve these problems.

14. Sentence 3: **Ninety-five percent of them are found in california.**

What correction should be made to this sentence?

(1) insert a comma after them
(2) change are to were
(3) change found to finding
(4) change california to California
(5) no correction is necessary

15. Sentence 5: **The American Wind Energy Association says it's possible to use wind to generate enough electricity to power residential use by nearly five and one-half million people for one year.**

If you rewrote sentence 5 beginning with

According to the American Wind Energy Association, wind can

the next word should be

(1) electrify
(2) use
(3) generate
(4) heat
(5) blow

16. Sentence 6: **The appeal of wind as a source of energy is that it is clean, it lessens dependence on foreign oil, and would lower utility rates for consumers.**

Which of the following is the best way to write the underlined portion of this sentence? If you think the original is the best way, choose option (1).

(1) and would lower utility rates for consumers
(2) and lowered utility rates for consumers
(3) and it would lower utility rates for consumers
(4) and would lower utility rates, for consumers
(5) and would lower utility rates. For consumers

17. Sentence 8: **Wind turbines can kill birds that fly into their blades or electrocute birds whose wings tamper with Electric Circuits.**

What correction should be made to this sentence?

(1) change turbines to Turbines
(2) insert a comma after blades
(3) change electrocute to electrocuted
(4) insert a comma after birds
(5) change Electric Circuits to electric circuits

To check your answers, turn to page 314.

Certain Words *Always* Begin with a Capital Letter

Distinguishing between the general and the specific lets you determine when to capitalize many words. But there are certain groups of words that always need to be capitalized. The best way to know what they are is to learn the following eight rules of capitalization.

Always capitalize the following:

1. Names of people and places

Shirley Chisholm, John F. Kennedy, Lincoln Center, Museum of Modern Art, Grand Canyon

2. Titles of works (books, movies, paintings) NOTE: Do not capitalize *and*, *or*, *the*, *a*, *an*, or prepositions of fewer than four letters in titles unless they are the first or last word of the title.

For Whom the Bell Tolls, *The Witches of Eastwick*, *Jurassic Park*, Leonardo's *The Last Supper*

3. Names of streets, cities, states, and countries

They live in the United States, at 555 Elm Street, Montgomery, Alabama.

4. Titles of people

Dr. Hobart, Mayor Wallace, Princess Diana, Aunt Ethel

5. Days of the week, months, and holidays (but not seasons)

The third Saturday in August is when we begin our vacation every summer, and we return after Labor Day.

6. Historic eras or events

the Renaissance, World War II

7. Languages or nationalities

He speaks Spanish and loves Mexican food.

8. Direction words when used as the name of a place

They moved to the West. Our cousins live in Northern Ireland.

Do not capitalize directions when they are used to describe something: The southern side of the house needs shade. Their house faces east.

EXERCISE 2

Directions: Using the capitalization rules, complete the following sentences. Exchange papers with your partner or a member of your group and correct each other's errors if you find any.

1. My favorite kind of ethnic food is _____ .

2. The historical event that most interests me is _____ .

3. _____ usually seems like a long day to me.

4. My street address is _____ .

5. If I could visit any city in the world, I'd choose _____ .

WRITE ON TARGET

Write one sentence to illustrate each of the eight capitalization rules on page 248.

Directions: Choose the one best answer to each item.

Items 6 to 8 refer to the following paragraph.

(1) My friend Gerry had to see a doctor at harborview hospital last Saturday because she tripped and twisted her ankle. (2) It was impossible for her to drive with her swollen ankle, so her uncle drove her to the hospital. (3) It was nearly an hour before Gerry saw a doctor. (4) While waiting, Uncle John found an outdated copy of *newsweek* and read a story about food shortages in Russia. (5) Gerry just waited quietly, feeling too uncomfortable to read.

6. Sentence 1: **My friend Gerry had to see a doctor at harborview hospital last Saturday because she tripped and twisted her ankle.**

    Which of the following is the best way to write the underlined portion of this sentence? If you think the original is the best, choose option (1).

    (1) doctor at harborview hospital
    (2) doctor at Harborview Hospital
    (3) Doctor at harborview hospital
    (4) doctor at Harborview hospital
    (5) Doctor at Harborview Hospital

7. Sentence 2: **It was impossible for her to drive with her swollen ankle, so her uncle drove her to the hospital.**

    What correction should be made to this sentence?

    (1) change swollen ankle to Swollen Ankle
    (2) change uncle to Uncle
    (3) insert John after uncle
    (4) change hospital to Hospital
    (5) no correction is necessary

8. Sentence 4: **While waiting, Uncle John found an outdated copy of *newsweek* and read a story about food shortages in Russia.**

    What correction should be made to this sentence?

    (1) change Uncle John to uncle John
    (2) change copy to Copy
    (3) change *newsweek* to *Newsweek*
    (4) change food shortages to Food Shortages
    (5) change Russia to russia

CONNECTIONS

In the Cultures theme pages in **CONNECTIONS** (at the back of the book), you'll find data on worldwide religious membership. Write a sentence to answer each question: (1) About how many Muslims are there worldwide, and where is this population concentrated? (2) About how many Hindus are there worldwide? Be sure to capitalize the appropriate words.

To check your answers, turn to page 314.

GED TEST PREVIEW

Directions: Choose the <u>one best answer</u> to each item.

<u>Items 1 to 5</u> refer to the following paragraph.

(1) The United States has almost fifty National Parks ranging from the western edge of the continent to the eastern edge. (2) Some, like yellowstone, cover territory in more than one state. (3) Each park boasts something beautiful and special. (4) For example, the Great Smoky Mountains are the largest eastern Mountain Range. (5) California's Yosemite national park is famous for having the nation's highest waterfall. (6) Mammoth cave in Kentucky has 144 miles of underground passages. (7) Our national parks preserve the scenic wonders of our land.

1. Sentence 1: **The United States has almost fifty National Parks ranging from the western edge of the continent to the eastern edge.**

What correction should be made to this sentence?

(1) change <u>United States</u> to <u>united states</u>
(2) change <u>National Parks</u> to <u>national parks</u>
(3) change <u>western</u> to <u>Western</u>
(4) change <u>continent</u> to <u>Continent</u>
(5) change <u>eastern</u> to <u>Eastern</u>

2. Sentence 2: **Some, like yellowstone, cover territory in more than one state.**

What correction should be made to this sentence?

(1) change <u>Some</u> to <u>some</u>
(2) change <u>yellowstone</u> to <u>Yellowstone</u>
(3) change <u>territory</u> to <u>Territory</u>
(4) change <u>state</u> to <u>State</u>
(5) no correction is necessary

3. Sentence 4: **For example, the Great Smoky Mountains are the largest eastern Mountain Range.**

What correction should be made to this sentence?

(1) change <u>example</u> to <u>Example</u>
(2) change <u>Great Smoky Mountains</u> to <u>great smoky mountains</u>
(3) change <u>largest</u> to <u>Largest</u>
(4) change <u>eastern</u> to <u>Eastern</u>
(5) change <u>Mountain Range</u> to <u>mountain range</u>

4. Sentence 5: **California's Yosemite national park is famous for having the nation's highest waterfall.**

What correction should be made to this sentence?

(1) change <u>Yosemite</u> to <u>yosemite</u>
(2) change <u>national park</u> to <u>National Park</u>
(3) change <u>nation's</u> to <u>Nation's</u>
(4) change <u>highest</u> to <u>Highest</u>
(5) change <u>waterfall</u> to <u>Waterfall</u>

5. Sentence 6: **Mammoth cave in Kentucky has 144 miles of underground passages.**

What correction should be made to this sentence?

(1) change <u>Mammoth</u> to <u>mammoth</u>
(2) change <u>cave</u> to <u>Cave</u>
(3) change <u>Kentucky</u> to <u>kentucky</u>
(4) change <u>underground</u> to <u>Underground</u>
(5) change <u>passages</u> to <u>Passages</u>

Items 6 to 10 refer to the following paragraphs.

(1) The Center for Marine conservation reports that America's beaches collect more than four million pieces of trash in a single year. (2) Some of it is washed up from the Sea, and the rest is left by people. (3) Vacationers leave a large amount of the trash, but most of it, the Report says, comes from commercial, military, and recreational boats. (4) In addition to aluminum cans, plastic bottles, and plastic food bags, tourists even leave things like charcoal grills on the beaches. (5) One of the most common kinds of beach trash is cigarette butts.

(6) The trash is unsightly, but more importantly, it devastates Wildlife. (7) Sea creatures, like turtles, whales, and dolphins, get caught in plastic nets, six-pack rings, or fishing line. (8) They might eat plastic bags or balloons, which also can kill them. (9) The Center for Marine Conservation directs volunteer beach cleanups along all of america's coastlines.

6. Sentence 1: **The Center for Marine conservation reports that America's beaches collect more than four million pieces of trash in a single year.**

What correction should be made to this sentence?

(1) change <u>Center</u> to <u>center</u>
(2) change <u>Marine</u> to <u>marine</u>
(3) change <u>conservation</u> to <u>Conservation</u>
(4) <u>beaches</u> to <u>Beaches</u>
(5) change <u>trash</u> to <u>Trash</u>

7. Sentence 2: **Some of it is washed up from the Sea, and the rest is left by people.**

What correction should be made to this sentence?

(1) change <u>Some</u> to <u>some</u>
(2) change <u>Sea</u> to <u>sea</u>
(3) change <u>rest</u> to <u>Rest</u>
(4) change <u>people</u> to <u>People</u>
(5) no correction is necessary

8. Sentence 3: **Vacationers leave a large amount of the trash, but most of it, the Report says, comes from commercial, military, and recreational boats.**

What correction should be made to this sentence?

(1) change <u>Vacationers</u> to <u>vacationers</u>
(2) change <u>Report</u> to <u>report</u>
(3) change <u>commercial</u> to <u>Commercial</u>
(4) change <u>military</u> to <u>Military</u>
(5) change <u>recreational</u> to <u>Recreational</u>

9. Sentence 6: **The trash is unsightly, but more importantly, it devastates Wildlife.**

What correction should be made to this sentence?

(1) change <u>The</u> to <u>the</u>
(2) change <u>trash</u> to <u>Trash</u>
(3) change <u>importantly</u> to <u>Importantly</u>
(4) change <u>it</u> to <u>It</u>
(5) change <u>Wildlife</u> to <u>wildlife</u>

10. Sentence 9: **The Center for Marine Conservation directs volunteer beach cleanups <u>along all of america's coastlines.</u>**

Which of the following is the best way to write the underlined portion of this sentence? If you think the original is the best way, choose option (1).

(1) along all of america's coastlines
(2) along All of america's coastlines
(3) along all of America's coastlines
(4) along all of America's Coastlines
(5) along all the coastlines of america

To check your answers, turn to page 315.

2 What About Commas?

ACHIEVEMENT GOALS
In this lesson, you will learn how to use commas to

- name items in a series

- create complex and compound sentences

In writing, punctuation is essential to make the meaning clear. Periods, question marks, and exclamation points appear at the ends of sentences and rarely present problems (unless they are missing—see Unit 1, Lesson 2 for information about run-on sentences).

Commas, on the other hand, are used internally in sentences for a variety of reasons. They indicate pauses in thought, and they show relationships among the ideas in a sentence. (You've already seen this in Unit 1, Lessons 2 and 3, where you learned how to use commas to combine ideas into complex and compound sentences.)

This lesson shows you how to use commas when you have a series of items in a sentence. You'll also have a chance to review using commas to combine ideas in complex and compound sentences.

Separating Items in a Series

Occasionally, you will write a sentence that lists three or more items. Consider the following sentence:

A good baseball player must be able *to bat, to run, to throw,* and *to catch.*

The items in the list of things a baseball player must be able to do are separated by commas. Notice that the last comma appears before *and.*

If you use a different conjunction or connecting word, you still use a comma in a series (see page 102 for more on conjunctions).

Reuben preferred football, basketball, or soccer.

Note that it's incorrect to place a comma <u>after</u> the *and* or the *or* that links the last two items in the series:

Incorrect: Everyone loved the movie's action, romance, and, suspense.

Correct: Everyone loved the movie's action, romance, and suspense.

It's also incorrect to place a comma at the end of the series:

Incorrect: The acting, the scenery, and the music, thrilled the audience.

Correct: The acting, the scenery, and the music thrilled the audience.

If your list contains only two items, you don't need a comma:

Marilee's strengths were *running and throwing.*

Mel could neither *run nor throw.*

If you use conjunctions between each item in the series, you don't need commas. Compare the following pairs of sentences. All are correct:

Ping-Lin, Danjiro, and Guillermo will stay on this side of the room.

Ping-Lin and Danjiro and Guillermo will stay on this side of the room.

They can find a chair or stand up or sit on the floor.

They can find a chair, stand up, or sit on the floor.

EXERCISE 1

Directions: In the following sentences, use commas to separate the items in a series. Not all the sentences require commas.

1. Mr. and Mrs. Suarez took their tent their cooking utensils and their fishing gear to the campsite in the woods.

2. They preferred camping in the summer when they could count on warm weather long days and good fishing.

3. They only had room for one extra lawn chair or a picnic basket or some extra blankets.

4. They forgot to bring the hot dogs and the mustard.

5. They did have plenty of equipment for swimming fishing and hiking.

6. Some people would rather vacation in cities than in mountains woods or the country.

7. They enjoy bustling city life with all that it offers, such as museums theater and restaurants.

8. Still others prefer to stay home to rest or work on projects around the house.

9. Winter vacations can be nice if you live in a climate that is cold or wet.

10. It can be fun to spend time exploring your own city neighborhood and community.

Directions: Choose the one best answer to each item.

Items 11 to 14 refer to the following paragraph:

(1) People plant trees for many reasons. (2) Large trees cool yards in summer both because of their shade, and their green color. (3) Some trees are chosen for their beauty. (4) They may be covered with flowers in spring or change color in fall or have unusual leaves. (5) Fruit trees have beautiful blossoms in spring, tasty peaches, or cherries in summer, and good climbing branches all year round. (6) Scientists now believe trees also help counteract the greenhouse effect. (7) Some local governments are considering communitywide tree-planting campaigns to keep cities cool and attractive.

11. Sentence 2: **Large trees cool yards in summer both because of their shade, and their green color.**

    What correction should be made to this sentence?

    (1) remove the comma after <u>shade</u>
    (2) remove <u>and</u>
    (3) insert a comma after <u>and</u>
    (4) insert a comma after <u>green</u>
    (5) no correction is necessary

12. Sentence 4: **They may be covered with flowers <u>in spring or change color in fall or have</u> unusual leaves.**

    Which of the following is the best way to write the underlined portion of this sentence? If you think the original is the best way, choose option (1).

    (1) in spring or change color in fall or have
    (2) in spring, or change color in fall or have
    (3) in spring or change color in fall or, have
    (4) in spring or change color in fall but have
    (5) in spring or change color in fall so have

13. Sentence 5: **Fruit trees have beautiful blossoms in spring, tasty peaches, or cherries in summer, and good climbing branches all year round.**

    What correction should be made to this sentence?

    (1) remove the comma after <u>spring</u>
    (2) remove the comma after <u>peaches</u>
    (3) remove the comma after <u>summer</u>
    (4) insert a comma after <u>and</u>
    (5) no correction is necessary

14. Sentence 7: **Some local governments are considering communitywide tree-planting campaigns <u>to keep cities cool and attractive.</u>**

Which of the following is the best way to write the underlined portion of this sentence? If you think the original is the best way, choose option (1).

(1) to keep cities cool and attractive
(2) to keep cities, cool, and attractive
(3) to keep cities cool, and attractive
(4) to keep cities cool and, attractive
(5) to keep cities cool, and, attractive

Items 15 to 18 refer to the following paragraphs.

(1) Under pressure from government and certain physicians, hospitals recently have begun to cut waste and save money for patients. (2) One of the causes of soaring hospital costs are the extravagant use of disposable supplies and instruments. (3) Hospitals use these disposable items and mark up the price as high as 400 percent on patients' bills. (4) Among the disposable items hospitals use are surgical gowns, and towels. (5) However, a new type of liquid-proof material that gowns are made of protects operating room personnel against diseases carried by blood, such as AIDS. (6) A growing industry offers facilities to launder and sterilize these gowns so that they can be reused. (7) Some hospitals are adding their own laundry and recycling facilities to their premises.

(8) Many hospitals are returning to reusable gowns, metal surgical trays, and, metal instruments. (9) These items may cost more to purchase than disposable ones, but their repeated use promises long-term savings.

15. Sentence 2: **One of the causes of soaring hospital costs are the extravagant use of disposable supplies and instruments.**

What correction should be made to this sentence?

(1) change causes of to causes. Of
(2) change hospital to Hospital
(3) change are to is
(4) insert a comma after supplies
(5) no correction is necessary

16. Sentence 4: **Among the disposable items hospitals use are surgical gowns, and towels.**

Which of the following is the best way to write the underlined portion of this sentence? If you think the original is the best way, choose option (1).

(1) are surgical gowns, and towels
(2) is surgical gowns, and towels
(3) are Surgical Gowns, and towels
(4) are surgical gowns and towels
(5) are surgical gowns and, towels

17. Sentence 5: **However, a new type of liquid-proof material that gowns are made of protects operating room personnel against diseases carried by blood, such as AIDS.**

If you rewrote sentence 5 beginning with

Gowns made of liquid-proof material

the next word should be

(1) operate
(2) carry
(3) spread
(4) infect
(5) protect

18. Sentence 8: **Many hospitals are returning to reusable gowns, metal surgical trays, and, metal instruments.**

What correction should be made to this sentence?

(1) change returning to returned
(2) change returning to return
(3) remove the comma after gowns
(4) remove the comma after trays
(5) remove the comma after and

To check your answers, turn to page 315.

Linking Ideas into One Sentence

To add variety to your writing, you will sometimes join two or more ideas together into one sentence. If each of the ideas is complete and can stand alone as a simple sentence, joining them results in a compound sentence. (See Unit 1, Lesson 3 for more about compound sentences.)

Simple sentences: Anita always eats dessert. She never seems to gain weight.

Compound sentence: Anita always eats dessert, but she never seems to gain weight.

TEST-TAKING TIP

A compound sentence can always be written as two separate sentences. If you're unsure where to place the comma and connector in a compound sentence, ask yourself where you could put a period to make two complete sentences.

You must use a comma between independent clauses when you join the clauses with the connecting words *and, so, but,* and *or.* The connecting word in compound sentences always appears in between the two clauses.

Late movies on television put me to *sleep, so* I don't watch them.

Certain connecting words in compound sentences take a semicolon and a comma. The semicolon precedes the connector, and the comma follows:

Movies on television put me to *sleep; however,* I never fall asleep in a movie theater.

These connectors usually take a semicolon and a comma:

however	nevertheless	otherwise	on the other hand
finally	instead	likewise	moreover
besides	furthermore	in addition	consequently
thus	therefore	as a result	for example

Writing complex sentences is another way to link ideas into a single sentence. In complex sentences, one of the ideas will have a connecting word attached to it that makes it dependent upon the rest of the sentence for its meaning. That dependent clause, with the connecting word attached, can appear at the beginning or at the end of the sentence. (See Unit 1, Lesson 4 for more about complex sentences.)

If the dependent clause appears at the beginning, before the independent clause, you must follow it with a comma:

Whenever I drink tea, I put lemon in it.

If the dependent clause appears at the end, after the independent clause, you do not use a comma:

I add lemon *whenever I drink tea.*

EXERCISE 2

Directions: Place commas in the complex and compound sentences below. When you find a simple sentence, add a dependent or an independent clause to it and punctuate as necessary. Exchange papers with your partner or members of your group to see a variety of clauses and check each other's comma placement.

1. Mary Ann lost her address book but she remembered the most important numbers in it.

2. If people are hungry enough they will beg for food.

3. Whenever it rains homeless people seek shelter inside abandoned buildings.

4. People can suffer from malnutrition even though they don't feel hungry.

5. Most Americans need more fiber in their diets.

6. Many laundromats are open all night.

7. Clothes dryers make towels soft but fresh air makes them smell nice.

8. Fresh blackberries are delicious and they make great pies.

9. Summer produces a greater variety of fruit than winter.

10. As temperatures rise outside some people become irritable.

11. Holidays are relaxing for most people but they are stressful for others.

12. Ice storms are unimaginable to people who live in warm climates.

13. Too many people misuse prescription drugs and doctors are concerned.

14. Your voice alone may be all you need to reach someone by telephone.

15. Computers are used in almost every business but many people still find them intimidating.

Directions: Choose the one best answer to each item.

Items 16 to 19 refer to the following paragraph.

(1) Enormous parking lots near shopping malls, hospitals, business districts, supermarkets, and movie theaters attest to the vast numbers of cars in America and the amount of time people spend in them. (2) Once people buck traffic jams to get to these parking lots they face the problem of finding a convenient parking place. (3) Because physical disabilities make it truly difficult for some people to walk long distances a few spaces for the disabled are often reserved close to the buildings. (4) Parking in these spots requires a special license plate. (5) It's not uncommon to find these spaces illegally occupied. (6) Illegally parking in these spaces carries a heavy fine. (7) Law enforcement officers have little time to patrol parking lots, but some communities have solved that problem with volunteers. (7) These volunteers cite illegally parked cars, inform the driver and report the car to the authorities.

16. Sentence 2: **Once people buck traffic jams <u>to get to these parking lots they face</u> the problem of finding a convenient parking place.**

Which of the following is the best way to write the underlined portion of this sentence? If you think the original is the best way, choose option (1).

(1) to get to these parking lots they face

(2) to get to these parking lots. They face

(3) to get to these, parking lots they face

(4) to get to these parking lots, they face

(5) to get, to these parking lots they face

17. Sentence 3: **Because physical disabilities make it truly difficult for some people to walk long distances a few spaces for the disabled are often reserved close to the buildings.**

What correction should be made to this sentence?

(1) insert a comma after <u>difficult</u>

(2) insert a comma after <u>distances</u>

(3) insert a comma after <u>spaces</u>

(4) insert a comma after <u>disabled</u>

(5) no correction is necessary

18. Sentences 4 and 5: **Parking in these spots requires a special license plate. It's not uncommon to find these spaces illegally occupied.**

The most effective combination of sentences 4 and 5 would include which of the following groups of words?

(1) Parking is not uncommon

(2) Illegally parked cars occupy

(3) Even though spaces are illegal

(4) Special license plates require

(5) Cars without spaces

19. Sentence 7: **These volunteers cite illegally parked cars, inform the driver and report the car to the authorities.**

What correction should be made to this sentence?

(1) insert a comma after <u>volunteers</u>

(2) remove the comma after <u>cars</u>

(3) insert a comma after <u>driver</u>

(4) insert a comma after <u>and</u>

(5) insert a comma after <u>report</u>

Items 20 to 23 refer to the following paragraphs.

(1) Television, newspapers, radio, and magazines bombard the public with information about current social and political issues. (2) Whether it's health care, the economy, rising crime or teenage pregnancy, powerful interest groups express their views and try to get the public to go along with them. (3) But research has found that people's opinions come from being based on interaction with other people about issues. (4) Most people would rather discuss ideas with their friends and acquaintances than just read what the press has to say. (5) Studies show that many people meet others at libraries, houses of worship, and community halls. (6) There they want to discuss problems and seek solutions.

(7) Rather than debating with each other, people seeking real understanding listen to each other carefully. (8) Personal experience contribute an emotional tone to these exchanges, which are often painful. (9) Personal experience, in fact, plays a larger role than statistics in people's forming of ideas. (10) When people see the reality of an issue reflected in their own lives, they are more likely to care about that issue.

20. Sentence 2: **Whether it's health care, the economy, rising crime or teenage pregnancy, powerful interest groups express their views and try to get the public to go along with them.**

What correction should be made to this sentence?

(1) insert a comma after <u>crime</u>

(2) change <u>pregnancy, powerful</u> to <u>pregnancy. Powerful</u>

(3) change <u>try</u> to <u>tried</u>

(4) change <u>public</u> to <u>Public</u>

(5) change <u>go</u> to <u>going</u>

21. Sentence 3: **But research has found that people's opinions come from being based on interaction with other people about issues.**

If you rewrote sentence 3 beginning with

<u>People base their opinions on</u>

the next word should be

(1) form
(2) interaction
(3) people's
(4) research
(5) issues

22. Sentences 5 and 6: **Studies show that many people meet others at <u>libraries, houses of worship, and community halls. There they want to discuss</u> problems and seek solutions.**

Which of the following is the best way to write the underlined portion of these sentences? If you think the original is the best way, choose option (1).

(1) libraries, houses of worship, and community halls. There they want to discuss
(2) libraries houses of worship, and community halls. There they want to discuss
(3) libraries, Houses of Worship, and community halls. There they want to discuss
(4) libraries, houses of worship, and community halls because they want to discuss
(5) libraries, houses of worship, and community halls, because they want to discuss

23. Sentence 8: **Personal experience contribute an emotional tone to these exchanges, which are often painful.**

What correction should be made to this sentence?

(1) change <u>experience</u> to <u>Experience</u>
(2) change <u>experience</u> to <u>expereince</u>
(3) change <u>contribute</u> to <u>contributes</u>
(4) change <u>contribute</u> to <u>contributed</u>
(5) change <u>which</u> to <u>who</u>

C O N N E C T I O N S

In the Leisure theme pages in **CONNECTIONS** (at the back of the book), you can see the different time zones in the United States. Find your own state and time zone on the map. Choose a vacation destination in another area and time zone. Write one compound sentence (use *and* or *but*) and one complex sentence (use *when*, *if*, or *because*) describing the time zone change between your home and your vacation spot. Be careful to place the commas correctly.

To check your answers, turn to page 316.

Directions: Choose the one best answer to each item.

Items 1 to 5 refer to the following paragraph.

(1) Picnics rank high among the many ways to enjoy a summer day. (2) Lunch or dinner in a park can be a nice escape from the noise and crowds, if you live in a city. (3) A picnic can be simple, and inexpensive. (4) All you need are a few sandwiches, some fruit, and something to drink. (5) Everyday food tastes especially good when you eat it under the shade of a tree on a hot day however it can also make you sick. (6) Mayonnaise, eggs, and other perishable foods can spoil quickly in hot weather so it's a good idea to pack some ice with your picnic. (7) Some people take food in its original packaging and make sandwiches at the picnic site but not even jars and plastic bags can protect food indefinitely. (8) Careless handling of food can not only spoil your picnic but also can make you seriously ill.

1. Sentence 2: **Lunch or dinner in a park can be a nice escape from the noise and crowds, if you live in a city.**

Which of the following is the best way to write the underlined portion of this sentence? If you think the original is the best way, choose option (1).

(1) crowds, if you live
(2) crowds. If you live
(3) crowds if you live
(4) crowds if, you live
(5) crowds; if you live

2. Sentence 3: **A picnic can be simple, and inexpensive.**

What correction should be made to this sentence?

(1) change simple, and to simple. And
(2) remove the comma
(3) replace and with or
(4) remove and
(5) no correction is necessary

3. Sentence 5: **Everyday food tastes especially good when you eat it under the shade of a tree on a hot day however it can also make you sick.**

Which of the following is the best way to write the underlined portion of this sentence? If you think the original is the best way, choose option (1).

(1) day however it
(2) day however. It
(3) day, however, it
(4) day; however it
(5) day; however, it

4. Sentence 6: **Mayonnaise, eggs, and other perishable foods can spoil quickly in hot weather so it's a good idea to pack some ice with your picnic.**

What correction should be made to this sentence?

(1) remove the comma after eggs
(2) insert a comma after foods
(3) insert a comma after weather
(4) insert a comma after idea
(5) insert a comma after ice

5. Sentence 7: **Some people take food in its original packaging and make sandwiches at the picnic site but not even jars and plastic bags can protect food indefinitely.**

What correction should be made to this sentence?

(1) change <u>packaging and</u> to <u>packaging. And</u>
(2) insert a comma after <u>sandwiches</u>
(3) insert a comma after <u>site</u>
(4) insert a comma after <u>jars</u>
(5) insert a comma after <u>bags</u>

<u>Items 6 to 10</u> refer to the following paragraph.

(1) The period of prehistory called the Stone Age gets its name from the way humans began to shape tools out of stone. (2) These early people used sharp rocks with jagged edges to cut, scrape and chop. (3) Each tool was designed to perform a particular task. (4) Because flint, sandstone, and volcanic rock were fine-grained the people used them to flake and polish the stones. (5) They used other rocks to chip away pieces from a stone and sharpen its edges. (6) The tools became more sophisticated, when wooden handles were added to the stones. (7) These early human beings developed a variety of tools and weapons including bird snares, blow guns, throwing sticks, slings, animal traps and nets. (8) They made harpoons and fishhooks out of bones. (9) These early devices were used only for hunting and gathering food.

6. Sentence 2: **These early people used sharp rocks with jagged edges to cut, scrape and chop.**

What correction should be made to this sentence?

(1) insert a comma after <u>rocks</u>
(2) change <u>edges to</u> to <u>edges. To</u>
(3) remove the comma
(4) insert a comma after <u>scrape</u>
(5) insert a comma after <u>and</u>

7. Sentence 4: **Because flint, sandstone, and volcanic rock were fine-grained the people used them to flake and polish the stones.**

What correction should be made to this sentence?

(1) remove the commas
(2) insert a comma after <u>rock</u>
(3) insert a comma after <u>fine-grained</u>
(4) insert a comma after <u>flake</u>
(5) no correction is necessary

8. Sentence 6: **The tools became more sophisticated, when wooden handles were added to the stones.**

Which is of the following is the best way to write the underlined portion of this sentence? If you think the original is the best way, choose option (1).

(1) sophisticated, when wooden
(2) sophisticated. When wooden
(3) sophisticated; when, wooden
(4) sophisticated when wooden
(5) sophisticated, when, wooden

9. Sentence 7: **These early human beings developed a variety of tools and weapons including bird snares, blow guns, throwing sticks, slings, animal traps and nets.**

What correction should be made to this sentence?

(1) insert a comma after <u>beings</u>
(2) remove the comma after <u>snares</u>
(3) remove the comma after <u>slings</u>
(4) insert a comma after <u>traps</u>
(5) insert a comma before <u>nets</u>

10. Sentence 9: **These early devices were used only for hunting and gathering food.**

What correction should be made to this sentence?

(1) insert a comma after <u>devices</u>
(2) insert a comma after <u>hunting</u>
(3) insert a comma after <u>and</u>
(4) insert a comma after <u>gathering</u>
(5) no correction is necessary

To check your answers, turn to page 317.

3 Using Commas to Set Off Parts of Sentences

ACHIEVEMENT GOALS
In this lesson, you will learn

- how to use commas to set off introductory material

- how to use commas to set off interrupting elements

- when *not* to use commas

Commas help readers understand your writing. Commas indicate a pause in thought. They tell the reader that some information is set apart from the main part of the sentence. You've already seen this with dependent clauses in compound sentences. Occasionally, the words to be set apart appear at the beginning of the sentence, like some dependent clauses:

Before the car started, all the passengers fastened their seat belts.

Other times, the words to be set apart appear in the middle of the sentence:

All the passengers, *eager to get going,* fastened their seat belts.

Fearful of making a mistake, some writers put in too many commas even though there is no reason for them.

Incorrect: Jonathan hurried to cafe, where he was to meet his friend, Cameron.

Correct: Jonathan hurried to the cafe where he was to meet his friend Cameron.

Using Commas with Introductory Material

You saw in Lesson 2 of this unit how to use commas with connecting words or conjunctions to link two independent clauses in a compound sentence (see Unit 1, Lessons 2 and 3 for more information on compound sentences):

The outside temperature rose rapidly, so everyone went swimming.

It cooled off early, but no one stopped swimming.

Lesson 2 also showed you how to use commas after a dependent clause that appears at the beginning of a sentence (see Unit 1, Lesson 4 for more on complex sentences):

Because it was late, the buses had stopped running.

Even though the buses had stopped running, they got home on time.

Single words or word *groups* (called **phrases**) sometimes appear at the beginning of sentences to give the reader additional information. Unlike a clause, a phrase does not contain a subject and a verb. Introductory words and introductory phrases must be followed by a comma (see Unit 1, Lesson 5 for more on introductory phrases):

Exploding with a loud bang, the tire went flat on the freeway.

Across town, crowds watched the Fourth of July parade.

Hoping for a miracle, Louis searched the house for his lost keys.

Eagerly, Yolanda opened the letter from her brother.

When addressing someone directly in a sentence, you use a comma to set off the person's name or title:

Benjamin, please see whether the water is boiling.

Colonel, will you be speaking to the troops next week?

Mother, please don't tell me what to wear.

TEST-TAKING TIP

If you're not sure whether a group of words is introductory material, read the sentence without those words. If the sentence still makes sense, the group of words is introductory and should be set apart with a comma.

E X E R C I S E 1

Directions: Some of the sentences below contain introductory elements that need to be set off with commas. Place a comma after the introductory material.

1. The governor tried to balance the state budget.

2. After arguing for weeks the two groups decided to put the issue to a vote.

3. Happily the program started on time.

4. Father would you show me how to bait the hook?

5. Nobody believed snow would close mountain roads in June.

6. His favorite breakfast was huevos rancheros.

7. According to the doctor the cast should come off in two weeks.

8. Unable to put down the books Rodolfo read three Stephen King novels in one month.

9. Angelo would rather read biographies of American presidents.

10. Eyeing the snake they held their breath.

11. Everyone was excited about the victory.

12. Nevertheless they planned to practice hard for the next game.

13. Surprisingly everyone voted for the incumbent.

14. Because she'd been accused of misusing campaign money no one expected her to win.

15. Jean please give that to me when you're finished with it.

Directions: Choose the <u>one best answer</u> to each item.

<u>Items 16 to 19</u> refer to the following paragraph.

(1) Dana had applications in for six jobs. (2) Of the six employers one called her in for an interview. (3) To prepare for the interview, Dana read about the company, jotted down her own experience that seemed to fit the job description, and wrote down a few questions she had about the job. (4) After preparing for the interview Dana felt confident about getting the job. (5) Nevertheless, she still felt somewhat nervous when she met the interviewer. (6) As it turned out she did fine and got the job.

16. Sentence 2: **Of the six <u>employers one called</u> her in for an interview.**

Which of the following is the best way to write the underlined portion of this sentence? If you think the original is the best way, choose option (1).

(1) employers one called
(2) employers. One called
(3) employers one, called
(4) employers, one called
(5) employers, one, called

17. Sentence 3: **<u>To prepare for the interview, Dana read</u> about the company, jotted down her own experience that seemed to fit the job description, and wrote down a few questions she had about the job.**

Which of the following is the best way to write the underlined portion of this sentence? If you think the original is the best, choose option (1).

(1) To prepare for the interview, Dana read
(2) To prepare, for the interview Dana read
(3) To prepare for the interview Dana, read
(4) To prepare for, the interview, Dana read
(5) To prepare for the interview Dana read

18. Sentence 4: **After preparing for the interview Dana felt confident about getting the job.**

What correction should be made to this sentence?

(1) insert a comma after <u>preparing</u>
(2) insert a comma after <u>interview</u>
(3) insert a comma after <u>Dana</u>
(4) insert a comma after <u>confident</u>
(5) insert a comma after <u>getting</u>

19. Sentence 6: **As it turned out she did fine and got the job.**

What correction should be made to this sentence?

(1) replace <u>turned out</u> with <u>was</u>
(2) change <u>out she</u> to <u>out. She</u>
(3) insert a comma after <u>out</u>
(4) change <u>fine and</u> to <u>fine. And</u>
(5) insert <u>immediately</u> after <u>job</u>

<u>Items 20 to 22</u> refer to the following paragraph.

(1) One of the most famous English writers of the last century was Charles Dickens, a novelist who lived form 1812 to 1870. (2) When he was alive his novels appeared in magazines in serial form. (3) Readers read the stories in monthly installments, and had to wait for the next issue to find out about the next plot twist. (4) Acclaimed during his lifetime, Dickens remains a popular novelist whose characters are well known to people around the world. (5) He filled his books with colorful villains and offbeat characters and used his novels to expose social injustice and hypocrisy. (6) Among his books are the well-known titles, *David Copperfield, Oliver Twist, A Tale of Two Cities,* and *A Christmas Carol.*

20. Sentence 2: **When he was alive his novels appeared in magazines in serial form.**

What correction should be made to this sentence?

(1) change <u>was</u> to <u>were</u>
(2) insert a comma after <u>alive</u>
(3) change <u>appeared</u> to <u>will appear</u>
(4) change the spelling of <u>magazines</u> to <u>magisines</u>
(5) no correction is necessary

21. Sentence 3: **Readers read the stories in <u>monthly installments, and had to wait</u> for the next issue to find out about the next plot twist.**

Which of the following is the best way to write the underlined portion of this sentence? If you think the original is the best way, choose option (1).

(1) monthly installments, and had to wait
(2) monthly installments, and have to wait
(3) monthly installments, and will wait
(4) monthly installments and had to wait
(5) Monthly Installments, and had to wait

22. Sentence 6: **Among his books are the well-known titles, *David Copperfield, Oliver Twist, A Tale of Two Cities,* and *A Christmas Carol.***

What correction should be made to this sentence?

(1) insert a comma after <u>are</u>
(2) change <u>titles</u> to <u>Titles</u>
(3) remove the comma after <u>titles</u>
(4) change <u>of</u> to <u>Of</u>
(5) remove the comma after *<u>Cities</u>*

To check your answers, turn to page 317.

Using Commas to Set Off Interrupting Elements

Occasionally, a sentence contains a word or a phrase that interrupts the main thought. If you remove the words or phrase, you still have a complete sentence. Consider the following example:

> Roy attended night school, exhausting himself in the process, to become a car mechanic.

The main idea of the sentence is that Roy attended school at night to become a car mechanic. The fact that he was exhausting himself in the process is informative, but not necessary to make the sentence clear. Notice that the interrupting phrase is separated from the rest of the sentence by commas.

Another kind of interrupter describes a noun in the sentence. The descriptive words or phrase can be removed without making the sentence incomplete. Consider these examples:

> Dmitri, *a Russian immigrant,* was eager to master English.
>
> His brother, *who had been in the United States for two years,* already spoke good English.

The main point of the first sentence is that Dmitri is eager to learn English. It's informative to know he's a Russian immigrant, but that information is set apart by commas because we could leave it out and still have a meaningful sentence. We lose some information about Dmitri, but it's not essential to the meaning of the sentence.

The main idea in the second sentence is that the brother speaks good English. Omitting the information that he's been in the United States for two years means we know less about him, but the sentence still works.

Common interrupters that are set off by commas include such expressions as *for example, I believe, they say, of course:*

> Consider, *for example,* yesterday's discussion.
>
> Too much attention, *I believe,* is harmful to some students.
>
> The food, *they say,* is excellent.
>
> There is, *of course,* too much food.

A person's name is occasionally an interrupter:

> Their favorite cousins, *Jeff and Lee,* were coming to visit.

You must not use commas to set apart information in the middle of a sentence if that information is *essential* to the meaning of the sentence. Compare the following two examples:

The hikers, who were in good physical condition, completed the hike.

The hikers who were in good physical condition completed the hike.

The important idea in the first sentence is that the hikers completed the hike. Apparently *all* of them completed the hike, and we assume, from the interrupter, that they probably did so because they were in good condition.

However, in the second sentence the idea is that *only* the hikers who were in good condition completed the hike. There may have been others who did not make it.

EXERCISE 2

Directions: Some of the following sentences contain interrupting elements. First, find those interrupters and set them off with commas. Next, rewrite every sentence that has an interrupting element. Replace the old interrupter with a new one, but do not change any other part of the sentence. Exchange papers with your partner or members of your group to see a variety of interrupters and to check each other's punctuation.

1. Vegetables for example are a great source of dietary fiber.

2. The host Mr. Yee made everyone feel welcome.

3. This year unlike past years there will be no fireworks display.

4. Their bowling team which is new this year won most of the games.

5. Drivers who check their rear-view mirror have fewer accidents.

6. Medical care that is available to everyone would improve the country's health.

7. Mr. Johnson's hobby which is woodworking gives him great satisfaction.

8. The map which we forgot to bring would have been useful.

9. Everyone of course enjoyed the magician.

10. Jeannette said she believed in astrology.

WRITE ON TARGET

Write two sentences using the following words as an interrupter: *who have natural talent.* Write one sentence so that the words interrupt the main idea and require commas. Write the other sentence so that the words are essential to the meaning of the sentence.

Directions: Choose the <u>one best answer</u> to each item.

<u>Items 11 to 14</u> refer to the following paragraph.

(1) Among other things, the French are known for their delicious pastry. (2) Mrs. Coulon who is from France owns a bakery in a small business district. (3) Nearly every day eager customers come to Mrs. Coulon's bakery to see what she has to sell. (4) Frank Alonso the shoe repairman next door is her best customer. (5) He comes in at least twice a day to buy some baked goods. (6) Mrs. Coulon sends her customers who need their shoes repaired to Frank.

11. Sentence 2: **Mrs. <u>Coulon who is from France owns</u> a bakery.**

Which of the following is the best way to write the underlined portion of this sentence? If you think the original is the best way, choose option (1).

(1) Coulon who is from France owns
(2) Coulon who is from France, owns
(3) Coulon, who is from France, owns
(4) Coulon, who is from France owns
(5) Coulon. Who is from France owns

12. Sentence 3: **Nearly every day eager customers come to Mrs. Coulon's bakery to see what she has to sell.**

What correction should be made to this sentence?

(1) insert a comma after <u>every day</u>
(2) insert a comma after <u>customers</u>
(3) change <u>Mrs.</u> to <u>mrs.</u>
(4) change <u>see what</u> to <u>see. What</u>
(5) no correction is necessary

13. Sentence 4: **Frank <u>Alonso the shoe repairman next door is</u> her best customer.**

Which of the following is the best way to write the underlined portion of this sentence? If you think the original is the best way, choose option (1).

(1) Alonso the shoe repairman next door is
(2) Alonso, the shoe repairman next door, is
(3) Alonso the shoe repairman next door, is
(4) Alonso who repairs shoes next door is
(5) Alonso who is the shoe repairman next door is

14. Sentence 6: **Mrs. Coulon sends her <u>customers who need their shoes repaired to Frank.</u>**

Which of the following is the best way to write the underlined portion of this sentence? If you think the original is the best way, choose option (1).

(1) customers who need their shoes repaired to
(2) customers. Who need their shoes repaired to
(3) customers, who need their shoes repaired to
(4) customers, who need their shoes repaired, to
(5) customers who, need their shoes, repaired to

<u>Items 15 to 18</u> refer to the following paragraph.

(1) Even in a depressed economy, workers claim to be less concerned about the size of their paychecks than about other job factors. (2) A major concern for most workers is how they are treated on the job. (3) They want some say in how to do their jobs and when to schedule their work. (4) They want to work for bosses that they can communicate with openly. (5) This means, for example that they want information to come from supervisors, not from gossip. (6) Although they value job security and financial reward workers also value a sense of fulfillment from their work. (7) They want to do work that is challenging and creative. (8) In past decades, workers felt more loyalty to companies than they do today because more workers stayed with one employer for a lifetime. (9) Today's workers are more concerned with his or her own welfare than that of the company, and they will work harder for a company that treats them well in return. (10) They want more time with their families and are less willing to disrupt family life for a job.

15. Sentence 4: **They want to work for <u>bosses that they can communicate with</u> openly.**

Which of the following is the best way to write the underlined portion of this sentence? If you think the original is the best way, choose option (1).

(1) bosses that they can communicate with
(2) bosses who they can communicate with
(3) bosses whom they can communicate with
(4) bosses which they can communicate with
(5) bosses that they communicated with

16. Sentence 5: **This <u>means, for example that they want</u> information to come from supervisors, not from gossip.**

Which of the following is the best way to write the underlined portion of this sentence? If you think the original is the best way, choose option (1).

(1) means, for example that they want
(2) means, for example, that they want
(3) means for example, that they want
(4) means, for example they want
(5) means, for example workers want

17. Sentence 6: **Although they value job security and financial reward workers also value a sense of fulfillment from their work.**

What correction should be made to this sentence?

(1) change <u>they</u> to <u>one</u>
(2) change <u>job security</u> to <u>Job Security</u>
(3) change <u>reward workers</u> to <u>reward. Workers</u>
(4) insert a comma after <u>reward</u>
(5) change <u>value</u> to <u>valued</u>

18. Sentence 9: **Today's workers are more concerned with his or her own welfare than that of the company, and they will work harder for a company that treats them well in return.**

What correction should be made to this sentence?

(1) change <u>are</u> to <u>were</u>
(2) change <u>his or her</u> to <u>one's</u>
(3) change <u>his or her</u> to <u>their</u>
(4) insert a comma after <u>a company</u>
(5) no correction is necessary

To check your answers, turn to page 318.

Avoiding Overuse of Commas

Inserting a comma that doesn't belong in a sentence can confuse readers just as much as omitting one that does. A misplaced comma forces the reader to pause when the meaning of the sentence doesn't call for a pause. This detracts from the smooth flow of a well-thought-out essay.

There are eight ways beginning writers commonly misuse commas. Study the following examples of comma errors so that you can avoid them in your own writing.

Avoid the following common errors:

1. Separating the subject and verb in a sentence

incorrect: Some gas *stations, let* you pay at the pump with a credit card.

correct: Some gas stations let you pay at the pump with a credit card.

2. Separating compound subjects and verbs

incorrect: *Ricardo, and* Cameron rented a truck to move furniture.

correct: Ricardo and Cameron rented a truck to move furniture.

3. Separating independent clauses without including a connecting word

incorrect: Oliver H. Perry was an important naval hero in the *1800s, he* defeated the British and their Indian allies.

correct: Oliver H. Perry was an important naval hero in the 1800s, and he defeated the British and their Indian allies.

4. Putting a comma after the connecting word

incorrect: There are many legends about the origins of the American flag *so, historians* aren't sure who designed the original.

correct: There are many legends about the origins of the American flag, so historians aren't sure who designed the original.

5. Putting a comma before the first item in a series

incorrect: Most school districts *require, history, English, science, and math* for high school graduation.

correct: Most school districts require history, English, science, and math for high school graduation.

6. Putting a comma after the conjunction that precedes the last item in a series

incorrect: The reasons people take the GED examinations include *preparing for higher education, seeking a better job, or, feeling a sense of accomplishment.*

correct: The reasons people take the GED examinations include preparing for higher education, seeking a better job, or feeling a sense of accomplishment.

7. Putting a comma after the last item in a series

incorrect: Americans often take things like *hot running water, telephones, and automobiles,* for granted.

correct: Americans often take things like hot running water, telephones, and automobiles for granted.

8. Separating an adjective from the noun it describes

incorrect: You can recognize black widow spiders by the *hourglass, markings* on their bodies.

correct: You can recognize black widow spiders by the hourglass markings on their bodies.

EXERCISE 3

Directions: Identify the unnecessary commas in the following sentences and make any necessary corrections. Not all of the sentences contain errors.

1. Rattlesnakes, range from two to eight feet in length.

2. The United States government issues passports to its citizens so that they can be identified as Americans in foreign countries.

3. During early morning and late afternoon rush hours, drivers, and their passengers benefit from carpool lanes.

4. Traffic was stopped by an accident, a flat tire, and, a stalled car.

5. A storm was indicated by the cloudy, dark sky.

6. The surfers hurried to shore, they weren't caught in the storm.

7. Trees blew, and shook in the fierce wind.

8. The sudden, roar frightened them.

9. After a flash of lightning came a burst of thunder, a downpour of rain, and, a violent wind.

10. The lights went out, but, they found their seats in the darkened theater.

Directions: Choose the one best answer to each item.

Items 11 to 14 refer to the following paragraph.

(1) The designers of the U.S. government, were radical thinkers in their day. (2) But that was more than 200 years ago. (3) Our nation's founders would be amazed today to see women in the President's Cabinet, on the Supreme Court and, in Congress. (4) Although they designed a democratic government, these men did not include women even among the voters.(5) Women have made huge strides in government participation, a woman probably will become president someday.

11. Sentence 1: **The designers of the U.S. government, were radical thinkers in their day.**

What correction should be made to this sentence?

(1) insert a comma after <u>designers</u>
(2) remove the comma after <u>government</u>
(3) insert a comma after <u>radical</u>
(4) insert a comma after <u>thinkers</u>
(5) no correction is necessary

12. Sentence 3: **Our nation's founders would be amazed today to see women <u>in the President's Cabinet, on the Supreme Court and, in Congress.</u>**

Which of the following is the best way to write the underlined portion of this sentence? If you think the original is the best way, choose option (1).

(1) in the President's Cabinet, on the Supreme Court and, in Congress
(2) in the President's Cabinet, on the Supreme Court, and, in Congress
(3) in the President's Cabinet, on the Supreme, Court, and in Congress
(4) in the President's Cabinet, on the Supreme Court, and in Congress
(5) in the President's Cabinet, on the Supreme Court and in Congress

13. Sentence 4: **Although they designed a democratic government, these men did not include women even among the voters.**

What correction should be made to this sentence?

(1) insert a comma after <u>Although</u>
(2) remove the comma after <u>government</u>
(3) insert a comma after <u>men</u>
(4) insert a comma after <u>women</u>
(5) no correction is necessary

14. Sentence 5: **Women have made huge strides in government <u>participation, a woman probably will become president someday</u>**

Which of the following is the best way to write the underlined portion of this sentence? If you think the original is the best way, choose option (1).

(1) participation, a woman
(2) participation a woman
(3) participation and, a woman
(4) participation, and a woman
(5) participation; and a woman

Items 15 to 18 refer to the following paragraphs.

(1) What is the impact working mothers have on today's families? (2) Compared with the 1950s, millions more women work outside the home today. (3) Many factors, contribute to this social change. (4) For one thing, many women must work for economic reasons. (5) For another, most people are having fewer children, which means they have more time to devote to activities outside the family. (6) Furthermore, women want to achieve equality in the workplace, and this often requires career commitment. (7) Finally, high divorce rates and the increasing independence of women requires them to earn a living outside the home.

(8) One change within the family is the disappearance of sit-down meals. (9) Families eat meals together much less frequently than in the past. (10) With mothers away from the home all day, schools and teachers have more responsibility for everything children learn. (11) Children even exhibit more tooth decay now than in the past because their eating of sweets and brushing of teeth are not well monitored. (12) Many families, split up, which leaves kids without stability or clear family role models. (13) Most women find it difficult to hold a full-time job, and maintain a family. (14) To do both, many women—and men—are seeking jobs they can do from their homes.

15. Sentence 3: **Many factors, contribute to this social change.**

What correction should be made to this sentence?

(1) insert a comma after <u>Many</u>
(2) remove the comma after <u>factors</u>
(3) change <u>contribute</u> to <u>contributes</u>
(4) insert a comma after <u>social</u>
(5) no correction is necessary

16. Sentence 7: **Finally, high divorce rates and the increasing independence <u>of women requires them to earn a living</u> outside the home.**

Which of the following is the best way to write the underlined portion of this sentence?

If you think the original is the best way, choose option (1).

(1) of women requires them to earn a living
(2) of women, requires them to earn a living
(3) of women requires them to earning a living
(4) of women requiring them to earn a living
(5) of women require them to earn a living

17. Sentence 12: **Many families, split up, which leaves kids without stability or clear family role models.**

What correction should be made to this sentence?

(1) remove the comma after <u>families</u>
(2) change <u>leaves</u> to <u>leave</u>
(3) change <u>which</u> to <u>who</u>
(4) insert a comma after <u>kids</u>
(5) insert a comma after <u>family</u>

18. Sentence 13: **Most women find it difficult <u>to hold a full-time job, and maintain a family</u>.**

Which of the following is the best way to write the underlined portion of this sentence? If you think the original is the best way, choose option (1).

(1) to hold a full-time job, and maintain a family
(2) to hold a full-time job, and maintain, a family
(3) to hold a full-time job and maintain, a family
(4) to hold, a full-time job and maintain a family
(5) to hold a full-time job and maintain a family

CONNECTIONS

In today's workforce, women work in almost every occupation. The Employment theme pages in **CONNECTIONS** give data on women in certain artistic or literary jobs. Write three sentences based on this data, each using either introductory material or an interrupting element. Proofread your work to be sure you haven't overused commas.

To check your answers, turn to page 319.

Directions: Choose the <u>one best answer</u> to each item.

<u>Items 1 to 5</u> refer to the following paragraph.

(1) For a variety of reasons more and more people are riding bicycles today. (2) Some people ride bicycles to work. (3) They want the exercise and feel they are helping to protect the environment against pollution. (4) Other people ride a bicycle for recreation. (5) Riding a bike is peaceful and quiet. (6) Still others ride bikes to run errands. (7) It's a good way to get from one place to another and still be out in the fresh air. (8) Automobile traffic however is also increasing, so bicycling can be dangerous. (9) It's important for cyclists to wear helmets, and to obey traffic rules. (10) In fact, strong, supporters of bicycle helmets believe they should be required by law. (11) Some states already have mandatory helmet laws for bicyclists.

1. Sentence 1: **For a variety of reasons more and more people are riding bicycles today.**

What correction should be made to this sentence?

(1) insert a comma after <u>variety</u>
(2) insert a comma after <u>reasons</u>
(3) insert a comma after <u>more and</u>
(4) insert a comma after <u>people</u>
(5) insert a comma after <u>bicycles</u>

2. Sentences 2 and 3: **Some people ride bicycles to work. They want the exercise and feel they are helping to protect the environment against pollution.**

The most effective combination of sentences 2 and 3 would include which of the following groups of words?

(1) the environment protects exercise
(2) bicycle riders exercise at work
(3) bicycles are part of the environment
(4) bicycle riding provides exercise and protects the environment
(5) exercising for the environment

3. Sentence 8: **Automobile <u>traffic however is</u> also increasing, so bicycling can be dangerous.**

Which of the following is the best way to write the underlined portion of this sentence? If you think the original is the best way, choose option (1).

(1) traffic however is
(2) traffic however, is
(3) traffic, however, is
(4) traffic; however, is
(5) traffic, however is

4. Sentence 9: **It's important for cyclists to wear helmets, and to obey traffic rules.**

What correction should be made to this sentence?

(1) insert a comma after <u>important</u>
(2) insert a comma after <u>cyclists</u>
(3) remove the comma after <u>helmets</u>
(4) insert a comma after <u>and</u>
(5) no correction is necessary

5. Sentence 10: **In fact, strong, supporters of bicycle helmets believe they should be required by law.**

What correction should be made to this sentence?

(1) remove the comma after <u>fact</u>
(2) remove the comma after <u>strong</u>
(3) insert a comma after <u>helmets</u>
(4) insert a comma after <u>believe</u>
(5) insert a comma after <u>required</u>

Items 6 to 10 refer to the following paragraph.

(1) According to scientists it's possible to lower hot summer temperatures in inner cities. (2) They point out that suburbs that surround cities are always a few degrees cooler than downtown because of the abundance of trees and lawn. (3) It would be simple they maintain for city planners to plant trees strategically to shade buildings and city streets. (4) Colors of buildings and streets also make a difference in temperatures. (5) Buildings, that are painted white on the outside, are easier to cool on the inside. (6) Some urban utility companies report that painting a building's roof white can cut air conditioning costs by as much as 50 percent. (7) Heat comes from sunlight reflecting off surfaces; therefore, blacktopped streets and dark buildings cause temperatures to rise. (8) Until people become conscious of depleting energy sources they will ignore these obvious solutions to overheated cities. (9) Anyone who moves from a busy downtown street to a grassy, tree-shaded park, appreciates the difference landscaping can make.

6. Sentence 1: **According to scientists it's possible to lower hot summer temperatures in inner cities.**

What correction should be made to this sentence?

(1) insert a comma after <u>scientists</u>
(2) insert a comma after <u>possible</u>
(3) insert a comma after <u>summer</u>
(4) insert a comma after <u>temperatures</u>
(5) insert a comma after <u>inner</u>

7. Sentence 3: **It would be <u>simple they maintain for</u> city planners to plant trees strategically to shade buildings and city streets.**

Which of the following is the best way to write the underlined portion of this sentence? If you think the original is the best way, choose option (1).

(1) simple they maintain for
(2) simple. They maintain for
(3) simple, they maintain for
(4) simple, they maintain, for
(5) simple; they maintain, for

8. Sentence 5: **Buildings, that are painted white on the outside, are easier to cool on the inside.**

What correction should be made to this sentence?

(1) remove the comma after <u>Buildings</u>
(2) remove the comma after <u>outside</u>
(3) remove both commas
(4) insert a comma after <u>cool</u>
(5) no correction is necessary

9. Sentence 8: **Until people become conscious of depleting <u>energy sources they will ignore</u> these obvious solutions to overheated cities.**

Which of the following is the best way to write the underlined portion of this sentence? If you think the original is the best way, choose option (1).

(1) energy sources they will ignore
(2) energy sources. They will ignore
(3) energy sources, they will ignore
(4) energy. Sources they will ignore
(5) energy sources they will ignore,

10. Sentence 9: **Anyone who moves from a busy downtown street to a grassy, tree-shaded park, appreciates the difference landscaping can make.**

What correction should be made to this sentence?

(1) remove the comma after <u>grassy</u>
(2) remove the comma after <u>park</u>
(3) insert a comma after <u>difference</u>
(4) insert a comma after <u>landscaping</u>
(5) no correction is necessary

To check your answers, turn to page 319.

4 Overcoming Spelling Problems

ACHIEVEMENT GOALS
In this lesson, you will learn how to

- spell changes in verb forms

- spell words that have confusing letter combinations

- change words from singular to plural

A good essay can be marred by misspelled words. Correct spelling helps keep your reader focused on your ideas rather than on mechanical errors in your writing. To improve your spelling skills, you must learn some basic rules, memorize exceptions to the rules, and practice what you have learned. The Master Spelling List provided on pages 300–304 can help you memorize words you have trouble spelling.

It's easier to spell words if you divide them into **syllables**. A syllable is a part of a word that is pronounced as a single unit: go + ing = going; fe + ver + ish = feverish. Say the word first, to hear how many syllables there are, and spell each one as you write. It will help if you remember that every syllable contains at least one vowel. Look at the following words that are broken into syllables.

char + ac + ter = character

con + cen + trate = concentrate

op + por + tu + ni + ty = opportunity

prob + a + bly = probably

As you study the Master Spelling List, pronounce each word carefully and then concentrate on each syllable as you practice spelling the word.

276 Unit 3 Handling Mechanics

Some Helpful Spelling Rules

Adding *ing* or *ed* to a verb

When you change verb tense or use verb phrases, you change the form of the verb, frequently by adding *ed* or *ing* to the main part of the verb. (See Unit 1, Lesson 5, and Unit 2, Lesson 3 for more about verb forms.) A few rules will help you spell verbs correctly when you add *ed* or *ing* to them:

1. If the verb ends in *e*, drop the *e* before adding *ing*:

use becomes *using*
ride becomes *riding*
shine becomes *shining*

2. If the verb has *one syllable and a single consonant preceded by a single vowel*, double the final consonant before adding *ed* or *ing*:

rap becomes *rapped*
hit becomes *hitting*
let becomes *letting*

3. If the word does not meet these criteria, do not double the consonant:

listen becomes *listened*
sleep becomes *sleeping*
eat becomes *eating*

Words with *ie* and *ei*

1. If the vowel sound is *ee*, put the *i* first, except after *c*:

believe, thief, niece, receive.

Exceptions to this rule include *seize, either, neither, leisure, weird*.

2. If the vowel sound is *a* or *i*, put the *e* before the *i*:

neighbor, freight, height.

Words that end in *cede, sede, ceed*

1. Only one word ends in *sede*:

supersede

2. Only three words end in *ceed*:

exceed, proceed, succeed

3. All the others end in *cede*:

precede, recede, secede, concede

Directions: Using the spelling rules above, correct the spelling in the following sentences. Some of the sentences contain more than one misspelled word. Some do not contain any.

Use the words that were misspelled in new sentences that you create. Compare your examples with those of your partner or a member of your group to be sure you have correctly spelled the words.

1. Jogging or danceing helps you acheive fitness.

2. The nieghbor was unavailable to work on the fence.

3. The mail carrier skipped our house yesterday.

4. Although the traffic was heavy, they steped off the curb and proceded to cross the street.

5. A breif summary of the program was all she had time for.

6. The stores advertised a product they didn't have.

7. After spliting logs all day, Tomas had a backache.

8. Niether one of you drives well enough to use my car.

9. Their neice and nephew arrived with six suitcases.

10. Simon knew he could succeed by working hard.

11. The sun was shineing all day yesterday.

12. A broken traffic light was stopping traffic at all four corners.

13. The wierd noise frightened all the guests.

14. His receding hairline changed his appearance.

15. Hearring was difficult in the crowded room.

Directions: Choose the one best answer to each item.

Items 16 to 18 refer to the following paragraph.

(1) People are living longer today than at any time in history. (2) It's not uncommon to find healthy people active well into their 80s. (3) This is due to advances in medical technology and to more healthful living. (4) Having more years of liesure time is one of the many benefits of living a long life. (5) However, long life brings some problems; an example is affordable housing for seniors. (6) As they become too old or too ill to live by themselves, senior citizens often move in with their children or have to live in costly nursing facilities. (7) Special housing for seniors does exist in many communities, but not everyone can afford it. (8) Both federal and local governments have started giving serious consideration to housing for an ageing population.

16. Sentence 4: **Having more years of liesure time is one of the many benefits of living a long life.**

What correction should be made to this sentence?

(1) change the spelling of Having to Haveing
(2) change the spelling of liesure to leisure
(3) insert a comma after time
(4) change the spelling of living to liveing
(5) no correction is necessary

17. Sentence 5: **However, long life brings some problems; an example is affordable housing for seniors.**

What correction should be made to this sentence?

(1) remove the comma after However
(2) change brings to bring
(3) change problems. An to problems an
(4) change the spelling of housing to houseing
(5) no correction is necessary

18. Sentence 8: **Both federal and local governments have started giving serious consideration to housing for an ageing population.**

What correction should be made to this sentence?

(1) change the spelling of <u>started</u> to <u>startted</u>
(2) change the spelling of <u>giving</u> to <u>giveing</u>
(3) change <u>giving</u> to <u>to give</u>
(4) change the spelling of <u>ageing</u> to <u>aging</u>
(5) no correction is necessary

<u>Items 19 to 21</u> refer to the following paragraph.

(1) To encourage recycling, some service stations and oil-changing facilities are begining to accept used motor oil from people who change the oil in their own cars. (2) Stations that recieve used oil have to pass government standards to obtain certification to recycle it. (3) Oil must not be contaminated, and there must be arrangements with waste-oil haulers to take the oil to recycling plants. (4) Many people, unsure how to dispose of their used motor oil, pour it down storm drains, into garbage cans, or directly into the ground. (5) Each gallon of oil has the potential to damage one million gallons of groundwater, but it is important that oil be disposed of properly.

19. Sentence 1: **To encourage recycling, some service stations and oil-changing <u>facilities are begining to accept used motor oil from people</u> who change the oil in their own cars.**

Which of the following is the best way to write the underlined portion of this sentence? If you think the original is the best way, choose option (1).

(1) facilities are begining to accept used motor oil from people
(2) facilities are begining to accept used motor oil, from people
(3) facilities are begining to accept used motor oil. From people
(4) facilities are beginning to accept used motor oil from people
(5) facilities are begun to accept used motor oil from people

20. Sentence 2: **<u>Stations that recieve used oil</u> have to pass government standards to obtain certification to recycle it.**

Which of the following is the best way to write the underlined portion of this sentence? If you think the original is the best way, choose option (1).

(1) Stations that recieve used oil
(2) Stations who recieve used oil
(3) Stations, that recieve used oil,
(4) Stations that receive used oil
(5) Stations that recieve old oil

21. Sentence 5: **Each gallon of oil has the potential to damage one million gallons of groundwater, but it is important that oil be disposed of properly.**

What correction should be made to this sentence?

(1) change <u>has</u> to <u>had</u>
(2) remove <u>to</u>
(3) change <u>damage</u> to <u>damaged</u>
(4) replace <u>but</u> with <u>or</u>
(5) replace <u>but</u> with <u>so</u>

To check your answers, turn to page 320.

Changing Nouns: Singular to Plural

If you write that Lorenzo drives *a truck*, you are using a singular noun. But if Lorenzo drives *several trucks*, you change the noun to plural.

You change words from singular to plural all the time, both in speaking and in writing. In English, there are several ways nouns get their plural form, so the trick is to spell the plural correctly. The following six rules will help you.

1. **Most nouns can be made plural by adding *s*. If the noun ends in *s*, *x*, *ch*, or *sh*, make it plural by adding *es*:**
   loss becomes *losses*
   fox becomes *foxes*
   wrench becomes *wrenches*
   lash becomes *lashes*

2. **Nouns that end in a consonant plus *y* become plural by changing the *y* to *i* and adding *es*:**
   city becomes *cities*
   penny becomes *pennies*

3. **Some nouns that end in a consonant plus *o* add *es*:**
   hero becomes *heroes*
   potato becomes *potatoes*

4. **Some nouns that end in *f* change the *f* to *v* and add *es* for the plural:**
   leaf becomes *leaves*
   wolf becomes *wolves*

5. **Some nouns that end in *fe* change the *f* to *v* and add *s*.**
   knife becomes *knives*
   wife becomes *wives*

6. **Some nouns don't change when they become plural:**
   The *deer* were hiding among the trees.
   I saw a *deer* by the side of the road.

EXERCISE 2

Directions: Find and correct the misspelled words in the sentences that follow. Not all of the sentences contain errors.

1. They had hopped to find more clues at the scene of the crime.

2. Some adults think there are no heros for youngsters to admire.

3. Guido's directions were so good, we found both address in less than an hour.

4. There were too many boxs to fit into the back of the car.

5. Marguerita planted tomatos and carrots in her garden.

6. After three trys, Madeline got the basketball through the hoop.

7. Early in the morning, the bus stop benchs are covered with dew.

8. Pruning trees is more difficult than mowing lawns.

9. Pablo and Saburo were friends at school but enemys during wrestling matches.

10. I get tired watching parades.

WRITE ON TARGET

Use each of the following words in a sentence: *foreign, loneliness, ridiculous, likelihood,* and *quite.*

Directions: Choose the <u>one best answer</u> to each item.

<u>Items 11 to 13</u> refer to the following paragraph.

(1) With a weak economy and high unemployment, people seek ways to save money. (2) Several books and articles have been written to help people save money and change bad spending habits. (3) There are even classes available for helping people reduce their debts. (4) Some people around the country have started newsletters that show how to save money. (5) Among a variety of ways to avoid exorbitent prices, they suggest cutting out coupons, buying food in bulk, making your own bread, and growing vegetables in a home garden. (6) Newspapers and magazines also publish ideas for saving money; there are plenty of tips for anyone who is serious about financiel cutbacks.

11. Sentence 3: **There are even classes available for helping people reduce their debts.**

What correction should be made to this sentence?

(1) change <u>classes</u> to <u>class's</u>
(2) change the spelling of <u>helpping</u> to <u>helping</u>
(3) change <u>their</u> to <u>thier</u>
(4) change the spelling of <u>debts</u> to <u>debtes</u>
(5) no correction is necessary

12. Sentence 5: **Among a variety of ways to avoid exorbitent prices, they suggest cutting out coupons, buying food in bulk, making your own bread, and growing vegetables in a home garden.**

What correction should be made to this sentence?

(1) change the spelling of <u>variety</u> to <u>vareity</u>
(2) change the spelling of <u>exorbitent</u> to <u>exorbitant</u>
(3) change the spelling of <u>making</u> to <u>makeing</u>
(4) change the spelling of <u>vegetables</u> to <u>vegetabels</u>
(5) no correction is necessary

13. Sentence 6: **Newspapers and magazines also publish ideas for saving money; there are plenty of tips for anyone who is serious about financiel cutbacks.**

What correction should be made to this sentence?

(1) change the spelling of <u>magazines</u> to <u>magezines</u>
(2) insert a comma after <u>ideas</u>
(3) replace the semicolon with a comma
(4) change <u>who</u> to <u>whom</u>
(5) change the spelling of <u>financiel</u> to <u>financial</u>

CONNECTIONS

The Lifestyles theme pages in **CONNECTIONS** give financial facts about raising a child. The costs rise each year to account for an estimated 6 percent inflation rate. Write one paragraph describing the effect these costs might have on family lifestyles. In your paragraph, use the *plural* form of some or all of these words: *family, child, parent, person, man, woman,* and *baby.*

To check your answers, turn to page 320.

Directions: Choose the <u>one best answer</u> to each item.

<u>Items 1 to 4</u> refer to the passage below.

(1) Perhaps it was inevitible that clothing would become part of the recycling movement. (2) Clothing manufacturer's have begun to use recycled rubber from tires, plastic from soda bottles, and many other kinds of throwaway materials to make new clothes. (3) One outdoor apparel company advertises lightwieght fleece sweaters they make by chopping up plastic bottles into pellets. (4) They spin the pellets into a polyester yarn and make sweaters from it. (5) The company says the sweater is warm and quick-drying. (6) One shoe company has put together old tire rubber, recycled wool, cardboard, and soda bottles to make hiking shoes. (7) For a natural look, the shoes' colors come from a dye made of tree bark, pecan shells, and vegetable oils. (8) Recycled clothing is not necessarily a bargain for consumers or particularly profitible for manufacturers. (9) It costs just as much as clothing made from virgin materials. (10) For one thing, recycled materials still cost manufacturers money. (11) Furthermore, the recycling process is complicated and expensive. (12) The companys that make and sell this recycled apparel, however, claim it is high quality.

1. Sentence 1: **Perhaps it was inevitible that clothing would become part of the recycling movement.**

What correction should be made to this sentence?

(1) change the spelling of <u>inevitible</u> to <u>inevitable</u>
(2) insert a comma after <u>inevitible</u>
(3) change the spelling of <u>clothing</u> to <u>clotheing</u>
(4) insert a comma after <u>recycling</u>
(5) no correction is necessary

2. Sentence 3: **One outdoor apparel company advertises lightwieght fleece sweaters they make by chopping up plastic bottles into pellets.**

What correction should be made to this sentence?

(1) change <u>apparel company</u> to <u>Apparel Company</u>
(2) change the spelling of <u>advertises</u> to <u>advertizes</u>
(3) change the spelling of <u>lightwieght</u> to <u>lightweight</u>
(4) insert a comma after <u>sweaters</u>
(5) insert a comma after <u>they</u>

3. Sentence 8: **Recycled clothing is not necessarily a bargain for consumers or particularly profitible for manufacturers.**

What correction should be made to this sentence?

(1) change the spelling of <u>necessarily</u> to <u>necesarily</u>
(2) change the spelling of <u>particularly</u> to <u>perticularly</u>
(3) change the spelling of <u>profitible</u> to <u>profitable</u>
(4) change the spelling of <u>profitible</u> to <u>profitibel</u>
(5) change <u>manufacturers</u> to <u>manufactureres</u>

4. Sentence 12: **The companys that make and sell this recycled apparel, however, claim it is high quality.**

What correction should be made to this sentence?

(1) change the spelling of <u>companys</u> to <u>companes</u>
(2) change the spelling of <u>companys</u> to <u>companies</u>
(3) insert a comma after <u>make</u>
(4) insert a comma after <u>apparel</u>
(5) insert a comma after <u>claim</u>

Items 5 to 8 refer to the following paragraph.

(1) Starting about 300 years before the Industrial Revolution, great changes took place in the economic life of Western Europe. (2) This era is known as the Commercial Revolution because it involved tremenduos changes in business practices, which changed Europe's economy. (3) The later Industrial Revolution signaled a change in the way products were manufacture, but the Commercial Revolution concerned the way people bought and sold goods. (4) During this time (late 1400s to mid-1700s), trade became worldwide. (5) Merchants avoided town craft guilds that set limits on production and controled prices. (6) In the English woolen business, for example, merchants decided to pay farmers directly to spin wool into cloth. (7) The farmers worked in their homes, and this kind of production continued until factorys emerged as part of the Industrial Revolution.

5. Sentence 2: **This era is known as the Commercial Revolution because it involved tremenduos changes in business practices, which changed Europe's economy.**

What correction should be made to this sentence?

(1) change <u>involved</u> to <u>involves</u>
(2) change the spelling of <u>tremenduos</u> to <u>tremendous</u>
(3) change the spelling of <u>business</u> to <u>buisness</u>
(4) change <u>changed</u> to <u>will change</u>
(5) change <u>economy</u> to <u>Economy</u>

6. Sentence 3: **The later Industrial Revolution signaled a change in the way products <u>were manufacture, but the Commercial Revolution concerned</u> the way people bought and sold goods.**

Which of the following is the best way to write the underlined portion of this sentence? If you think the original is the best way, choose option (1).

(1) were manufacture, but the Commercial Revolution concerned
(2) were manufacture, but the Commercial Revolution concerns
(3) were manufacture but the Commercial Revolution concerned
(4) were manufactured, but the Commercial Revolution concerned
(5) were manufacture, the Commercial Revolution concerned

7. Sentence 5: **Merchants avoided town craft guilds <u>that set limits on production and controled prices.</u>**

Which of the following is the best way to write the underlined portion of this sentence? If you think the original is the best way, choose option (1).

(1) that set limits on production and controled prices
(2) that set limits on production and control prices
(3) that set limits on production and controlled prices
(4) that sets limits on production and controls prices
(5) that sets production limits and price controls

8. Sentence 7: **The farmers worked in their homes, and this kind of production continued until factorys emerged as part of the Industrial Revolution.**

What correction should be made to this sentence?

(1) remove the comma after <u>homes</u>
(2) change <u>continued</u> to <u>continues</u>
(3) change the spelling of <u>factorys</u> to <u>factories</u>
(4) insert a comma after <u>emerged</u>
(5) no correction is necessary

To check your answers, turn to page 321.

5 Adding Syllables to Words

ACHIEVEMENT GOALS
In this lesson, you will learn how to

- add prefixes to words
- add suffixes to words

Many words are created by adding syllables to smaller words that you already know how to spell. A few rules about adding letters at the beginning or end of words will increase considerably the number of words you can spell easily.

These syllables are called prefixes and suffixes. A **prefix** is one or more letters or syllables added to the *beginning* of a word to change its meaning. A **suffix,** similarly, is one or more letters or syllables added to the *end* of a word to change its meaning. Common suffixes you have already worked with are *ed* and *ing*.

Adding Prefixes

Prefixes do not change the spelling of the word they are added to:

il + legal = illegal

mis + use = misuse

When you spell a word with a prefix, think of the main word first, and then add the syllable or syllables that precede it.

Sometimes a complete word can serve as a prefix:

under + estimate = underestimate

Be careful not to join two separate words unless one is meant to be the prefix of the other. For example, *a lot* must always be written as two separate words. Likewise, do not separate a word from its prefix if the two parts are meant to be a single word. *Upstairs* is written as a single word.

EXERCISE 1

Directions: Match the prefixes from the list on the left to the main words from the list on the right to form words that could replace the words in parentheses in the sentences that follow.

im	check
non	view
pre	natural
un	mature
re	stop
super	cover

1. Next Saturday, they will (remove the cover from) the statue.

2. She asked the lab to (check again) the results of her blood test.

3. The (view of some of the scenes) will give you an idea of the kind of movie it is.

4. Even though they are (more than natural), some people do believe in ghosts.

5. They were too (not yet mature) to handle that kind of problem.

6. The (didn't stop) music seemed to last all night.

Directions: Choose the <u>one best answer</u> to each item.

<u>Items 7 to 9</u> refer to the following paragraph.

(1) Living with a roomate is different from living with your family because at first everything is unfamiliar. (2) When you've grown up with people, you understand them and know what to expect from them even if you don't get along well. (3) Over a period of years, you and your family develop certain patterns of behavior that everyone reconizes. (4) When you share housing with someone new undoubtedly you will be in for some surprises.

7. Sentence 1: **Living with a roomate is different from living with your family because at first everything is unfamiliar.**

What correction should be made to this sentence?

(1) change the spelling of <u>Living</u> to <u>Liveing</u>
(2) change the spelling of <u>roomate</u> to <u>roommate</u>
(3) change the spelling of <u>different</u> to <u>diffrent</u>
(4) change <u>unfamiliar</u> to <u>unfamilier</u>
(5) no correction is necessary

8. Sentence 3: **Over a period of years, you and your family develop certain patterns of behavior that everyone reconizes.**

What correction should be made to this sentence?

(1) remove the comma after <u>years</u>
(2) insert a comma after <u>family</u>
(3) change <u>reconizes</u> to <u>reconises</u>
(4) change <u>reconizes</u> to <u>recognizes</u>
(5) no correction is necessary

9. Sentence 4: **When you share housing with someone new undoubtedly you will be in for some surprises.**

Which of the following is the best way to write the underlined portion of this sentence? If you think the original is the best way, choose option (1).

(1) housing with someone new undoubtedly
(2) houseing with someone new undoubtedly
(3) housing with someone new. Undoubtedly
(4) housing with someone, new, undoubtedly
(5) housing with someone new, undoubtedly

To check your answers, turn to page 321.

Adding Suffixes

Some words change their spelling when a suffix is added to them, and others don't. A few rules will help you correctly spell words that have suffixes.

1. When a word ends in a consonant and the suffix begins with a consonant, just add the suffix:

fear + ful = fearful; mind + less = mindless.

2. When a word ends with the letter *e* and the suffix begins with a consonant, just add the suffix:

care + ful = careful; sense + less = senseless

Exceptions include *truly, argument, ninth, wholly,* and *judgment.*

3. When a word ends with the letter *e* and the suffix begins with a vowel, drop the final *e*:

value + able = valuable; confuse + ion = confusion

Words that end in *ce* or *ge* are often exceptions to this rule:

advantageous, replaceable, courageous, noticeable.

4. Add *ly* and *ness* without changing the spelling of the main word:

final + ly = finally; eager + ly = eagerly; careless + ness = carelessness

5. If a word ends in *y* following a consonant, change the *y* to *i* before adding a suffix:

silly + er = sillier; forty + eth = fortieth

6. Don't change the *y* before adding *ing*:

cry + ing = crying

7. If a word ends in *y* following a vowel, do not change the *y*:

pay + ment = payment; annoy + ed = annoyed

Exceptions include *paid* and *said.*

TEST-TAKING TIP

Make a list of the common exceptions to spelling rules and memorize the spelling of those words.

EXERCISE 2

Directions: Add a suffix from the list below to a main word from the numbered list. You may use some suffixes more than once. Compare your paper with that of your partner or member of your group to see other combinations and to check each other's spelling.

ment	ly
able	ness
ing	ive
ful	less
ous	iest

1. like
2. hate
3. joy
4. sad
5. make

6. expense
7. noise
8. pay
9. expand
10. hope

WRITE ON TARGET

List five words that have a prefix or a suffix. Use each word in a written sentence.

Items 11 to 13 refer to the following paragraph.

(1) Medical technology is so far advanced that it's possible for a team of surgeons to operate on an unborn baby with out removing it from the mother's body. (2) If doctors see that a fetus is not developing normaly, they may be able to fix it surgically. (3) If, for example, a fetus's organs are not in the proper location, doctors can relocate the organs within the tiny body of the fetus. (4) Fetal surgery involves operating on the mother, too. (5) To reach the fetus, the surgeons have to make one incision in the mother to reach the womb, and then they have to open the womb to reach the fetus. (6) After the fetal operation, they seal the uterus with staples and a material like glue. (7) Then they stitch the mother's incision. (8) It takes couragous parents and highly skilled doctors to give babies this chance at a healthy life.

11. Sentence 1: **Medical technology is so far advanced that it's possible for a team of surgeons to operate on an unborn baby with out removing it from the mother's body.**

What correction should be made to this sentence?

(1) change possible to posible
(2) change the spelling of operate to oporate
(3) change with out to without
(4) change the spelling of removing to removeing
(5) no correction is necessary

12. Sentence 2: **If doctors see that a fetus is not developing normaly, they may be able to fix it surgically.**

What correction should be made to this sentence?

(1) change the spelling of developing to developeing
(2) change the spelling of normaly to normally
(3) remove the comma after normaly
(4) change the spelling of surgically to surgicaly
(5) no correction is necessary

13. Sentence 8: **It takes couragous parents and highly skilled doctors to give babies this chance at a healthy life.**

Which of the following is the best way to write the underlined portion of this sentence? If you think the original is the best way, choose option (1).

(1) It takes couragous parents and highly skilled doctors
(2) It take couragous parents and highly skilled doctors
(3) It took couragous parentes and highly skilled doctors
(4) It takes courageous parents and highly skilled doctors
(5) It takes couragous parents and highely skilled doctors

CONNECTIONS

Lasers are an important scientific and artistic tool, as the Technology theme pages in **CONNECTIONS** show. Write a paragraph describing the laser light show photograph. Use one or more descriptive words that end in a suffix such as *al, ity,* and *ful,* and one or more words that begin with a prefix such as *re* or *im.*

To check your answers, turn to page 322.

GED TEST PREVIEW

Directions: Choose the <u>one best answer</u> to each item.

<u>Items 1 to 5</u> refer to the following paragraph.

(1) If you're tired of the same old fruits and vegetables, you might like to experiment with kiwi fruit. (2) It's an increasingly popular, egg-shaped, fuzzy-skinned fruit that looks like a green banana inside and tastes vaguely like berries. (3) The fruit grows abundantely in New Zealand, but it originally came from China, where it was considered a delicacy in ancient times. (4) Because of its Chinese origins, when it was first importted into the United States it was called "Chinese gooseberries." (5) In 1962, its name was changed, and it underwent a profiteable increase in popularity. (6) Ninety-five percent of the 8,000 acres of kiwi fruit that is grown in the United States today comes from northern California. (7) The green meat of the kiwi makes it prettyer than most fruit. (8) It's also nutritious. (9) It's a good source of vitamin C, potassium, and fiber. (10) Kiwi is an unusual, pleasant-tasting fruit that more and more people are discovering in supermarket produce departments.

1. Sentence 1: **If you're tired of the same old fruits and <u>vegetables, you might like to experment with</u> kiwi fruit.**

Which of the following is the best way to write the underlined portion of this sentence? If you think the original is the best way, choose option (1).

(1) vegetables, you might like to experment with

(2) vegetables you might like to experment with

(3) vegetables, you might like to experiment with

(4) vegetables, you might like to experement with

(5) vegtables, you might like to experment with

2. Sentence 3: **The fruit grows in abundance in New Zealand, but it originaly came from China, where it was considered a delicacy in ancient times.**

What correction should be made to this sentence?

(1) change <u>grows</u> to <u>grow</u>

(2) change the spelling of <u>abundance</u> to <u>abundence</u>

(3) change the spelling of <u>originaly</u> to <u>originally</u>

(4) change <u>China</u> to <u>china</u>

(5) change the spelling of <u>ancient</u> to <u>anceint</u>

3. Sentence 5: **In 1962, its name was changed, and it underwent a profiteable increase in popularity.**

What correction should be made to this sentence?

(1) replace the comma with a semicolon

(2) change <u>underwent</u> to <u>under went</u>

(3) change the spelling of <u>profiteable</u> to <u>profitable</u>

(4) change the spelling of <u>increase</u> to <u>increace</u>

(5) no correction is necessary

4. Sentence 6: **Ninety-five percent of the 8,000 acres of kiwi fruit that is grown in the United States today comes from northern California.**

What correction should be made to this sentence?

(1) replace <u>that</u> with <u>who</u>

(2) change <u>grown</u> to <u>growed</u>

(3) change <u>today</u> to <u>to day</u>

(4) change <u>northern</u> to <u>Northern</u>

(5) change <u>California</u> to <u>california</u>

5. Sentence 7: **The green meat of the <u>kiwi</u> <u>makes it prettyer than most fruit.</u>**

Which of the following is the best way to write the underlined portion of this sentence? If you think the original is the best way, choose option (1).

(1) kiwi makes it prettyer than most fruit
(2) kiwi make it prettyer than most fruit
(3) kiwi, makes it prettyer than most fruit
(4) kiwi. Makes it prettyer than most fruit
(5) kiwi makes it prettier than most fruit

<u>Items 6 to 9</u> refer to the following paragraphs.

(1) There is a way buisnesses can earn more money and cut down on national health expenses at the same time. (2) They can do this by offering their employees a fitness program at work. (3) Employees who are fit and healthy cost their employers less money on health insurance claims. (4) About 60 percent of our population does not get regular exersize, and this costs the nation money in health care. (5) Doctors believe moderate exercise five times a week can make a big difference in people's risk for heart disease. (6) The exercise could be as simple as walking or working in the yard for 30-minute periods.

(7) Fit workers are healthyer mentally as well as physically. (8) On the job, this contributes to productive work. (9) Some companies offer their employees exercise classes, an on-site gym, and exercise equipment. (10) Such businesses claim they save nearly $7.00 in health costs and productivity for every dollar they spend on fitness for their workers.

6. Sentence 1: **There is a way buisnesses can earn more money and cut down on national health expenses at the same time.**

What correction should be made to this sentence?

(1) change the spelling of <u>buisenesses</u> to <u>busineses</u>
(2) change the spelling of <u>buisnesses</u> to <u>businesses</u>
(3) insert a comma after <u>money</u>
(4) change <u>national</u> to <u>National</u>
(5) change the spelling of <u>expenses</u> to <u>expences</u>

7. Sentence 4: **About 60 percent of our <u>population does not get regular exersize, and this costs</u> the nation money in health care.**

Which of the following is the best way to write the underlined portion of this sentence? If you think the original is the best way, choose option (1).

(1) population does not get regular exersize, and this costs
(2) population does not get regular exersize, and this cost
(3) population does not get regular exercize, or this costs
(4) population does not get regular exercise, and this costs
(5) population does not get regular exercize; nevertheless, this costs

8. Sentence 7: **Fit workers are healthyer mentally as well as physically.**

What correction should be made to this sentence?

(1) insert a comma after <u>workers</u>
(2) change the spelling of <u>healthyer</u> to <u>healthier</u>
(3) change the spelling of <u>mentally</u> to <u>mentaly</u>
(4) insert a comma after <u>mentally</u>
(5) change the spelling of <u>physically</u> to <u>physicaly</u>

9. Sentences 8 and 9: **On the job, this contributes to productive work. Some companies offer their employees exercise classes, an on-site gym, and exercise equipment.**

The most effective combination of sentences 8 and 9 would include which of the following groups of words?

(1) Although many companies offer exercise opportunities
(2) Productivity contributes to exercise
(3) To enhance productivity
(4) after-hours workouts
(5) productive exercise equipment

To check your answers, turn to page 322.

6 What Is the Apostrophe For?

The **apostrophe** is the punctuation mark that looks like a comma but appears at the top of a word ('). Apostrophes cause problems for writers who don't understand their function. Writers who are uncertain about when and how to use the apostrophe seem either to ignore it altogether or to insert one here and there for no apparent reason.

ACHIEVEMENT GOALS
In this lesson, you will learn how to

• form contractions

• show ownership

When you understand that there are only three uses for the apostrophe, you can master this tiny punctuation mark and use it to make your writing clear and correct. Like all punctuation, the apostrophe serves one or more purposes, and misusing it detracts from your writing.

Use Apostrophes to Combine Words

A **contraction** combines two words into one by omitting one or more letters:

are + not becomes *aren't*

The apostrophe takes the place of the missing *o*. Here's another example:

would + have becomes *would've*

The apostrophe replaces the missing *h* and *a*.

EXERCISE 1

Directions: Place apostrophes in the contractions in the following sentences. Identify the missing letters.

1. Being late so often, youre going to have trouble keeping the job.
2. Itll be hard to find any place open at this hour.
3. They arent selling that item any longer.
4. He hasnt missed a single game all season.
5. Youll have to wait until the report is published.
6. Sam saw that theyd been there already.
7. Shes completely dependable.
8. Take whatever theyll give you.
9. It really isnt hard to understand.
10. By now, its too late to get tickets.

Directions: Choose the <u>one best answer</u> to each item.

<u>Items 11 to 13</u> refer to the following paragraph.

(1) Nutritionists agree that snacks are an important part of our food intake. (2) Snacks keep us from feeling hungry before the next meal. (3) It's also fun to eat. (4) However, most people who work all day depend on vending machines for snacks, and theyre more likely to buy candy bars than a more healthful snack like pretzels. (5) Apparently, its necessary to bring something from home if we want a healthful snack during the work day.

11. Sentence 3: **It's also fun to eat.**

    What correction should be made to this sentence?

    (1) change <u>It's</u> to <u>Its</u>
    (2) change <u>It's</u> to <u>They're</u>
    (3) insert a comma after <u>fun</u>
    (4) change <u>fun to</u> to <u>fun. To</u>
    (5) no correction is necessary

12. Sentence 4: **However, most people who work all day depend on vending machines for snacks, and theyre more likely to buy candy bars than a more healthful snack like pretzels.**

    What correction should be made to this sentence?

    (1) remove the comma after <u>However</u>
    (2) remove the comma after <u>snacks</u>
    (3) change <u>theyre</u> to <u>they're</u>
    (4) change <u>theyre</u> to <u>theyr'e</u>
    (5) change the spelling of <u>healthful</u> to <u>healthfull</u>

13. Sentence 5: **Apparently, its necessary to bring something from home if we want a healthful snack during the work day.**

    What correction should be made to this sentence?

    (1) remove the comma after <u>Apparently</u>
    (2) change <u>its</u> to <u>its'</u>
    (3) change <u>its</u> to <u>it's</u>
    (4) insert a comma after <u>home</u>
    (5) change <u>snack during</u> to <u>snack. During</u>

To check your answers, turn to page 323.

Use Apostrophes to Show Possession

TEST-TAKING TIP

Before you use an apostrophe in a word, ask yourself two questions: Does this word show possession? Is this word a contraction? Unless the answer is *yes* to one of the questions, do not use the apostrophe.

The second most common reason to use an apostrophe is to show that one thing belongs to another:

the *soldier's* weapon

the *truck's* front wheel

Note, however, that we use apostrophes to show possession *only with nouns*. Pronouns that show possession (*yours, hers, his, theirs, ours, its, whose*) do not take apostrophes:

Her house is around the corner.

Their values are different from *ours*.

To show possession with a singular noun, add an *apostrophe + s*:

Marci's coat looks warm.

The *boss's* car was stolen yesterday.

With nouns that become plural by adding *s* or *es*, put the apostrophe after the *s*:

The *bosses'* privileges seemed more numerous than ours.

The sentence above shows that there was more than one boss.

The *boxes'* contents were a mystery.

According to this sentence, there was more than one box with mysterious contents.

With nouns that become plural in other ways, add *apostrophe + s* to show possession:

Women's fashions change more dramatically than *men's* fashions.

The *oxen's* strength made them essential on farms before tractors were invented.

NOTE: *Do not use an apostrophe to indicate a noun is plural. We do use apostrophes to show plurals with numbers and letters, but never with words:*

His report card showed two *A's*, three *B's*, and one C.

There are too many *7's* in your answer.

EXERCISE 2

Directions: Place apostrophes in the possessive words in the sentences below.

1. It was steamy in the mens locker room.

2. The girls softball team won all but two games last season.

3. Governor Cuomos speech held the audience spellbound.

4. Congresss failure to pass the bill irritated the president.

5. The science museums latest exhibit won national recognition.

WRITE ON TARGET

Use each of the following words in a written sentence: *Seth's, musicians', explosions, Patricia's, women's.* Pay attention to the apostrophes.

Directions: Choose the <u>one best answer</u> for each item.

<u>Items 6 to 8</u> refer to the following paragraph.

(1) A resurgence of hate crimes throughout America and in Europe worries world leaders and ordinary citizens. (2) It is not uncommon during times of economic hardship for people to seek scapegoats to blame their problems on. (3) It's easy to victimize people who look different and have different custom's. (4) When large numbers of immigrants enter a country, some of the native residents may feel threatened. (5) They worry about losing their job's or paying higher taxes to help settle newcomers. (6) Economic troubles and influxes of immigrants into countries provide great opportunities for people to cooperate and learn from each other. (7) The attitudes of extremist's lead to hate crimes, but all of us can fight the trend by helping each other change attitudes and learn to embrace cultural differences.

6. Sentence 3: **It's easy to victimize people who look different and have different custom's.**

What correction should be made to this sentence?

(1) change <u>It's</u> to <u>Its</u>
(2) insert a comma after <u>people</u>
(3) replace <u>who</u> with <u>whom</u>
(4) insert a comma after <u>different</u>
(5) change <u>custom's</u> to <u>customs</u>

7. Sentence 5: **They worry about losing their job's or paying higher taxes to help settle newcomers.**

What correction should be made to this sentence?

(1) change <u>their</u> to <u>their's</u>
(2) change <u>job's</u> to <u>jobs</u>
(3) change <u>taxes</u> to <u>taxes'</u>
(4) change <u>newcomers</u> to <u>newcomer's</u>
(5) no correction is necessary

8. Sentence 7: **The attitudes of extremist's lead to hate crimes, but all of us can fight the trend by helping each other change attitudes and learn to embrace cultural differences.**

What correction should be made to this sentence?

(1) change <u>attitudes of</u> to <u>attitude's of</u>
(2) change <u>extremist's</u> to <u>extremists</u>
(3) change <u>extremist's</u> to <u>extremists'</u>
(4) change <u>differences</u> to <u>differences'</u>
(5) change <u>differences</u> to <u>difference's</u>

CONNECTIONS

Do movie dialogues sound like real-life speech? Find out in the News Media theme pages in **CONNECTIONS.** With a small group, read the dialogue from the screenplay aloud, each person taking one part. As you read, pronounce the contractions as full words: *it is* or *it has* for *it's, that is* for *that's,* and so on. Discuss how this sounds—does it sound like real-life speech? What does this tell you about contractions?

To check your answers, turn to page 323.

G E D TEST PREVIEW

Directions: Choose the <u>one best answer</u> for each item.

<u>Items 1 to 6</u> refer to the following paragraph.

(1) Most school districts in the United States teach American History two or three times during a childs' education. (2) Starting in about the fifth grade, every American child learns about the origins of their country. (3) For generation's, these schoolchildren learned that Christopher Columbus discovered America. (4) Columbus Day is still a holiday in many parts of the country. (5) However, it is no longer believed that Columbus's voyages to America were the first one's. (6) Most scholars believe Viking's from Norway were the first Europeans to discover America around the year 1000. (7) Some people claim it is inaccurate to credit any Europeans with the "discovery" of America when the Indians were already populating the land. (8) History is far more complicated than people might think.

1. Sentence 1: **Most school districts in the United States teach American History two or three times during a childs' education.**

What correction should be made to this sentence?

(1) change <u>districts</u> to <u>district's</u>
(2) change <u>times</u> to <u>time's</u>
(3) change <u>times</u> to <u>times'</u>
(4) change <u>childs'</u> to <u>child's</u>
(5) change <u>childs'</u> to <u>childs</u>

2. Sentence 2: **Starting in about the fifth grade, every American <u>child learns about the origins of their country.</u>**

Which of the following is the best way to write the underlined portion of this sentence? If you think the original is the best way, choose option (1).

(1) child learns about the origins of their country
(2) child learn about the origins of their country
(3) child learns about the origins of their Country
(4) child learns about the origin's of their country
(5) child learns about the origins of his or her country

3. Sentence 3: **For generation's, these schoolchildren learned that Christopher Columbus discovered America.**

What correction should be made to this sentence?

(1) change <u>generation's</u> to <u>generations</u>
(2) change <u>generation's</u> to <u>generations'</u>
(3) change <u>Columbus</u> to <u>Columbus's</u>
(4) change <u>America</u> to <u>america</u>
(5) no correction is necessary

4. Sentence 4: **Columbus Day is still a holiday in many parts of the country.**

What correction should be made to this sentence?

(1) change <u>Day</u> to <u>day</u>
(2) change <u>holiday</u> to <u>Holiday</u>
(3) change <u>parts</u> to <u>parts'</u>
(4) change <u>country</u> to <u>Country</u>
(5) no correction is necessary

5. Sentence 5: **However, it is no longer believed that Columbus's voyages to America were the first one's.**

What correction should be made to this sentence?

(1) change the spelling of <u>believed</u> to <u>beleived</u>
(2) change <u>Columbus's</u> to <u>Columbuses</u>
(3) change <u>voyages</u> to <u>voyage's</u>
(4) change <u>one's</u> to <u>ones</u>
(5) change <u>one's</u> to <u>ones'</u>

6. Sentence 6: **Most scholars believe Viking's from Norway were the first Europeans to discover America around the year 1000.**

What correction should be made to this sentence?

(1) change <u>scholars</u> to <u>scholars'</u>
(2) change <u>scholars</u> to <u>scholar's</u>
(3) change <u>scholars</u> to <u>Scholars</u>
(4) change <u>Viking's</u> to <u>Vikings</u>
(5) change <u>Europeans</u> to <u>European's</u>

<u>Items 7 to 10</u> refer to the following paragraph.

(1) A college computer students' project led to a fascinating discovery about jumprope rhymes. (2) While watching some children jumping rope on a school playground, the student decided to research the origins of their jingles. (3) Children who jump rope and chant jingles while they jump usually think they invented the rhymes. (4) Their older brothers and sisters claim the rhymes are their's. (5) However, the project revealed that the same or similar rhymes are sung by rope-jumping children all over the world. (6) Not only do the rhymes cross national boundaries, they cross generations. (7) They're the same rhymes that have been sung by children for decade's. (8) The projects conclusions led not only to information about jumprope rhymes, but show the similarity among people, no matter where they live or when they lived.

7. Sentence 1: **A college computer students' project led to a fascinating discovery about jumprope rhymes.**

What correction should be made to this sentence?

(1) change <u>students'</u> to <u>students</u>
(2) change <u>students'</u> to <u>student's</u>
(3) change the spelling of <u>fascinating</u> to <u>fasinating</u>
(4) insert a comma after <u>discovery</u>
(5) no correction is necessary

8. Sentence 4: **Their older brothers and sisters claim the rhymes are their's.**

What correction should be made to this sentence?

(1) change <u>brothers</u> to <u>brother's</u>
(2) change <u>sisters</u> to <u>sister's</u>
(3) change <u>claim</u> to <u>claims</u>
(4) change <u>their's</u> to <u>theirs</u>
(5) change <u>their's</u> to <u>theirs'</u>

9. Sentence 7: **They're the same rhymes that have been sung by children for decade's.**

What correction should be made to this sentence?

(1) change <u>They're</u> to <u>Theyre</u>
(2) change <u>sung</u> to <u>sang</u>
(3) change <u>sung</u> to <u>singed</u>
(4) change <u>children</u> to <u>children's</u>
(5) change <u>decade's</u> to <u>decades</u>

10. Sentence 8: **The projects conclusions led not only to information about jumprope rhymes, but show the similarity among people, no matter where they live or when they lived.**

Which of the following is the best way to write the underlined portion of this sentence? If you think the original is the best way, choose option (1).

(1) the projects conclusions
(2) the projects' conclusions
(3) the project's conclusion
(4) the project's conclusions
(5) the projects conclusion's

To check your answers, turn to page 323.

7 Words to Watch Out For

**ACHIEVEMENT GOALS
In this lesson, you will learn how to**

- distinguish among sound-alike words

- spell the words on the Master Spelling List

Memory and practice are essential tools for mastering spelling. You'll find it helpful to be aware of words that often cause spelling problems. In this lesson you'll find a GED Master Spelling List and a list of word pairs or groups that sound the same but have different meanings and different spellings. Study the lists and use them for reference when you're not sure about the spelling of a word.

Ask your partner or a member of your group to read the words from both lists as you write them down. Check your spelling against the lists. If you memorize the spelling of the words you missed, you'll improve your overall spelling and the quality of your essays.

Words That Sound Alike

Words that have the same sound but different spellings and meanings present special spelling problems. If you learn these words and practice using them correctly, you will eliminate many common spelling errors. You need to study the meanings as well as the spellings of these words to be sure you use the correct one.

The table on the next two pages shows some of the most commonly confused word pairs and groups.

Table 7-1 Commonly confused word pairs and groups

WORD PAIR	MEANING	EXAMPLE
affect	verb meaning to have an impact	How did the exercise affect you?
effect	noun meaning a result	Did it have the effect you hoped for?
already	previously	He had already filled the gas tank.
all ready	entirely prepared	The class was all ready for the field trip.
altar	table or stand in a church	The altar boys lit the candles.
alter	to change	They altered the strategy for the game's second half.
altogether	entirely	She was altogether confused by the map.
all together	everyone or everything in the same place	The books were all together on the correct shelves.
bored	not interested	The lecture bored most of the audience.
board	a piece of wood, a group of policy-makers	The board wouldn't fit in the truck. The board voted to raise fees.
brake	device to stop something	The bicycle's brake gripped the back wheel.
break	to destroy	Someone will have to break a window.
capitol	the building in which government officials work	Pictures on the capitol walls show all the governors.
capital	the city that serves as the seat of government	The capital of the United States is Washington, D.C.
desert	a dry arid place	The desert blooms in the spring.
dessert	the last course of a meal	Ice cream is a popular dessert.
for	a preposition	These papers are for you.
fore	a prefix	The outcome was a foregone conclusion
four	a number	Four of the five panel members voted to adjourn.
heard	past tense of the verb *to hear*	They heard the train coming.
herd	a group of animals	A herd of cattle stampeded in the night.
lead	a metal, the graphite in a pencil	A lead weight is hard to move.
led	past tense of the verb *to lead*	The captain led his team to victory.
miner	someone who works in a mine	They rescued the miner after four days.
minor	under legal age, not important	No minors were allowed in the bar. It was a minor offense, so he was put on probation.
passed	past tense of the verb *to pass*	She passed the exam easily.
past	time that has gone by	In the past, dress was more formal.
peace	the absence of war	The entire world longed for peace
piece	a part of something	A piece of pie after dinner would be nice.
principal	head of a school, most important	The principal kept the school running smoothly. It is our principal demand.
principle	basic law or rule	He liked to study the principles of chemistry.

Table 7-1 Continued

WORD PAIR	MEANING	EXAMPLE
role	a part in a play	She wanted to play the role of the detective.
roll	to move over and over, a shape of a bread, a list of names	The car would roll down the hill if the brake slipped. A roll and butter make a good snack. After roll call, the class started.
stationary	not moving	Riding a stationary bicycle is good exercise.
stationery	paper	She found note cards at the stationery store.
there	in that place	The ball is over there.
their	belonging to them	It's their problem.
they're	contraction of *they are*	They're able to solve it.
to	indicates direction	Turn to the left.
too	also, excessive	I'll go too. Too many movies are disappointing.
two	a number	Two people lost their cameras.
waist	a part of the body	The belt was too small for his waist.
waste	to squander	Try not to waste space in the room.
weak	not strong	The wind grew too weak to do damage.
week	a period of seven days	It had been storming for a week.
weather	the climate	It depends on the weather.
whether	if	I don't know whether we can go this time.
who's	contraction of *who is* or *who has*	Who's riding in the station wagon?
whose	possessive pronoun	Whose jacket is this?

EXERCISE 1

Directions: Identify the correct word from each pair in the sentences below. Then write sentences using the other words in the pairs. Exchange papers with your partner or a member of your group to see whether you have used the words correctly.

1. (Your/You're) late for the interview.

2. This is beautiful (stationary/stationery).

3. He did a great job explaining the general (principal/principle).

4. That car (passed/past) me on the right.

5. How did you (brake/break) your arm?

6. The drum major (lead/led) the band in the parade.

7. A little (peace/piece) and quiet would help.

8. That's (too/to/two) heavy for you to carry.

9. The job is (altogether/all together) too boring.

10. Some people never eat (desert/dessert).

11. She can't decide (weather/whether) to apply for that job.

12. I (heard/herd) you had a great trip.

13. There are at least (to/too/two) choices.

14. Were you (board/bored) by that book?

15. Give it to (their/there/they're) supervisor.

Directions: Choose the one best answer to each item.

Items 16 to 20 refer to the following paragraph.

(1) The sene of the collision was a four-way-stop intersection. (2) It was hard to tell who's fault it was. (3) Three cars were involved, but their were no other witnesses to the accident. (4) Even after questioning the three drivers, the police were not sure what had happened. (5) One driver claimed neither of the other two applied the breaks. (6) Another driver said he was already to go when the other one ran the stop sign.

16. Sentence 1: **The sene of the collision was a four-way-stop intersection.**

What correction should be made to this sentence?

(1) change the spelling of sene to scene
(2) change collision to Collision
(3) change four-way to for-way
(4) change four-way to fore-way
(5) change intersection to inter section

17. Sentence 2: **It was hard to tell who's fault it was.**

What correction should be made to this sentence?

(1) replace to with too
(2) replace to with two
(3) replace who's with whose
(4) replace who's with who is
(5) change it to its

18. Sentence 3: **Three cars were involved, but their were no other witnesses to the accident.**

What correction should be made to this sentence?

(1) replace their with there
(2) replace their with they're
(3) replace no with know
(4) replace to with too
(5) replace to with two

19. Sentence 5: **One driver claimed neither of the other two applied the breaks.**

What correction should be made to this sentence?

(1) replace one with won
(2) change the spelling of neither to niether
(3) replace two with to
(4) replace breaks with brakes
(5) no correction is necessary

20. Sentence 6: **Another driver said he was already to go when the other one ran the stop sign.**

What correction should be made to this sentence?

(1) insert a comma after said
(2) change already to all ready
(3) change ran to run
(4) change stop sign to Stop Sign
(5) no correction is necessary

To check your answers, turn to page 324.

GED Master List of Frequently Misspelled Words

The following pages list the most commonly misspelled words. To determine which ones you need to study, ask your partner or a member of your group to read the words to you, and then write them down as you hear them. Check your words against the list, and underline those you missed. Practice spelling those words. Remember to think about syllables and to apply the basic spelling rules, but also remember that some of the words present problems because they are exceptions to the rules.

Some words you simply have to memorize because there is no logic to the way they are spelled. Others, however, you probably misspell for one of the reasons listed below. As you study the words you have trouble with, ask yourself whether your spelling error resulted from any of the following:

- an exception to a rule
- adding a suffix
- adding a prefix
- confusing words that sound alike
- doubling letters
- omitting letters
- using the wrong vowel

TEST-TAKING TIP

As you revise your essay, you may discover you've misspelled a word. Draw a single line through the misspelled word and write the correct word above it neatly and clearly.

Table 7-2 Practice spelling the words in Table 7-2 before taking the GED Writing Skills Test.

MASTER LIST OF FREQUENTLY MISSPELLED WORDS			
a lot	acquire	aggressive	answer
ability	across	agree	antiseptic
absence	address	aisle	anxious
absent	addressed	all right	apologize
abundance	adequate	almost	apparatus
accept	advantage	already	apparent
acceptable	advantageous	although	appear
accident	advertise	altogether	appearance
accommodate	advertisement	always	appetite
accompanied	advice	amateur	application
accomplish	advisable	American	apply
accumulation	advise	among	appreciate
accuse	advisor	amount	appreciation
accustomed	aerial	analysis	approach
ache	affect	analyze	appropriate
achieve	affectionate	angel	approval
achievement	again	angle	approve
acknowledge	against	annual	approximate
acquaintance	aggravate	another	argue

Table 7-2 Continued

MASTER LIST OF FREQUENTLY MISSPELLED WORDS			
arguing	breadth	commitment	curiosity
argument	breath	committed	cylinder
arouse	breathe	committee	daily
arrange	brilliant	communicate	daughter
arrangement	building	company	daybreak
article	bulletin	comparative	death
artificial	bureau	compel	deceive
ascend	burial	competent	December
assistance	buried	competition	deception
assistant	bury	compliment	decide
associate	bushes	conceal	decision
association	business	conceit	decisive
attempt	cafeteria	conceivable	deed
attendance	calculator	conceive	definite
attention	calendar	concentration	delicious
audience	campaign	conception	dependent
August	capital	condition	deposit
author	capitol	conference	derelict
automobile	captain	confident	descend
autumn	career	conquer	descent
auxiliary	careful	conscience	describe
available	careless	conscientious	description
avenue	carriage	conscious	desert
awful	carrying	consequence	desirable
awkward	category	consequently	despair
bachelor	ceiling	considerable	desperate
balance	cemetery	consistency	dessert
balloon	cereal	consistent	destruction
bargain	certain	continual	determine
basic	changeable	continuous	develop
beautiful	characteristic	controlled	development
because	charity	controversy	device
become	chief	convenience	dictator
before	choose	convenient	died
beginning	chose	conversation	difference
being	cigarette	corporal	different
believe	circumstance	corroborate	dilemma
benefit	congratulate	council	dinner
benefited	citizen	counsel	direction
between	clothes	counselor	disappear
bicycle	clothing	courage	disappoint
board	coarse	courageous	disappointment
bored	coffee	course	disapproval
borrow	collect	courteous	disapprove
bottle	college	courtesy	disastrous
bottom	column	criticism	discipline
boundary	comedy	criticize	discover
brake	comfortable	crystal	discriminate

Table 7-2 Continued

MASTER LIST OF FREQUENTLY MISSPELLED WORDS			
disease	exceed	grievance	intelligence
dissatisfied	excellent	grievous	intercede
dissection	except	grocery	interest
dissipate	exceptional	guarantee	interfere
distance	exercise	guess	interference
distinction	exhausted	guidance	interpreted
division	exhaustion	half	interrupt
doctor	exhilaration	hammer	invitation
dollar	existence	handkerchief	irrelevant
doubt	exorbitant	happiness	irresistible
dozen	expense	healthy	irritable
earnest	experience	heard	island
easy	experiment	heavy	its
ecstasy	explanation	height	it's
ecstatic	extreme	heroes	itself
education	facility	heroine	January
effect	factory	hideous	jealous
efficiency	familiar	himself	judgment
efficient	fascinate	hoarse	journal
eight	fascinating	holiday	kindergarten
either	fatigue	hopeless	kitchen
eligibility	February	hospital	knew
eligible	financial	humorous	knock
eliminate	financier	hurried	know
embarrass	flourish	hurrying	knowledge
embarrassment	forcibly	ignorance	labor
emergency	forehead	imaginary	laboratory
emphasis	foreign	imbecile	laid
emphasize	formal	imitation	language
enclosure	former	immediately	later
encouraging	fortunate	immigrant	latter
endeavor	fourteen	incidental	laugh
engineer	fourth	increase	leisure
English	frequent	independence	length
enormous	friend	independent	lesson
enough	frightening	indispensable	library
entrance	fundamental	inevitable	license
envelope	further	influence	light
environment	gallon	influential	lightning
equipment	garden	initiate	likelihood
equipped	gardener	innocence	likely
especially	general	inoculate	literal
essential	genius	inquiry	literature
evening	government	insistent	livelihood
evident	governor	instead	loaf
exaggerate	grammar	instinct	loneliness
exaggeration	grateful	integrity	loose
examine	great	intellectual	lose

Table 7-2 Continued

MASTER LIST OF FREQUENTLY MISSPELLED WORDS

losing	occasion	perseverance	principal
loyal	occasional	persevere	principle
loyalty	occur	persistent	privilege
magazine	occurred	persuade	probably
maintenance	occurrence	personality	procedure
maneuver	ocean	personal	proceed
marriage	offer	personnel	produce
married	often	persuade	professional
marry	omission	persuasion	professor
match	omit	pertain	profitable
material	once	picture	prominent
mathematics	operate	piece	promise
measure	opinion	plain	pronounce
medicine	opportune	playwright	pronunciation
million	opportunity	pleasant	propeller
miniature	optimist	please	prophet
minimum	optimistic	pleasure	prospect
miracle	origin	pocket	psychology
miscellaneous	original	poison	pursue
mischief	oscillate	policeman	pursuit
mischievous	ought	political	quality
misspelled	ounce	population	quantity
mistake	overcoat	portrayal	quarreling
momentous	paid	positive	quart
monkey	pamphlet	possess	quarter
monotonous	panicky	possession	quiet
moral	parallel	possessive	quite
morale	parallelism	possible	raise
mortgage	particular	post office	realistic
mountain	partner	potatoes	realize
mournful	pastime	practical	reason
muscle	patience	prairie	rebellion
mysterious	peace	precede	recede
mystery	peaceable	preceding	receipt
narrative	pear	precise	receive
natural	peculiar	predictable	recipe
necessary	pencil	prefer	recognize
needle	people	preference	recommend
negligence	perceive	preferential	recuperate
neighbor	perception	preferred	referred
neither	perfect	prejudice	rehearsal
newspaper	perform	preparation	reign
newsstand	performance	prepare	relevant
niece	perhaps	prescription	relieve
noticeable	period	presence	remedy
o'clock	permanence	president	renovate
obedient	permanent	prevalent	repeat
obstacle	perpendicular	primitive	repetition

Table 7-2 Continued

MASTER LIST OF FREQUENTLY MISSPELLED WORDS

representative	siege	surely	university
requirements	sight	surprise	unnecessary
resemblance	signal	suspense	unusual
resistance	significance	sweat	vacuum
resource	significant	sweet	useful
respectability	similar	syllable	usual
responsibility	similarity	symmetrical	valley
restaurant	sincerely	sympathy	valuable
rhythm	site	synonym	variety
rhythmical	soldier	technical	vegetable
ridiculous	solemn	telegram	vein
right	sophomore	telephone	vengeance
role	soul	temperament	versatile
roll	source	temperature	vicinity
roommate	souvenir	tenant	vicious
sandwich	special	tendency	view
Saturday	specified	tenement	village
scarcely	specimen	therefore	villain
scene	speech	thorough	visitor
schedule	stationary	through	voice
science	stationery	title	volume
scientific	statue	together	waist
scissors	stockings	tomorrow	weak
season	stomach	tongue	wear
secretary	straight	toward	weather
seize	strength	tragedy	Wednesday
seminar	strenuous	transferred	week
sense	stretch	treasury	weigh
separate	striking	tremendous	weird
service	studying	tries	whether
several	substantial	truly	which
severely	succeed	twelfth	while
shepherd	successful	twelve	whole
sheriff	sudden	tyranny	wholly
shining	superintendent	undoubtedly	whose
shoulder	suppress	United States	wretched
shriek			

EXERCISE 2

Directions: Identify and correct the misspelled words in the following sentences.

1. A competant gardener knows how much to water.

2. With practice, you can concquer most spelling problems.

3. It's important to take advantage of any guidence you can find.

4. Daily practice is advantagous to anyone learning a new skill.

5. Wensday falls in the middle of the week.

6. Helping others can be a priviledge.

304 Unit 3 Handling Mechanics

7. Misunderstanding something in class is inevitible.

8. A good teacher doesn't mind repeeting something.

9. After hearing the story, he felt simpathy for her.

10. Sometimes it's better to wait until tommorow.

Directions: Choose the <u>one best answer</u> to each item.

<u>Items 11 to 13</u> refer to the following paragraph.

(1) Isabel and Felix attended a sychology seminar. (2) They hoped to learn some things that would help them solve problems with their families. (3) Isabel felt she had to sholder most of the responsibility in her family because her younger brothers wouldn't help around the house. (4) Felix was especially interested in learning how to deal with his demanding boss. (5) They found the seminar helpful in those and other areas as well. (6) There were talks on marriage, tragedy, and predjudice. (7) By the time they left, they had much to think about.

11. Sentence 1: **Isabel and Felix attended <u>a sychology seminar.</u>**

    Which of the following is the best way to write the underlined portion of this sentence? If you think the original is the best way, choose option (1).

    (1) a sychology seminar
    (2) a sychology semnar
    (3) a psychology semnar
    (4) a psychology seminar
    (5) a psychology semanar

12. Sentence 3: **Isabel felt she had to sholder most of the responsibility in her family because her younger brothers wouldn't help around the house.**

    What correction should be made to this sentence?

    (1) change the spelling of <u>sholder</u> to <u>shuolder</u>
    (2) change the spelling of <u>sholder</u> to <u>shoulder</u>
    (3) change the spelling of <u>responsibility</u> to <u>responsability</u>
    (4) change the spelling of <u>responsibility</u> to <u>responsibleity</u>
    (5) no correction is necessary

13. Sentence 6: **There were talks on marriage, tragedy, and predjudice.**

    What correction should be made to this sentence?

    (1) replace <u>There</u> with <u>They're</u>
    (2) change the spelling of <u>marriage</u> to <u>marrage</u>
    (3) change the spelling of <u>marriage</u> to <u>marrige</u>
    (4) change the spelling of <u>tragedy</u> to <u>tradgedy</u>
    (5) change the spelling of <u>predjudice</u> to <u>prejudice</u>

To check your answers, turn to page 324.

GED TEST PREVIEW

Directions: Choose the <u>one best answer</u> to each item.

<u>Items 1 to 5</u> refer to the following paragraph.

(1) Among nature's animals are many that can harm human beings. (2) Most people know insects and snake's can be poisonous. (3) Wary campers, hikers, and picnickers watch out for these creatures. (4) Not everyone realizes, however, that the oceon is also home to poisonous creatures. (5) One such animal is a deadly jellyfish. (6) It's sting affects the victim's circulatory system. (7) The impact of the vicious sting is felt immediately. (8) A disasterous encounter with such a creature could amount to a tragedy that ends in death. (9) Because of their dramatic impact, we usually think of sharks when we think of the dangers of the sea. (10) Clearly, sharks are not the only fish to avoid.

1. Sentence 2: **Most people know insects and snake's can be poisonous.**

What correction should be made to this sentence?

(1) replace <u>know</u> with <u>no</u>
(2) change <u>insects</u> to <u>insect's</u>
(3) change <u>snake's</u> to <u>snakes'</u>
(4) change <u>snake's</u> to <u>snakes</u>
(5) no correction is necessary

2. Sentence 4: **Not everyone realizes, however, that the oceon is also home to poisonous creatures.**

What correction should be made to this sentence?

(1) change <u>realizes</u> to <u>realize's</u>
(2) remove the comma before <u>however</u>
(3) change the spelling of <u>oceon</u> to <u>ocean</u>
(4) replace <u>to</u> with <u>too</u>
(5) change the spelling of <u>poisonous</u> to <u>poisinous</u>

3. Sentence 6: **It's sting affects the victim's circulatory system.**

What correction should be made to this sentence?

(1) change <u>It's</u> to <u>Its</u>
(2) change <u>affects</u> to <u>effects</u>
(3) change <u>victim's</u> to <u>victims</u>
(4) change the spelling of <u>circulatory</u> to <u>sirculatory</u>
(5) no correction necessary

4. Sentence 7: **The impact of the vicious sting is felt immediatelly.**

What correction should be made to this sentence?

(1) change <u>impact</u> to <u>Impact</u>
(2) change the spelling of <u>vicious</u> to <u>visious</u>
(3) change <u>is</u> to <u>was</u>
(4) change the spelling of <u>immediatelly</u> to <u>imediatelly</u>
(5) change the spelling of <u>immediatelly</u> to <u>immediately</u>

5. Sentence 8: **A disasterous encounter with such a creature could amount to a tragedy that ends in death.**

What correction should be made to this sentence?

(1) change the spelling of <u>disasterous</u> to <u>disastrous</u>
(2) change <u>encounter</u> to <u>Encounter</u>
(3) insert a comma after <u>creature</u>
(4) change the spelling of <u>amount</u> to <u>ammount</u>
(5) change the spelling of <u>death</u> to <u>deth</u>

Items 6 to 9 refer to the following paragraph.

(1) There was a time when banks offered people toasters and other gifts for opening checking and savings accounts. (2) Those days are gone, and now banks charge customers fees for just about every service. (3) Some banks charge customers for using the automated teller machine, and others charge customers for not using the ATM often enough. (4) Penalties for bounced checks have also increased. (5) There are service charges for checking accounts and savings accounts, so some banks even charge consumers for closing accounts. (6) Banks claim they must charge all these fees because they have to pay fees as well. (7) Federal regulations, such as those that govern deposit insurance, costs financial institutions money; they, in turn, pass those charges on to the consumer. (8) Consumers could protest by shopping around for banks that charge fewer fees, but many consumers apparently choose a bank for its convenient location rather than for its costs or services.

6. Sentence 2: **Those days are gone, and now banks charge customers fees for just about every service.**

If you rewrote sentence 2 beginning with

For just about every service, some banks

the next word should be

(1) save
(2) serve
(3) automate
(4) charge
(5) use

7. Sentence 3: **Some banks charge customers for using the <u>automated teller machine, and others charge customers</u> for not using the ATM often enough.**

Which of the following is the best way to write the underlined portion of this sentence? If you think the original is the best way, choose option (1).

(1) automated teller machine, and others charge customers
(2) automated teller machine and others charge customers
(3) automated teller machine, and others charged customers
(4) automated, teller machine, and others charge customers
(5) automated teller machine, and others charging customers

8. Sentence 5: **There are service charges for checking accounts and savings accounts, so some banks even charge consumers for closing accounts.**

What correction should be made to this sentence?

(1) change <u>are</u> to <u>is</u>
(2) insert a comma after <u>checking accounts</u>
(3) change the spelling of <u>savings</u> to <u>saveings</u>
(4) remove the comma after <u>savings accounts</u>
(5) replace <u>so</u> with <u>and</u>

9. Sentence 7: **Federal <u>regulations, such as those that govern deposit insurance, costs financial institutions</u> money; they, in turn, pass these charges on to the consumer.**

Which of the following is the best way to write the underlined portion of this sentence? If you think the original is the best way, choose option (1).

(1) regulations, such as those that govern deposit insurance, costs financial institutions
(2) regulations, such as those that govern deposit insurance, costs Financial Institutions
(3) Regulations like federal deposit insurance, costs financial institutions
(4) regulations, such as those that govern deposit insurance, cost financial institutions
(5) regulations such as those that govern deposit insurance, cost financial institutions

To check your answers, turn to page 325.

3 Handling Mechanics
R E V I E W

You've learned the mechanics of writing that will help you edit your essay. If you think about these points as you write, you'll have less to do when it's time to edit.

You've learned there are rules of capitalization that affect words other than the first one in a sentence. You've learned to capitalize particular names within a group (*General* MacArthur), but not the group itself *(generals)*. You've also learned that certain words, like dates, names, languages, and nationalities, *always* take a capital letter, no matter where they appear in the sentence.

You know now that commas serve many purposes. You had already learned how to use commas to separate the clauses in compound sentences. Now you know how to use commas to separate items in a series. You've learned to use commas to set introductory material apart from the rest of the sentence. In addition, you've learned to use commas to set off interrupting elements so that the reader can follow your thoughts without becoming confused.

By learning where you *do* use commas, you have also learned where you *do not* use them. If you think about the rules that govern the use of commas, you can avoid the problem of overusing them.

Key Terms to Review

apostrophe	a punctuation mark that is used to indicate either ownership or that a letter has been omitted
contraction	a word formed by combining two words; one or more letters are omitted and an apostrophe is put in their place
mechanics	rules of capitalization, punctuation, and spelling
phrase	a word group that does not contain a subject and verb; a phrase often appears at the beginning of a sentence as introductory material
prefix	one or more letters or syllables added to the beginning of a word to change its meaning
suffix	one or more letters or syllables added to the end of a word to change its meaning
syllable	a part of a word that is pronounced as a single unit; a syllable always contains a vowel

You've learned rules that govern spelling, too. These rules will help you avoid common spelling errors. You've learned how to use apostrophes to form one word from two separate words (a contraction). You've also learned to use apostrophes with nouns to show ownership.

You have a list of the most commonly misspelled words, including words that have the same sound but different meanings and spellings. You also have some tips for studying this list so you can focus on those words you need to learn how to spell.

EXERCISES

Directions: Choose the <u>one best answer</u> to each item.

<u>Items 1 to 7</u> refer to the following paragraph.

(1) Workplace safety is an issue that interests Government officials and business owners. (2) Today's workers face substantial riskes from many more sources than just heavy machinery. (3) Everyone recognizes the dangers faced by roofers, miners, firefighters and police officers who don't work inside offices. (4) Technology has brought new hazards to office workers. (5) People who work with computers for example can develop back problems from sitting in inappropriate chairs. (6) If the keyboard isn't at just the right level, computer operators can incur wrist injuries that could require surgery. (7) Fatigue and eyestrain, trouble workers who spend their day looking at computer monitors. (8) Ergonomics is a growing scients that addresses these issues. (9) It deals with features of the work enviorment, including design of office furniture, office lighting, and use of space. (10) It's costly for everyone if a worker is injured on the job.

1. Sentence 1: **Workplace safety is an issue that interests Government officials and business owners.**

What correction should be made to this sentence?

(1) change the spelling of <u>safety</u> to <u>safty</u>
(2) change the spelling of <u>interests</u> to <u>intrests</u>
(3) change <u>Government</u> to <u>government</u>
(4) insert a comma after <u>officials</u>
(5) no correction is necessary

2. Sentence 2: **Today's workers face substantial riskes from many more sources than just heavy machinery.**

Which of the following is the best way to write the underlined portion of this sentence? If you think the original is the best way, choose option (1).

(1) Today's workers face substantial riskes from
(2) Todays workeres face substantial riskes from
(3) Today's workers, face substantial riskes from
(4) Today's workers face substantial risks from
(5) Today's workers' faced substantial riskes from

3. Sentence 3: **Everyone recognizes the dangers faced by roofers, miners, firefighters and police officers who don't work inside offices.**

What correction should be made to this sentence?

(1) change the spelling of <u>recognizes</u> to <u>reconizes</u>
(2) remove the comma after <u>roofers</u>
(3) remove the comma after <u>miners</u>
(4) insert a comma after <u>firefighters</u>
(5) change <u>don't</u> to <u>dont</u>

4. Sentence 5: **People who work with computers for example can develop back problems from sitting in inappropriate chairs.**

Which of the following is the best way to write the underlined portion of this sentence? If you think the original is the best way, choose option (1).

(1) computers for example can
(2) computers. For example can
(3) computers for, example can
(4) computers, for example, can
(5) computers for example, can

5. Sentence 7: **Fatigue and eyestrain, trouble workers who spend their day looking at computer monitors.**

What correction should be made to this sentence?

(1) change the spelling of Fatigue to Fatige
(2) remove the comma after eyestrain
(3) change trouble to troubles
(4) change their to there
(5) change their to they're

6. Sentence 8: **Ergonomics is a growing scients that addresses these issues.**

Which of the following is the best way to write the underlined portion of this sentence? If you think the original is the best way, choose option (1).

(1) growing scients that addresses these issues
(2) growing scients that address these issues
(3) growing science that addresses these issues
(4) growing scients who addresses these issues
(5) growing scients whom addresses these issues

7. Sentence 9: **It deals with features of the work enviorment, including design of office furniture, office lighting, and use of space.**

Which of the following is the best way to write the underlined portion of this sentence? If you think the original is the best way, choose option (1).

(1) work enviorment, including
(2) works enviorment, including
(3) work enviorment, including
(4) work environment, including
(5) work enviorment, includeing

Items 8 to 15 refer to the following paragraph.

(1) One of technologys most frustrating achievements is voice mail. (2) Voice mail is a recording that answers when you phone certain business's or government offices. (3) You don't actualy speak to a person. (4) Instead, you are invited by a recorded voice to answer a series of questions by pushing buttons on your telephone. (5) The recording gives you some choices and tells you to push a perticuler button on your touch-tone telephone to choose the item you want. (6) Sometimes the list of choices is so long you forget what the choices were by the end. (7) But voice mail is ready to help with that problem, to. (8) The last choice is usually a number to push to hear the entire list of choices again. (9) The best choice however is the one that tells you to stay on the line if you wish to speak to a person. (10) If your willing to wait long enough, you might get to talk to somebody. (11) Then, you might even get your question answered.

8. Sentence 1: **One of technologys most frustrating achievements is voice mail.**

What correction should be made to this sentence?

(1) change technologys to technology's
(2) change the spelling of technologys to technologies
(3) insert a comma after achievements
(4) change the spelling of achievements to acheivements
(5) no correction is necessary

9. Sentence 2: **Voice mail is a recording that answers when you phone <u>certain business's or government offices</u>.**

Which of the following is the best way to write the underlined portion of this sentence? If you think the original is the best way, choose option (1).

(1) certain business's or government offices
(2) certain Business's or government offices
(3) certain business's or Government offices
(4) certain business's or goverment offices
(5) certain businesses or government offices

10. Sentence 3: **You don't actualy speak to a person.**

What correction should be made to this sentence?

(1) replace <u>You</u> with <u>We</u>
(2) change <u>don't</u> to <u>dont</u>
(3) change the spelling of <u>actualy</u> to <u>actually</u>
(4) change <u>to</u> to <u>too</u>
(5) no correction is necessary

11. Sentence 5: **The recording gives you a series of choices and tells you to push a perticuler button on your touch-tone telephone to choose the item you want.**

What correction should be made to this sentence?

(1) insert a comma after <u>choices</u>
(2) change the spelling of <u>perticuler</u> to <u>particular</u>
(3) change <u>touch-tone telephone</u> to <u>Touch-Tone Telephone</u>
(4) change the spelling of <u>telephone</u> to <u>telphone</u>
(5) change the spelling of <u>choose</u> to <u>chose</u>

12. Sentence 6: **Sometimes the list of choices is so long you forget what the choices were by the end.**

If you rewrote sentence 4 beginning with

<u>By the time you get to the end of a long list of choices,</u>

the next word should be

(1) we
(2) they
(3) they're
(4) his
(5) you

13. Sentence 7: **But voice mail is ready <u>to help with that problem, to</u>.**

Which of the following is the best way to write the underlined portion of this sentence? If you think the original is the best way, choose option (1).

(1) to help with that problem, to
(2) to help with that problem, two
(3) to help with that problem, too
(4) too help with that problem, to
(5) two help with that problem, to

14. Sentence 9: **The best <u>choice however is</u> the one that tells you to stay on the line if you wish to speak to a person.**

Which of the following is the best way to write the underlined portion of this sentence? If you think the original is the best way, choose option (1).

(1) choice however is
(2) choice, however, is
(3) choice. However is
(4) choice however, is
(5) choice; however, is

15. Sentence 10: **If you're willing to wait long enough you might get to talk to somebody.**

What correction should be made to this sentence?

(1) replace <u>you're</u> with <u>your</u>
(2) change the spelling of <u>enough</u> to <u>enuff</u>
(3) insert a comma after <u>enough</u>
(4) insert a comma after <u>get to</u>
(5) no correction is necessary

Items 16 to 22 refer to the following paragraph.

(1) There is considerable debate among politicians and voters as to weather English should be noted as the official language of the United States. (2) Supporters of an official language policy argue that it costs to much to provide education, voter ballots, and other services in several different languages. (3) Opponents argue that its important to serve the millions of nonEnglish speakers in their native languages so that they can more quickly learn to function productively in American society. (4) Teaching school in languages other than English, they argue, helps children learn the basic skills everyone needs. (5) An opposing view says immigrants should, on the other hand, not be able to avoid English so easily. (6) Without English language skills, the argument goes, people are stuck in jobs with low pay. (7) Such jobs also offer little opportunity for advancment. (8) America's earlier waves of immigrants had less available in their native languages, so they were forced to learn english. (9) Which approach is better? (10) The experts, who hold widely different opinions may not come to agreement on this issue for a long time.

16. Sentence 1: **There is considerable debate among politicians and voters as to weather English should be noted as the official language of the United States.**

What correction should be made to this sentence?

(1) replace <u>There</u> with <u>Their</u>
(2) change the spelling of <u>considerable</u> to <u>considerible</u>
(3) replace <u>weather</u> with <u>whether</u>
(4) change <u>English</u> to <u>english</u>
(5) change the spelling of <u>language</u> to <u>langauge</u>

17. Sentence 2: **Supporters of an official language policy argue that <u>it costs to much to provide education</u>, voter ballots, and other services in several different languages.**

Which of the following is the best way to write the underlined portion of this sentence? If you think the original is the best way, choose option (1).

(1) it costs to much to provide education
(2) it cost to much to provide education
(3) it costs to much too provide education
(4) it costs too much to provide education
(5) it costs to much to provide, education

18. Sentence 3: **Opponents argue that its important to serve the millions of nonEnglish speakers in their native languages so that they can more quickly learn to function productively in American society.**

What correction should be made to this sentence?

(1) change the spelling of <u>argue</u> to <u>argu</u>
(2) change <u>its</u> to <u>it's</u>
(3) change the spelling of <u>millions</u> to <u>milions</u>
(4) insert a comma after <u>languages</u>
(5) no correction is necessary

19. Sentence 5: **An opposing view says immigrants should, on the other hand, not be able to avoid English so easily.**

If you rewrote sentence 5 beginning with

<u>On the other hand, opponents believe it's too easy for</u>

the next word should be

(1) everyone
(2) teachers
(3) Americans
(4) politicians
(5) immigrants

20. Sentence 7: **Such jobs also offer <u>little opportunity for advancment.</u>**

Which of the following is the best way to write the underlined portion of this sentence? If you think the original is the best way, choose option (1).

(1) little opportunity for advancment
(2) little oppertunity for advancment
(3) little opportunity, for advancment
(4) little opportunity to advancment
(5) little opportunity for advancement

21. Sentence 8: **America's earlier waves of immigrants had less available in their native languages, so they were forced to learn english.**

What correction should be made to this sentence?

(1) change <u>America's</u> to <u>Americas</u>
(2) change the spelling of <u>available</u> to <u>avalable</u>
(3) change <u>native languages</u> to <u>Native Languages</u>
(4) remove the comma after <u>languages</u>
(5) change <u>english</u> to <u>English</u>

22. Sentence 10: **The experts, who hold widely different opinions may not come to agreement on this issue for a long time.**

What correction should be made to this sentence?

(1) change <u>experts</u> to <u>expert's</u>
(2) change <u>experts</u> to <u>experts'</u>
(3) remove the comma after <u>experts</u>
(4) insert a comma after <u>opinions</u>
(5) no correction is necessary

To check your answers, turn to page 325.

Answers and Explanations

Lesson 1: Using Capital Letters

Exercise 1 (page 246)

1. Dr.
2. July
3. Correct
4. *Casablanca*
5. Japanese, English, French
6. Fifth Avenue
7. Mane Tamers
8. Correct
9. *The Autobiography of Malcolm X*
10. Commodore County Animal Protection Society

11. (3) change <u>senator</u> to <u>Senator</u>   In this sentence, Senator must be capitalized because it is a title used as part of someone's name. Option (1) is incorrect because the first word in a sentence must be capitalized. Option (2) is incorrect because *legislator* is a general term, and option (4) is incorrect because a person's name must be capitalized.

12. (5) meetings at a public library   Option (5) is the only one that doesn't capitalize *public* or *library*. These words are used in a general sense in the sentence. Option (2) capitalizes the general word *meeting*.

13. (4) change <u>public library</u> to <u>Public Library</u>   Option (4) capitalizes both words because in this sentence they are part of the name of a specific public library. The other options either capitalize general words or fail to capitalize specific names.

14. (4) change <u>california</u> to <u>California</u>   Option (4) capitalizes the name of a state. Option (1) inserts a comma for no reason, option (2) shifts to the past tense, and option (3) uses a present, instead of a past, participle.

15. (3) generate   Option (3) is the only one that maintains the meaning of the original sentence.

16. (3) and it would lower utility rates for consumers   Option (3) uses parallel structure. Option (1) lacks parallel structure, option (2) shifts to the past tense, option (4) inserts a comma for no reason, and option (5) creates a fragment.

17. (5) change <u>Electric Circuits</u> to <u>electric circuits</u>   Option (5) is correct because *electric circuits* is a general term. Option (1) capitalizes a general word, option (2) separates the parts of a compound verb, option (3) shifts tense, and option (4) incorrectly places a comma before a modifier.

Exercise 2 (page 249)

Answers will vary. Here are some samples.

1. My favorite ethnic food is *Chinese.*
2. The historical even that most interests me is the *Civil War.*
3. *Monday* usually seems like a long day to me.
4. My street address is *7321 Mission Bay Avenue.*
5. If I could visit any city in the world, I'd choose *Hong Kong.*

Write on Target

Answers will vary. Here are some sample sentences to illustrate the capitalization rules:

1. Walter Cronkite is a famous television news commentator.
2. I enjoyed reading *Catcher in the Rye.*
3. The store is at the corner of Pine and Stewart.
4. They said Mother will be late.
5. School starts in the fall, usually in early September.
6. The French and Indian War began America's westward expansion.
7. The Swedish visitors loved the amusement park.
8. The East Coast states are smaller than those in the West.

6. (2) doctor at Harborview Hospital   Option (2) capitalizes the entire name of a particular hospital. Options (1) and (4) don't capitalize the name of the hospital, and option (3) capitalizes *doctor* although no specific doctor is named.

7. (5) no correction is necessary

8. (3) change <u>*newsweek*</u> to <u>*Newsweek*</u>   Option (3) capitalizes the name of a particular magazine. Option (1) is incorrect because *Uncle*, as part of *John's* name, must be capitalized. There is no reason to capitalize the nouns in options (2) and (4). Option (5) is incorrect because the name of a country must be capitalized.

Connections

Sentences will vary. Here are some sample sentences:

1. There are more than 900,000,000 Muslims worldwide; this population is concentrated in northern Africa and in the Middle East.

2. Most of the world's approximately 700,000,000 Hindus live in India.

GED Test Preview (page 250)

1. **(2) change <u>National Parks</u> to <u>national parks</u>** Option (2) is correct because the writer is speaking of national parks in general, so there is no need for capital letters. Option (1) is incorrect because the name of a country must be capitalized. Option (3) is incorrect because we do not capitalize directions unless they are used as the name of a place. There is no reason to capitalize the nouns in options (4) and (5).

2. **(2) change <u>yellowstone</u> to <u>Yellowstone</u>** Option (2) capitalizes the name of a specific national park. Option (1) is incorrect because the first word of a sentence must be capitalized. There's no reason to capitalize the words in options (3) and (4).

3. **(5) change <u>Mountain Range</u> to <u>mountain range</u>** Option (5) is correct because there is no need to capitalize when speaking of mountain ranges in general. There is no reason to capitalize the words in options (1), (3), and (4). Option (2) is incorrect because the entire name of a specific mountain range must be capitalized.

4. **(2) change <u>national park</u> to <u>National Park</u>** Option (2) capitalizes all the words that are part of a name. Option (1) fails to capitalize all the words in a name, and there is no reason to capitalize the words in options (3), (4), and (5).

5. **(2) change <u>cave</u> to <u>Cave</u>** Option (2) capitalizes the name of a particular cave. Option (1) is incorrect because the first word of a sentence and the name of a particular place must be capitalized. Option (3) fails to capitalize the name of a state, and there is no reason to capitalize the words in options (4) and (5).

6. **(3) change <u>conservation</u> to <u>Conservation</u>** Option (3) correctly capitalizes all the words in a specific name. Options (1) and (2) fail to capitalize all the words in a name, and there is no reason to capitalize the words in options (4) and (5).

7. **(2) change <u>Sea</u> to <u>sea</u>** Option (2) is correct because there is no reason to capitalize *sea* when the sentence is not referring to any particular sea. Option (1) is incorrect because the first word of a sentence must be capitalized. There is no reason to capitalize the words in options (3) and (4).

8. **(2) change <u>Report</u> to <u>report</u>** Option (2) recognizes that report is a general term, not the name of a particular report, so it doesn't take a capital letter. Option (1) fails to capitalize the first word of a sentence, and there is no reason to capitalize in options (3), (4), and (5).

9. **(5) change <u>Wildlife</u> to <u>wildlife</u>** A general noun does not take a capital letter. Option (1) fails to capitalize the first word of a sentence, and there is no reason to capitalize the words in options (2), (3), and (4).

10. **(3) along all of America's coastlines** Option (3) capitalizes the name of a country, the only word in the sentence, besides the first word, that requires a capital letter. Options (1), (2), and (4) capitalize other words for no reason. Option (5) doesn't correct the capitalization error.

Lesson 2: What About Commas?

Exercise 1 (page 254)

1. Mr. and Mrs. Suarez took their tent, their cooking utensils, and their fishing gear to the campsite in the woods.

2. They preferred camping in the summer when they could count on warm weather, long days, and good fishing.

3. Correct

4. Correct

5. They did have plenty of equipment for swimming, fishing, and hiking.

6. Some people would rather vacation in cities than in mountains, woods, or the country.

7. They enjoy bustling city life with all that it offers, such as museums, theater, and restaurants.

8. Correct

9. Correct

10. It can be fun to spend time exploring your own city, neighborhood, and community.

11. **(1) remove the commas after <u>shade</u>** Option (1) omits the comma because there are only two items in the list. Option (2) uses a comma instead of a conjunction between the two items. It's incorrect to place a comma after the *and* that precedes the last item in a series, as in option (3), and there is no reason for the comma in option (4).

12. **(1) in spring or change color in fall or have** Option (1) uses no commas because the conjunction is repeated. Options (2) and (3) incorrectly use commas, and options (4) and (5) use inappropriate connecting words.

13. **(2) Remove the comma after <u>peaches</u>** Option (2) omits the comma because the last item in the list is *tasty peaches or cherries in summer*. Options (1) and (3) remove the required comma between items in a series. Option (4) incorrectly places a comma after the *and* that precedes the last item in a series.

14. (1) to keep cities cool and attractive Option (1) correctly links two items with a conjunction and no comma. The other options insert unnecessary commas.

15. (3) change are to is Option (3) uses a singular verb (*is*) to agree with a singular subject (*one*). Option (1) creates a fragment, option (2) capitalizes a general word, and option (4) uses a comma when there are only two items in the series.

16. (4) are surgical gowns and towels Option (4) removes a comma between items in a series of two. Option (1) uses a comma to separate items in a series of two, option (2) lacks subject-verb agreement, option (3) capitalizes general words, and option (5) puts a comma after *and* and between items in a series of only two.

17. (5) protect Option (5) uses the only word that maintains the meaning of the original sentence.

18. (5) remove the comma after and Option (5) removes the comma after *and* at the end of a series. Options (1) and (2) are not present participles, and options (3) and (4) remove commas between items in a series of three.

Exercise 2 (page 257)
Answers will vary for numbers 5, 6, 9, 12, and 14.

1. Mary Ann lost her address book, but she remembered the most important numbers in it.

2. If people are hungry enough, they will beg or for food.

3. Whenever it rains, homeless people seek shelter inside abandoned buildings.

4. People can suffer from malnutrition even though they don't feel hungry.

5. *If they are to remain healthy,* most Americans need more fiber in their diets.

6. *Because not everyone has time to do laundry during the day,* many laundromats are open all night.

7. Clothes dryers make towels soft, but fresh air makes them smell nice.

8. Fresh blackberries are delicious, and they make great pies.

9. Summer produces a greater variety of fruit than winter, *but winter fruit tastes just as good.*

10. As temperatures rise outside, some people become irritable.

11. Holidays are relaxing for most people, but they are stressful for others.

12. Ice storms are unimaginable to people who live in warm climates even though they see pictures of them on TV.

13. Too many people misuse prescription drugs, and doctors are concerned.

14. Your voice alone may be all you need to reach someone by telephone when the new technology becomes commonplace.

15. Computers are used in almost every business, but many people still find them intimidating.

Write on Target
Paragraphs will vary. Here is a sample:

One of my favorite books is *To Kill a Mockingbird*. The story is suspenseful, and the characters are believable. Because the main character is a child, the book reminds me of my own childhood. This book taught me about life in the South, about prejudice, and about good parenting. I love the book even though it's sad.

16. (4) to get to these parking lots, they face Option (4) places a comma after the dependent clause at the beginning of the sentence. Option (1) omits the comma, option (2) creates a fragment, and options (3) and (5) put the comma in the wrong places.

17. (2) insert a comma after distances Option (2) places a comma after the dependent clause at the beginning of the sentence. The other options put commas in the wrong places.

18. (2) illegally parked cars occupy Option (2) is the only option that maintains the meaning of the original sentence.

19. (3) insert a comma after driver Option (3) places a comma before the last item in a series. There's no reason for the comma in the other options.

20. (1) insert a comma after crime Option (1) places a comma before the last item in a series. Option (2) creates a fragment, option (3) shifts to the past tense, option (4) capitalizes a general word, and option (5) uses a participle as part of an infinitive.

21. (2) interaction Option (2) is the only option that maintains the original meaning of the sentence.

22. (4) libraries, houses of worship, and community halls because they want to discuss Option (4) changes sentence 6 to a dependent clause and adds it to the end of the first sentence for smoother reading. Option (1) is not incorrect, but it is less fluent than option (4). Option (2) omits a comma between items in a series, option (3) capitalizes a general term, and option (5) inserts a comma before a dependent clause.

15. (3) bosses whom they can communicate with
Option (3) uses the correct relative pronoun for its position in the clause (they can communicate with *whom*). Options (1) and (4) assume nonhuman antecedents, option (2) uses the wrong relative pronoun, and option (5) shifts to the past tense.

16. (2) means, for example, that they want Option (2) uses commas to set off an interrupting element. Options (1), (4), and (5) omit the comma that follows the interrupter. Option (3) omits the comma that precedes the interrupter.

17. (4) insert a comma after <u>reward</u> Option (4) uses a comma after a dependent clause. Option (1) shifts to a singular pronoun, option (2) capitalizes a general term, option (3) creates a fragment, and option (5) shifts to the past tense.

18. (3) change <u>his or her</u> to <u>their</u> Option (3) uses a plural pronoun (*their*) to agree with a plural antecedent (*workers*). Option (1) shifts to the past tense, option (2) uses a singular pronoun, and there's no reason for the comma in option (4).

Exercise 3 (page 271)

1. *Rattlesnakes range* from two to eight feet in length.

2. Correct

3. During early morning and late afternoon rush hours, *drivers and* their passengers benefit from carpool lanes.

4. Traffic was stopped by an accident, a flat tire, *and a* stalled car.

5. Correct

6. The surfers hurried to *shore, and* they weren't caught in the storm.

7. Trees *blew and* shook in the fierce wind.

8. The *sudden roar* frightened them.

9. After a flash of lightning came a burst of thunder, a downpour of rain, *and a* violent wind.

10. The lights went out, *but they* found their seats in the darkened theater.

11. (2) remove the comma after <u>government</u> Option (2) does not separate a subject and verb with a comma. There is no reason for the commas in the other options.

12. (4) in the President's Cabinet, on the Supreme Court, and in Congress Option (4) places a comma after the last item in the series *before* the connecting word. Do not put a comma *after* the connecting word. The other options punctuate the series incorrectly.

13. no correction is necessary

14. (4) participation, and a woman Option (4) places a comma before the connecting word that links two independent clauses into a compound sentence. Options (1) and (2) create run-on sentences. Option (3) incorrectly places a comma after the conjunction rather than before, and option (5) uses a semicolon instead of a comma.

15. (2) remove the comma after <u>factors</u> Option (2) removes a comma between a subject and a verb. Options (1) and (4) use a comma to separate a noun from its adjective, and option (3) introduces an error in subject-verb agreement.

16. (5) of women require them to earn a living Option (5) uses a plural verb (*require*) to agree with a plural subject (*women*). Option (1) lacks subject-verb agreement, option (2) uses a comma for no reason, option (3) uses an incorrect form for the infinitive, and option (4) uses a participle as a verb.

17. (1) remove the comma after <u>families</u> Option (1) removes the comma that incorrectly separates subject and verb. Option (2) lacks subject-verb agreement, option (3) uses a pronoun that assumes a human antecedent, option (4) uses a comma for no reason, and option (5) uses a comma to separate an adjective from its noun.

18. (5) to hold a full-time job and maintain a family Option (5) removes the comma between two parts of a compound verb. Option (1) separates the parts of a compound verb, option (2) uses commas to set off part of a compound verb, and options (3) and (4) use commas for no reason.

Connections

Sentences will vary. Here are three sample sentences:

1. (introductory material) **In 1991,** 53 percent of the authors employed in the United States were female.

2. (interrupting element) Only 33 percent of actors and directors, **of which there are 87,000 employed,** are female.

3. (introductory material) **Of the eight occupations listed on the chart,** five employ at least as many women as men.

GED Test Preview (page 274)

1. (2) insert a comma after <u>reasons</u> Option (2) uses a comma after the introductory phrase. The other options do not place the comma at the end of the introductory phrase.

2. (4) bicycle riding provides exercise and protects the environment Option (4) combines the two sentences and maintains the original meaning. The other options change the meaning of the sentence.

3. (3) traffic, however, is Option (3) sets off the interrupter *however* with commas. Option (1) omits the commas, and options (2) and (5) use only one comma. Option (4) incorrectly uses a semicolon.

4. (3) remove the comma after <u>helmets</u> Option (3) removes the comma between the parts of a compound verb (*wear and obey*). There's no reason for the commas in the other options.

5. (2) remove the comma after <u>strong</u> Option (2) removes the comma between a noun and its adjective. There is no reason for the commas in the other options.

6. (1) insert a comma after <u>scientists</u> Option (1) places a comma after an introductory phrase. There's no reason for the commas in options (2) and (4). Options (3) and (5) separate adjectives from the nouns they modify.

7. (4) simple, they maintain, for Option (4) uses commas to set off an interrupting element. Option (1) doesn't set the interrupter apart, option (2) changes the meaning of the sentence, option (3) places a comma only *before* the interrupter and not after it, and option (5) uses a semicolon instead of a comma before the interrupter.

8. (3) remove both commas Option (3) omits commas around words that are essential to the meaning of the sentence. Options (1) and (2) remove only one of the unnecessary commas, and there's no reason for the comma in option (4).

9. (3) energy sources, they will ignore Option (3) sets off the introductory material with a comma. Option (1) has no comma, option (2) creates a fragment, option (4) creates a fragment and a meaningless sentence, and option (5) places a comma far beyond the end of the dependent clause.

10. (2) remove the comma after <u>park</u> Option (2) removes a comma that separates a subject from its verb. Option (1) removes a comma that separates two adjectives, there's no reason for the comma in option (3), and option (4) uses a comma to separate a subject from its verb.

Lesson 4: Overcoming Spelling Problems

Exercise 1 (page 278)

1. dancing, achieve
2. neighbor
3. Correct
4. stepped, proceeded
5. brief
6. Correct
7. splitting
8. Neither
9. niece
10. Correct
11. shining
12. Correct
13. weird
14. Correct
15. Hearing

16. (2) change the spelling of <u>liesure</u> to <u>leisure</u> *Leisure* is an exception to the *i* before *e* rule. Options (1) and (4) don't drop the *e* before adding *ing* to a verb that ends in *e*. Option (3) uses a comma to separate the subject from the verb.

17. (5) no correction is necessary

18. (4) change the spelling of <u>ageing</u> to <u>aging</u> Option (4) drops the *e* before adding *ing* to a verb that ends in *e*. Option (1) is incorrect because the final consonant is doubled only if it is preceded by a vowel. Option (2) doesn't drop the *e* before adding *ing*, and option (3) doesn't correct the spelling error.

19. (4) facilities are beginning to accept used motor oil from people Option (4) doubles the final consonant before adding *ing* to spell *beginning*. Option (1) misspells the participle, option (2) inserts a comma for no reason, option (3) creates a fragment, and option (5) uses a past participle.

20. (4) stations that receive used oil Option (4) correctly spells *receive*. Option (1) misspells the word, option (2) uses a pronoun that assumes a human antecedent, option (3) sets off an essential clause with commas, and option (5) doesn't correct the spelling error.

21. (5) replace <u>but</u> with <u>so</u> Option (5) uses the correct connecting word to show contrast. Option (1) shifts to the past tense, option (2) omits part of a verb, option (3) uses a past participle as part of the infinitive, and option (4) uses an inappropriate connecting word.

Exercise 2 (page 280)

1. hoped
2. heroes
3. addresses
4. boxes
5. tomatoes
6. tries
7. benches
8. Correct
9. enemies
10. Correct

Write on Target

Sentences will vary. Here are some sample sentences:

- Our school has a large *foreign* population.

- Moving to a new country can result in *loneliness.*

- No one will believe that *ridiculous* excuse.

- There's not much *likelihood* of rain this week.

- It was *quite* difficult to figure out the puzzle.

11. (2) change the spelling of <u>helpping</u> to <u>helping</u>
Option (2) is correct because the consonant is doubled before *ing* is added to a one-syllable verb only if the consonant is preceded by a vowel. Option (1) incorrectly changes a plural noun to a possessive. Option (3) reverses the *ei* in *their.* Option (4) adds *es* to a noun that becomes plural simply by adding *s.*

12. (2) change the spelling of <u>exorbitent</u> to <u>exorbitant</u>
Options (1) and (4) misspell words by reversing letters, and option (3) fails to drop the *e* before adding *ing.*

13. (5) change the spellng of <u>financiel</u> to <u>financial</u> Option (1) is a misspelling. There is no reason for the comma in option (2). Option (3) is incorrect because a comma between independent clauses requires a connecting word. Option (4) is the incorrect form of the relative pronoun.

Connections

Paragraphs will vary. Here is a sample paragraph:

Rising costs of raising **children** can add a lot of stress to **families. Women** who had **babies** in 1990 spent an average of $4,000 the first year. However, by the time the **children** are 17 years old, their **parents** will be spending about $14,700 on them. This causes stress for both **men** and **women. Parents** need to provide for their **children,** which may mean working at a job they do not like, taking on part-time work for extra money, or carefully watching where the money goes. This kind of responsibility can be tough on **people.**

GED Test Preview (page 282)

1. (1) change the spelling of <u>inevitible</u> to <u>inevitable</u>
There is no reason for the comma in option (2), option (3) is a misspelling, and there should be no comma separating an adjective and the noun it modifies, as in option (4).

2. (3) change the spelling of <u>lightwieght</u> to <u>lightweight</u>
Option (3) is an exception to the rule of *i* before *e* except after *c.* Option (1) capitalizes general words that do not name a specific company. Option (2) is a misspelling, there's no reason for the comma in option (4), and option (5) uses a comma to separate a subject from its verb.

3. (4) change the spelling of <u>profitible</u> to <u>profitable</u>
Options (1), (2), and (3) are misspellings, and option (5) is a misspelling.

4. (2) change the spelling of <u>companys</u> to <u>companies</u>
Option (2) is correct because when a noun ends in *y,* you change the *y* to *i* and add *es* to make it plural. Option (1) drops the *i.* Option (3) uses a comma to separate the verbs in a compound verb, option (4) uses a comma to separate a subject from its verb, and there is no reason for the comma in option (5).

5. (2) change the spelling of <u>tremenduos</u> to <u>tremendous</u> Option (1) shifts from past to present tense, option (3) is a misspelling, option (4) shifts to future tense, and option (5) capitalizes a general word.

6. (4) were manufactured, but the Commercial Revolution concerned Option (4) uses the correct past participle of *manufacture.* Option (1) is not the correct past participle, option (2) shifts from past to present tense, option (3) omits the comma that must precede the connecting word between two independent clauses, and option (5) omits the connecting word that must follow the comma.

7. (3) that set limits on production and controlled prices
Option (3) correctly spells *controlled.* Option (1) misspells *controlled,* option (2) switches from past to present tense, and options (4) and (5) lack subject-verb agreement.

8. (3) change the spelling of <u>factorys</u> to <u>factories</u>
Option (3) changes the *y* to *i* and adds *es* to make the plural. Option (1) omits the comma before the connecting word that connects two independent clauses, option (2) shifts from past to present tense, and there is no reason for the comma in option (4).

Lesson 5: Adding Syllables to Words

Exercise 1 (page 285)

1. uncover
2. recheck
3. preview
4. supernatural
5. immature
6. nonstop

7. (2) change the spelling of roomate to roommate
Option (2) is correct because adding a prefix (*room*) does not change the spelling of the main word (*mate*). Option (1) fails to drop the final *e* before adding *ing,* options (3) and (4) misspell words.

8. (4) change <u>reconizes</u> to <u>recognizes</u> Option (1) removes a comma after an introductory phrase, and option (2) uses a comma to separate subject from verb. Option (3) doesn't correct the spelling error.

9. (5) housing with someone new, undoubtedly
Option (5) places a comma after a dependent clause. Option (1) omits that comma. Option (2) misspells *housing,* option (3) creates a fragment, and option (4) uses two commas to set off a word that is not an interrupting element.

Exercise 2 (page 286)
Answers will vary.

1. likeness
2. hateful
3. joyous
4. sadly
5. making
6. expensive
7. noisiest
8. payment
9. expandable
10. hopeless

Write on Target
Answers will vary. Here are some sample words and sentences:

1. *handful:* There was a huge clatter when the boy dropped a handful of marbles.

2. *immodest:* Their immodest clothing shocked the others.

3. *looking:* Charlene thought no one was looking when she tossed the bag out of the car window.

4. *irregular:* The doctor heard an irregular heartbeat.

5. *income:* Her new job guaranteed a larger income.

11. (3) change with out to without   Do not separate prefixes and suffixes from the main word even if the suffix or prefix is a complete word. Options (1) and (2) are misspellings, and option (4) fails to drop the final *e* before adding *ing.*

12. (2) change the spelling of normaly to normally
Option (2) adds the suffix *ly* without changing the spelling of the main word. Option (1) fails to drop the final *e* before adding *ing.* Option (3) removes the comma after a dependent clause in a compound sentence, and option (4) changes the spelling of the main word before adding the suffix *ly.*

13. (4) It takes courageous parents and highly skilled doctors   Option (4) correctly spells *courageous.* Options (1) and (5) misspell words, option (2) lacks subject-verb agreement, and option (3) shifts to the past tense.

Connections
Paragraphs will vary. Here is a sample paragraph:

> Based on the photograph, it is clear that laser light shows can be **incredibly colorful.** The photograph looks three-**dimensional,** as if an **explosion** of light surrounds the audience. The light has **remarkable clarity** as well. Now that I have seen the photograph, I would like to see an **artistic** show like this one in person.

GED Test Preview (page 288)

1. **(3) vegetables, you might like to experiment with**
Option (3) correctly spells the word *experiment.* Option (1) misspells *experiment.* Option (2) misspells *experiment* and also removes the comma after an introductory phrase. Option (4) misspells *experiment,* and option (5) misspells *vegetables* and *experiment.*

2. **(3) change the spelling of <u>originaly</u> to <u>originally</u>**
Option (3) adds the suffix *ly* without changing the main word. Option (1) lacks subject-verb agreement, option (2) is a misspelling, option (4) doesn't use a capital letter for the name of a country, and option (5) is a misspelling.

3. **(3) change the spelling of <u>profiteable</u> to <u>profitable</u>**
Option (3) adds a suffix without changing the main word. Option (1) incorrectly uses a semicolon, option (2) separates the prefix from the main word, and option (4) misspells *increase.*

4. **(4) change <u>northern</u> to <u>Northern</u>**   Option (4) capitalizes a direction that is part of the name of a place. Option (1) uses an incorrect relative pronoun, option (2) uses an incorrect past participle, option (3) separates the prefix from the main word, and option (5) fails to capitalize the name of a state.

5. **(5) kiwi makes it prettier than most fruit**   Option (1) misspells *prettier;* option (2) misspells the word and lacks subject-verb agreement. Option (3) uses a comma to separate a subject from its verb, and option (4) creates two sentence fragments.

6. **(2) change the spelling of <u>buisnesses</u> to <u>businesses</u>**
Option (1) misspells *businesses.* Option (3) uses a comma to separate the parts of a compound verb, there's no reason to capitalize the word in option (4), and option (5) misspells *expenses.*

7. **(4) population does not get regular exercise, and this costs**   Option (4) correctly spells *exercise.* Option (1) misspells *exercise,* option (2) misspells the word and lacks subject-verb agreement, and options (3) and (5) use inappropriate connecting words.

8. (2) change the spelling of <u>healthyer</u> to <u>healthier</u>
Option (2) changes the *y* to *i* before adding a suffix that begins with a vowel. Option (1) uses a comma to separate the subject from the verb, option (3) changes the spelling of the main word before adding *ly*, and there's no reason for the comma in option (4).

9. (3) To enhance productivity Option (3) provides an introductory phrase that tells why companies offer fitness opportunities to their workers. The other options change the meaning of the sentence.

Lesson 6: What Is the Apostrophe For?

Exercise 1 (page 291)

1. Being late so often, *you're* going to have trouble keeping the job. *a*
2. *It'll* be hard to find any place open at this hour. *wi*
3. They *aren't* selling that item any longer. *o*
4. He *hasn't* missed a single game all season. *o*
5. *You'll* have to wait until the report is published. *wi*
6. Sam saw that *they'd* been there already. *ha*
7. *She's* completely dependable. *i*
8. Take whatever *they'll* give you. *wi*
9. It really *isn't* hard to understand. *o*
10. By now, *it's* too late to get tickets. *i*

11. **(2) change <u>It's</u> to <u>They're</u>** Option (2) uses a plural pronoun (*they*) to agree with a plural antecedent (*snacks*). Option (1) removes an apostrophe from a contraction, option (3) uses a comma for no reason, and option (4) creates a fragment.

12. **(3) change <u>theyre</u> to <u>they're</u>** Option (3) makes a contraction out of *they are*. Options (1) and (2) remove necessary commas, option (4) puts the apostrophe in the wrong place, and option (5) misspells *healthful*.

13. **(3) change <u>its</u> to <u>it's</u>** Option (3) makes a contraction out of *it is*. Option (1) removes a comma after an introductory word, and option (2) misplaces the apostrophe. Option (4) places a comma before a dependent clause, and option (5) creates a fragment.

Exercise 2 (page 293)

1. It was steamy in the *men's* locker room.

2. The *girls'* softball team won all but two games last season.

3. Governor *Cuomo's* speech held the audience spellbound.

4. *Congress's* failure to pass the bill irritated the president.

5. The science *museum's* latest exhibit won national recognition.

Write on Target

Sentences will vary. Here are some sample sentences:

1. *Seth's* paper was excellent.
2. The *musicians'* instruments filled the trailer.
3. We heard several *explosions*.
4. That one must be *Patricia's*.
5. You'll find it by the *women's* coats.

6. **(5) change <u>custom's</u> to <u>customs</u>** Option (5) removes an apostrophe from a word that is neither possessive nor a contraction. Option (1) removes the apostrophe in a contraction. There's no reason for the comma in option (2), option (3) uses an incorrect relative pronoun, and option (4) uses a comma to separate an adjective from the noun it modifies.

7. **(2) change <u>job's</u> to <u>jobs</u>** Option (2) changes a possessive to a plural. Option (1) uses an apostrophe with a pronoun, option (3) uses an apostrophe for a word that is neither possessive nor a contraction, and option (4) changes a plural to a possessive.

8. **(2) change <u>extremist's</u> to <u>extremists</u>** Option (2) removes the apostrophe from a word that is neither possessive nor a contraction. The other options place an apostrophe in words that are neither possessive nor contractions.

Connections

Your group probably found that pronouncing the contractions as the original words sounded more formal and less like real-life speech. This tells us that in everyday language—as well as in plays, movies, and TV shows—contractions are very common. However, in formal writing such as essay writing, you may choose to avoid contractions.

GED Test Preview (page 294)

1. **(4) change <u>childs'</u> to <u>child's</u>** Option (4) places the apostrophe to show that the noun is singular. Options (1) and (2) change a plural to a possessive, and option (3) changes a plural to a plural possessive for no reason. Option (5) does not use an apostrophe to show possession.

2. **(5) child learns about the origins of his or her country** Option (5) uses a singular pronoun, *his* or *her,* for a singular antecedent, *child.* Option (1) lacks pronoun-antecedent agreement, option (2) lacks subject-verb agreement, option (3) capitalizes a general word, *country,* and option (4) changes a plural to a possessive.

3. **(1) change <u>generation's</u> to <u>generations</u>** Option (1) removes the apostrophe from a word that is neither possessive nor a contraction. Option (2) uses an apostrophe for a word that is neither possessive nor a contraction, there's no reason for the possessive in option (3), and option (4) fails to capitalize the name of a place.

4. **(5) no correction is necessary**

5. **(4) change <u>one's</u> to <u>ones</u>** Option (4) removes the apostrophe from a word that is neither possessive nor a contraction. Option (1) misspells the word, option (2) changes a possessive to a plural, and options (3) and (5) change plural words to possessives.

6. **(4) change <u>Vikings'</u> to <u>Vikings</u>** Option (4) removes the apostrophe from a word that is neither possessive nor a contraction. Options (1), (2), and (5) change plural words to possessives, and option (3) capitalizes the general word *scholars.*

7. **(2) change <u>students'</u> to <u>student's</u>** Option (2) places the apostrophe to indicate that the possessive noun is singular. Option (1) fails to use an apostrophe for a possessive noun. Option (3) misspells *fascinating,* and there's no reason for the comma in option (4).

8. **(4) change <u>their's</u> to <u>theirs</u>** Possessive pronouns do not use apostrophes. Options (1) and (2) change plural words to singular possessives, option (3) lacks subject-verb agreement, and option (5) uses an apostrophe with a possessive pronoun.

9. **(5) change <u>decade's</u> to <u>decades</u>** Option (5) removes the apostrophe from a word that is neither possessive nor a contraction. Option (1) removes the apostrophe from a contraction, options (2) and (3) use incorrect past participles, and option (4) makes a noun possessive for no reason.

10. **(4) the project's conclusions** Option (4) uses the apostrophe for the possessive and leaves it out of the plural word. Option (1) has no possessive, option (2) places the apostrophe after the *s* in a singular possessive, option (3) changes a noun from plural to singular and will result in faulty subject-verb agreement *(conclusion show),* and option (5) reverses the plural and the possessive words.

Lesson 7: Words to Watch Out For

Exercise 1 (page 298)
Sentences will vary. Here are some sample sentences.

1. You're (Your coat looks warm.)
2. stationery (The fence post isn't stationary.)
3. principle (The principal character is played by a professional.)

4. passed (The past few surveys have been disappointing.)
5. break (Watch out for faulty brakes on your truck.)
6. led (Toxic levels of lead were found in the paint.)
7. peace (May I have a clean piece of paper please?)
8. too (Let me have two of those. She went to the store.)
9. altogether (Let's try it all together on the count of three.)
10. dessert (Have you seen the desert in bloom?)
11. whether (May brings beautiful weather.)
12. heard (Those kids sound like a herd of elephants.)
13. two (Let me have those, too. She went to the store.)
14. bored (One more board will finish the project.)
15. their (They're coming tomorrow. Set it down over there.)

16. **(1) change the spelling of <u>sene</u> to <u>scene</u>** There's no reason to capitalize collision, as in option (2). Options (3) and (4) use the wrong sound-alike words, and option (5) is incorrect because there's no reason to separate the prefix from the main word.

17. **(3) replace <u>who's</u> with <u>whose</u>** Option (3) uses *whose,* which is the possessive pronoun, rather than *who's,* the contraction of *who is.* Options (1) and (2) use the wrong sound-alike words. Option (4) doesn't make sense, and option (5) is incorrect because *Its* is a possessive.

18. **(1) replace <u>their</u> with <u>there</u>** Option (1) uses *there* to indicate place. The other options use the wrong sound-alike words.

19. **(4) replace <u>breaks</u> with <u>brakes</u>** Option (4) uses *brakes,* which stop cars. Options (1) and (3) use the wrong sound-alike words, and option (2) is incorrect because *neither* is an exception to the *ie* rule.

20. **(2) change <u>already</u> to <u>all ready</u>** *Already* means *previously,* and *all ready* means *entirely ready.* Option (1) is incorrect because we only use a comma before a quotation. Option (3) is the wrong verb tense, and there is no reason to capitalize the words in option (4).

Exercise 2 (page 304)

1. competent
2. conquer
3. guidance
4. advantageous
5. Wednesday
6. privilege
7. inevitable
8. repeating
9. sympathy
10. tomorrow

Write on Target
Answers will vary, depending upon the words *you* need to learn to spell. Here's an example: *accomplish:* I can accomplish all the work by the end of the day.

11. (4) a psychology seminar   Option (4) is the only one that spells both the words correctly.

12. (2) change the spelling of <u>sholder</u> to <u>shoulder</u>   Option (2) is the only one that doesn't misspell a word.

13. (5) change the spelling of <u>predjudice</u> to <u>prejudice</u>   Option (5) is the only one that doesn't misspell a word. Option (1) also uses the wrong sound-alike word.

Connections

Sentences will vary. Here are some sample sentences:

1. I am **already** employed in the Transportation and Utilities industry, which is expected to grow by the year 2005.

2. I think I have worked in my job for **too** many years, and I need a change.

3. Passing the GED Tests should have a positive **effect** on my job prospects.

GED Test Preview (page 306)

1. (4) change <u>snake's</u> to <u>snakes</u>   Option (4) uses the plural, not the possessive. Option (2) changes a plural to a possessive, and option (3) uses a possessive.

2. (3) change the spelling of <u>oceon</u> to <u>ocean</u>   There's no reason for the apostrophe in option (1). Option (2) is incorrect because an interrupting word must be set apart by commas, option (4) uses the wrong sound-alike word, and option (5) spells *poisonous* incorrectly.

3. (1) change <u>It's</u> to <u>Its</u>   Option (1) uses the possessive rather than the contraction. Option (2) uses the wrong sound-alike word, option (3) changes a possessive to a plural, and option (4) uses the wrong initial letter.

4. (5) change the spelling of <u>immediatelly</u> to <u>immediately</u>   Option (5) adds *ly* to a word without changing the main word's spelling. There's no reason to capitalize the word in option (1), option (2) misspells *vicious,* and option (3) uses the incorrect verb tense. Option (4) misspells the main word.

5. (1) change the spelling of <u>disasterous</u> to <u>disastrous</u>   Option (1) is the correct spelling of *disastrous.* Pronounce the word carefully to hear that it has only three syllables. There's no reason to capitalize the word in option (2), there's no reason the for the comma in option (3), and options (4) and (5) misspell words.

6. (4) charge   Option (4) is the only one that maintains the meaning of the original sentence.

7. (1) automated teller machine, and others charge customers   Option (1) correctly links two independent clauses with a comma and a connecting word (*and*). Option (2) removes the comma that links the sentence's two independent clauses. Option (3) shifts to the past tense, option (4) uses a comma to separate an adjective from its noun, and option (5) uses a participle as a verb.

8. (5) replace <u>so</u> with <u>and</u>   Option (5) uses the appropriate connecting word to show similarity between the ideas in the two independent clauses. Option (1) lacks subject-verb agreement, option (2) uses a comma for no reason, option (3) fails to drop the *e* before adding *ing* to a word that ends in a vowel, and option (4) removes the comma that joins a connecting word to separate the two independent clauses in a compound sentence.

9. (4) regulations, such as those that govern deposit insurance, cost financial institutions   Option (4) uses a plural verb (*cost*) to agree with a plural subject (*regulations*). Option (1) lacks subject-verb agreement, options (2) and (3) capitalize general terms, and option (5) omits a comma that is needed to set off an interrupting element.

Unit Review

1. (3) change the spelling of <u>Government</u> to <u>government</u>   Option (3) is correct because there is no reason to capitalize government when it is a general term. Options (1) and (2) are misspellings, and there's no reason for the comma in option (4).

2. (4) Today's workers face substantial risks from   Option (4) adds an *s* to *risk* to make it plural. The other options add *es,* and option (2) also incorrectly spells workers. Option (3) separates a subject from its verb, using a comma. Option (5) shifts to the past tense.

3. (4) insert a comma after <u>firefighters</u>   Option (4) places a comma after the last item in a series. Option (1) misspells a word, options (2) and (3) omit commas in a series, and option (5) omits the apostrophe in a contraction.

4. (4) computers, for example, can   Option (4) uses commas to set off an interrupting element. Option (1) has no commas, option (2) creates a fragment, and options (3) and (5) use only one comma to set off an interrupter.

5. (2) remove the comma after <u>eyestrain</u>   Option (2) removes a comma that separates a subject from its verb. Option (1) misspells a word, option (3) lacks subject-verb agreement, and options (4) and (5) use the wrong sound-alike word.

6. (3) growing science that addresses these issues
Option (3) spells *science* correctly. Option (1) misspells *science,* option (2) lacks subject-verb agreement, and options (4) and (5) use incorrect relative pronouns.

7. (4) work environment, including Option (4) spells *environment* correctly. Option (2) misspells it, option (3) continues to misspell *environment,* and option (5) also misspells *including.*

8. (1) change technologys to technology's Option (1) uses an apostrophe to show possession. Option (2) uses a plural instead of a possessive. Option (3) uses a comma to separate the subject from the verb, and option (4) misspells a word.

9. (5) certain businesses or government offices
Option (5) makes *business* plural rather than possessive. The other options misspell *businesses.* Options (2) and (3) also capitalize general terms, and option (4) misspells *government.*

10. (3) change the spelling of actualy to actually
Option (3) adds the suffix *ly* without changing the spelling of the main word. Option (1) shifts to first person in midparagraph. Option (2) omits the apostrophe in a contraction, and option (4) uses the wrong sound-alike word.

11. (2) change the spelling of perticuler to particular
Option (2) is the correct spelling. Option (1) separates a compound verb. Option (3) capitalizes a general term, and option (4) misspells *telephone.*

12. (5) you Option (5) uses the pronoun that is consistent with the rest of the paragraph. Options (1), (2), and (3) shift person, and option (4) uses a possessive pronoun.

13. (3) to help with that problem, too Option (3) uses the correct sound-alike word. The other options use incorrect sound-alike words.

14. (2) choice, however, is Option (2) sets off an interrupter with commas. Option (1) uses no commas, option (3) creates a fragment, option (4) uses only one comma, and option (5) uses a semicolon instead of the first comma.

15. (3) insert a comma after enough Option (3) places a comma after a dependent clause in a complex sentence. Option (1) uses the wrong sound-alike word, option (2) misspells a word, and option (4) separates the parts of an infinitive.

16. (3) replace weather with whether Option (3) uses the correct word. Option (1) uses the wrong sound-alike word, options (2) and (5) misspell a word, and option (4) fails to capitalize the name of a language.

17. (4) it costs too much to provide Option (4) uses the correct sound-alike words. Options (1), (3), and (5) use the wrong sound-alike words, option (5) uses a comma for no reason, and option (2) lacks subject-verb agreement.

18. (2) change its to it's Option (2) uses an apostrophe for a contraction. Options (1) and (3) misspell words, and there is no reason for the comma in option (4).

19. (5) immigrants Option (5) is correct because the sentence speaks of immigrants having it too easy. The other options change the meaning of the sentence.

20. (5) little opportunity for advancement Option (5) correctly spells *advancement.* Options (1) and (2) misspell words, and option (3) inserts a comma for no reason. Option (4) is incorrect because the infinitive is *to advance.*

21. (5) change english to English Option (5) capitalizes the name of a language. Option (1) omits the apostrophe in a possessive, option (2) misspells the word, option (3) capitalizes a general word, and option (4) removes the comma required before a connecting word in a compound sentence.

22. (4) insert a comma after opinions Option (4) places a comma after the interrupter. Options (1) and (2) change plurals to possessives, and option (3) removes the comma at the beginning of an interrupter.

SKILLS ANALYSIS CHART

You may use this chart to determine your strengths and weaknesses in handling mechanics. The numbers in the boxes represent the items in the GED test previews and the unit review exercises. The column on the left shows you where to find more information about the items you missed.

LESSONS	EXERCISES	SENTENCE CORRECTION	SENTENCE REVISION	CONSTRUCTION SHIFT	SCORE
Capitalization	Test Preview	1, 2, 3, 4, 5, 6, 7, 8, 9	10		
(Lesson 1, pp. 244–251)	Unit Review	1, 21			_____ of 12
Commas	Test Preview	2, 4, 5, 6, 7, 9, 10	1, 3, 8		
(Lesson 2, pp. 252–261)	Unit Review	3, 15		12	_____ of 13
Commas	Test Preview	1, 4, 5, 6, 8, 10	3, 7, 9	2	
(Lesson 3, pp. 262–275)	Unit Review	5, 22	4, 14	19	_____ of 15
Spelling	Test Preview	1, 2, 3, 4, 5, 8,	6, 7		
(Lesson 4, pp. 276–283)	Unit Review		2, 9		_____ of 10
Prefixes and suffixes	Test Preview	2, 3, 4, 6, 8	1, 5, 7	9	
(Lesson 5, pp. 284–289)	Unit Review	10	20		_____ of 11
Apostrophes	Test Preview	1, 3, 4, 5, 6, 7, 8, 9	2, 10		
(Lesson 6, pp. 290–295)	Unit Review	8, 18			_____ of 12
Spelling	Test Preview	1, 2, 3, 4, 5, 8,	7, 9	6	
(Lesson 7, pp. 296–307	Unit Review	11, 16	6, 7, 13, 17		_____ of 15
SCORE		_____ of 58	_____ of 25	_____ of 5	_____ of 88

For further practice, see:

📖 *GED Writing Skills Exercises,* Unit 3, pages 64–95

💾 *GED ADVANTAGE—Writing Skills Software*

Simulated GED Writing Skills Test

Part I

Directions

The Writing Skills Test is intended to measure your ability to use clear and effective English. It is a test of English as it should be written, not as it might be spoken. This test includes both multiple-choice questions and an essay. These directions apply only to the multiple-choice section; a separate set of directions is given for the essay.

The multiple-choice section consists of paragraphs with numbered sentences. Some of the sentences contain errors in sentence structure, usage, or mechanics (spelling, punctuation, and capitalization). After reading the numbered sentences, answer the multiple-choice questions that follow. Some questions refer to sentences that are correct as written. The best answer for these questions is the one that leaves the sentence as originally written. The best answer for some questions is the one that produces a sentence that is consistent with the verb tense and point of view used throughout the paragraph.

You should spend no more than 75 minutes on the multiple-choice questions and 45 minutes on your essay. Work carefully, but do not spend too much time on any one question. You may begin working on the essay part of this test as soon as you complete the multiple-choice section.

Do not mark in this test booklet. Record your answers on the separate answer sheet provided. Be sure that all requested information is properly recorded on the answer sheet.

To record your answers, mark one numbered space on the answer sheet beside the number that corresponds to the question in the test booklet.

FOR EXAMPLE:

Sentence 1: **We were all honored to meet governor Phillips.**

What correction should be made to this sentence?

(1) insert a comma after <u>honored</u>
(2) change the spelling of <u>honored</u> to <u>honered</u>
(3) change <u>governor</u> to <u>Governor</u>
(4) replace <u>were</u> with <u>was</u>
(5) no correction is necessary

① ② ● ④ ⑤

In this example, the word "governor" should be capitalized; therefore, answer space 3 would be marked on the answer sheet.

Do not rest the point of your pencil on the answer sheet while you are considering your answer. Make no stray or unnecessary marks. If you change an answer, erase your first mark completely. Mark only one answer space for each question; multiple answers will be scored as incorrect. Do not fold or crease your answer sheet.

GED Test

① ② ③ ④ ⑤

NAME _____

DATE _____

- Use a No. 2 pencil.
- Mark one numbered space beside the number that corresponds to each question you are answering.
- Erase cleanly and completely.

---

1 ① ② ③ ④ ⑤		23 ① ② ③ ④ ⑤		45 ① ② ③ ④ ⑤
2 ① ② ③ ④ ⑤		24 ① ② ③ ④ ⑤		46 ① ② ③ ④ ⑤
3 ① ② ③ ④ ⑤		25 ① ② ③ ④ ⑤		47 ① ② ③ ④ ⑤
4 ① ② ③ ④ ⑤		26 ① ② ③ ④ ⑤		48 ① ② ③ ④ ⑤
5 ① ② ③ ④ ⑤		27 ① ② ③ ④ ⑤		49 ① ② ③ ④ ⑤
6 ① ② ③ ④ ⑤		28 ① ② ③ ④ ⑤		50 ① ② ③ ④ ⑤
7 ① ② ③ ④ ⑤		29 ① ② ③ ④ ⑤		51 ① ② ③ ④ ⑤
8 ① ② ③ ④ ⑤		30 ① ② ③ ④ ⑤		52 ① ② ③ ④ ⑤
9 ① ② ③ ④ ⑤		31 ① ② ③ ④ ⑤		53 ① ② ③ ④ ⑤
10 ① ② ③ ④ ⑤		32 ① ② ③ ④ ⑤		54 ① ② ③ ④ ⑤
11 ① ② ③ ④ ⑤		33 ① ② ③ ④ ⑤		55 ① ② ③ ④ ⑤
12 ① ② ③ ④ ⑤		34 ① ② ③ ④ ⑤		56 ① ② ③ ④ ⑤
13 ① ② ③ ④ ⑤		35 ① ② ③ ④ ⑤		57 ① ② ③ ④ ⑤
14 ① ② ③ ④ ⑤		36 ① ② ③ ④ ⑤		58 ① ② ③ ④ ⑤
15 ① ② ③ ④ ⑤		37 ① ② ③ ④ ⑤		59 ① ② ③ ④ ⑤
16 ① ② ③ ④ ⑤		38 ① ② ③ ④ ⑤		60 ① ② ③ ④ ⑤
17 ① ② ③ ④ ⑤		39 ① ② ③ ④ ⑤		61 ① ② ③ ④ ⑤
18 ① ② ③ ④ ⑤		40 ① ② ③ ④ ⑤		62 ① ② ③ ④ ⑤
19 ① ② ③ ④ ⑤		41 ① ② ③ ④ ⑤		63 ① ② ③ ④ ⑤
20 ① ② ③ ④ ⑤		42 ① ② ③ ④ ⑤		64 ① ② ③ ④ ⑤
21 ① ② ③ ④ ⑤		43 ① ② ③ ④ ⑤		65 ① ② ③ ④ ⑤
22 ① ② ③ ④ ⑤		44 ① ② ③ ④ ⑤		66 ① ② ③ ④ ⑤

Directions: Choose the one best answer to each item.

Items 1 to 7 refer to the following paragraphs.

(1) Some of the worlds largest cities depend on underground railway systems for urban transportation. (2) These underground trains called subways are powered by electricity and run through tunnels built beneath city streets. (3) The trains carry large numbers of people, thereby freeing the streets of a significant amount of traffic. (4) We who walk, drive or travel by bus on surface streets are unaware of the vast maze of tunnels and tracks transporting people continually beneath our feet. (5) The occasional rumble of a train through a tunnel only reminds us of the underground transit system.

(6) Unfortunately, it costs millions of dollars to build a subway system. (7) Building a subway system tears up a city and creates even more traffic problems above ground until it's finished. (8) It can take months or even years to complete a system. (9) Then more government funds are needed to maintain the trains and stations and to provide security for travellers. (10) Some cities are building less expensive rail lines above ground these visible light- rail systems interfere with other traffic and usually cover a smaller area than do subways.

1. Sentence 1: **Some of the worlds largest cities depend on underground railway systems for urban transportation.**

What correction should be made to this sentence?

(1) change worlds to Worlds
(2) change worlds to world's
(3) change the spelling of cities to citys
(4) insert a comma after cities
(5) change systems for to systems. For

2. Sentence 2: **These underground trains called subways are powered by electricity and run through tunnels built beneath city streets.**

Which of the following is the best way to write the underlined portion of this sentence?

If you think the original is the best way, choose option (1).

(1) underground trains called subways are powered
(2) underground trains called subways are power
(3) underground trains, called subways are powered
(4) underground trains, called subways, are powered
(5) underground trains, called subways, is powered

3. Sentence 3: **The trains carry large numbers of people, thereby freeing the streets of a significant amount of traffic.**

What correction should be made to this sentence?

(1) change carry to carries
(2) insert a comma after numbers
(3) change the spelling of significant to significant
(4) change the spelling of amount to ammount
(5) no correction is necessary

4. Sentence 4: **We who walk, drive or travel by bus on surface streets are unaware of the vast maze of tunnels and tracks transporting people continually beneath our feet.**

What correction should be made to this sentence?

(1) remove the comma after walk
(2) insert a comma after drive
(3) insert a comma after streets
(4) change the spelling of continually to continualy
(5) no correction is necessary

5. Sentence 5: **The occasional rumble of a train through a tunnel only reminds us of the underground transit system.**

Which of the following is the best way to write the underlined portion of this sentence? If you think the original is the best way, choose option (1).

(1) The occasional rumble of a train through a tunnel only reminds us
(2) The occasional rumble only of a train through a tunnel reminds us
(3) The occasional rumble of a only train through a tunnel reminds us
(4) Only the occasional rumble of a train through a tunnel reminds us
(5) Through only a tunnel the occasional rumble of a train reminds us

6. Sentence 7: **Building a subway system tears up a city and creates even more traffic problems above ground until it's finished.**

If you rewrote sentence 7 beginning with

While a subway system is being built, traffic above ground

the next word should be

(1) tears
(2) creates
(3) increases
(4) decreases
(5) finishes

7. Sentence 10: **Some cities are building less expensive rail lines above ground these visible light-rail systems interfere with other traffic and usually cover a smaller area than do subways.**

Which of the following is the best way to write the underlined portion of this sentence? If you think the original is the best way, choose option (1).

(1) above ground these visible light-rail systems
(2) above ground while these visible light-rail systems
(3) above ground because these visible light-rail systems
(4) above ground if these visible light-rail systems
(5) above ground, but these visible light-rail systems

Items 8 to 14 refer to the following paragraph.

(1) During the Great Depression, more than five thousand banks closed, which resulted in many people losing all there savings. (2) Wealthy people that had made fortunes in the stock market lost everything, and many of them committed suicide. (3) Unemployment reached 25 percent, with 15 million people out of jobs. (4) Many young people who were ready to go to work for the first time had no hope of employment, so they wander around the country riding freight trains. (5) Because so many of these young wanderers sought shelter in railcars the railroads added empty cars to their trains to help them. (6) Years of drought in the part of the country known as the great plains drove people west. (7) Families abandoned their unproductive farms, loaded their possessions onto their beat-up cars, and headed to California, hoping to find a better life. (8) However they found no help when they got there. (9) *The Grapes of Wrath* is a great book by John Steinbeck, it tells the story of some of these people.

8. Sentence 1: **During the Great Depression, more than five thousand banks closed, which resulted in many people losing all there savings.**

What correction should be made to this sentence?

(1) change Great Depression to great depression
(2) remove the comma after Depression
(3) remove the comma after closed
(4) change the spelling of losing to loosing
(5) change the spelling of there to their

9. Sentence 2: **Wealthy people <u>that had made fortunes in the stock market lost</u> everything, and many of them committed suicide.**

Which of the following is the best way to write the underlined portion of this sentence? If you think the original is the best way, choose option (1).

(1) that had made fortunes in the stock market lost
(2) whom had made fortunes in the stock market lost
(3) who had made fortunes in the stock market lost
(4) that had made fortunes in the stock market lose
(5) that had make fortunes in the stock market lost

10. Sentence 4: **Many young people who were ready to go to work for the first time had no hope of employment, so they wander around the country riding freight trains.**

What correction should be made to this sentence?

(1) replace <u>who</u> with <u>that</u>
(2) remove the comma after <u>employment</u>
(3) change <u>wander</u> to <u>wandered</u>
(4) change the spelling of <u>riding</u> to <u>rideing</u>
(5) change the spelling of <u>riding</u> to <u>ridding</u>

11. Sentence 5: **Because so many of these young wanderers sought shelter in railcars the railroads added empty cars to their trains to help them.**

What correction should be made to this sentence?

(1) replace <u>Because</u> with <u>Nevertheless</u>
(2) change <u>sought</u> to <u>seek</u>
(3) change <u>added</u> to <u>add</u>
(4) insert a comma after <u>railcars</u>
(5) change <u>help</u> to <u>helped</u>

12. Sentence 6: **Years of drought in the part of the country known as the great plains drove people west.**

What correction should be made to this sentence?

(1) change <u>country</u> to <u>Country</u>
(2) insert a comma after <u>country</u>
(3) change <u>known</u> to <u>knowed</u>
(4) change <u>great plains</u> to <u>Great Plains</u>
(5) change <u>drove</u> to <u>drive</u>

13. Sentence 8: **However they found no help when they got there.**

What correction should be made to this sentence?

(1) insert a comma after <u>However</u>
(2) replace <u>they</u> with <u>he</u>
(3) insert a comma after <u>help</u>
(4) change <u>got</u> to <u>get</u>
(5) replace <u>there</u> with <u>their</u>

14. Sentence 9: ***The Grapes of Wrath* is a great book by John Steinbeck, it tells the story of some of these people.**

If you rewrote sentence 9 beginning with

<u>In his great book, *The Grapes of Wrath*,</u>

the next word should be

(1) these
(2) John
(3) people
(4) readers
(5) you

Items 15 to 20 refer to the following paragraph.

(1) Thirty-four million Americans who need dental treatment don't get it because they are afraid of pain. (2) Even though dentists can deaden pain with local anesthetics, many people become quiet anxious about dental work. (3) Now, there is a new laser available for several dental procedures. (4) The new technology promise treatment with little or no pain. (5) The laser can, with little harm to the surrounding area, remove damaged gum tissue. (6) With laser treatment, neither fillings nor root canals are painful. (7) Cavities can be simply rinsed away, leaving the tooth more resistant to decay because the laser leaves a densely packed tooth surface. (8) Root canal procedures treat infected tissue around the roots of teeth and usually require two sessions. (9) In just one session, the laser destroys the damaged tissue and killed the bacteria that cause disease. (10) When the Federal Drug Administration approves laser treatment for all these procedures, fearful people may be able to get the dental treatment they need.

15. Sentence 2: **Even though dentists can deaden pain with local anesthetics, many people become quiet anxious about dental work.**

What correction should be made to this sentence?

(1) insert a comma after though
(2) remove the comma after anesthetics
(3) change become to became
(4) change the spelling of quiet to quite
(5) change the spelling of anxious to anxsious

16. Sentence 3: **Now, there is a new laser availeable for several dental procedures.**

What correction should be made to this sentence?

(1) change the spelling of there to they're
(2) change the spelling of availeable to available
(3) insert a comma after availeable
(4) change the spelling of for to four
(5) change the spelling of several to sevral

17. Sentence 4: **The new technology promise treatment with little or no pain.**

Which of the following is the best way to write the underlined portion of this sentence? If you think the original is the best way, choose option (1).

(1) technology promise treatment
(2) technology promised treatment
(3) technology promises treatment
(4) technology, promise treatment
(5) technology. Promise treatment

18. Sentence 5: **The laser can, with little harm to the surrounding area, remove damaged gum tissue.**

If you rewrote sentence 5 beginning with

The laser can remove damaged gum tissue without

the next word should be

(1) removing
(2) surrounding
(3) cleaning
(4) harming
(5) treating

19. Sentence 6: **With laser treatment, neither fillings nor root canals are painful.**

What correction should be made to this sentence?

(1) remove the comma after treatment
(2) change the spelling of neither to niether
(3) insert a comma after canals
(4) change are to be
(5) change are to is

20. Sentence 9: **In just one session, the laser destroys the damaged tissue and killed the bacteria that cause disease.**

What correction should be made to this sentence?

(1) change destroys to destroy
(2) change destroys to destroyed
(3) change killed to killing
(4) change killed to kills
(5) change cause to causing

Items 21 to 27 refer to the following paragraph.

(1) When you shop for a used car experts say you should check the car thoroughly inside and out. (2) Look for signs of a rolled-back odometer. (3) Such as scratches around the ignition, a sagging driver's seat, and worn brake and accelerator pedals. (4) Make sure all the cars gadgets, turn signals, headlights, taillights, and brake lights work. (5) Check for warning lights on the gauges when you turn on the ignition. (6) Listen for dashboard noises, exhaust noises, and sounds that are peculiar from the engine. (7) Take it for at least a half-hour test drive, and note whether it pulls to one side. (8) Try to let the engine idle for five minutes with newspaper beneath the car to check for fluid leaks. (9) Test brakes by stopping suddenly from a speed of 40 to 45 miles per hour. (10) If the brakes feel mushy after several tries, beware. (11) After putting the car through your own tests, it's a good idea to take them to a trusted mechanic for an expert examination.

21. Sentence 1: **When you shop for a used car experts say you should check the car thoroughly inside and out.**

Which of the following is the best way to write the underlined portion of this sentence? If you think the original is the best way, choose option (1).

(1) used car experts say you should check the car
(2) used car experts said you should check the car
(3) used car, experts say you should check the car
(4) used car. Experts say you should check the car
(5) used car, experts say you should, check the car

22. Sentences 2 and 3: **Look for signs of a rolled-back odometer. Such as scratches around the ignition, a sagging driver's seat, and worn brake and accelerator pedals.**

Which of the following is the best way to write the underlined portion of these sentences? If you think the original is the best way, choose option (1).

(1) rolled-back odometer. Such as scratches
(2) rolled-back odometer, such as scratches
(3) rolled-back odometer. Like scratches
(4) rolled-back odometer. With scratches
(5) rolled-back odometer. Scratches

23. Sentence 4: **Make sure all the cars gadgets, turn signals, headlights, taillights, and brake lights work.**

What correction should be made to this sentence?

(1) change cars to car's
(2) change gadgets to gadget's
(3) remove the comma after taillights
(4) change work to works
(5) no correction is necessary

24. Sentence 6: **Listen for dashboard noises, exhaust noises, and sounds that are peculiar from the engine.**

Which of the following is the best way to write the underlined portion of this sentence? If you think the original is the best way, choose option (1).

(1) sounds that are peculiar from the engine
(2) sounds that is peculiar from the engine
(3) sound that are peculiar from the engine
(4) sounds from the engine that are peculiar
(5) peculiar engine sounds

25. Sentence 7: **Take it for at least a <u>half-hour test drive, and note</u> whether it pulls to one side.**

Which of the following is the best way to write the underlined portion of this sentence? If you think the original is the best way, choose option (1).

(1) half-hour test drive, and note
(2) half-hour test drive and note
(3) half-hour Test Drive, and note
(4) half-hour test drive. And note
(5) half-hour test drive; and note

26. Sentence 10: **If the brakes feel mushy after several tries, beware.**

What correction should be made to this sentence?

(1) insert a comma after <u>mushy</u>
(2) change <u>tries</u> to <u>trys</u>
(3) change <u>tries</u> to <u>try</u>
(4) remove the comma after <u>tries</u>
(5) no correction is necessary

27. Sentence 11: **After putting the car through your own tests, it's a good idea to take them to a trusted mechanic for an expert examination.**

What correction should be made to this sentence?

(1) remove the comma after <u>tests</u>
(2) replace <u>your</u> with <u>their</u>
(3) change <u>it's</u> to <u>its</u>
(4) replace <u>them</u> with <u>it</u>
(5) replace <u>them</u> with <u>him</u>

<u>Items 28 to 34</u> refer to the following paragraphs.

(1) Many Americans express concern about the declining ethics of their country's leaders. (2) They look at the federal government and see instances of sexual harassment, misspending of campaign money, and personal travel at the taxpayers' expense. (3) Federal officials are not the only ones that behave immorally. (4) State and local officials also abused the power of their positions. (5) People have become used to wasteful, extravagant spending on the part of politicians. (6) Who claim to be eager to save money. (7) Our leaders say they are concerned about law and order nevertheless many of them break the laws they expect everyone else to obey.

(8) It is fortunate, that reformers, public watchdogs, and the media keep an eye on public officials. (9) Newspapers and television especially try to keep people informed about political scandals. (10) Reporters publish probing articles about the behavior of political figures so that citizens can look at candidates carefully before they vote for them.

28. Sentence 3: **Federal officials are not the only ones that behave immorally.**

What correction should be made to this sentence?

(1) replace <u>that</u> with <u>whom</u>
(2) replace <u>that</u> with <u>who</u>
(3) change <u>behave</u> to <u>behaves</u>
(4) change the spelling of <u>immorally</u> to <u>immoraly</u>
(5) no correction is necessary

29. Sentence 4: **<u>State and local officials also abused</u> the power of their positions.**

Which of the following is the best way to write the underlined portion of this sentence? If you think the original is the best way, choose option (1).

(1) State and local officials also abused
(2) State and local officials, also abused
(3) State and local officials also, abused
(4) State and local officials also abuse
(5) State and local officials abused

30. Sentences 5 and 6: **People have become used to wasteful, extravagant spending on the part of politicians. Who claim to be eager to save money.**

Which of the following is the best way to write the underlined portion of this sentence? If you think the original is the best way, choose option (1).

(1) the part of politicians. Who claim
(2) the part of politicians. Who claiming
(3) the part of politicians who claim
(4) the part of politicians. Who claims
(5) the part of politicians who, claim

31. Sentence 7: **Our leaders say they are concerned about law and order nevertheless many of them break the laws they expect everyone else to obey.**

Which of the following is the best way to write the underlined portion of this sentence? If you think the original is the best way, choose option (1).

(1) law and order nevertheless many of them break
(2) law and order, nevertheless many of them break
(3) law and order; nevertheless, many of them break
(4) law and order nevertheless, many of them break
(5) law and order nevertheless. Many of them break

32. Sentence 8: **It is fortunate, that reformers, public watchdogs, and the media keep an eye on public officials.**

What correction should be made to this sentence?

(1) remove the comma after <u>fortunate</u>
(2) remove the comma after <u>watchdogs</u>
(3) insert a comma after <u>media</u>
(4) change <u>keep</u> to <u>kept</u>
(5) change <u>kept</u> to <u>will keep</u>

33. Sentence 9: <u>**Newspapers and television especially try**</u> **to keep people informed about political scandals.**

Which of the following is the best way to write the underlined portion of this sentence? If you think the original is the best way, choose option (1).

(1) Newspapers and television especially try
(2) Newspapers, and television especially try
(3) Newspapers and Television especially try
(4) Newspapers and television especially tries
(5) Newspapers and television, especially, try

34. Sentence 10: **Reporters publish probing articles about the behavior of political figures so that citizens can look at candidates carefully before they vote for them.**

If you rewrote sentence 10 beginning with

<u>To help citizens vote wisely,</u>

the next word should be

(1) probing
(2) reporters
(3) politicians
(4) write
(5) voters

Items 35 to 41 refer to the following paragraph.

(1) For more than a decade, Americans have worked conscientiously to change their eating habits. (2) Now, it looks as though they may be slipping back into unhealthful behavior. (3) A nation concerned with wieght control, cholesterol levels, and blood pressure readings, America cut back its intake of high-fat foods. (4) Between 1970 and 1990, for example, consumption of red meat dropped twenty pounds per person. (5) Articles on heart-healthy dieting filled magazines and books on the subject appeared on best-seller lists. (6) Low-fat or nonfat foods appeared on grocery store shelves. (7) But it appear that some people are fed up with eating well and are indulging themselves with old-fashioned rich foods. (8) Ice cream manufacturers find consumers eager to buying extra-rich flavors despite their high fat content. (9) Fast-food restaurants find it's easier to sell high-calorie double burgers than the leaner meats it have tried to market. (10) This worries physicians, who warn that high-fat, high-cholesterol food still poses serious health threats.

35. Sentences 1 and 2: **For more than a decade, Americans have worked conscientiously to change their eating habits. Now, it looks as though they may be slipping back into unhealthful behavior.**

The best combination of sentences 1 and 2 would include

(1) after a decade of habitual behavior
(2) after a decade of slipping back
(3) after a decade of eating well
(4) after a decade of unhealthful eating habits
(5) after a decade of working to change their eating habits

36. Sentence 3: **A nation concerned with wieght control, cholesterol levels, and blood pressure readings, America cut back its intake of high-fat foods.**

What correction should be made to this sentence?

(1) change nation to Nation
(2) change the spelling of wieght to weight
(3) insert a comma after and
(4) change its to it's
(5) change the spelling of intake to inntake

37. Sentence 5: **Articles on heart-healthy dieting filled magazines and books on the subject appeared on best-seller lists.**

What correction should be made to this sentence?

(1) change the spelling of dieting to dietting
(2) change filled to fill
(3) insert a comma after magazines
(4) insert a comma after books
(5) change appeared to will appear

38. Sentence 7: **But it appear that some people are fed up with eating well and are indulging themselves with old-fashioned rich foods.**

What correction should be made to this sentence?

(1) change appear to appears
(2) change people are to people be
(3) insert a comma after well
(4) change indulging to indulge
(5) no correction is necessary

39. Sentence 8: **Ice cream manufacturers find consumers eager to buying extra-rich flavors despite their high fat content.**

What correction should be made to this sentence?

(1) change find to finds
(2) change buying to buy
(3) change buying to bought
(4) change the spelling of their to there
(5) change the spelling of their to they're

40. Sentence 9: **Fast-food restaurants find it's easier to sell high-calorie double burgers than the leaner meats it have tried to market.**

What correction should be made to this sentence?

(1) change <u>find</u> to <u>will find</u>
(2) change the spelling of <u>it's</u> to <u>its</u>
(3) change the spelling of <u>easier</u> to <u>easyer</u>
(4) replace <u>it</u> with <u>they</u>
(5) no correction is necessary

41. Sentence 10: <u>**This worries physicians, who warn**</u> **that high-fat, high-cholesterol food still poses serious health threats.**

Which of the following is the best way to write the underlined portion of this sentence? If you think the original is the best way, choose option (1).

(1) This worries physicians, who warn
(2) This worry physicians, who warn
(3) This worries physicians, that warn
(4) This worries physicians, who warns
(5) This change in eating habits worries physicians, who warn

<u>Items 42 to 48</u> refer to the following paragraph.

(1) Are television a major source of the violence in our society? (2) The television industry says no even though the average American child, while still in elementary school, saw 8,000 murders and 100,000 acts of violence on television. (3) Is it possible to curb television violence without governmental censorship? (4) Some people believe warning labels for violent programs, similar to the movie rating system, will solve the problem others advocate use of a computer chip that would allow viewers at home to program violent programs out of their television sets. (5) Still others say the best way to curbing violence is to stop watching the programs. (6) Refusing to patronize the sponsors of violent programs are another view. (7) The theory is that, if people stop buying products that are advertise on violent television shows, the sponsors will withdraw their support and the shows will go off the air. (8) Television may or may not be guilty of causing violence in our society. (9) If it is, the solution may lie in a combination of all these ideas.

42. Sentence 1: **Are television a major source of the violence in our society?**

What correction should be made to this sentence?

(1) change <u>Are</u> to <u>Were</u>
(2) change <u>Are</u> to <u>Was</u>
(3) change <u>Are</u> to <u>Is</u>
(4) change <u>major source</u> to <u>Major Source</u>
(5) change <u>society</u> to <u>Society</u>

43. Sentence 2: **The television industry says no even though the average American child, while still in elementary school, saw 8,000 murders and 100,000 acts of violence on television.**

What correction should be made to this sentence?

(1) insert a comma after <u>even</u>
(2) remove the comma after <u>child</u>
(3) remove the comma after <u>school</u>
(4) change <u>elementary school</u> to <u>Elementary School</u>
(5) change <u>saw</u> to <u>sees</u>

44. Sentence 4: **Some people believe warning labels for violent programs, similar to the movie rating system, will <u>solve the problem others advocate</u> use of a computer chip that would allow viewers at home to program violent programs out of their television sets.**

Which of the following is the best way to write the underlined portion of this sentence? If you think the original is the best way, choose option (1).

(1) solve the problem others advocate
(2) solve the problem, others advocate
(3) solve the problem that others advocate
(4) solve the problem. Others advocate
(5) solve the problem, so others advocate

45. Sentence 5: **Still others say the best way <u>to curbing violence is to stop watching</u> the programs.**

Which of the following is the best way to write the underlined portion of this sentence? If you think the original is the best way, choose option (1).

(1) to curbing violence is to stop watching
(2) to curbing violence is to stop watch
(3) to curbing violence is to stopping watching
(4) to curbing violence is to stopping watch
(5) to curb violence is to stop watching

46. Sentence 6: **Refusing to patronize the sponsors of violent programs are another view.**

What correction should be made to this sentence?

(1) remove <u>to</u>
(2) change <u>violent programs</u> to <u>Violent Programs</u>
(3) change <u>are</u> to <u>is</u>
(4) change <u>are</u> to <u>were</u>
(5) change <u>are</u> to <u>will be</u>

47. Sentence 7: **The theory is that, if people stop buying products that are advertise on violent television shows, the sponsors will withdraw their support and the shows will go off the air.**

What correction should be made to this sentence?

(1) change <u>is</u> to <u>being</u>
(2) change <u>advertise</u> to <u>advertised</u>
(3) remove the comma after <u>shows</u>
(4) change the spelling of <u>their</u> to <u>there</u>
(5) change <u>will go</u> to <u>went</u>

48. Sentences 8 and 9: **Television may or may not be guilty of causing violence in our society. If it is, the solution may lie in a combination of all these ideas.**

The most effective combination of sentences 8 and 9 would include which of the following groups of words?

(1) television's cure for violence
(2) violent solutions
(3) society is guilty
(4) if television causes violence
(5) a guilty combination

Items 49 to 55 refer to the following paragraph.

(1) Llamas, once thought of as exotic creatures, are becoming more widely understood in the United States even though people thought they were found only in the South American Andes Mountains. (2) You can see them in zoos and on exhibit at state and county fairs. (3) A growing number of individuals raises the animals for wool, to use as pack animals, for sheep herding, or for pets. (4) Llamas are quiet graceful animals; their presence many find soothing. (5) People who work with them claim they are loving. (6) They're noted for being responsive to humans. (7) With their gentle ways and soft coats, he or she comfort the elderly and the ill. (8) However, these animals can get upset. (9) When they do, they emit a humming noise. (10) To signal that something is not right. (11) Another way they signal distress is to point their ears back, so they also spit at their enemies. (12) They can also deliver a swift kick although they usually display this behavior only in the wild.

49. Sentence 1: **Llamas, once thought of as exotic creatures, are becoming more widely understood in the United States even though people thought they were found only in the South American Andes Mountains.**

If you rewrote sentence 1 beginning with

Once thought of as exotic creatures found only in the South American Andes Mountains,

the next word would be

(1) people
(2) understanding
(3) United States
(4) llamas
(5) animals

50. Sentence 3: **A growing number of individuals raises the animals for wool, to use as pack animals, for sheep herding, or for pets.**

What correction should be made to this sentence?

(1) change raises to raise
(2) replace to use as with for
(3) remove the comma after pack animals
(4) insert a comma after or
(5) no correction is necessary

51. Sentence 4: **Llamas are quiet graceful animals; their presence many find soothing.**

If you rewrote sentence 4 beginning with

Many people find llamas soothing

the next word should be

(1) so
(2) because
(3) even though
(4) or
(5) but

52. Sentence 5: **People who work with them claim they are loving.**

Which of the following is the best way to write the underlined portion of this sentence? If you think the original is the best way, choose option (1).

(1) who work with them claim they are
(2) that work with them claim they are
(3) who have worked with them claim they are
(4) who work with llamas claim they are
(5) who work with them claim llamas are

53. Sentence 7: **With their gentle ways and soft coats, he or she comfort the elderly and the ill.**

What correction should be made to this sentence?

(1) remove the comma after <u>coats</u>
(2) replace <u>he or she</u> with <u>they</u>
(3) insert a comma after <u>she</u>
(4) change <u>comfort</u> to <u>comforts</u>
(5) change <u>comfort</u> to <u>comforted</u>

54. Sentences 9 and 10: **When they do, they emit a <u>humming noise. To signal</u> that something is not right.**

Which of the following is the best way to write the underlined portion of these sentences? If you think the original is the best way, choose option (1).

(1) humming noise. To signal
(2) huming noise. To signal
(3) humming noise, to signal
(4) humming noise to signal
(5) humming noise; to signal

55. Sentence 11: **Another way they signal distress is to <u>point their ears back, so they also spit at their enemies</u>.**

Which of the following is the best way to write the underlined portion of this sentence? If you think the original is the best way, choose option (1).

(1) point their ears back, so they also spit at their enemies
(2) point their ears back so they also spit at their enemies
(3) point their ears back, so they also spit at their enemys
(4) point their ears back, and they also spit at their enemies
(5) point their ears back, even though they also spit at their enemies

To check your answers, turn to page 344.

Part II

Directions

This part of the Writing Skills Test is intended to determine how well you write. You are asked to write an essay that explains something or presents an opinion on an issue. In preparing your essay, you should take the following steps.

1. Read carefully the directions and the essay topic given below.

2. Plan your essay carefully before you write.

3. Use scratch paper to make any notes.

4. Read carefully what you have written and make any changes that will improve your essay.

5. Check your paragraphs, sentence structure, spelling, punctuation, capitalization, and usage, and make any necessary corrections.

You will have 45 minutes to write on the topic below. Write legibly and use a ballpoint pen.

TOPIC

Telephone answering machines are becoming nearly as common in private homes as they are in offices. Some people appreciate these machines and rely on them to send and to receive telephone messages. Others resent answering machines and refuse to use them. They will neither have one in their home nor leave messages on one.

In an essay of about 200 words, tell whether you find answering machines a convenience, an annoyance, or both. Use examples from your experience and your observations.

To check your answer, turn to page 347.

Answers and Explanations

1. (2) change worlds to world's   Option (2) uses an apostrophe to show possession. Option (1) capitalizes a general word; option (3) introduces a spelling error; option (4) inserts an unneeded comma, which separates the subject from its verb; and option (5) creates a sentence fragment.

2. (4) underground trains, called subways, are powered   Option (4) uses commas to set off an interrupting element. Option (1) omits the commas, option (2) uses an incorrect verb form for the past participle, option (3) omits one of the required commas, and option (5) lacks subject-verb agreement.

3. (5) no correction is necessary

4. (2) insert a comma after drive   Option (2) places a comma between items in a series of three. Option (1) deletes the comma between items in the series, option (3) incorrectly places a comma after the last item in the series, and option (4) introduces a spelling error.

5. (4) Only the occasional rumble of a train through a tunnel reminds us   Option (4) places the modifier, *only,* near the words it modifies, *occasional rumble*. The other options misplace the modifier and change the meaning of the sentence.

6. (3) increases   Option (3) captures the meaning of the original sentence: the building of a subway temporarily increases traffic above ground. The other options change the meaning of the sentence.

7. (5) above ground, but these visible light-rail systems   Option (5) uses an appropriate connecting word to show the proper relationship between the independent clauses in this compound sentence. The other options change the meaning of the sentence.

8. (5) change the spelling of there to their   Option (5) correctly uses the possessive *their*. Option (1) fails to capitalize the name of an historical era, option (2) omits the comma after an introductory phrase, option (3) deletes a necessary comma, and option (4) introduces a spelling error.

9. (3) who had made fortunes in the stock market lost   Option (3) uses the correct relative pronoun for antecedents that are people. Options (1), (4), and (5) use the wrong relative pronoun for people, and option (2) uses the wrong form of the pronoun for its role in the clause.

10. (3) change wander to wandered   Option (3) uses the past tense to be consistent with the rest of the paragraph. Option (1) uses the wrong relative pronoun, option (2) removes a comma that is required with the connecting word between two independent clauses, option (4) fails to drop the *e* before adding *ing*, and the misspelling in option (5) changes the word (*ride* not *rid*).

11. (4) insert a comma after railcars   Option (4) uses a comma after a dependent clause in a complex sentence. Option (1) changes the meaning of the sentence, options (2) and (3) shift to the present tense, and option (5) uses the wrong verb form for the infinitive.

12. (4) change great plains to Great Plains   Option (4) capitalizes the name of a place. Option (1) capitalizes a general word, there's no need for the comma in option (2), option (3) uses the wrong verb form for the past participle, and option (5) shifts the tense to the present.

13. (1) insert a comma after However   Option (1) places a comma after an introductory word. Option (2) shifts to a singular pronoun, option (3) uses a comma before a dependent clause, option (4) shifts to the present tense, and option (5) uses the wrong sound-alike word.

14. (2) John   Option (2) supplies the only word that logically refers back to the pronoun *his* in the introductory phrase.

15. (4) change the spelling of quiet to quite   Option (4) correctly spells the intended word and maintains the sentence's meaning. Option (1) places a comma in the middle of the dependent clause, option (2) removes the comma required after the dependent clause, option (3) shifts to the past tense, and option (5) introduces a spelling error.

16. (2) change the spelling of availeable to available   Option (2) does not add an *e* before adding a suffix to *avail*. Option (1) uses the wrong sound-alike word, there is no need for the comma in option (3), option (4) uses the wrong sound-alike word, and option (5) introduces a spelling error.

17. (3) technology promises treatment   Option (3) corrects the error in subject-verb agreement. Option (1) lacks subject-verb agreement, option (2) shifts to the past tense, option (4) incorrectly inserts a comma between the subject and its verb, and option (5) creates sentence fragments.

18. (4) harming Option (4) accurately introduces the rest of the sentence (*harming the surrounding area*).

19. (5) change are to is Option (5) uses a singular verb, *is*, to agree with the singular subject, *neither*. Option (1) omits the comma after an introductory phrase, option (2) introduces a spelling error, option (3) incorrectly inserts a comma between the subject and its verb, and option (4) uses part of the infinitive alone as a verb.

20. (4) change killed to kills Option (4) maintains the present tense. Option (1) lacks subject-verb agreement, option (2) shifts to the past tense, and options (3) and (5) use the present participle alone as a verb.

21. (3) used car, experts say you should check the car Option (3) uses a comma to set off the dependent clause. Option (1) omits the comma. Option (2) shifts to the past tense, option (4) creates a fragment, and option (5) uses unnecessary commas.

22. (2) rolled-back odometer, such as scratches Option (2) eliminates the sentence fragment. The other options create fragments.

23. (1) change cars to car's Option (1) uses an apostrophe to show possession. Option (2) changes a plural to a possessive, option (3) removes one of the commas between items in a series, and option (4) lacks subject-verb agreement.

24. (5) peculiar engine sounds Option (5) is the only option that maintains parallel structure. Options (2) and (3) also lack subject-verb agreement.

25. (2) half-hour test drive and note Options (1), (3), (4), and (5) use punctuation to separate the verbs in a compound verb. Option (3) also capitalizes a general term.

26. (5) no correction is necessary

27. (4) replace them with it Option (4) uses the singular pronoun, *it*, to agree with the singular antecedent, *car*.

28. (2) replace that with who Option (2) uses *who*, the correct relative pronoun when the antecedent is a person. Option (1) uses the wrong relative pronoun, option (3) lacks subject-verb agreement, and option (4) introduces a spelling error.

29. (4) State and local officials also abuse Option (4) maintains present tense and is consistent with the rest of the paragraph. The other options do not correct the shift in tense. Options (2) and (3) also insert unneeded commas.

30. (3) the part of politicians who claim Option (3) corrects the sentence fragment by attaching it to the rest of the sentence. Option (1) creates a fragment, option (2) uses the participle instead of the proper verb form, option (4) lacks subject-verb agreement, and option (5) inserts an unneeded comma.

31. (3) law and order; nevertheless, many of them break Option (3) uses the correct punctuation with the connecting word *nevertheless* in a compound sentence. The other options use incorrect punctuation.

32. (1) remove the comma after fortunate Option (1) removes an unnecessary comma. Option (2) omits the comma before the last item in a series, option (3) places a comma after the last item in a series, and options (4) and (5) shift tense.

33. (5) Newspapers and television, especially, try Option (5) is the only one that uses commas to set off interrupting material. Option (4) also lacks subject-verb agreement.

34. (2) reporters Option (2) is the only option that maintains the meaning of the original sentence.

35. (5) after a decade of working to change their eating habits Option (5) is the only one that maintains the meaning of the original sentence.

36. (2) change the spelling of wieght to weight Option (1) obeys the rule for words in which *ei* sounds like *a*. Option (1) capitalizes a general word, option (3) places a comma after the conjunction in a series, option (4) uses the wrong sound-alike word, and option (5) adds a letter to a prefix.

37. (3) insert a comma after magazines Option (3) uses a comma with the connecting word *and*, which separates the two clauses in a compound sentence. Option (1) doubles the final consonant of a multisyllable word before adding *ing*, option (2) shifts to the present tense, there's no need for the comma in option (4), and option (5) shifts to the future tense.

38. (1) change appear to appears Option (1) uses a singular verb to agree with the singular subject (*it*). Option (2) uses part of the infinitive as a verb, option (3) uses a comma to separate the verbs in a compound verb, and option (4) uses the wrong verb form for the present participle.

39. (2) change buying to buy Option (2) uses the correct verb form for the infinitive. Option (1) lacks subject-verb agreement, option (3) uses the past participle as part of the infinitive, and options (4) and (5) use the wrong sound-alike words.

40. (4) replace it with they Option (4) uses a plural pronoun, *they*, to match its plural antecedent, *restaurants*. Option (1) shifts to the future tense, option (2) changes *it's* from a contraction to a possessive, and option (3) fails to change the *y* to *i* before adding the suffix.

41. (5) This change in eating habits worries physicians who warn   Option (5) is the only option that doesn't use a pronoun with an unclear antecedent.

42. (3) change <u>Are</u> to <u>Is</u>   Option (3) matches a singular verb, *is,* with the singular subject, *television.* Option (1) shifts to the past tense and lacks subject-verb agreement, option (2) shifts to the past tense, and options (4) and (5) capitalize general words.

43. (5) change <u>saw</u> to <u>sees</u>   Option (5) keeps the verb in present tense and maintains tense consistency throughout the paragraph. There's no need for the comma in option (1), options (2) and (3) omit commas that set off an interrupting element, and option (4) capitalizes a general term.

44. (4) solve the problem. Others advocate   Option (4) corrects the run-on sentence by making two separate sentences out of it. Option (1) is a run-on, option (2) is incorrect because a comma without a connecting word between two independent clauses results in a run-on, option (3) changes the meaning of the sentence, and option (5) uses an inappropriate connecting word.

45. (5) to curb violence is to stop watching   Option (5) uses the correct verb form for the infinitive. The other options have incorrect infinitives.

46. (3) change <u>are</u> to <u>is</u>   Option (3) uses a singular verb, *is,* to match the singular subject, *refusing.* Option (1) removes part of the infinitive, option (2) capitalizes a general term, option (4) shifts to the past tense, and option (5) shifts to the future tense.

47. (2) change <u>advertise</u> to <u>advertised</u>   Option (5) uses the correct verb form for the past participle. Option (1) uses a present participle alone as a verb, option (3) omits the comma that follows a dependent clause, option (4) uses the wrong sound-alike word, and option (5) shifts to the past tense.

48. (4) if television causes violence   Option (4) is the only option that maintains the meaning of the original sentence.

49. (4) llamas   Option (4) provides a logical subject for the main clause that follows the long introductory phrase. The other options change the meaning of the sentence.

50. (2) replace <u>to use as</u> with <u>for</u>   Option (2) maintains parallel structure. Option (1) uses a plural verb with the singular subject, *number.* Option (3) omits a comma between items in a series, and option (4) inserts a comma after the conjunction in a series.

51. (2) because   Option (2) is the only option that makes sense and that maintains the meaning of the original sentence.

52. (5) who work with them claim llamas are   Option (5) clarifies the antecedent, *llamas,* for the pronoun, *them.* The other options don't correct the unclear antecedent, and option (2) also uses the wrong relative pronoun for people.

53. (2) replace <u>he or she</u> with <u>they</u>   Option (2) uses the plural third-person pronoun to be consistent with the other pronoun in the sentence, *their.* Option (1) omits the comma after an introductory element, option (3) uses a comma to separate a subject from its verb, option (4) lacks subject-verb agreement, and option (5) shifts to the past tense.

54. (4) humming noise to signal   Option (4) corrects the sentence fragment by attaching it to the preceding independent clause. Options (1) and (2) create fragments, and option (2) also misspells *humming.* There's no need for the comma in option (3), and option (5) incorrectly uses a semicolon.

55. (4) point their ears back, and they also spit at their enemies   Option (4) is the only one that uses the appropriate connecting word between the two independent clauses in this compound sentence.

Part II

The scoring information on page 349 will help you estimate a score for your essay. If you can, ask an instructor to read and score your essay. For your use, make a list of its strengths and weaknesses based on the checklist below.

With 6 as the top score and 1 as the bottom, rank your essay for each item in the checklist. Put a check in the box that you think reflects the quality of that particular part of your essay.

DOES MY ESSAY . . .	1	2	3	4	5	6
discuss the topic?						
have a clear controlling idea that is developed throughout?						
have a clear structure (introduction, body, conclusion)?						
tell the reader in the introduction what the topic is and what I am going to say about it?						
use details and examples to support each point?						
sum up the essay in the conclusion?						
have practically no errors in sentence structure, usage, or punctuation?						

TEST ANALYSIS CHART

You may use this chart to determine your strengths and weaknesses. The numbers in the boxes represent the items in Part I of the simulated test. The column on the left shows you where to find information on the items you missed.

CATEGORIES	SENTENCE CORRECTION	SENTENCE REVISION	CONSTRUCTION SHIFT	SCORE
Part I Sentence Structure (pp. 77–165)	3, 11, 37, 50	5, 7, 22, 24, 30, 31, 44, 54, 55	14, 18, 35, 49, 51	_____ of 18
Usage (pp. 167–238)	10, 19, 20, 27, 28, 38, 39, 40, 42, 43, 46, 47, 53	9, 17, 29, 41, 45, 52	34, 48	_____ of 21
Mechanics (pp. 241–327)	1, 4, 8, 12, 13, 15, 16, 23, 26, 32, 36	2, 21, 25, 33	6	_____ of 16
SCORE	_____ of 28	_____ of 19	_____ of 8	_____ of 55
Part II GED Essay (pp. 25–73)	Strengths: Weaknesses:			

Scoring Guide: Simulated GED Writing Skills Test Part II

Two trained readers will read your GED essay and score it *holistically*. This means that they will read the essay through quickly for an overall impression. The readers will neither count nor mark every error on your paper. They will be concerned with the overall effectiveness of the composition: its structure, logic, use of examples, freedom from errors, and flow of writing.

Each reader will give the essay a ranking of 1 through 6, and the two scores will be averaged to determine your score on Part II of the GED Writing Skills Test. The essay score, together with your score on Part I of the test, becomes your GED Writing Skills Test score. The merging of the two scores is done on a special grid used by the GED test scorers.

If your essay makes a point, has a clear structure, uses logical examples, and is relatively free from errors in sentence structure, usage, and mechanics, it will fall in the upper half of the point range with a score of 4 to 6. An essay that is not legible or not on the topic will receive no points.

- The *6 essay* develops ideas clearly, uses particularly sophisticated and vivid examples, flows smoothly, and has almost no errors.

- The *5 essay* develops ideas pretty well, but the writing is not as smooth, the examples aren't as good, and the essay has noticeably more errors than a 6 essay.

- The *4 essay* develops ideas adequately, but the writing is a bit more awkward, the examples less extensive and less effective, and the essay has noticeably more errors than the 5 essay.

- A *3 essay* shows some evidence of planning, but the examples are weak or underdeveloped. It also contains repeated errors in sentence structure, usage, and mechanics.

- A *2 essay* is weak in organization or inadequate in the development of ideas. It contains many errors.

- A *1 essay* lacks structure, purpose, and control. It contains many errors.

The following student essays illustrate the GED scoring criteria discussed above.

A SAMPLE 6 ESSAY

Hook and thesis, with three subtopics stated

Advertisers spend billions of dollars each year persuading consumers to buy their products. To sell products, they exploit human desires to be healthy, to save money, and to be happy.

First subtopic

Example

It's pretty hard to resist a product that promises health and long life. Actors posing as doctors appear in advertisements to sell cold medicines, headache remedies, and even health insurance. These actors look authentic and authoritative, so we pay attention to what they say. They use

Explanation

charts and graphs, along with testimonials from "ordinary people," to convince us that one product is more beneficial to our health than another.

Second subtopic

Example

Explanation

Just as we all want to be healthy, most of us also want to save money. With free samples, coupons, and low prices, advertisers urge us to try a product. If it costs less, we might try it. Then we might continue to buy it, get used to it, and keep buying it even if the price goes up a little.

Third subtopic

Example and explanation

When an ad shows people having fun or falling in love, it suggests that a particular product brings happiness. Advertisers would like us to believe that the right toothpaste, drink, car, perfume, or aftershave is all that is needed to find true love and happiness.

Conclusion, with thesis implied

As consumers, we must be careful shoppers if we are to avoid the awesome power and influence of advertisers.

A 6 essay has a clear structure, develops the topic with excellent examples, and concludes neatly. The conclusion does not repeat the three-point thesis but implies it in the closing sentence.

A SAMPLE 5 ESSAY

Consumers are influenced in many ways by advertisers who have billions of dollars to spend on radio, television, newspapers, magazines and billboards. The most vulnerble consumers are the ones with children, and advertisers that sell toys and food are quick to take advantage of that.

Most kids watch television, and TV bombards them with commercials that show how much fun they could have if they owned a particlar toy. Maybe it's the latest movie character, a dinosaur or a mermaid. It could even be a character they see on television, but not necessarily in commercials. The television shows themselves serve as advertisements because often the characters in the programs are available as dolls in toy stores. If children see enough ads for a particlar product, there desire to have it will increase. On top of advertisements, kids can apply plenty of their own pressure on parents.

Kids play with toys, but they eat food too, especially cereal. One cereal commercial actually states that "unless your kids are weird, they'll eat it." This implies that kids who don't like this cereal are not normal. Most parents, sure that their own kids ar perfectly normal, probly will buy this particular brand of breakfast food.

Advertisers count on parents to buy anything it takes to keep their children happy and normal.

Hook and thesis with two subtopics

First subtopic
Several examples

Example and explanation

Second subtopic
Example and explanation

This essay is a *5* because the second subtopic is not developed as completely as the first. There are also a few misspellings.

Hook and thesis with two subtopics

Wherever we turn, we see advertisements. Ads are on television, on the radio, in the papers, everywhere. Sometimes they try to get us to buy products by pretending to be scientific. Other times they try to make us think we'll change for the better if we have the product, sometimes they just pressure us with time limits.

Weak development, confusing sentence structure

Sometimes advertisers try to get us to buy products by they'll pretend to be real science. They use charts and make it look like they're in a laboratory or a doctors office or something like that.

Example is developed, but writing contains too many errors

Some ads try to make us think we'll be better if we have the product. For example, sleep on a certain kind of mattress, the ad says you did a better job at work or school the next day. Another is use the right car for a happy picnic in the woods or some place.

Example needs more explanation

Some ads just pressure us with time limits. They say a special price is over by some date pretty soon. They'll say hurry, don't wait, and they make you feel like you better run right out this very minute or you'll be sorry.

Thesis is restated, but sentence structure is weak

Pressure, pretend science, and promising to change us is how advertisements influence consumers.

This essay is a *4* because the support is weak and there are errors in sentence structure and mechanics even though it does develop a thesis with a clear structure.

A SAMPLE 3 ESSAY

Its pretty hard to avoid the pressures of advertisers. Because they use athleets and movie stars to sell products and ordnary people.

Everybody reconizes athleets and movie stars, so you shouldn't be surprized that they appear in ads on television and elsewhere. Take Michael Jordan. hes a great basketball player, so he wears shoes anybody would like to buy them when they see him wearing them on television.

The same with movie stars. If you see Al Pacino or somebody like that useing a credit card in Europe on vacation, who wouldn't want to use that same credit card?

Sometimes it's just regular people in advertisements. Well, they they look like regular people, but you know there just actors. Anyway, you see them having fun with their familys, so you buy that kind of film, too.

Weather there famous or ordinary, consumers buy things that athletes and movie stars say to buy because we look up to them. Regular people can make us buy things, too. But only if the product seem to make them happy.

Thesis is stated, but it is not logical.

This essay is a *3* because the support is weak and the errors confuse the reader.

A SAMPLE 2 ESSAY

Television is where most advertising is on. Kids programs, sports, news, everything has it. Then kids nag there parents all day to buy the stuff they seen on television this just gets parents mad and the kids wont get anything. Which serve them right if they act bratty like that.

Sports is another thing. You cant even watch a football or baseball without too many commercals. Why do they have to ruin a perfecly good ballgame with those dumb commercals. Then they use the same guys to brake into other programs, I mean sport guys who get millions of dollars I bet just to tell you to buy some kind of razer and you cant even see them play there game. Because the ads ruin the game right in the middle.

So in conclusion, I think there's too many commercials in the cartoons and the sports. News, too.

This essay is a *2* because it lacks a clear thesis, the support details wander from the topic, the conclusion doesn't match the thesis, and there are many errors.

A SAMPLE 1 ESSAY

I think advertising is horrible. Because they lie and you waist your hard earned money. I can't think of any place where you dont see ads there everywhere and all they do is lie and tell you to buy stuff you don't need and you cant aford to anyway so it's kind of rotten to do that. Besides that stuff isnt ture anybody knows that.

So how do they do it? Well, there is alot of ways. Television for example. People just leave the room when the comershal come on, because it gets loud and its like their yelling at you to buy something. Who wants to listen to stuff like that. That why remote controls are good. Because you can just change the chanel or turn off the sound. The best thing is to go get something to eat, and it probly wont even be what they advertise. Which shows you that the ads just lie anyway.

This essay is a *1* because the ideas are jumbled together. It lacks a clear thesis, subtopics, and examples to support them. The writer has no control over the topic.

Glossary

A

action verb a word that shows what the subject of a sentence is doing. *(page 86)*

> The leaves *turn* red and gold in the fall.

adjective a word that modifies a noun. *(page 129)*

> The *delicious* dessert was tempting.

adverb a word that modifies a verb, an adjective, or another adverb. *(page 129)*

> The office staff worked *overtime* on that project.

antecedent the noun for which a pronoun is substituted or to which a pronoun refers. *(page 210)*

> Whenever *Greg* comes over, he makes us laugh.

apostrophe a punctuation mark used to indicate ownership or a contraction. *(page 290)*

> John's book   She doesn't cook.

B

body the middle paragraphs in an essay that appear between the introduction and the conclusion. *(page 26)*

brainstorm to write down, in random form, all your thoughts about an essay's topic; the first step in planning an essay. *(page 31)*

C

clause a word group that contains a subject and a verb but is not necessarily a complete thought. *(page 88)*

closing thought a concluding sentence or two that completes an essay and leaves the reader with something to think about. *(page 53)*

comma splice one kind of run-on sentence in which a series of complete thoughts is punctuated only by commas. *(page 96)*

> Sally is young, Frank is younger.

complete sentence a word group that contains a subject and a complete verb and that expresses a complete thought. *(page 80)*

complete subject the subject of a sentence plus any additional information that modifies it. *(page 84)*

> *The speeding red car* swerved around the corner.

complex sentence a sentence that contains an independent clause and a dependent clause. *(page 118)*

> *Even though I like to cook, I'm too tired to make dinner tonight.*

compound sentence a sentence that contains two or more independent clauses. *(page 107)*

> *Pablo likes to cook; he can make dinner tonight.*

compound subject two subjects that use the same verb. *(page 100)*

> *The cake and the pie* are delicious.

compound verb two verbs that have the same subject. *(page 100)*

> Sally *rides* a bike and *swims* for exercise.

conclusion the final paragraph in an essay; restates the thesis and contains a closing thought. *(page 26)*

conjunction a connecting word used to link other words, phrases, or clauses. *(page 102)*

> Marj *and* George requested bottles *and* cans for recycling, *but* no one had any.

contraction two words combined into one, with an apostrophe substituting for the missing letter or letters. *(page 290)*

> *can't*

D

dependent clause a clause that depends on an independent clause for its meaning. *(page 88)*

> *Before the snow fell,* the Leonards put up storm windows.

F

fragment a word group that lacks either a subject, a verb, or part of a verb and is not a complete thought; therefore, it is not a complete sentence. *(page 80)*

> *Wishing things could be better.*

G

gerund a present participle used as a noun in a sentence. *(page 189)*

> *Skating* is good exercise.

H

hook the opening sentence or sentences in an essay, designed to grab the reader's interest. *(page 46)*

I

independent clause a clause that can stand alone as a complete thought; a simple sentence. *(page 88)*

infinitive the form of a verb that consists of the word *to* followed by the present tense form of the verb. *(page 194)*

> It's important *to deliver* this package on time.

introduction the first paragraph of an essay; contains a hook and the essay's thesis. *(page 26)*

irregular verb a verb that changes form in a pattern that differs from most English verbs. *(page 26)*

L

linking verb a verb that tells what the subject of a sentence is, feels, or seems to be. *(page 86)*

> Jeannette *is* strong.

M

mechanics the aspect of writing that includes capitalization, punctuation, and spelling. *(page 242)*

modifier a word or word group that describes another word or word group in a sentence. *(page 128)*

> Marlene, *eager to please,* agreed to test the product.

N

noun a word that names a person, place, or thing. *(page 129)*

> The *repairman* came to *Lexington* to fix my roof.

O

outline a written plan or guide to the structure of an essay. *(page 140)*

P

parallel structure a series of words or word groups written in the same form to achieve clarity. *(page 140)*

> They wanted *to ride* a bus, *to see* the country, and *to visit* major cities.

participle the form of a verb used with a helping verb. *(page 189)*

> We have *seen* that movie already. Joe is *seeing* it tonight.

phrase a word group that does not contain a subject and a verb and acts like another part of speech. *(pages 129; 263)*

> They found it *in the yard*. (*In the yard* acts as an adverb in the example.)

plural more than one. *(page 171)*

prefix one or more letters or syllables added to the beginning of a word to change its meaning. *(page 284)*

> Everyone was *un*happy about the change.

preposition a word that shows the relationship of a noun to some other word in the sentence. *(page 129)*

> The ball rolled *under* the table.

prepositional phrase a phrase that begins with a preposition. *(page 129)*

> The bus stop is *across the street*.

prompt one, two, or three paragraphs that contain the GED essay topic, along with background information and specific direction for writing the essay. *(page 30)*

pronoun a word that substitutes for or refers to a noun in the same or another sentence. *(page 206)*

> Clouds threatened rain. *They* were dark and moving swiftly.

R

relative pronoun a word that refers to a noun rather than replaces it. *(page 218)*

> I wanted a hat *that* covered my ears.

run-on sentence a string of two or more independent clauses written without proper punctuation or connecting words, as if they were one sentence. *(page 94)*

S

simple sentence a sentence containing one complete thought. *(page 106)*

simple subject the noun that a sentence is about; the actor in the sentence, without any other information. *(page 84)*

> Our helpful *neighbor* from across the street fixed the broken door.

singular one. *(page 171)*

standard English English usage that obeys the rules of the language and is considered correct by educated writers and speakers. *(page 66)*

subject the noun that a sentence is about; the actor in the sentence. *(page 84)*

subject-verb agreement singular subjects take singular verbs, and plural subjects take plural verbs. *(page 171)*

> *He walks* to school. *Helen and Charlie ride* the bus.

suffix a syllable added to the end of a word that changes the word's meaning. *(page 284)*

> They certain*ly* didn't mean to hurt anyone.

syllable part of a word that is pronounced as a single unit; contains at least one vowel. *(page 276)*

> *hap-py*

T

thesis statement a sentence that connects the essay's topic with the points the writer intends to make about the topic; the central idea of an essay. *(page 38)*

topic sentence   a sentence, usually appearing at the beginning of a paragraph, that tells the reader what the paragraph is about. *(page 50)*

transition   the smooth flow from one paragraph to the next in an essay; helped by words like *however, therefore, also. (page 51)*

V

verb   the word in a sentence that shows what the subject is or does. *(page 86)*

Computers *save* time.

verb phrase   **(1)** a phrase that begins with some form of a verb and answers questions about other words in the sentence. Example: *Stretching their muscles*, all the runners took their positions. (The phrase tells how the runners took their positions.) **(2)** a verb form that contains more than one word. *(page s 129; 188)*

They *have heard* this warning many times.

verb tense   the form of a verb that indicates a change in the time of the action. *(page 188)*

I *will exercise* for an hour today because yesterday I *exercised* for only twenty minutes.

Acknowledgments

Literary Credits

page C9
"Yeah, You're Right. I'm Not Your 'Real' Father" reproduced from *I Wanna Be the Kinda Father My Mother Was* with the permission of New Readers Press. Copyright 1993 by New Readers Press. All rights reserved.

page C14
"Dust Bowl" reproduced from *10,000 Maniacs Blind Man's Zoo* with the permission of Natalie Merchant. Copyright 1989 by Christian Burial Music. All rights reserved.

pages 329, 343
Reprinted with permission of the American Council on Education.

Photo Credits

page 80
© Photo Edit, Amy Etra

page 94
© Wendt World Wide

page 106
© Bod Daemmrich, Stock Boston

page 118
© Wendt World Wide

page 128
© Bill Ross, West Light

page 140
© Wendt World Wide

page 188
© Eric Neurath, Stock Boston

page 198
© Comstock, Inc.

page 206
© Gemma LaMana, Shooting Star

page 216
© James Holland, Stock Boston

page 244
© Christopher S. Johnson, Stock Boston

page 252
© Lionel J-M Delevingne

page 262
© Wendt World Wide

page 276
©Akos Szilvasi, Stock Boston

page 284
© Lawrence Migdale, Stock Boston

page 290
© Frances M. Cox, Stock Boston

page 296
© Wendt World Wide

page C3
Laser Image by LASERIUM®/Laser Images, Inc.

page C7
© Murray & Associates/Tony Stone Images

Index

A

Action verbs, 86, 100, 148
Active verbs, 199
Adjectives, 129, 148
Adverbs, 129, 148
Agreement
    antecedent-pronoun, 210–211
    subject-verb, 170–177, 222
        sentence structure and errors in, 184
Antecedent-pronoun agreement, 210–211
Antecedents, 210, 222
Apostrophes, 290, 308
    using to combine words, 290
    using to show possesssion, 292

B

Body (of essay), 26, 27, 42
    details and examples in, 42, 60–61
    developing, 50–51
Brainstorming (essay ideas), 31–34, 40

C

Capitalization, 242–249
    checking for errors in, 65
    eight rules of, 248
    of specific nouns, 244–245
Clauses, 88, 148
    dependent, 88, 89, 118, 119, 148, 180, 256
    independent, 88, 89, 118, 148, 180, 256
        linking, 106–107, 110, 112–113
    relative pronoun, 218
Clichés, avoiding, 61
Closing thought (of essay), 53
Commas, 243, 252–259, 262–273
    avoiding overuse of, 270–721
    common errors in using, 270–271
    and independent clauses, 112
    with introductory phrases, 263
    linking ideas with, 256
    and run-on sentences, 96
    using, to separate items in a series, 252–253
    using, to set off interrupting elements, 266–267
    using, to set off parts of sentences, 262–273
Comma splice, 96, 148. *See also* Run-on sentences
Complete sentences, 80, 148, 149
Complete subject, 84, 148

Complex sentences, 122–123, 148, 149, 252, 256
    identifying, 118–119
    relative pronouns in, 218
Compound sentences, 112–113, 148, 149, 252, 256
    identifying, 106–107
    relative pronouns in, 218
Compound subject, 100, 148
Compound verb, 100
Computer, organizing essay using, 38
Conclusion (of essay), 26–28, 53–54
    things to avoid in, 54
    writing, 54
Conjunctions, 148
    choosing appropriate, 149
    and commas, 256
    for complex sentences, 122–123
    for compound sentences, 113
    using, to correct run-on sentences, 102
    and punctuation, 112
Connecting words. *See* Conjunctions
CONNECTIONS activities, explanation of, 21
Construction shift questions, 2, 3
Contractions, 290, 308

D

Dangling modifiers, 136
Dependent clauses, 88, 89, 118, 119, 148, 180, 256
Details, in body of essay, 42

E

Errors
    finding, in essay, 64–66
    grammatical, 66
    spelling, 65, 296–305
    standard English, 66
    subject-verb agreement, 184
    in using commas, 270–271
Essay
    body, 26, 27, 42
    developing, 50–51
    collecting ideas for, 31–34
    conclusion, 26–28, 53–54
    editing, 64–66
    hook, defined, 46
    introduction, 26–28, 42, 48
    keeping focused, 56
    main points of, developing, 40
    organizing and planning, 36–44
    outline for, 40–44, 49, 60

    preliminary steps in writing, 44
    prompt, for GED exam, 30
    revising, 56–62
    sample, 27
    structure of, 26–29, 58–59
    taking control of, 40
    thesis statement for, 38, 39, 40, 46, 47
    topic of, 26, 31, 39, 46
    topic sentence, 28
    writing, 46–54
Essay section, on GED Writing Skills Test, 6
Examples, using, in body of essay, 42, 60–61

F

Foundation skills, for GED Writing Skills Test, 18
Fragments, sentence, 79, 148, 149
    avoiding, 80–93, 81
    lacking subject, 84
    lacking verb, 86–87

G

GED Master List of Frequently Misspelled Words, 300–304
GED Test Previews, explanation of, 19
GED Writing Skills Test
    essay section, 6
    introduction to, 2–14
    multiple-choice questions, 2–5
    preparing for, 18–23
    simulated, explanation of, 22
Gerunds, 189, 222
Grammar, table of common errors in, 66
Grouping ideas, for essay, 36–38

H

Homonyms, spelling, 296–298
Hook, to introduce essay subject, 46

I

Ideas
    for essay
        collecting, 31–34
        condensing, 38–39
        grouping, 36–38
    linking, of equal importance, 106–117, 149
    linking, of unequal importance, 118–127, 149
    using commas to link, 256

Independent clauses, 88, 89, 118, 148, 180, 256
  linking, 106–107, 110, 112–113
Infinitives, 194, 222
Interactive instruction, explanation of, 20
Interrupting elements, using commas to set off, 266–267
Introduction (of essay), 26, 27–28, 42
  outline of, 46
  things to avoid in, 47
  writing, 48
Introductory words, using commas with, 263
Irregular verbs, 188, 192, 222
  chart of frequently used, 193

L

Language
  using, 167–238
  overview, 168–169
  review, 222–226
Lesson format, explanation of, 20
Lesson openers, explanation of, 20
Linking verbs, 86, 100, 148

M

Mechanics of writing
  defined, 242–243
  handling, 241–313
  overview, 242–243
  review, 308–313
Misspelled words, 300–304
Modifiers, 79, 128, 148
  adding information with, 128–139
  correct placement of, 132, 149
  dangling, 136
  recognizing, 128–130
Multiple-choice questions, on GED Writing Skill Test, 2–5

N

Nonparallel sentence structure, 140
Nouns, 129, 148
  singular, changing to plural, 280
  specific, capitalization of, 244–245
Noun substitutes, 206–213. *See also* Pronouns

O

Organization, of essay ideas, 36–38
Outlines
  creating, 40–44
  defined, 40
  of introduction, 46
  logical order in, 43, 50
  as map of essay, 43, 50
  sample, 41, 43, 49
  types of, 41
  working with, 60
  writing, 44

P

Paragraphs, consistent verb tense in, 202

Parallel sentence structure, 79, 148, 149
  achieving, by repeating words, 141
  balancing writing style with, 144
  and clear meaning, 141
  understanding, 140–147
Participles, 189, 192–194, 222
Passive verbs, 199
Past participles, 189, 192, 193
Past perfect, 199
Past tense, 189, 192–194, 199, 202
Personal pronouns, 176, 210
Phrases, 148, 180, 308
  introductory, 263
  prepositional, 129, 148
  verb, 129, 148, 188–190, 194, 222
Planning essay, 40–44
Plural, 171, 222
  subjects, 170–171, 174, 176–177
Possession, using apostrophes to show, 292
Practice exercises, explanation of, 20
Prefixes, 308
  adding to words, 284
Prepositional phrases, 129, 148
Prepositions, 129, 148
Present participles, 189
Present tense, 192–194, 199, 202
Prompt, essay
  background information in, 30
  example, 30
  for GED exam essay, 30
  instructions in, 30
Pronoun-antecedent agreement, 210–211
Pronouns, 169, 206–213, 222
  choosing correct, 210–211
  keeping references clear, 216–217
  personal, 176, 210
  recognizing, 207
  relative, 218, 222
Punctuation, 64, 242, 243
  checking for errors in, 65
  proper, 149
  using, to correct run-on sentences, 98

Q

Questions
  construction shift, 2, 3
  multiple-choice, 2–5
  sentence correction, 2, 3
  sentence revision, 2, 4
  types of, on GED Writing Skills Test, 2–5

R

Relative pronouns, 218, 222
Repetition, avoiding, 61
Run-on sentences, 79, 94, 148, 149
  avoiding, 94–105
  and comma splice, 96
  recognizing, 94–96
  using punctuation to correct, 98
  using conjunctions to correct, 102

S

Semicolons, 256
  and independent clauses, 112
Sentence correction questions, 2, 3
Sentence fragments, 79, 148, 149
  avoiding, 80–93
  lacking subject, 84
  lacking verb, 86–87
  recognizing, 81
Sentence revision questions, 2, 4
Sentences
  building, 78–153
  complete, 80, 148, 149
  complex, 122–123, 148, 149, 252, 256
    identifying, 118–119
    relative pronouns in, 218
  compound, 112–113, 148, 149, 252, 256
    identifying, 106–107
    relative pronouns in, 218
  consistent verb tense in, 198–199
  review, 148–153
  run-on, 79, 94, 148, 149
    avoiding, 94–105
    and comma splice, 96
    recognizing, 94–95, 96
    using conjunctions to correct, 102
    using punctuation to correct, 98
  simple, 106, 107, 148, 256
    relative pronoun clauses in, 218
  unclear
    and dangling modifiers, 136
    and misplaced modifiers, 132
    and nonparallel structure, 141
  using complete, 64–65
Sentence structure
  nonparallel, 140
  parallel, 79
    understanding, 140–147
  and subject-verb agreement errors, 184
Series, using commas to separate items in, 252–253
Simple past tense, 189, 192
Simple sentences, 106, 107, 148, 256
  relative pronoun clauses in, 218
Simple subject, 84, 148
Simulated GED Writing Skills Test, explanation of, 22
Singular, 171, 222
  nouns, changing to plural, 280
  subjects, 170–171, 174, 176–177
Skill checkups, explanation of, 18
Slang, avoiding, 61
Spelling, 242, 243
  checking for errors in, 65
  common errors in, 296–305
  GED Master List of Frequently
Misspelled Words, 300–304
  helpful rules for, 277
  overcoming problems with, 276–281
  and words that sound alike, 296–298
Standard English
  table of common errors in, 66
  using, 66
  written, conventions of, 2

Subject, 84, 148, 149
    complete, 84, 148
    compound, 100, 148
    separated from verb, 180–181
    simple, 84, 148
    singular or plural, 170–171, 174
    special case, 176–177
Subject-verb agreement, 170–177, 222
    sentence structure and errors in, 184
Suffixes, 284, 308
    adding to words, 286
Syllables, 276, 308
    adding to words, 284–287

T

Tense, 189–190, 192–194, 198–203, 222
    consistent
        in paragraphs, 202
        in sentences, 198–199
    defined, 188
    simple, 190
Test preparation tips, 22–23
Test-taking tips, explanation of, 20
Thesis, developing, 57
Thesis statement, 38, 39, 40, 46, 47
    using, to stay on topic, 58
    writing, 40

Topic (of essay), 26, 31, 39, 46
    keeping to, 56–57, 58
    stating, 31
    understanding, 30–31
Topic sentences
    essay, 28
    using, 50–51
Transitional words and phrases, table
    of, 52
Transitions, 51
    using, in essay, 51–53

U

Unit overviews, explanation of, 19
Unit reviews, explanation of, 19

V

Verb form, using correct, 192–194
Verb phrases, 129, 148, 188, 194, 222
    using, 188–190
Verbs, 86, 129, 148, 149
    action, 86, 100, 148
    active, 199
    compound, 100
    irregular, 188, 192, 222
        chart of frequently used, 193
    linking, 86, 100, 148

passive, 199
    placed before subjects, 184
    placement in sentences, 180–185
    recognizing parts of, 188–915
Verb-subject agreement, 170–177, 222
Verb tense, 169, 188, 189–190, 192–194,
    198–203, 222
    keeping consistent
        in paragraphs, 202
        in sentences, 198–199

W

Word choice, 61–62
Words, misused, avoiding, 62
Write on Target activities, explanation
    of, 20
Writing mechanics
    defined, 242–243
    handling, 241–313
    overview, 242–243
    review, 308–313
Writing Skills Test, GED, introduction
    to, 2–14
Writing style, balancing, with parallel
    structure, 144

Answer Guide

Technology (pages C2–C3)

The Writing Connection

Outline contents and styles will vary. Here is a sample outline:

1. Introduction
   - Hook (communications technology affects my life at home)
   - Thesis (communicate with **family**, get **information**, pay **bills**)
2. Telephones help me communicate with **family**
   - I call my mother every day to find out if she is OK
   - My children call to tell me where they are going, so I know they're safe
3. Technology helps me get **information**
   - I use television to find out what's going on in the world
   - I watch cable television to find out what the weather will be like
   - The computer network at Job Service helps me find job openings
4. Computerized information helps me when I pay **bills**
   - I can call a number to have a computer tell me what my bank balance is, so I won't bounce a check
   - My phone bill is computerized; if there's a problem, I just call the phone company, and my bill can be quickly fixed
5. Conclusion
   - Restate thesis, using different words (communications technology helps me get through my day)
   - Closing thought (technology has made my life easier)

Problem Solver

92,120,000 households have televisions.

94,000,000	×	.98	=	92,120,000
total households	×	percentage of households with television	=	households with televisions

1,880,000 households do not have televisions.

94,000,000	−	92,120,000	=	1,880,000
total households	−	households with television	=	households with no televisions

55,460,000 households have cable television.

94,000,000	×	.59	=	55,460,000
total households	×	percentage of households with cable television	=	households with cable television

38,540,000 households do not have cable television.

94,000,000	−	5,460,000	=	38,540,000
total households	−	households with cable television	=	households without cable television

Employment (pages C4–C5)

The Writing Connection

Answers will vary. Here is a sample brainstorm list based on the job choice of home health aides:

- More elderly people will need medical help
- Patients may want to avoid the high cost of long hospital stays
- Hospitals may send patients home as soon as possible; patients still need help recovering
- Adult children of elderly parents may hire help
- Advances in technology make it possible to do some procedures in home
- Advances in medicine help patients recover from once-fatal diseases, but recovery is slow and patients still need help

Here is a sample of how the list may be categorized into groups:

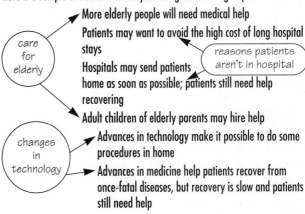

care for elderly

- More elderly people will need medical help
- Patients may want to avoid the high cost of long hospital stays

reasons patients aren't in hospital

- Hospitals may send patients home as soon as possible; patients still need help recovering
- Adult children of elderly parents may hire help

changes in technology

- Advances in technology make it possible to do some procedures in home
- Advances in medicine help patients recover from once-fatal diseases, but recovery is slow and patients still need help

Problem Solver

1. The service-producing industries have the better outlook. Growth is shown by bars above the line marked *0* (positive numbers). Decline is shown by bars below the line marked *0* (negative numbers).

2. The services industry will have the greatest job growth. It will experience growth that is about 10 percent greater than growth in retail trade, the industry with the second-highest expected job growth of the industries listed.

Cultures (pages C6–C7)

The Writing Connection

Paragraphs will vary. Reread your paragraph or have a partner read it. Answer these questions as you read: Is your position clearly stated? Is it presented logically? Are there sufficient reasons given to support your opinion?

Problem Solver

Christianity does *not* have more members than all other religions combined. When added together, Muslims, Hindus, Buddhists, Jews, Tribal Religionists, and Chinese Folk Religionists outnumber Christians.

Family Life (pages C8–C9)

The Writing Connection

Paragraphs will vary. Here are two sample paragraphs:

Omanii Abdullah's poem entitled "Yeah, You're Right. I'm Not Your 'Real' Father" uses pictures to show that being a good father does not require being related by blood to your children. The pictures he shows us—getting up in the night to put more blankets on his son, comforting his son when he sprains his wrist, cheering him on in a football game—let us see that he's there for his son in good times and in bad. He is someone his son can really count on. The reader gets a good picture of the relationship between son and father.

The sound of the poem also helps get the poet's message across. When you read it aloud, the poem's short everyday words sound like natural speech. A few of the lines are shorter than the rest, which emphasizes them and makes them stand out. Finally, many of the stanzas begin with the words "I'm the one." This repetition keeps reminding us that the father can give lots of reasons why he is a good father to his son.

Problem Solver

Answers will vary. Your answer may have included some of the following ideas:

As the graphs Families Maintained by Women and U.S. Families: Marital Status and Income show, families maintained by women tend to have lower income levels than do other types of families listed. As the number of families headed by women grows, it is likely that more families will have lower incomes. Because women generally make less money than men, this create financial hardships for their families.

News Media (pages C10–C11)

The Writing Connection

Paragraphs will vary. Here is a sample paragraph:

Recently, I read a newspaper article about a gang summit held in Chicago. The gangs wanted to promote peace on the streets and to increase the political activism of minorities. In my opinion, the article was fair and unbiased. The reporter described the summit: where, when, and why it was held, who attended, and what was said. The reporter interviewed people with different opinions about the summit. Some supported the summit; some didn't. Finally, the reporter did not insert any of her own opinions into the article.

Problem Solver

Your estimates of the numbers in the chart should have been similar to these:

AUDIENCE TYPE	NEWS PROGRAMS	SITUATION COMEDIES
Women, 18 and over	7,000,000	9,000,000
Men, 18 and over	5,000,000	6,000,000
Teens (12–17)	400,000	2,000,000
Children (2–11)	700,000	3,000,000

Based on the estimates above, estimated averages are as follows:
3,275,000   5,000,000

Based on the actual numbers in the chart, actual averages are as follows:
3,432,500   4,810,000

Leisure (pages C12–C13)

The Writing Connection

Paragraphs will vary. Here is a sample paragraph:

Americans take summer vacations of all kinds. Most Americans choose to travel within the United States; in fact, the majority chooses to travel south—maybe to the beaches of Florida or South Carolina; maybe to famous cities like New Orleans or Atlanta; or maybe to Graceland, the Grand Ole Opry, or to Disney World. Wherever it is they choose to go, summer vacationers generally spend only four or five nights away from home. Most people travel by car or other motor vehicle and choose not to stay at a hotel. Finally, summer travelers aren't necessarily the wealthiest Americans: nearly 60 percent of summer vacationers have household incomes of less than $40,000.

Problem Solver

1. 460.5 million
2. 18 percent

Lifestyles (pages C14–C15)

The Writing Connection

Paragraphs will vary. Here is a sample paragraph:

Our group had spending patterns that were very similar to the spending information presented. For example, all four of us agreed that we spend more money on entertainment technology than on reading material. We also spend a lot more money on entertainment technology now than in the past. We don't buy very expensive technology—we just buy more of it, which can really add up. For example, in the past, Renaldo would buy about two cassette tapes a month. Now, he buys one compact disc a month; however, he also spends money on videocassette rentals and video games for his kids. Renaldo is the only one in our group with kids. He says he definitely spends more money on each child each year.

Problem Solver

Sales of entertainment material by region, from highest to lowest, are as follows:

1. West
2. Midwest
3. Northeast
4. South

CONNECTIONS Skills Analysis Chart

The CONNECTIONS activities within the lessons of this book and on the theme pages themselves will help you develop the skills you need to pass the GED Writing Skills Test. The chart below lists the skill or skills you will build in each CONNECTIONS activity.

LESSON ACTIVITY	SKILLS APPLIED
Unit 1: Building Sentences	
Lesson 1 (page 91)	writing a paragraph; proofreading for fragments
Lesson 2 (page 103)	writing sentences; proofreading for fragments
Lesson 3 (page 115)	writing compound sentences
Lesson 4 (page 125)	writing complex sentences
Lesson 5 (page 137)	writing a paragraph; using modifiers
Lesson 6 (page 145)	analyzing parallel structure in a passage
Unit 2: Using Language	
Lesson 1 (page 177)	writing sentences with "tricky" subject-verb agreement
Lesson 2 (page 185)	matching subjects and verbs with "tricky" placement
Lesson 3 (page 195)	writing sentences; using verb phrases
Lesson 4 (page 203)	writing a paragraph; proofreading for verb-tense errors
Lesson 5 (page 213)	writing a paragraph; using noun substitutes
Lesson 6 (page 219)	writing sentences; using relative pronouns
Unit 3: Handling Mechanics	
Lesson 1 (page 249)	writing sentences; checking capitalization
Lesson 2 (page 259)	using commas in compound and complex sentences
Lesson 3 (page 273)	using commas to set off parts of a sentence
Lesson 4 (page 281)	writing a paragraph; spelling plurals of words
Lesson 5 (page 287)	writing a paragraph; using words with suffixes and prefixes
Lesson 6 (page 293)	reading aloud; analyzing contractions
Lesson 7 (page 305)	writing sentences; spelling homonyms

THEME ACTIVITY	SKILLS APPLIED
Technology	
The Writing Connection (page C2)	organize: create an outline
Problem Solver (page C3)	number relationships: percents
Employment	
The Writing Connection (page C4)	organize: group ideas
Problem Solver (page C5)	data analysis: interpreting graphs
Cultures	
The Writing Connection (page C6)	write: write a paragraph
Problem Solver (page C7)	data analysis: interpreting graphs
Family Life	
The Writing Connection (page C9)	write: write multiple paragraphs
Problem Solver (page C8)	data analysis: interpreting graphs
News Media	
The Writing Connection (page C11)	write: write headlines
Problem Solver (page C11)	problem solving: estimation
Leisure	
The Writing Connection (page C12)	write: write a paragraph
Problem Solver (page C13)	data analysis: charts and tables
Lifestyles	
The Writing Connection (page C15)	write: write a paragraph
Problem Solver (page C15)	data analysis: graphs and maps

CONNECTIONS

CONNECTIONS is a unique, high-interest, thematic section of information, colorful graphic displays, and activities that you can use to prepare for the GED Tests. The information here— from the subject areas of writing, social studies, science, literature and the arts, mathematics, and from the world of work—may also be important to you as an individual. "The GED Essay: 45-Minute Plan for Success" on page C16 can be useful throughout your work in this book.

CONTENTS

THEMES	PAGES
Technology	C2 – C3
Employment	C4 – C5
Cultures	C6 – C7
Family Life	C8 – C9
News Media	C10 – C11
Leisure	C12 – C13
Lifestyles	C14 – C15
The GED Essay: 45-Minute Plan for Success	C16

USING CONNECTIONS

You can use CONNECTIONS in two ways:

- Complete the CONNECTIONS activities that appear in each lesson of Section Three: Preparing for the Test of this book. The answers appear in the answer key for each lesson.

- Turn to the theme pages listed above and complete The Writing Connection and Problem Solver activities. These activities will focus your energies on two of the most challenging tasks in passing the GED — writing and math problem solving. Answers to these activities appear in the Connections Answer Guide beginning on page A1.

CONNECTIONS AND THE GED TESTS

Completing CONNECTIONS activities will give you an opportunity to build the thinking, writing, and problem solving skills that you need to pass the GED. Even though you are using this book to prepare for the Writing Skills Test, CONNECTIONS will allow you to practice skills that are needed to pass all of the tests. You will also be working constantly with topics that can appear on any part of the GED.

Remember, passing the GED Test is just one stage in a lifetime of learning. The topics on the following pages will also prepare you for further studies, the world of work, and your own personal goals. We hope that you enjoy CONNECTIONS.

KEY TO ELEMENTS IN CONNECTIONS

 Writing Skills

 Social Studies

 Science

 Literature and the Arts

 Mathematics

Technology

Communications Satellites

Communications satellites transmit thousands of telephone calls at one time nearly anywhere in the world. Orbiting the earth, these satellites receive phone calls through radio waves beamed from a transmitting station on earth. When a satellite receives radio waves, it strengthens and retransmits them to another ground station. This second station connects the call. If we did not use satellites, we would need extensive networks of wires and cables to connect telephone calls around the world.

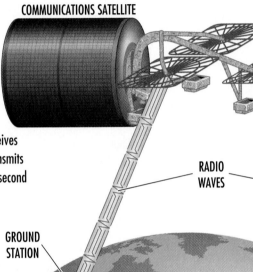

COMMUNICATIONS SATELLITE

RADIO WAVES

GROUND STATION

WORKING WORLD

The phrase "global economy" means that the economies of different nations are becoming linked together as countries share information, goods, and services with each other. What effect will this global emphasis have on the typical U.S. workplace? Workers will rely more and more on technology for instant, worldwide communication. Each of us will need to develop computer and other technical skills. Communications skills—the ability to speak and listen well—will also grow in importance, as will an appreciation for other cultures and the ability to speak more than one language.

THE WRITING CONNECTION

Suppose you are presented with the following GED essay prompt:

Changes in communications technology have revolutionized the way Americans live and work. We rely on the quick transfer of information through telephones, radios, televisions, facsimile (FAX) machines, and computer networks.

In an essay of 200 words, explain how communications technology affects your life, either at home, at work, or both.

What you would say in an essay on this topic? You may want to use information presented on this page. Then, create a sentence outline to organize your ideas. If you're not sure how to make an outline, refer to Foundation Skill 2 pages 40–44.

Answers will vary. Turn to page A1 for ideas.

Timeline: The Telephone

• **1876** American inventor Alexander Graham Bell creates the first working model of the telephone

1860   1880   1900

• **1877** Bell Telephone Company sells the first commercial telephones

• **1885** AT&T is formed, begins to create a national long-distance service

• **1892** First long distance service connects Chicago and New York

Communications in U.S. Households

Presence of Various Technology, 1990

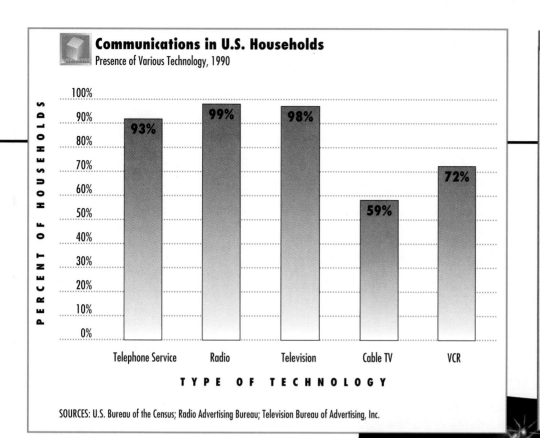

Bar chart — PERCENT OF HOUSEHOLDS (vertical axis) by TYPE OF TECHNOLOGY (horizontal axis):

- Telephone Service: 93%
- Radio: 99%
- Television: 98%
- Cable TV: 59%
- VCR: 72%

SOURCES: U.S. Bureau of the Census; Radio Advertising Bureau; Television Bureau of Advertising, Inc.

PROBLEM SOLVER

Study the graph on the left. You can see that the percentage of households with each technology is represented by the vertical bars. Practice calculating the numerical value of these percentages. If the total number of households is 94,000,000, how many households have televisions? How many don't have televisions? How many households have cable TV? How many don't?

To find the answers, turn to page A1.

Lasers

The laser—invented in 1960—is integral to much of the new communications technology, including fiber optic telephone and television signals, TV video discs and compact disc players. Lasers also are used in popular art forms such as holograms and light shows. A hologram is a photograph that looks three-dimensional and seems to change as the viewer changes places. A laser light show allows light images to surround an audience. The image to the right is from a laser light concert. Have you ever seen this type of concert?

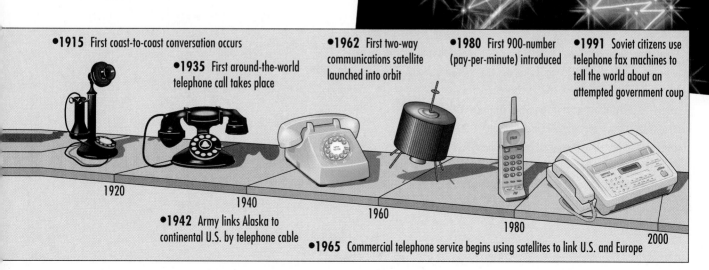

- **1915** First coast-to-coast conversation occurs
- **1935** First around-the-world telephone call takes place
- **1942** Army links Alaska to continental U.S. by telephone cable
- **1962** First two-way communications satellite launched into orbit
- **1965** Commercial telephone service begins using satellites to link U.S. and Europe
- **1980** First 900-number (pay-per-minute) introduced
- **1991** Soviet citizens use telephone fax machines to tell the world about an attempted government coup

Timeline markers: 1920, 1940, 1960, 1980, 2000

Employment

10 Fastest Growing Occupations: 1990 to 2005

- HOME HEALTH AIDES
- SYSTEMS ANALYSTS AND COMPUTER SCIENTISTS
- PERSONAL AND HOME CARE AIDES
- MEDICAL ASSISTANTS
- HUMAN SERVICES WORKERS
- RADIOLOGIC TECHNOLOGISTS AND TECHNICIANS
- MEDICAL SECRETARIES
- PSYCHOLOGISTS
- TRAVEL AGENTS
- CORRECTIONS OFFICERS

0   25   50   75   100

P E R C E N T   I N C R E A S E

SOURCE: Chart prepared by U.S. Bureau of the Census

THE WRITING CONNECTION

The service industry—healthcare, business, automotive, legal, educational, social, and personal services—presents the best employment outlook for the next decade. Many occupations in the graph on the left are in the service industry.

On your own or in a small group, pick one job from the graph on the left. Brainstorm ideas about why that job is expected to grow over the next 10 years. For example, you might say that more home health aides will be needed to care for America's growing elderly population.

Finally, categorize your ideas into groups as if you were organizing an essay on this topic. If you're not sure how to group your ideas, refer to Foundation Skill 2 pages 36–37.

Answers will vary. Turn to page A1 for ideas.

WORKING WORLD

According to a recent survey, 50% of all new jobs created in the 1990s will require some education beyond a high school diploma or a GED certificate. In fact, 33% of the new jobs will require a college degree. Today that number is only 22%. Many other jobs will require an associate's degree from a community college or a certificate from a vocational or trade school. Some occupations offer apprenticeship programs in which you can earn money while you learn new job skills. And, it is becoming increasingly common for companies to help upgrade their employees' skills by providing them additional skills training.

Literary or Artistic Occupations in the U.S.

Job Characteristics, 1991

Occupation	Total Employed	Females Employed (percent of total)
Authors	91,000	53%
Technical Writers	62,000	50%
Designers	527,000	53%
Musicians and composers	156,000	31%
Actors and directors	87,000	33%
Painters, sculptors, craft-artists, and printmakers	208,000	55%
Editors and reporters	279,000	51%
Photographers	136,000	23%

SOURCE: U.S. Bureau of Labor Statistics

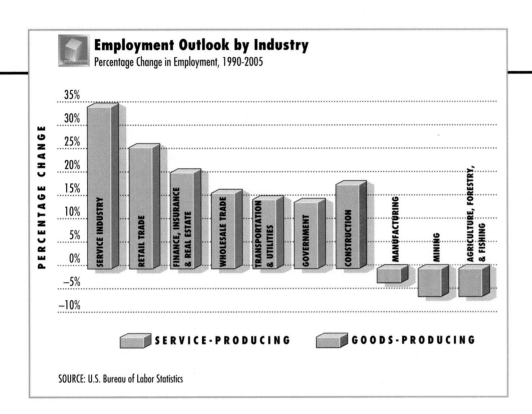

Employment Outlook by Industry
Percentage Change in Employment, 1990-2005

PERCENTAGE CHANGE

- SERVICE INDUSTRY
- RETAIL TRADE
- FINANCE, INSURANCE & REAL ESTATE
- WHOLESALE TRADE
- TRANSPORTATION & UTILITIES
- GOVERNMENT
- CONSTRUCTION
- MANUFACTURING
- MINING
- AGRICULTURE, FORESTRY, & FISHING

■ SERVICE-PRODUCING   ■ GOODS-PRODUCING

SOURCE: U.S. Bureau of Labor Statistics

PROBLEM SOLVER

Study the graph to the left. *Employment outlook*—expected gain or loss of jobs within an industry over a period of time—is given for two main industry categories: service-producing and goods-producing. Answer the following questions:

1 Which type of industry has the better employment outlook— service-producing or goods-producing? How can you tell?

2 Within the service-producing industry, which particular industry has the best employment outlook? What is the difference in percentage of job growth between this industry and the industry with the second highest growth?

To check your answers, turn to page A2.

Expected Job Growth in Science-Related Occupations
1990-2005

Occupation	Selected Jobs	Percent Increase	Comments
Technicians and related support	health technicians, surgical technologists, computer programmers	37%	fastest growing occupational cluster in the economy
Professional speciality	computer specialists, health diagnosing and treating, engineers	32%	workers in these occupations are employed in almost every industry
Mechanics, installers, and repairers	computer and office machine repairers	16%	employment growth due to increased use of mechanical and electronic equipment

SOURCE: U.S. Bureau of Labor Statistics

Cultures

C O N N E C T I O N S

The Creationism/Evolution Conflict

Religious beliefs sometimes conflict with scientific theories. In the United States, one of the most controversial of these conflicts revolves around this question: Where did human beings come from?

Two schools of thought answer this question very differently. Some people support a theory called Creation Science, which ties scientific explanations to parts of the Bible's creation story. Others support the theory of evolution, which proposes that human beings evolved from lower forms of animals over a period of millions of years.

In 1925, this conflict was first brought to court in a famous trial known as the "Monkey Trial." A Tennessee high school teacher was arrested for teaching the theory of evolution, which was against the law in his state. He was found guilty, but the state supreme court later overturned the verdict.

Today, the conflict rages on. Supporters of Creation Science believe that it should be taught in public schools along with the theory of evolution. Critics disagree; they feel that Creationism is strictly a religious viewpoint, and that as such it does not belong in public schools. Exactly how this conflict is handled usually varies from state to state, even from one local school district to another.

THE WRITING CONNECTION

Read the information on the right. What is your position on the creationism/evolution conflict? What do you believe should be taught in schools—one theory or both theories? What reasons can you give to support your opinion?

Write one paragraph explaining your position. Be sure that your paragraph has a topic sentence and plenty of supporting details. Give yourself time to revise and edit your paragraph when you've finished writing.

Paragraphs will vary. Turn to page A2 for a sample.

Religions of the World

Christian
- Roman Catholic
- Eastern Orthodox
- Protestant
- Mormon
- Mixed Christian

- Hindu
- Jewish
- Sunni Muslim
- Shia Muslim
- Tribal Religions, Anamist
- Buddhist
- Buddhist and Shintoist
- Buddhist, Taoist, and Confucianist

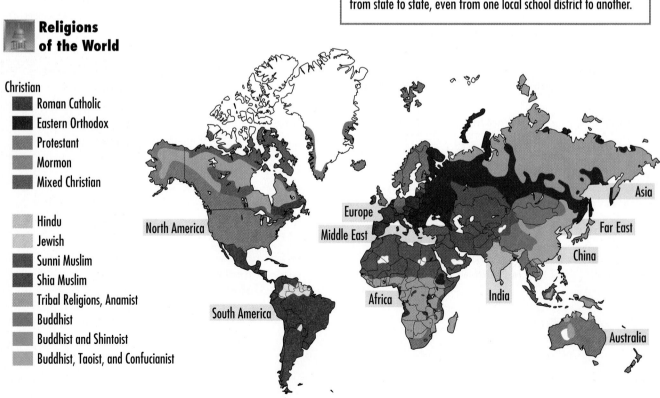

North America
Europe
Middle East
Asia
Far East
China
Africa
India
South America
Australia

Castillo at Chichén Itzá, Yucatán Peninsula, Mexico

This pyramid, built in the Mayan city of Chichén Itzá in 1000-1100 A.D., holds both an upper temple and a lower temple. The lower temple was enclosed as a large pyramid, and the upper temple was built around it. This lower temple still contains a stone altar on which sacrifices were placed and a jade-decorated sculpture known as the Throne of the Red Jaguar—both of which are nearly 1,000 years old.

WORKING WORLD

In the United States, more than 50 percent of the work force is women. By comparison, in Saudi Arabia, women comprise only 5 percent of the workforce. Why the huge difference? Religious and cultural beliefs in many parts of the Middle East discourage women from working outside the home.

Religions–Worldwide Membership
Estimated Membership of Principal Religions

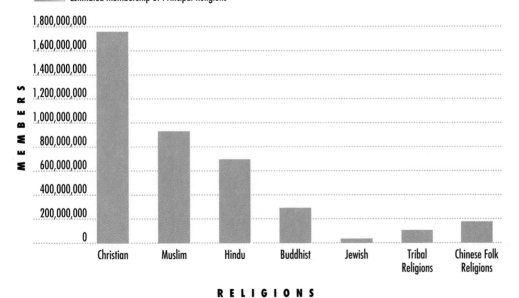

SOURCE: Britiannica Book of the Year, 1991

PROBLEM SOLVER

According to the graph to the left, Christianity has more members worldwide than any other *single* religion. Answer this question: Does Christianity have more members than all of the other religions on the graph *combined*? What data on the graph supports your conclusion?

To check your answer, turn to page A2.

Family Life

PROBLEM SOLVER

The graph to the left shows that the number of families maintained by women in the United States is growing. How does the economic status of families headed by women compare to that of other types of families? Analyze the information on this page.

In one or two sentences, summarize the relationship between this growing trend in families and its economic implications. Use data from more than one graph on this page.

To check your answer, turn to page A2.

Families Maintained by Women, 1960-1991

No Husband Present

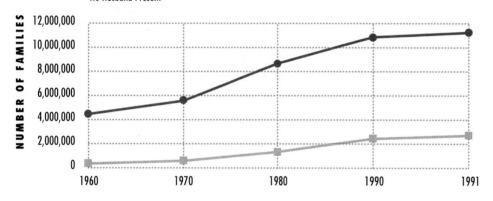

NUMBER OF FAMILIES

- 12,000,000
- 10,000,000
- 8,000,000
- 6,000,000
- 4,000,000
- 2,000,000
- 0

1960   1970   1980   1990   1991

● TOTAL FAMILIES   ■ WOMEN NEVER MARRIED

SOURCE: U.S. Bureau of the Census

WORKING WORLD

More than 58 percent of the mothers in the United States work outside the home. Where do they turn for childcare? More than 40 percent turn to relatives for help. Others rely on family daycare homes (in-home sitters or care in private homes). About 30 percent enroll their children in childcare centers. If you needed to find childcare, where would you look? Who would you ask for information?

U.S. Families: Marital Status and Income

1990 Data

- 50,000
- 40,000
- 30,000
- 20,000
- 10,000
- 0

30,298	21,849	2,907	11,268
$46,777	$30,265	$29,046	$16,932
Married, Two Incomes	Married, Male Income Only	Male, No Wife Present	Female, No Husband Present

NUMBER (IN THOUSANDS)   MEDIAN INCOME

SOURCE: U. S. Bureau of the Census

Yeah, You're Right.
I'm Not Your "Real" Father

Mama said there'd be days like this
There'd be days like this Mama said

You know it bothers me when I watch TV
And I always see these athletes waving
And saying "hi" to their moms
Not that I have anything against mothers
Mind you
But I just wonder
Don't none of y'all have daddies
You wanna say "hi" to?

So the next time
You wanna jump in my face with
"Yo man, you ain't my real daddy"
Yeah, you're right
I'm not your "real" father

I'm just the man who gets up out of his bed
To put extra blankets on you
When I think your room is too cold

I'm the one that stands out in the rain
To watch you while you play
Little league football

I'm the one who held you
And tried to comfort you
When you sprained
Your wrist and thought you were dying

I'm the one who feels bad
'Cause all your teammates have $100 Nikes on
But I can't afford to buy you a pair
But yeah, you're right
I'm not your "real" father

I'm just the one
Who picks you up from work
So you don't have to
Stand out in the rain
Waiting for a bus

I'm the one
That your principal has gotten to know
On a first-name basis
Because he sees me so often
And it's not because your ass is so good
Either

I'm the one who took a part-time job
So that I could afford to buy you
And your brother a bicycle

I'm the one who compliments you
On jobs well done

I'm the one who's trying to give you
A sense of direction
So that maybe one day
When you grow up
And if you should have an athletic son
That ever has a need
To look into a TV camera
He just might want to say
"Hi Dad"

So yeah, you're right
I'm not your "real" father
I'm just the man who loves you!

—Omanii Abdullah

THE WRITING CONNECTION

Like many 20th-century poems, the poem on this page is in free verse—its structure depends on neither rhyme nor rhythm. Yet the poem effectively conveys the father's strong emotions. Read the poem aloud. Listen to the sounds of the poem. Now read the poem silently. Try to picture the scenes described.

Write a few short paragraphs describing the poem. You might discuss the poet's word choices, the theme (main idea) of the poem, or the images or pictures it suggests to you.

Answers will vary. Turn to page A2 for ideas.

Life Expectancy

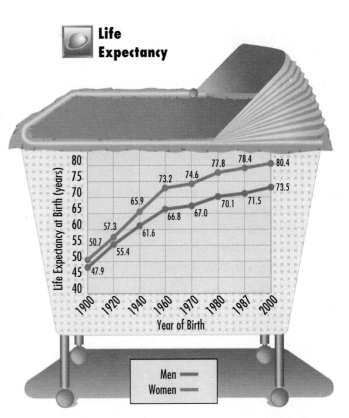

Life Expectancy at Birth (years) vs. Year of Birth

Men: 47.9 (1900), 55.4 (1920), 61.6 (1940), 66.8 (1960), 67.0 (1970), 70.1 (1980), 71.5 (1987), 73.5 (2000)

Women: 50.7 (1900), 57.3 (1920), 65.9 (1940), 73.2 (1960), 74.6 (1970), 77.8 (1980), 78.4 (1987), 80.4 (2000)

Men —
Women —

News Media

Circulation of Morning and Evening News
1970-1990

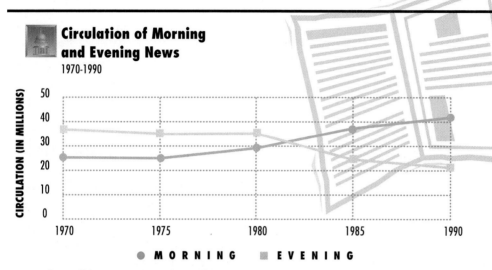

CIRCULATION (IN MILLIONS)

50				
40				
30				
20				
10				
0				

| 1970 | 1975 | 1980 | 1985 | 1990 |

● MORNING ▪ EVENING

SOURCE: Editor & Publisher Co., New York, NY, *Editor & Publisher International Year Book*.

Paper collected and transported to recycling bank

What Can You Do with Old News?

In the past, most Americans would read the newspaper, then throw it away. These days, however, we know that recycling newsprint (and many other items, such as glass and aluminum) not only reduces the amount of garbage in our landfills, but also reduces the environmental harm caused by harvesting and working with raw materials. The diagram to the right shows how newsprint and other paper are recycled.

Paper used in home or office

Recycled paper de-inked, then immersed in a chemical bath to separate its fibers

New paper for use by consumers

Who's Watching the News?

Average Audience for Evening News and Situation Comedies

Audience Type	News Programs	Situation Comedies
Women, 18 and over	7,170,000	8,940,000
Men, 18 and over	5,470,000	5,700,000
Teens (12-17)	370,000	1,780,000
Children (2-11)	720,000	2,820,000

SOURCE: Nielsen Media Research

PROBLEM SOLVER

Using the data in the chart above, estimate and then find the average number of people who watch news programs. Next, estimate and find the average number of people who watch situation comedies. Finally, find the average based on the actual numbers in the chart. Were your estimates close?

To check your answers, turn to page A2.

from *Citizen Kane*

This 1941 movie documents the life of Charles Kane, a fictional character who builds a communications empire and who experiences fame, fortune, and, finally, ruin. In the following scene, an ambitious young Kane makes plans for his first newspaper.

(*Scene: The office of Charles Kane at the New York Inquirer, very early dawn, 1890*)

LELAND: It's been a tough day.

KANE: A wasted day.

BERNSTEIN: Wasted?

LELAND: Charlie?

BERNSTEIN: You just made the paper over four times tonight, Mr. Kane—that's all—

KANE: I've changed the front page a little, Mr. Bernstein. That's not enough—There's something I've got to get into this paper besides pictures and print—I've got to make the New York "Inquirer" as important to New York as the gas in that light.

LELAND: What're you going to do, Charlie?

KANE: My Declaration of Principles—don't smile, Jed— (*Getting the idea*) Take dictation, Mr. Bernstein—

BERNSTEIN: I can't write shorthand, Mr. Kane—

KANE: I'll write it myself.
Kane grabs a piece of rough paper and a grease crayon. Sitting down on the bed next to Bernstein, he starts to write.

BERNSTEIN: (*Looking over his shoulder*) You don't wanta make any promises, Mr. Kane, you don't wanta keep.

KANE: (*As he writes*) These'll be kept. (*Stops and reads what he has written*) I'll provide the people of this city with a daily paper that will tell all the news honestly. (*Starts to write again; reading as he writes*) I will also provide them—

LELAND: That's the second sentence you've started with "I"—

KANE: (*Looking up*) People are going to know who's responsible. And they're going to get the news—the true news—quickly and simply and entertainingly. (*With real conviction*) And no special interests will be allowed to interfere with the truth of that news. (*Writes again; reading as he writes*) I will also provide them with a fighting and tireless champion of their rights as citizens and human beings—Signed—Charles Foster Kane.

—Screenplay by Herman J. Mankiewicz and Orson Welles

Leisure

 from *Travels with Charley*

Once a journey is designed, equipped, and put in process, a new factor enters and takes over. A trip, a safari, an exploration, is an entity, different from all other journeys. It has personality, temperament, individuality, uniqueness. A journey is a person in itself; no two are alike. And all plans, safeguards, policing, and coercion are fruitless. We find after years of struggle that we do not take a trip; a trip takes us. Tour masters, schedules, reservations, brass-bound and inevitable, dash themselves to wreckage on the personality of the trip. Only when this is recognized can the blown-in-the-glass bum relax and go along with it. Only then do the frustrations fall away. In this a journey is like marriage. The certain way to be wrong is to think you control it. I feel better now, having said this, although only those who have experienced it will understand it.

—John Steinbeck

THE WRITING CONNECTION

The data given on these pages present a picture of the "typical" American vacation. For example, the data on the chart show that only 37 percent of vacationers stayed in a hotel; therefore, the majority of Americans typically did *not* stay in a hotel while on vacation. On your own or in a small group, compile the data given. Where did most Americans travel? How did they get there? How long were their trips?

With a group or on your own, write one paragraph that describes the "typical" American vacation. Add creative details if you'd like: what people might travel to see or do, whom they might visit, or where they might stay if not in a hotel. When you've finished writing, discuss the paragraph. Does it accurately portray the data on these pages?

Answers will vary. Turn to page A3 for ideas.

U.S. Time Zones

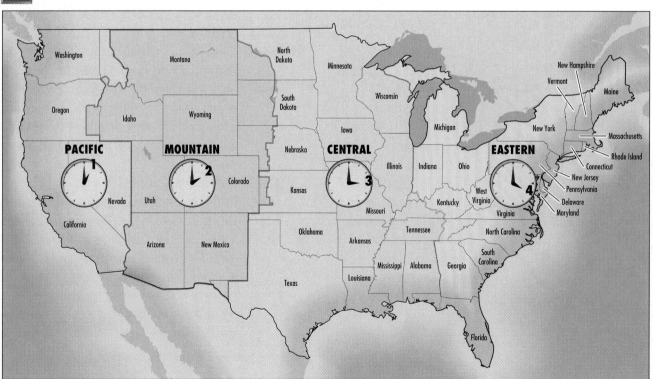

The travel industry is one of the fastest growing industries in the United States. In 1990, there were approximately 132,000 travel agents employed in this country. By 2005, there will be an estimated 214,000 travel agents. This represents a 62 percent increase in employment in this occupation. Many local community colleges, as well as specialized trade schools, offer programs to prepare people to become travel agents.

Characteristics of U.S. Pleasure Trips

CHARACTERISTIC	UNIT	DATA
total trips	millions	460.5
average household members on trip	number	2.1
average nights per trip	number	4.4
traveled primarily by motor vehicle	percent	77
traveled primarily by air	percent	18
stayed in a hotel	percent	37
household income less than $40,000	percent	59
household income $40,000 or more	percent	41

SOURCE: U.S. Travel Data Center, Washington, D.C., 1990

When you read a chart or graph, you need to pay attention to more than the numbers. You need to understand the units of measurement as well. Answer these questions based on the chart on the left. Be sure to give the correct *unit* in your answer.

1 How many total trips were taken in the U.S. in 1990?

2 What is the percentage difference between trips taken by households with an income less than $40,000 and households with an income over $40,000?

To check your answers, turn to page A3.

Summer Vacation Destinations for U.S. Travelers
Averages Based on 1991 Data

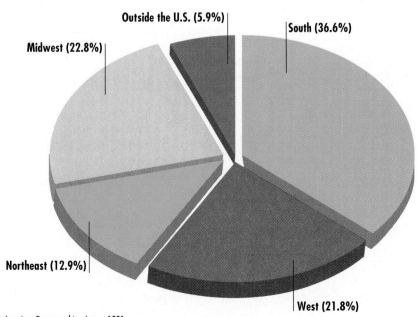

- Outside the U.S. (5.9%)
- South (36.6%)
- Midwest (22.8%)
- Northeast (12.9%)
- West (21.8%)

SOURCE: American Demographics, August,1991

Lifestyles

CONNECTIONS

Dust Bowl

I should know to leave them home. They follow me through the store with these toys I can't afford. "Kids, take them back, you know better than that." Dolls that talk, astronauts, T.V. games, airplanes, they don't understand and how can I explain? I try and try but I can't save. Pennies, nickels, dollars slip away. I've tried and tried but I can't save.

My youngest girl has bad fever, sure. All night with alcohol to cool and rub her down. Ruby, I'm tired, try and get some sleep. I'm adding doctor's fees to remedies with the cost of three day's work lost. I try and try but I can't save. Pennies, nickels, dollars slip away. I've tried and tried but I can't save. The hole in my pocketbook is growing.

There's a new wind blowing they say, it's gonna be a cold, cold one. So brace yourselves my darlings, it won't bring anything much our way but more dust bowl days.

I played a card in this week's game. Took the first and the last letters in three of their names. This lottery's been building up for weeks. I could be lucky me with the five million prize, tears of disbelief spilling out of my eyes. I try and try but I can't save. Pennies, nickels, dollars slip away. I've tried and tried but I can't save. The hole in my pocketbook is growing.

There's a new wind blowing they say, it's gonna be a cold, cold one. So brace yourselves my darlings, it won't bring anything much our way but more dust bowl days.

— song by the 10,000 Maniacs (music: Robert Buck; words: Natalie Merchant)

WORKING WORLD

It's a known fact: Americans like to spend money. In the 1990s and beyond, we'll be spending more money in specialty stores, mass merchandise stores, and discount stores. And that's where most of the 922,000 new jobs in retail sales will open up by the year 2000. Retail sales offers full-time, part-time, and temporary job opportunities. Most retail sales jobs require a high school diploma or a GED, but most entry-level jobs do not require previous sales experience. Workers in this field should have excellent communication skills and should enjoy working with clients and customers.

Average Spending on Entertainment* and Reading Material
(per person, by region of residence, 1990)

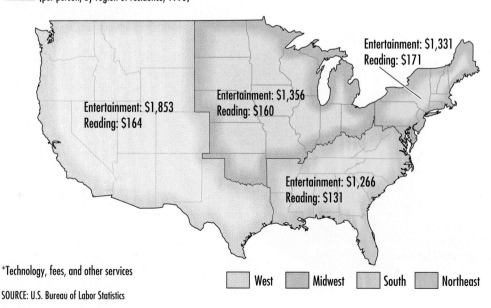

Entertainment: $1,331
Reading: $171

Entertainment: $1,356
Reading: $160

Entertainment: $1,853
Reading: $164

Entertainment: $1,266
Reading: $131

West   Midwest   South   Northeast

*Technology, fees, and other services

SOURCE: U.S. Bureau of Labor Statistics

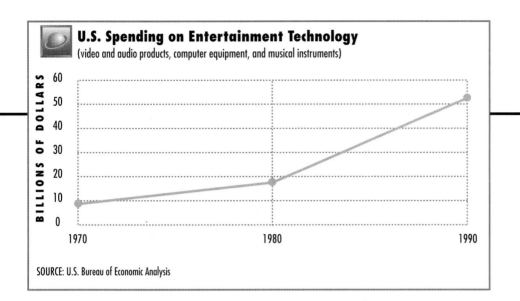

U.S. Spending on Entertainment Technology
(video and audio products, computer equipment, and musical instruments)

SOURCE: U.S. Bureau of Economic Analysis

Bringing Up Baby
Estimated Annual Spending on a Child Born in 1990*

YEAR	AGE OF CHILD	AMOUNT SPENT
1990	under 1	$ 4,330
1991	1	4,590
1992	2	4,870
1993	3	5,510
1994	4	5,850
1995	5	6,200
1996	6	6,550
1997	7	6,950
1998	8	7,360
1999	9	7,570
2000	10	8,020
2001	11	8,500
2002	12	10,360
2003	13	10,980
2004	14	11,640
2005	15	13,160
2006	16	13,950
2007	17	14,780
TOTAL		**$151,170**

*estimated spending for a married couple family with income under
$29,000 in 1990; **projection assumes 6 percent annual inflation.**

SOURCE: American Demographics, August 1991

PROBLEM SOLVER

Consumer spending on entertainment technology has skyrocketed since 1980. Based on this information, it's a good guess that jobs selling entertainment material—including technology—are increasing as well.

Using the information on these two pages, decide which region of the country would have the highest sales in entertainment material, which region the second highest, the third highest, and the lowest. List the regions in order.

To check your answers, turn to page A3.

THE WRITING CONNECTION

The information on these two pages presents some facts about how Americans spend money. Do these facts fit with your own experience or the experience of people you know?

Discuss the information with two or three other people. Compare and contrast the spending patterns given here with the spending patterns of your group. For example, do you and your group spend more on recreational technology now than in the past? Do you spend more on children each year? Finally, write one paragraph discussing how your group's spending is similar to or differs from the information provided.

Answers will vary. Turn to page A3 for ideas.

The GED Essay
45-MINUTE PLAN FOR SUCCESS

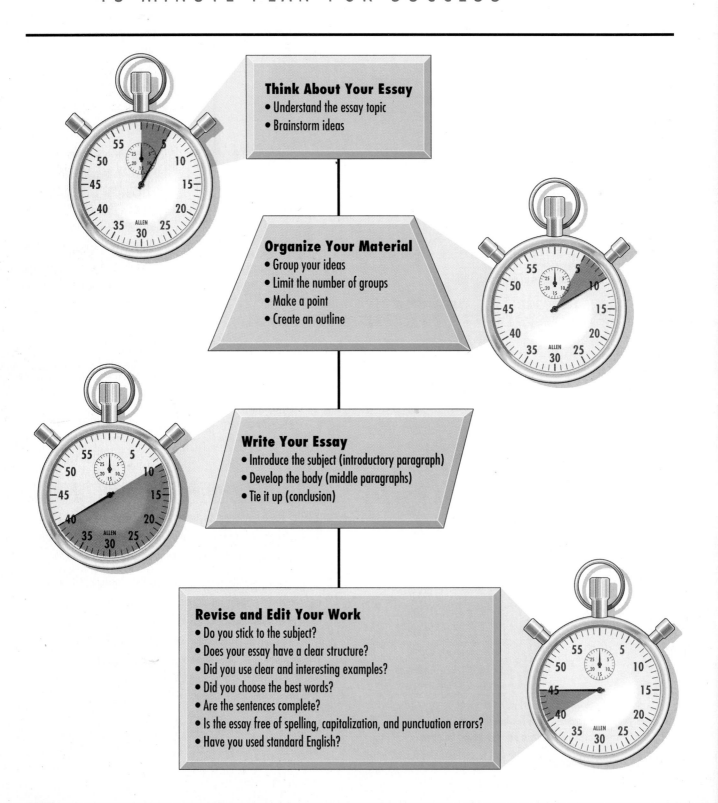

Think About Your Essay
- Understand the essay topic
- Brainstorm ideas

Organize Your Material
- Group your ideas
- Limit the number of groups
- Make a point
- Create an outline

Write Your Essay
- Introduce the subject (introductory paragraph)
- Develop the body (middle paragraphs)
- Tie it up (conclusion)

Revise and Edit Your Work
- Do you stick to the subject?
- Does your essay have a clear structure?
- Did you use clear and interesting examples?
- Did you choose the best words?
- Are the sentences complete?
- Is the essay free of spelling, capitalization, and punctuation errors?
- Have you used standard English?